F

Presenting Gender

Changing Sex in Early-Modern Culture

Edited by
Chris Mounsey

Lewisburg
Bucknell University Press
London: Associated University Presses

Associated University Presses
440 Forsgate Drive
Cranbury, NJ 08512

Associated University Presses
16 Barter Street
London WC1A 2AH, England

Associated University Presses
P.O. Box 338, Port Credit
Mississauga, Ontario
Canada L5G 4L8

The paper used in this publication meets the requirements of the American National Standards for Permanence of Paper for Printed Library Materials Z39.48-1984.

Library of Congress Cataloging-in-Publication Data

Presenting gender : changing sex in early-modern culture / edited by Chris Mounsey.
    p.   cm. — (Bucknell studies in eighteenth-century literature and culture)
    Includes bibliographical references and index.
    ISBN 0-8387-5477-5 (alk. paper)
    1. English literature—Women authors—History and criticism.   2. Women and literature—Great Britain—History—18th century.   3. Women and literature—Great   Britain—History—17th century.   4. English literature—18th century—History and criticism.   5. English literature—Early modern, 1500–1700—History and criticism.   6. Passing   (Identity) in literature.   7. Gender identity in literature.   8. Masculinity in literature.   9. Femininity in literature.   10. Sex role in literature.   I. Mounsey, Chris, 1959–   II. Series.

PR448.W65 P74   2001
820.9′9287′09032—dc21

00-068068

PRINTED IN THE UNITED STATES OF AMERICA

Contents

List of Illustrations

Acknowledgements

THE IDEA FOR THIS BOOK OF ESSAYS BEGAN WITH A CONFERENCE held at King Alfred's College, Winchester in September 1997, entitled "Passing: Assumed Identities in Literature, Art and Film." The intention of the conference was to offer a forum for debate about the cultural significance of cross-identification in all its forms — sexual, racial, and class-based — from the early modern period right up to the present day. I am indebted to Amanda Boulter and Natalie McGrath who helped me with the organization of it, and to Roger Lowman who encouraged us to go ahead with the project.

The collection is of a much narrower focus that its parent conference, even though, as will become clear, it is separated into two sections. I would hope therefore, that it will be read not only as a series of examples of early modern cross-dressing, literary or otherwise, but also, in the spirit of the original conference, as a glimpse at a general theory of "passing."

Introduction

In an age in which feminism is still a curricular item in our universities and a current subject for debate on early morning radio talk shows, it is not out of the question to argue that one of the most immediate things we notice about other people, and they notice about us, concerns sex and gender. When we see a member of either sex, a woman or a man, some degree of our perception and interaction with them is predicated upon whether we can fit them into the gender categories feminine or masculine. We designate rightly or wrongly, but if we withhold judgment, language makes it difficult for us to speak to or about the person whom we have seen. We fumble with "he/she" and "him/her" out loud or in our minds, but always feel self-conscious and imprecise. While giving a paper recently at a large conference, I shared a panel with a person whose sex I could not decide. When reporting back to my students on the paper I had heard, which concerned the way homosexuals recognize one another, I was torn between using the pronoun "he" which best described the person's dress and way of speaking, and "she," which best described the person's physicality. However, the decision, if made, would have been so fundamental it would have affected the way I explained the paper, and I was reduced to silence. The very point the speaker was making seemed to have become dependent upon how I perceived the speaker's sex and gender.

But what is the basis upon which such designations are made? The expectation that gender characteristics will lead us correctly to know the sex of a person is shown by the foregoing example to be misguided. Expectation from gender traits did not lead to a decision: it was as if there was no truth about biological sex. But the shift in language between my use of "he" and "she" was no mere political correctness since the gender neutral pronoun "it" would have reduced the experiences of gay men and gay women to a homogeneity that lacked the subtlety of each experience. The appeal to the neuter could not have made the situation clearer since that word is still based on the idea (which would appear to be inherent in language, at least it caused my problem in the first place) that sex is stable and essential (or absent), while gender may be discussed, and therefore socially constructed.

11

However, the case of Agnes, described by Laurel Richardson in *The Dynamics of Sex and Gender* would suggest the opposite. Agnes was born male, but felt she "was female, misunderstood and mislabeled." Although Agnes had to learn socially acceptable feminine traits from the age of seventeen, she believed that it was "moral and correct" for her to be female and asked for corrective surgery so that she "could have what nature had intended all along." What nature had intended was not her sex but her feeling of femininity. For Agnes, sex was unstable and correctable, and gender essential and immutable.[1] Of course there are other possible interpretations of each of my examples, but I present them, such as they are, to open up the problematic of whether sex and gender are some kind of performance or essential to the body. Are they socially constructed or genetic?

The language we use to describe sex and gender would therefore seem to offer an account that is not borne out by lived experience, and it is in this fissure that the present collection locates itself. It is articulated around an artificial separation of the sex/biology and gender/culture opposition, which is used as a practical tool for exploring each issue in order to force some reconceiving of each term as well as of their relationships to one another. In so doing, the collection is an intervention into the growing debate about sex and gender in the early modern period, between 1650 and 1800, addressing the available historical and theoretical models. The current situation may be characterized approximately as a debate between historians and theorists, where the former privilege sex and the latter privilege gender as a basis for their conclusions. By addressing early modern texts about gender passing, which also tend to privilege either sex or gender, the essays suggest the argument that the choice between strategies may be argued to derive from the purpose of the writer.

The debate between the historians and theorists finds its roots in two influential texts of the end of the 1970s. Lawrence Stone's history, *The Family, Sex and Marriage, in England, 1500–1800,*[2] argues that while the sexes became more politically equal, gender roles came to be defined as stable and incommensurable. The same perceived binary opposition between sexes and genders made the early modern period a prime site for deconstruction by the recent wave of theorists, led by Michel Foucault's *History of Sexuality,*[3] who declare that early modern sexes and genders were, on the contrary, unstable and ambiguous.

While Stone's history has become so popular it has appeared in an abridged volume, it has not been without its detractors among historians. The New Historicists argued from their insistence upon reading for subversion that its focus on familial relationships avoided the ideological impact of the dissident. Their argument is borne out by the fact that a book that purports to be on "sex" gives only cursory mention of homosexuality, and thereby excludes the experience of ten percent of the population under study. However, to take the New Historicist approach to its ultimate conclusion can also lead to problems. Beth Fowkes Tobin, for example, argues in *History, Gender and Eighteenth-Century Literature* that the area of the problematic of gender in literary studies lies entirely in ideology. She claims that "we have to interrogate the ideological production and circulation of gender."[4] In so doing, she gives us a book of theories rather than a book that believes it is able to interrogate texts directly for accounts of personal experiences of gender. Arguing against such an approach is Janet Todd, who suggests in *Gender, Art and Death*: "A reconstruction of the past after some archival study and wide reading over a long period of time has, I think, some authority. It is as partial as memory is, but its authority has to be asserted."[5]

Thus, Todd acts as an authority for at least a partial reconstructing of personal experience of gender from a study of texts within their historical contexts with which to examine the propounded gender imperatives, whether they be subversive or within the dominant ideology. The move, which marks to some extent the return of the intention of the author, is balanced by Todd's skepticism toward the absolute referentiality imputed by Stone, but her methodology is crucial for the functioning of the readings that follow.

Applying such an historical reconstructionist approach to sex and gender, Thomas Laqueur's *Making Sex* consults medical texts to demonstrate that the Renaissance one-sex account of the body gave way to two sexes in the early modern period: "In the late seventeenth and eighteenth centuries, science fleshed out, in terms acceptable to the epistemology, the categories 'male' and 'female' as opposite and incommensurable biological sexes. A notion of order and coherence is replaced by corporeal wiring."[6] Following the example of the stabilized sexed body, gender and its roles was also separated and designated as essential, and early modern men could argued that: "the uterus naturally disposes women toward domesticity."[7] As such, the stability of the body and of its gender may be seen, from a historical perspective (though not agreed by all historicists), to follow Stone's view, as "state of the art" early modern science.[8]

From as early as 1976, gender theorists, such as Patricia Meyer Spacks, argued that fixity of the self (and by default the gendered self) and social challenges to it represented the most important adventure for the protagonist in the eighteenth-century novel. In *Imagining a Self*, she wrote: "To remain essentially the same, in many eighteenth-century

novels, constitutes the central character's triumph. People are rewarded
. . . for being themselves. . . . If the optimism of the nineteenth century
focuses on the possibilities of change, that of the eighteenth depends on
the reassurances of stability."[9] Thus, Spacks may be said to argue that
gender was unstable in a society that did not wish it to be so and demanded ideological support from its fictions.

Entering the debate on the theoretical side,[10] Paul-Gabriel Boucé, G.
S. Rousseau and Roy Porter,[11] among others, brought us many interesting studies of the dissident sexes, genders, and sexualities of the period.
Collections such as these centered on the binary of body/sex : mind/
gender and its malcontents, showing how, as scientific attempts continued to separate bodies into two clearly defined sexes, gender roles became increasingly subject to ideological control and its concomitant
subversion. For example, Lynne Friedli, in her essay "Passing
Women," concludes her study of women who dressed as men with the
argument that " 'woman' is invented as a social category from around
the end of the seventeenth century."[12] "Woman," whom she argues became "the Woman question" was invented by masculine patriarchal discourse. Invention would necessarily lead to female education and follow
the form of Shawn Lisa Maurer's reading of the *Tatler* essays, where
the male "author" of the text — Isaac Bickerstaff — teaches his female
pupil how to be a "Woman."[13]

Julia Epstein and Kristina Straub's *Body Guards* developed Friedli's
cultural political argument about the study of the body and gender in
cases of cross-gendering along anthropological lines:

> We agree [they write] with anthropologist Thomas Csordas that "the body
> is not an *object* to be studied in relation to culture, but is to be considered as
> the *subject* of culture, or in other words as the existential ground of culture."
> The thesis of [*Body Guards*] is that distinctions between male and female
> bodies are mapped by cultural politics onto an only apparently clear biologi-
> cal foundation. As a consequence, sex/gender systems are always unstable
> sociocultural constructions.[14]

Their collection of essays might be argued to be the high point of the
theoretical argument for the constructedness and ambiguity of sex and
gender, though it did not concentrate on the early modern period alone.

As noted above, much written by theorists of sex and gender in the
early modern period focuses on the dissident: cross-dressing, cross-gendering, prostitution, rape, homosexuality. Concentration on the dissident was important as the method not only followed the deconstructive
technique of bringing the marginal into the center of the debate, but
since it was one of the few places in which sex and gender were dis-

cussed in available contemporary texts, which include many law reports, autobiographies, and heated outbursts in magazines and newspapers about "counterfeit ladies" and "molly houses."[15] On the other hand, little is written, since little is known, about those whose "transgression" was successful and unnoticed. In fact Kristina Straub goes as far as arguing that in order to protect gender ideology in a specular society, where: "one can see with particular vividness . . . the ongoing process of naturalization by which the powerful, gendered tropes of the male spectator and the female spectacle become encoded"[16] it was important that in ritual transgressions: "obvious travesty was crucial to the acceptance of male cross-dressing . . . (the actor must be seen as a bad parody of femininity)."[17] Parody had to be bad in order to protect dominant masculinity from charges of effeminacy, since the feminine, Straub argues, was defined by being oppressed and in terms of the pain of suffering oppression.

Other anthropologists, such as Natalie Zemon Davis, would disagree. For her, ritual transgression is the locus of political power: "With their women's garb, they [the men] also appropriated for political rebellion the carnival licence allowed members of 'the unruly sex,' assumed to be enslaved to passion and not responsible for their actions."[18] So much so, that, as Victor Turner argues: "Out of ludic disorder may come the potential for social change."[19]

The following essays attempt to explore the gulf between such apparently opposed interpretations of sex and gender. They concern gender passing—that is, where a member of one designated biological sex takes on attributes of the other for the purpose of being *successfully* mistaken for a member of the assumed sex. Together, the conclusion they suggest is that early modern people in England subscribed to both sides of the opposition between the historical and theoretical approaches to gender. "Passers," by presenting themselves, whether in life or in text, as members of the opposite sex, required that sex and gender roles and stereotypes be stable enough to be successfully recognized. At the same time the fact of their successful passing showed that they believed that sex and gender were not essential to one particular biological body, as they could be taken on by the other.

If, as Epstein and Straub suggest, the body is the existential ground for culture, it may be argued that it interacts with others in two different ways, the sexual and the political. Both areas are more or less ideological, but they are not indissociable. Personal sexual expression may be policed by the political sphere, but, as the cases of the academic and of Agnes cited above suggest, however panoptical the external oppression, the existence of sexual dissidents demonstrates that the body's needs somehow escape complete subjugation to ideological norms. By artificially separating the sexual and the political, we can perhaps examine the opposition between the views that sex and gender are stable or unstable, in a new way. To this end, the present study of successful cross-gendering opens up a useful space for such an analysis, since, as will be seen, it reduces slippage between the sexual and political spheres to a minimum.

The essays that follow demonstrate that early modern people presented themselves across gender for a variety of reasons, but largely to follow the dictates of personal and sexual identity or for reasons of political expression. They therefore explore the debate from each perspective and from a combination of both historical and theoretical approaches. However, in order to investigate the complexities of passing to study sex and gender, the essays must be neither too strictly historical nor too strictly theoretical. To err on the side of historicity is to ignore the valuable work on gender and identity carried out since the late nineteenth century. But to err on the side of theoretical analysis is to impose twentieth-century ideas upon seventeenth- and eighteenth-century examples: the time, it may be argued, that twentieth-century theories were in their infancy. The approach of each essay therefore follows the rubric of exploring cases of textual or social gender passing in the way in which they might have been received by contemporary readers or witnesses, using theoretical tools where necessary, and where possible developing such tools from the source material itself. As such, each essay is a detailed historical contextualization and reading of a particular textual or actual passing.

Following this general methodology, the contributors show that those who passed for sexual reasons tended to suggest that the sexual body was stable (though it may be categorized into more than two sexes), while those who passed for political reasons privileged its cultural construction. The opposite was true for gender. Those who passed for sexual reasons suggested that gender was unstable, and those who passed for political reasons suggested its stability (or at least created meanings within an ideological framework in which gender was stable).

The (rather tendentious) opposition between passing for sexual or political reasons that articulates this collection may itself be thought to privilege an autonomous self over a model of cultural construction and so distort the conclusions of a group of analyses that claim to be inclusive of both theoretical and historical methodologies. This is not necessarily so. Both versions of desire, sexual and political, are examples of desire in relation to an other or others. But while "passing" is necessarily a personal choice, it occurs within a social system that requires for its completion recognition of whether or not the passing has been successful. Thus it is predicated upon an expectation of relationality and cannot be defined as being purely in the ownership of the "passer." The successful passer wants to be recognized as having passed by someone who does not know they are being taken in. Thus the viewer, although unknowing, is a necessary participant in the act of passing. In this sense, the viewer may be argued to construct the sex and gender of the passer as much as the individual who passes. The system that is thereby illuminated may also act as a model for nonpassing sexes and genders.

It may therefore be argued that, as living people, we are constructed and self-constructing according to the situations in which we find ourselves: in a dynamic process. Since the situations we find ourselves in differ from the sexual to the political, we construct and are constructed accordingly. But the fact that the sex and gender we display is in dynamic process does not reduce the reality of the sex or gender constructed, nor does the reality of the sex or gender constructed preclude their reconstruction in a new circumstance. Only a fluidity of sex and gender, and its construction and reconstruction into real events, will account for the early modern passers' experience, of which the following essays offer a schematic snapshot. Underlying the schema, however, is the certainty that both sex and gender are fluid *and* stable and depend upon the context of their existence and analysis for their reality.

What is perhaps most striking, however, is that where sex or gender is seen to be mutable, the other is seen to be stable. From the brief account of the historical and theoretical approaches, the phenomenon might have appeared to be a product of the analysis, but with the results of the following essays as evidence, it appears to be a given of the sex/gender binary: that one remains stable while the other shifts.

To give some kind of point zero from which to begin, Conrad Brunstrom's essay explores the question of males trying and often failing to pass as masculine. With respect to an ABC of eighteenth-century explorations of gender by John Armstrong (in his "unspeakable sex georgic"), "Estimate" Brown (in his *Estimate of the Manners and Morals of the Times*), and Charles Churchill (in his abuse of the Earl of Bute), Brunstrom demonstrates that men's attempts to be solely masculine constantly fell victim to the return of prescientific accounts of one sex. Masculinity, he argues, was in crisis from its very invention and needed to maintain constant activity or it would lapse back into passive effeminacy. His essay is also important as it explores contemporary links made between gender and nationality, and as such introduces the two parts into which the rest of the essays are placed: Passing Identities and Passing Politically.

Passing for reasons of personal sexual identity was brought into clear focus in the late twentieth century when reconstructive surgery and hormone treatment made it possible to cross the abyss of the body/sex more or less successfully to the other side. What Roy Porter calls "the cherished ideal of 'being yourself,' "[20] in terms of the history of identity, is not, however, a new phenomenon. The essays in the first section of this collection offer passing seen as a privileged site of analysis of the early modern understanding of the gender choices open to individuals in their relationship with a stable sexual body, their own or other people's.

Carolyn D. Williams's essay, "Women Behaving Well," argues from a multitude of sources that demonstrate female bravery that women who presented themselves as weak and feminine to attract strong, masculine husbands were passing in their passive role, rather than passing in the role of "Female Warrior" as has long been argued. Her accumulation of evidence points to the conclusion that men and women were more the same than different in terms of gender in the early modern period, and that the roles expected of masculine men and feminine women were socially constructed and unstable. But by working backward from the obvious passers such as the pirate Ann Bonny and the female soldier Hannah Snell to the extraordinary feats of ordinary women in ordinary marriages, Williams demonstrates that behind the mask of the socially gendered self is not another mask, or nothing at all, but a body with various different potentials and choices. The passer may follow differently gendered roles at each passing, but s/he is an irreducible fact by whom the play of gender is acted out.

Karina Williamson's essay on verse epistles by both men and women poets explores how the classical inheritance was used for female subversion and is also a more thoroughgoing questioning of gender and genre. Williamson's reading of Mary Leapor's "To Artemisia" explores how the genre expectations of verse epistles are exploited by the "kitchen-maid poet" to challenge the gender and class assumptions of male poets of the Augustan club and to demonstrate their instability. Leapor is also seen to privilege the actuality of the private "here and now" of the hospitality offered and the "you and me" who reside behind the addresser and addressee of the epistle. This private space is gendered feminine, although the Horatian model for it is a masculine retreat from the cares of the political world. But Leapor's subversion lies in not only the apparent ease with which gender is put on and off like a garment (or rather, two garments, one made to measure for each), but once again, in the residual female body that remains to be fed and to enjoy company in the private space. Likewise, John Wilmot, the Earl of Rochester's "Letter from Mistress Price," ought to be written by a woman, not only from its superscription, but also to be true to its

Ovidian model. But whereas, as Williamson shows, gender is completely subverted in the verse epistle's execution, the body of the author, in either male or female form, remains in the indeterminacy of the Earl's passing, for the reader to reconstruct using the available biographical reasons for his passing as Mistress Price.

Thomas King's essay, "The Fop, the Canting Queen, and the Deferral of Gender," begins by exploring not so much passing itself, as the question of what happened when passers no longer had to pass. King argues that after the restoration of the monarchy, when female impersonators such as Edward Kynaston were no longer needed to play women's roles in the theater, their "feminine" language of gestures, voices, and grimaces did not simply disappear but was redeployed as the cant of the emergent "sodomite." Hogarth's contemporary theory in his *Analysis of Beauty* and how to make the consciousness visible on the surface of the body is then used to show how an athletic barge-man, a Herculean coal-heaver, and a deaf tyre-smith may pass as Fanny Murry, Lucy Cooper, and Kitty Fisher. In such situations, the choice of alternate gendering is made despite the body whose sex is stable but outside the agent's capacity for dissimulation or trickery. The body does not disappear, but its successful passing (successful at least to the passer) lies in learning the behaviors demanded by the sexual body to take on the gender that it desires, though it appears freakish to the norm. The behaviors are learned; the desire to be gendered is stable in the sexual body. Colley Cibber's attempts at a more successful passing as a nonhomosexual male are then set against his theory of acting in which Kynaston's gestures were explained to an early modern audience.

Julie Shaffer's paper, "Cross-Dressing and the Nature of Gender in Mary Robinson's *Walsingham*," appears to be a paper that concerns a more political passing than passing in terms of the desire for alternative sexual identity. In Robinson's novel, Sidney Aubrey, the heroine, passes as a boy in order to stave off the legal minefield that would become the plot motor of all Jane Austen's novels—male entailed inheritance. However, since Sidney's passing as a man is so successful that even her (male) cousin, with whom she is in love, does not recognize her biological sex, the novel generates a space for a discussion of gender and sex in terms of sexual desire. For, as Shaffer argues, the gender of the protagonist, who is entirely educated as a male, though little distinguishable from her female transformation, is subject to a process of unlearning during a period of illness at the end of the novel. Ultimately Robinson cannot decide about what makes up the different attributes of masculine or feminine gendered behavior. At the same time, however, the sex of Sidney is never in doubt. Her desire for her cousin,

Walsingham, is the cause of many of the novel's incidents as she chases away her rivals for his affection. The desires of Sidney's body beneath the surface of its gender performance are not in question. Tricks may be played with and by gender, a woman may be misrecognized as a man, but Sidney's heterosexual desire for Walsingham, like Kynaston's desire for men in King's essay, is stable and cannot be constructed.

We have four very different views of the stability of sex(es—more than two) amid the changes wrought in gender, where questions of identity are at stake. Williams argues that sex is a ground base, which enacts gendered behavior attributable to either, depending on the circumstance. Williamson shows that though the gender of a genre may be subverted by an alteration of the sex of the letter writer, the interplay between the assumed and the actual sex of the writer has a more radical effect, giving the reader a crucial role in the text, which she explains in terms of his/her *jouissance*. King demonstrates that where a new sex— the sodomite—was emergent as a social group, it appropriated a gender role that had unexpectedly become available, rather than it being an essential character. Shaffer explores how despite gender being learnable, the sex and sexual desires of the subject remain unaltered and unalterable. This is not the case where sex and gender are counterfeited for political reasons.

David Robinson's essay, "The Metamorphosis of Sex(uality): 'Iphis and Ianthe' in the Seventeenth and Eighteenth Centuries," leads into the group of papers on passing for political reasons with an account of Ovid's *Metamorphosis* tale of the change of Iphis from a girl into a boy. Robinson's perspective on the tale is to explore the ideological constructions of female homosexuality and is predicated against the "impossible" change of sex and the negative attitude society (both classical and early modern) held toward lesbianism. Robinson argues that in order to maintain phallic control, the patriarchal hegemony must "unknow" lesbianism. That is to say "unnatural" sexual acts, those that occur without a penetrating penis, must be deemed impossible, even at the expense of allowing a magical, though equally impossible, change of sex of Iphis from female to male in order that the marriage be consummated "normally." The result of political discourse, therefore, is that sex may be considered unstable to maintain the stability of gender "norms" so that they may become the loci of ideological enforcement.

Successful political passers play with this rigid gender ideology, and therefore change their bodies at will in order to make their political statements with impunity. Of course, as in Ovid, bodily changes are magical or fictional, but in an ideology where fixed gender expectation is a force of social control, passers have gotten away with murder by pretending to be members of the opposite sex. If the feminine is deemed irrational and unfit to enter the political arena, there can be no political threat from women's writing: it is scandal and gossip. If the masculine is ideologically defined as immutably heterosexual, accusations of homosexuality are not merely scandal but political opposition. The question at the heart of the papers in this section lies in what can be said by the two genders—or at least what is expected of them.

Ruth Herman's paper, "Enigmatic Gender in Delarivier Manley's *New Atalantis*," explores this now famous text from the point of view of its sex reversals. Herman argues that Manley regularly changed the sex of a character in her representation of a political figure, in order to make scandalous suggestions about the character's sexuality. While the accusation of heterosexual misdeeds tended to enhance the reputation of politicians (as it still does today), the accusation of homosexual misdeeds was potentially more devastating. Set against the author's imprisonment for the apparently less scandalous second volume of the novel, Manley's sexual innuendo is argued to be a political act. By indirectly accusing the Earl of Sunderland of homosexuality in her use of sex reversal, Manley is argued to employ the rigid gender ideology of masculine-equals-heterosexual to denounce the Whig government as effeminate and therefore ineffectual. The fact the Whigs lost the next election perhaps demonstrates the effectiveness of this type of Tory propaganda.

Elizabeth Kubek's essay, "The Key to Stowe: Toward a Patriot Whig Reading of Eliza Haywood's *Eovaai*," describes the way Haywood changed her own sex in order to be taken seriously as a political writer. After she had been famously offered by Alexander Pope as a prize in a urinating competition between rival publishers, her status as a serious propagandist was put in doubt, and her role in writing superficial feminine scandal highlighted. Kubek argues that the novel *Eovaai* is Haywood's attempt to reconstruct herself as a political writer, in fact as "an alternative-universe Bolingbroke" writing for the opposition Whigs. This narrator, in which she doubly passes as male and Chinese, speaks from a pre-Adamic, that is to say prepatriarchal, times to show how gender constructions became "naturalized" as a source of ideological control under the Whigs. At the same time the novel legitimizes the political opposition of the Patriot Whig political discourse, and in so doing sets Haywood among the "worthies" in the Patriot Whig pantheon in the temple in the gardens at Stowe.

The debate about Haywood's writing on politics and gender is continued in Rachel K. Carnell's "The Very Scandal of Her Tea Table: Eliza Haywood's Response to the Whig Public Sphere." Where Kubek argues that Haywood constructed herself as a prepatriarchal Asian man in order to create an objective position from which to write about the construction of gender as a method of Whig ideological control, Carnell applies the same argument to the *Parrot*. The androgynous bird is above gender, and what is more writes only what it hears, parrot-fashion. It cannot therefore be biased toward either gender, though its green feathers suggests its Jacobitism. Carnell argues that Haywood's later texts show an increasing pessimism about the possibility of a woman's voice being heard in the public political sphere due to the separation of gender roles. Her parrot voice, therefore, must encode her political position in somewhat the same way that Manley encoded her political assault upon Sunderland thirty years earlier. The male bastion of political discourse, the coffee-house, is "bugged" by the parrot, who exposes the methods of exclusion of the political opposition, and gives yet another a disguised voice for the woman propagandist for the Jacobite cause.

Chris Mounsey's essay, ' "To the Women of Both Sexes': Christopher Smart, Mrs. Mary Midnight, and the Voice of the Dissident Woman Writer," builds on the idea of feminine gendered political writing. It is a study of the periodical *The Midwife, or Old Woman's Magazine*, which Christopher Smart wrote and edited as Mrs. Mary Midnight. Mounsey argues that Smart's sex change from male to female was used to disguise the political nature of the magazine in stereotyped female gossip and scandal-mongering. The essay argues further that, if this was so, it necessarily followed in a tradition of women's political writing. *The Midwife* was immensely successful from its first number, but since its surface meaning is neither funny nor witty, the readership must have been able to recognize the underlying content and been easily able to decode it.

What is important to note is that in all five papers on passing for political reasons, the case studies show that gender is exposed to be only ideologically fixed, rather than essential, but that this exposure is always explored through the dominant discourse. Passers find their voice by ironizing the stabilizing of gender as a means of political control. They use the stable genders of the dominant discourse and change their sex, race, and even species rather than allow for the impossible: a woman to talk sense about politics or a man to gossip about scandal. It may have been this complexity, brought about by the fact that passers themselves were happy to play with sex and gender roles, that has led to the oppositions between the historians and theorists of gender.

NOTES

1. See Laurel Richardson, *The Dynamics of Sex and Gender* (New York: Harper and Row, 1988).

2. Lawrence Stone, *The Family, Sex and Marriage, In England, 1500–1800* (London: Weidenfeld and Nicholson, 1977).

3. Michel Foucault, *The History of Sexuality*, trans. R. Hurley (London: Allen Lane, 1979).

4. Beth Fowkes Tobin, *History, Gender and Eighteenth-Century Literature* (Athens: University of Georgia Press, 1994), 4.

5. Janet Todd, *Gender Art and Death* (Cambridge: Polity Press, 1994), 7.

6. Thomas Laqueur, *Making Sex, Body and Gender from the Greeks to Freud* (Cambridge: Harvard University Press, 1990), 154.

7. Ibid., 155.

8. It has to be said that Laqueur's study falls into the same problem as Stone's and might be called *Making Heterosex* as it contains only four references to homosexuality in the main text and two notes, only one of which describes homosexual behavior.

9. Patricia Meyer Spacks, *Imagining a Self: Autobiography and the Novel in Eighteenth-Century England* (Cambridge, Mass.: Harvard University Press, 1976), 8–9.

10. It is necessary to note that Porter and Rousseau do not claim to be "theorists," though their contribution to the side of the debate that I have labeled "theoretical" makes a useful shorthand so to designate them.

11. *Sexuality in the Eighteenth Century*, ed. P-G. Boucé (Manchester: Manchester University Press, 1982) and *Sexual Underworlds of the Enlightenment*, eds. G. S. Rousseau and Roy Porter (Manchester: Manchester University Press, 1987).

12. In *Sexual Underworlds of the Enlightenment*, eds. Rousseau and Porter, 250.

13. Shawn Lisa Maurer, "Father-Son Relations in the *Tatler* and *Spectator*," in *History, Gender and Eighteenth-Century Literature*, ed. Beth Fowkes Tobin (Athens: Georgia University Press, 1994).

14. *Body Guards: The Cultural Politics of Gender Ambiguity*, eds. Julia Epstein and Kristina Straub (New York: Routledge, 1991), 2.

15. See, for example, Janet Todd and Elizabeth Spearing, eds., *Counterfeit Ladies: The Life and Death of Moll Cutpurse, The Case of Mary Carelton* (London: William Pickering, 1994), and Rictor Norton, *Mother Clap's Molly House* (London: Gay Man's Press, 1992).

16. Kristina Straub, *Sexual Suspects: Eighteenth-Century Players and Sexual Ideology* (Princeton: Princeton University Press, 1992), 19.

17. Ibid., 127.

18. Natalie Zemon Davis, "Women on Top: Symbolic Sexual Inversion and Political Disorder in Early Modern Europe," in *The Reversible World: Symbolic Inversion in Art and Society*, ed. Barbara Babcock (Ithaca: Cornell University Press, 1978). Quoted in Anna K. Nardo, *The Ludic Self in Seventeenth-Century English Literature* (Albany: State University of New York Press, 1991), 37.

19. Victor Turner, "Liminal to Liminoid, in Play, Flow, and Ritual: An Essay in Comparative Symbology," in *The Anthropological Study of Human Play*, ed. Edward Norbeck, *Rice University Studies* 60 (1974): 59–61. Quoted in Nardo, *The Ludic Self*, 37.

20. *Rewriting the Self: Histories from the Renaissance to the Present*, ed. Roy Porter (London: Routledge, 1997), 1.

Presenting Gender

1

Passing Identities

"Be Male and Female Still":
An ABC of Hyperbolic Masculinity in the Eighteenth Century

Conrad Brunstrom

THE FLEXIBILITY AND PERFORMATIVITY OF GENDER IN THE EIGH-
teenth century can be registered not only instancing those who "pass"
as the opposite gender, but also by gauging the urgency and the persis-
tence of the rhetoric used to reinforce traditional gender roles. The measure of the flow can be extrapolated from the effort of resistance. In this
essay, I intend to examine the reactions to gender ambiguity as represented by influential authors of the mid-century. Following George
Cheyne, John Armstrong offers a holistic, medical context for sexual
expression and control. John Brown offers a paranoid social context
for perceived sexual ambivalence, whereas Charles Churchill exploits
his own precious heterosexual stability as a political weapon.

One of the earliest and perhaps the most thoughtful of these analyses
of national effeminacy is offered by Cheyne in his most famous work
The English Malady (1733).

> All Nervous Distempers whatsoever from Yawning and Stretching up to
> a mortal Fit of Apoplexy, seem to me to be but one continued Disorder, or
> the several Steps and Degrees of it, arising from a Relaxation or Weakness,
> and the Want of a Sufficient Force and Elasticity in the Solids in general,
> and the Nerves in particular, in Proportion to the Resistance of the Fluids,
> in order to carry on the Circulation, remove Obstructions, carry of the Re-
> cremants, and make the Secretions.[1]

Nerves need exercise. The human body is moralized as a site of sustained energy.[2] This energy is gendered from the outset, a morality that
precedes the birth of the patient defines the male patient as a trustee of
his own natural masculinity:

> The original Stamina, the whole System of the Solids, the Firmness, Force,
> and Strength of the Muscles, of the Viscera, and great Organs, are they not

29

owing to the Male? And does the Female contribute any more but as convenient Habitation, proper Nourishment, and an Incubation to the seminal
Animalcul for a Time, to enable the living Creature to bear the Air, Sun,
and Day the sooner.[3]

This (Walter) Shandean doctrine enforces masculine vigor as a form of
Burkeian compact with one's seminal ancestry. The true parent is the
father, the sperm is the verb to the womb's passive noun, and exercise
is the guarantee not only of bodily health but of seminal continuity.
Cheyne's health-care regime is at once intransigent and fragile; masculinity is natural and normative, but is constantly put at risk by corrupt
habits and dissipated fashions:

And whoever is acquainted with the History of the Origin of Nations, and
the Manner in which they liv'd, preserv'd themselves in Health, and got rid
of their Diseases, while they liv'd in their Simplicity, and had not yet grown
luxurious, rich and wanton, or had frequent Commerce with other Nations,
and communicated with their Luxury and Arts, will be pretty well satisfy'd
of this Truth. But where the Luxury and Disease of all the Nations on the
Globe are brought together, mingled and blended, and perhaps heighten'd
by the Difference of Climates, there is an absolute Necessity that the Materials of Physick, and the Methods of Cure, should be various and extended
in equal Proportion.[4]

If his advice sounds familiar, it is because the vogue for novelty, for the
*un*familiar, is the true enemy of securely gendered health.

"BE TEMPERATE STILL: WHEN NATURE BIDS, OBEY": JOHN ARMSTRONG'S UNSPEAKABLE SEX GEORGIC

A securely masculinized health regimen inevitably appeals to traditional rather than pioneering treatments. Georgic poetry is almost inevitably enlisted as the most eloquent means of revivifying ancient
"common sense" advice. John Armstrong (1709–1779) is remembered
as one of a number of blank versifiers to trail in the wake of James
Thomson, Edward Young, and Mark Akenside. He remains, however,
of abiding interest to anyone wishing to chart histories of medicalized
and poeticized sexuality. He is also interesting for anyone concerned
with the history of masculinism as a paranoid ideology.

The maintenance of normative masculinity is a key aspect of *The Oeconomy of Love* (1737), the sex georgic that almost made and almost destroyed Armstrong's name as a poet. The title alone invites Foucauldian
fascination, and this georgic is surely the most important poem Fou-

cault never read. The poem reduces the expenditure of sex into a calcu-
lable regime of observable procedure. Armstrong's few biographers
clearly found this, his most interesting poem, acutely embarrassing. Alexander Chalmers laments:

> In 1737, he published A Synopsis of the History and Care of the Venereal
> Disease, probably as an introduction to practice in that lucrative branch:
> but it was unfortunately followed by his poem, The Economy of Love,
> which, although it enjoyed a rapid sale, has been very properly excluded
> from every collection of poetry, and is supposed to have impeded his profes-
> sional career.[5]

Armstrong's poem is eminently reasonable and startlingly offensive by
turns. By terming it a "sex georgic" I intend to argue that it concerns
itself with the *cultivation* of sex. In this poem, sex is both agriculture and
profitable labor. The poem is about the ergonomics, not just of procre-
ation, but of pleasure itself. What Armstrong offers is not so much the
function of the orgasm as the function of the whole theater of sexual
enterprise, the *work* of heterosexual expression. Serious and detailed
celebration of sexuality makes for a far more complex and nuanced sexual morality than either straightforward prohibitionism or unfettered
hedonism. Time and place are crucial to a morality that depends on
agriculture and horticulture for its imagery. Sowing one's wild oats is
not to be undertaken without checking the soil and the season. "Hus-
banding one's resources" is the key to nuptial bliss. Sowing one's highly
organized oats is (needless to say) all a matter of timing:

> The rising Down
> Then too begins to skirt the hallow'd Bounds
> Of Venus' blest Domain. In either Sex
> This sign obtains. For Nature, provident,
> Now when both Sides stand equal for the Fray,
> This graceful Armour spreads, and, but for this
> Excoriate oft the tender parts would rue
> The close Encounter;
>
> *The Oeconomy of Love*, 70–77[6]

Pubic hair is treated almost as a crop to be cultivated by some divine
farmer and breeder as a variety of fertile topsoil and as a sign of ripe-
ness indicating the right time of harvest.

However, if God objectifies humanity, then man (his viceroy) in turn,
objectifies woman. Sometimes this objectification becomes extreme and
paranoid. At one point, Armstrong alarms his male readers with the
threat of a terrifying wedding night discovery.

> But hapless he,
> In nuptial Night, on whom a horrid Chasm
> Yawns dreadful, waste and wild; like to that thro' which
> The wand'ring *Greek*, and *Cytherea's Son*,
> Diving, explor'd Hell's adamantine Gates:
> An unessential Void; where neither Love
> Nor pleasure dwells, where warm Creation dies
> Starv'd in th'abortive Gulph; the dire Effects
> Of Use too frequent, or for Love or Gold.
>
> *The Oeconomy of Love*, 246–52

In a deliberately repulsive inversion, the doors to paradise are transformed at once into the Gates of Hell. Sex is cloyed by overuse; there is a rhythmic stickiness, associated with loving out of season: the heavy use of the caesura accentuates the halting, abortive travesty of sex that is meant to traumatize the careless bridegroom. The "unessential void" is a place where the male risks annihilating himself, being destroyed and swallowed up by the overactive site of sheerest femininity.

If young women should avoid "use too frequent," then old men should abandon sexual exercise altogether. (Writing as a young man) Armstrong describes the use of flagellation employed by the dotard struggling to "rouse the Venus loitering in his Veins!" (531). In opposition to the misuse and overuse of sex, Armstrong attempts to produce a holistic, almost tantric view of sex as the measure and the test of healthy retention and control of forces. It would be very tempting to produce an elegantly straightforward Foucaultian reading of Armstrong that imagines him as an Enlightenment visionary, subjecting and reducing the dangerous expenditure of sexuality to a clinical authorial gaze. Fortunately, Armstrong does everything he can to resist this approach, leaving us with the valuable opportunity to construct a difficult Foucaultian reading. Foucault himself makes it clear that it is impossible to establish any clear separation between *ars erotica* and *scientia sexualis* and that the sexualized pleasures of knowing, telling and exposing sexualized pleasures inhabit a shared terrain, destabilizing both "pure" unintellectual sex and "pure" dispassionate inquiry.[7] To understand Armstrong's view of sexuality, it is necessary to understand something of his erratic medical conservatism and advanced philosophical scepticism.

Although Peter Wagner has described him as a "true follower of enlightenment ideas,"[8] there was nothing clinical, objective, or enlightened about John Armstrong, nothing suggestive of calm Benthamite surveillance. James Boswell, who knew Armstrong in later life, refers to him as a "violent Scot"—an entertainingly splenetic exhibition of unrestrained prejudice. As a personality, he was generally regarded as being "disordered," abrupt, and quick to take offense. His personality spilled easily into prose. Armstrong appears to have written in much the same way that he talked, and he talked and behaved very much for effect. The preface to the *Miscellanies* illustrates his persistent misanthropy: "If the best judges of this age honour him with their approbation, all the worst of the next will favour him [the author] with theirs, when by Heaven's grace, he'll be too far beyond the reach of their unmeaning praise to receive any disgust from them."[9] Armstrong's essays are bizarrely phlegmatic, full of contractions and hyphens. Exclamation marks seem from time to time to actually outnumber full stops. Nor does he admit to any delight in the Dunciadic fertility of literary exchange: "I have for a long time in sad earnest, considered the art of printing as a most pernicious invention. It puts it in the power of every blockhead and scoundrel to propagate stupidity, brutality, bad morals, deceit, and imposture throughout the land."[10] Armstrong is persistently disgusted at having to live in a country where people less intelligent than he have any right to express their opinions. Throughout his *Medical Essays* (1773) he claims that anyone pretending to differ from him can only ever be motivated by ignorant malevolence. His first and last publications are attacks on autodidacts and opportunists, on anyone who threatens the closed shop of medical learning.

The usually restrained and benevolent poet and philosopher James Beattie reacted with bemused horror to the appearance of Armstrong's *Miscellanies* in 1770: " 'I know not,' says Dr. Beattie to his friend Sir William Forbes, 'what is the matter with Armstrong, but he seems to have conceived a rooted aversion at the whole human species, except a few friends, who, it seems, are dead.' "[11] All those who knew him well regarded splenetic misanthropy as an indispensable element of his unique character. James Thomson writing in 1748 remarks that Armstrong "increases in business," but "does not decrease in spleen," and he goes on to compare his friend to Jacques from *As You Like It*.[12] A cherishable spleen is, I think, indicated, since Armstrong was invited that same year by Thomson to contribute the last (appropriately medical) stanzas of the first canto of *The Castle of Indolence*.[13]

Armstrong's personal and rhetorical "imbalance" is related to a profound belief in the nonperfectibility of the human animal, physically and spiritually. *Medical Essays*, the intended culmination of his professional experience, is a fiercely antitheoretical work. Armstrong even suggests in this text that the theory of the circulation of the blood has brought with it no practical medical benefits. The theory may be true, but it was not worth the trouble of finding out: "It is surely enough for the physician to know the natural and usual effects of the materials he employs."[14] Modern physicians are undone it seems by a hubristic desire to systematize individual units of data in a vain and futile desire to relate one curative procedure to another. Armstrong asserts that medicine, if it is to be of any practical use, *must* be kept fragmentary, humble, and repetitive. When it comes to causation, he adopts an almost Humean posture of extreme scepticism: "In short, to explain the phenomena of nature beyond a certain line, we must humbly return to the honest, ancient, ineffectual; expedient of occult properties."[15] Writing itself must preserve a whimsical eclecticism if the reader is to be spared the unhealthy experience of a sustained argument. Digression is good for the mind and body alike. Instead of four humors, Armstrong offers four dimensions of health care: environment, diet, exercise, and "the passions." In this last section he picks up much of the central thread of the *Oeconomy of Love*.

> Be temperate still: when Nature bids, obey;
> Her wild impatient sallies bear no curb:
> But when the prurient habit of delight,
> Or loose imagination spurs you on
> To deeds above your strength, impute it not
> To Nature.
>
> *The Art of Preserving Health*, Book IV[16]

This is not "nature methodis'd" but nature "fetishized." Armstrong asserts a circular definition of and appeal to nature, offering no means of telling how a natural instinct is to be distinguished from an unnatural one. This circularity is related to his preference for digression rather than equilibrium as the natural state of the healthy body. Sane sexual health and sexual identity is a matter of restless momentum not calm resolution.

The Oeconomy of Love is similarly circular and unhelpful about Nature, and Nature's ability to regulate sexuality:

> We know great Nature's power,
> Mother of Things, whose vast unbounded Sway
> From the deep Center all around extends
> Beyond the flaming Barriers of the World.
> We feel her power; we strive not to repress
> (Vainly repress'd, or to Deformity)
> Her lawful Growth; ours be the Task alone
> To check her rude Excrescences, to prune
> Her wanton Overgrowth, and where she strays
> In uncouth Shapes to lead her gently back,
> With prudent Hand, to Form and better Use.
>
> *The Oeconomy of Love* (1737), 276–85

How to prune, where to prune, when to prune: these are not outlined. There is only instinctive good taste versus depraved habit; humans (specifically males) are expected to govern their passions according to a principle of rational expenditure. The true source of Armstrong's vision of healthy sexual equilibrium is *Paradise Lost*, itself the most important source of sex-georgic writing in the English language. Milton is the poet who decisively linked sex and gardening in order to argue that the *essence* of sexual morality is not "what," but "when," "where," and "why." Paradise has been long lost, of course, and Milton and Armstrong were both concerned to manage rather than ignore or transcend conflict in "the real world." *The Oeconomy of Love* represents a studied extrapolation of Books IV, IX, and X of *Paradise Lost* and is also a vindication of the fact that wholesome sexual freedom prefers blank verse to couplets.

> What *Nature* bids
> Is good, is wise, and faultless we obey.
> We must obey; howe'er hard *Stoick* dreams
> Of *Apathy*, much vaunted, seldom prov'd:
> For oft beneath the philosophic Gloom
> Sly *Lewdness* lurks, and oftener mazy *Guile*,
> That with well-mimicked Love th'unwary Heart
> Lures to its Fate, and hails while it betrays.
>
> *The Oeconomy of Love*, 263–70

Overt sexuality is always preferable to covert sexuality; expression is better than repression; honesty is always the best policy. For Armstrong, as for Milton, denial of sexuality is regarded as "monkish" and associated with the abuse of power. The prophets of abstinence are autocrats within a polity of privation and ignorance. As Milton says:

> . . . nor *Eve* the Rites
> Mysterious of connubial love refus'd:
> Whatever Hypocrites austerely talk
> Or puritie and place and innocence,
> Defaming as impure what God declares
> Pure, and commands to som, leaves free to all.
>
> *Paradise Lost*, IV, 742–46

Armstrong's sexual freedom is defined negatively however. Like Charles Churchill, with whom he was briefly acquainted, Armstrong uses an ideal of healthy heterosexuality to condemn homosexuality as a dangerous import and a threat to national security.

Britons, for shame! be Male and Female still.
Banish this foreign Vice, it grows not here,
It dies neglected; and in Clime so chaste
Cannot but by forc'd Cultivation thrive.

The Oeconomy of Love, 42.

Armstrong's xenophobic homophobia is interesting in terms of the way it asserts unambiguous sexual identity as a precious but desperately fragile British characteristic. *The Art of Preserving Health* (1744) concludes with reference to "music" and the Cure of Saul. John "Estimate" Brown would compose an ode entitled the "The Cure of Saul," which is a celebration of a Doric measure of masculine integrity. The degenerate, sexually ambivalent metropolitan is regenerated and remasculinized by simple melodies from the pastoral margins. The measure, not the message, of song is that which effeminizes, according to Brown's attack on Italianate arias in his *Estimate of the Manners and Principles of the Times* (1757). The constant reiteration of the threat is in itself significant.

It is at this point that georgic invites the attention of critical theory. Judith Butler has argued that gender is something that has to be performed on a regular and predictive basis.[17] "Being male and female still" is something that requires effort, the maintenance of gender is a cyclic labor that is agricultural in shape and style. Gender is performance and citation at one and the same time. Genre, like gender, is performative in a reiterative way; it is an effort of will, but is patterned will. Julia Kristeva remarks: "Art—this semiotization of the symbolic—thus represents the flow of jouissance into language. . . . In cracking the sociosymbolic, splitting it open, changing vocabulary, syntax, the word itself, the and releasing the drives borne by vocalic or kinetic difference, *jouissance* works its way into the social and symbolic."[18] If poetic language "releases the drives," georgic poetic language generally does so in a referential, citational context. In the medium to long term, Armstrong failed to establish a poetic language of sexual honesty. Although the *Oeconomy of Love* went through a number of editions without being revised in any significant way, the text was finally self-censored in 1768.[19] The revised version is only 550 lines long, as opposed to the original 616. Lines 194–252 of the original are gone; the description of jagged vaginal lips disappears, as does (for some reason) the description of menstruation (lines 56–69 in the 1737 edition). These cuts may have been imperfect attempts to reinforce Armstrong's growing reputation as a successful doctor. The splenetic manner in which Dr. Armstrong conducted medical debate, however, attributing the mildest criticisms of his work to malice and ignorance, prevented any securely respectable repu-

tation from surviving. A need to control is undermined by a refusal to
theorize and a rage for order is subverted by disordered prose. Knowledge can never be systematized, but neither can it be allowed freely to
circulate (a recipe for quackocracy), even if blood must reluctantly be
permitted to do so.

Armstrong offers not an Enlightenment defense and delimitation of
sexual energy, but rather, an oscillation between competing energies.
His binding authority is not, in the final analysis, medical at all but literary. It is command of language that empowers and curtails sexuality,
not control of the body. Armstrong's literary failure, his inability to discipline language, becomes part of a larger repeated failure to discipline
the body. The defense of masculine health emerges essentially as a paranoid effort, and gender evades his every attempt to secure and delimit
its scope.

"SINKING INTO EFFEMINACY":
JOHN "ESTIMATE" BROWN AND THE CRISIS OF BRITISH
MASCULINITY

A thoroughly masculine ideal of active citizenship is continually appealed to by moralists of the mid century. John "Estimate" Brown was
a clergyman, controversialist, poet, and essayist, briefly famous in the
late 1750s as author of *An Estimate of the Manners and Morals of the Times*
(1757). He was born near to the Scottish border, the son of a suspected
Jacobite. In 1766 he committed suicide by cutting his jugular vein with
a large knife, apparently because he could not honorably disengage
himself from a trip to Russia (where he had been contracted to help
reorganize the educational system). His most persistent political anxiety
was the selfish effeminacy supposedly rife among the British ruling
classes. The *Estimate* literally made his name. His earliest biographer,
Andrew Kippis, writes: "it was, in part indebted to its being well-timed.
It came out when the minds of the people had been extremely depressed
by some unprosperous events; and when, consequently, they were the
more ready to listen to the melancholy, and perhaps too just representation that was given of the Manners and Principles of the Times."[20] A
"sane" securely gendered aesthetic is not constructed not merely as a
public health issue in the eighteenth century, but also as a matter of
national security:

> To promote the fine arts in Britain, has become of greater importance than is
> generally imagined. A flourishing commerce begets opulence; and opulence,
> inflaming our appetite for pleasure, is commonly vented on luxury, and on

every sensual gratification. Selfishness rears its head; becomes fashionable; and infecting all . . . extinguishes every spark of public spirit.[21]

So urged Lord Kames, dedicating his epic *Elements of Criticism* to George III in 1761, at the height of the most international war Britain had yet fought with France. It appears that a judicious program of arts sponsorship is an essential aspect of any war economy. Fine arts combat the effects of luxury, which is supportive of a selfish want of patriotic spirit. Whereas Kames identifies effeminate selfishness as the key issue, Brown uses the phrase "selfish effeminacy" to conclude many sections of his *Estimate*. The crisis thereby elides from the moral to the viral from the social (or antisocial) to the sexual. Brown highlights effeminacy for reasons that are, I will argue, ergonomic in their basis, related to a growing awareness of the division of labor. Selfish effeminacy is, in part, the result of men subcontracting many of the human faculties that ought to comprise the totality of the active citizen. In Brown's lesser-known book, *A Dissertation on the Rise, Union, and Power, the Progressions, Separations, and Corruptions of Poetry and Music*, he explains that the totality of aesthetic, political, and moral endeavor has been ruptured by the specialization of artistic effort: "the *moral* End being now *forgot*, and nothing but *Amusement* attended to, a higher Proficiency in these arts became necessary, and consequently a more severe Application to each."[22] Ends have been sacrificed to means. Vision is sacrificed to skill. Overspecialism encourages a minute fastidiousness in the consumption of any particular cultural product: whether it be an aria, an Ode, a sleeve, or a ragout. The transferability of the terms of effeminacy from one cultural and economic sphere to another is anticipated by George Cheyne's dedication (to Lord Bateman) prefacing *The English Malady*:

> It would ill suit, *my Lord*, with such a Design, to introduce it with a Dedication, cook'd up to the height of a *French* or *Italian* taste. Addresses of this Kind are generally a sort of *Ragous* and *Olios*, compounded of Ingredients as pernicious to the Mind as such unnatural Meats are to the Body. Servile Flattery, fulsome Compliments, and *bombast Panegyrick* make up the *nauseous* Composition.[23]

Within the holistic masculinism of Cheyne and Brown's worldview, the dietary terms are more than metaphors. Promiscuous consumption promotes a consumptive aesthetic. Brown's particular obsession, however, his controlling discourse of gendering value, was musical: "The divine Art, capable of inspiring every thing that is great or excellent, of rouzing every nobler Passion of the Soul, is at length dwindled into a Woman's or a Eunuch's effeminate Thrill."[24] The pairing of "woman" and "eunuch" assumes that all that is not male is lack, is sexless diminution. This sexless lack is sponsored primarily by a type of selfish egotism, of a kind to be expected in a large consumerist metropolis such as London.

Xenophobia, pastoralism, and sexual ambiguity form a continuum of paranoia. As Cheyne and Armstrong demonstrate, in the mid-eighteenth century effeminacy and/or homosexuality is usually figured as an imported rather than an indigenous crisis. Men would have stayed men and the sexes would have remained admirably demarcated had Britons been content to restrain their tastes to the domestic. In the *Estimate*, Brown also seems to hint that unambiguous heterosexuality is hard to find in London. The stage is an important point of reference:

> As Excess of Delicacy hath destroyed our *Force* of *Taste*, it hath at least one laudable Effect; for along with this it hath carried off our *Grossness* of *Obscenity*. A strong Characteristic, this, of the Manners of the Times: The untractable Spirit of Lewdness is sunk into gentle Gallantry, and *Obscenity* itself is grown Effeminate.
>
> BUT what *Vice* hath lost in *Coarseness* of Expression, she hath gained in a more easy and general Admittance: In ancient Days, *bare* and *impudent Obscenity*, like a common Woman of the Town, was confined to *Brothels*: Whereas the *Double-Entendre*, like a modern fine Lady, is now admitted into the *best Company*, while her *transparent Covering* of Words, like a thin fashionable *Gawze*, delicately thrown across, *discloses*, while it seems to *veil* her *Nakedness* of Thought.[25]

An opposite but allied point had been made forty years previously by John Dennis, replying to William Law's *Absolute Unlawfulness of the Stage Entertainment*. Dennis had argued that the recent raids on molly houses and consequent convictions for sodomy had shown that a dangerously homoerotic culture required the corrective remedy of healthily heterosexual bawdiness on stage.[26] Forty years on, Brown is arguing that vice has become harder to isolate and combat as a result of the effeminacy of public manners. However, John Brewer is right to point out that Brown's jeremiad does not assume any necessary elision between effeminacy and homosexuality, and that although this elision was often assumed, it was equally possible to condemn some forms of obsessive heterosexuality as "effeminate": "A libertine like Richardson's Lovelace in *Clarissa* was effeminate, though he embodied what we now would consider aggressive male heterosexuality."[27] Effeminacy erodes the categories of moral judgment that make ethical reflection possible.

A responsible legislature would treat aesthetics as a matter of national security. In his *Dissertation*, Brown admiringly describes how Sparta protected its citizens from the debilitating effects of a ten-string lyre (seven-string simplicity being regarded as essential to preserve Doric martial vigor among the citizenry):

> There hath been much ill-founded Ridicule thrown on the *Spartans* for this Decision. For if we consider the dangerous Effects of mere *Innovation* in small Republics, and the close Connexion between the *Melody* and the *Subject* in ancient *Music*, together with the early and continued Application of *These* to the *Education* of their Youth, we shall find, that in this Instance the *Spartans* only acted a cautious and consistent Part. Their Principle was, to admit *no Change* in *Manners*, and therefore *no Change* in Music.[28]

Morality is as much dictated by form as by content. Sensual luxuriance blurs categories and smudges the human capacity of rational decision making. Continually passing from one form to another corrodes stable appreciation of classical form.

Brown's gendered nationalism becomes all the more suggestive in terms of the more familiar history of aesthetic theory. Brown was one of the first people to celebrate the scenery of the Lake District. He was nicknamed "The Columbus of Keswick" by one early tourist in 1755.[29] Still more significant is the fact that Brown was a close friend of the young William Gilpin, and Brown would write to Gilpin, reinforcing Gilpin's youthful enthusiasm for (specifically) Cumbrian landscape. The massive contours of a mountain landscape served as a dramatic contrast with the effeminate ambiguities of London, the decadent Italianate metropolis. Is it possible that Burkeian categories of the Sublime and Beautiful are infected with xenophobia and sexual paranoia from their very inception? Brown repaired regularly to the north of England thereby renovating his sense of the large and masculine. The scenery of sublime intransigence is patriotically masculine and abstraction represents the very opposite of confusion. The Cumbrian sublime is obscure but not ambiguous; it may be vague but it is masculinely vague rather than vaguely masculine.

Masculine patriotism is about taking the broad view. In a sermon in 1746, Brown describes virtue thus:

> the Knowledge of God's Goodness and Perfections, — of his Hatred to Injustice and Oppression — all these elevate the human Soul, and raise it to a Love of Freedom: Not of that Licentiousness which is the Off-spring of Vice, but that true Greatness of Mind which is the Parent of every Virtue. It is this *extended View* of Things, which drives every partial and ungenerous Thought from the Breasts of Mankind; and inspired them with that *modest Pride*, that *noble Humility*, which expects indeed and even demands the Possession of its own Rights, but is equally zealous in securing the Rights of Others.[30]

The "extended view" of the masculine patriot is more than metaphorically associated with access to a sublime perspective. Effeminate metropoles rarely extend theirs by venturing out of doors and are therefore inclined to "narrow" selfishness.

Masculinity is (throughout Brown's works) the only norm of value. In the *Estimate*, Brown explains why (unlike Pope and Young) he has neglected to satirize female modern manners:

> It may probably be asked, why the ruling Manners of our Women have not been particularly delineated? The Reason is, because they are essentially the same with those of the Men, and are therefore included in the Estimate. The sexes have now little other apparent Distinction, beyond that of Person and Dress: their peculiar and characteristic Manners are confounded and lost: the one Sex having advanced into Boldness, as the other have sunk into Effeminacy.[31]

He glosses this passage in Part II of the *Estimate* (1758), arguing that as men become less chivalrous and protective, "The Women, finding themselves neglected by the Men, choose that System of Manners which is most agreeable to their own Views and Passions."[32] Women are masterful wherever Men are servile. It is of course depressingly predictable to see that masculinity is regarded as an advance, whereas effeminacy is a species of retreat. This zero-sum game is reminiscent of Cheyne's description of the feminine as mere passivity, as absence and as "lack." The idea that men and women could learn from one is, of course, never entertained (by Cheyne or Brown), although Carolyn Williams has directed my attention to this passage in Johnson's *Idler*, which is almost contemporary with Brown:

> Our masculine squadrons will not suppose themselves disgraced by their auxiliaries, till they have done something which women could not have done. The troops of Braddock never saw their enemies, and perhaps were defeated by women. If our American general had headed an army of girls, he might still have built a fort, and taken it. Had Minorca been defended by a female garrison, it might have been surrendered, as it was, without a breach; and I cannot but think, that seven thousand women might have ventured to look at Rochfort, sack a village, rob a vineyard, and return in safety. (*The Idler*, No. 5. Saturday, 13 May 1758)[33]

Johnson is concerned to castigate effeminate men rather than masculine women, but Brown clearly regards masculinity in zero-sum terms. There is only a finite quantity of masculinity to go around. Women cannot acquire masculinity without men losing theirs (and presumably vice versa?): "it is remarkable that the Sexes have changed Characters: The

Men capering about on Hobbys of thirteen Hands, while the Women are galloping full speed on sized and fiery Hunters."[34] Brown's horror of gender confusion resembles Burke's. It is worth making the point that Brown and Burke's gendered opposites tend ultimately toward each other. The sublime, supposedly masculine, figures as a solitary, passive, antisocial and emotional experience, while the beautiful is a social, active, analysable phenomenon.

However, if Estimate Brown were merely a heated masculinist champion of old-fashioned morality, he would be of no very special interest. The century is full of moralist tracts advocating a return to traditional values. What makes Brown's hyperbolic masculinity distinctively interesting is, first, his partial admission of the impossibility of reconciling republican identity with imperial destiny, and, second, a gendered aesthetics that connects him with the aesthetic and sexual apartheid proclaimed by Burke's categories of the sublime and beautiful. Where men are effeminate, the somber sublime of patriotic endeavor is eroded: "where Humanity hath its chief Foundation in effeminate Manners, as at present, there it amount to no more than temporary Starts of Pity, according as Objects of Distress occasionally present themselves: And hence, this Species of Humanity, and a total Defect of Public Spirit, are not only compatible, but naturally connected."[35] Brown's historical vision (highly moralized as it is) is organicist in a way that recalls Adam Ferguson. It is possible to construct Brown as a sort of third-rate Adam Ferguson, whose famous *Essay on the History of Civil Society* was first published in 1767, only a year after Brown's suicide, and whose own distaste for effeminacy was based on classical categories that regarded public service as a quintessentially masculine priority. If so, Brown's extremism can help illuminate the logical affinities and connections that Ferguson's more restrained rhetoric implicitly suggests.

Brown was neither a great or original thinker nor a great expressive writer, but his idiosyncracies are sufficiently urgent and representative to make him a figure of enduring interest. Brown articulates the absurd extremity of patterns of thinking made respectable by Adam Ferguson and Edmund Burke. Through him we can connect the dynamics of sexual paranoia with the paranoid dynamics of empire building. National identity and sexual identity become merged and preserved by and within the politicized aesthetics of pastoral.

"SNIVELLING VIRTUES AND LOOSE DIGRESSIONS": CHARLES CHURCHILL'S URSINE HETEROSEXUALITY

Go where we will, at ev'ry time and place,
SODOM confronts, and stares us in the face;

They ply in public at our very doors
And take the bread from much more honest Whores.

(The Times, 293–95)[36]

Churchill's homophobic paranoia, as here expressed in The Times (1764), has the single but not unimportant virtue of being amusing:

> Let not one brother be to t'other known,
> Nor let his father sit with him alone.
> Be all his servants female, young and fair,
> And if the pride of Nature spur thy heir
> To deeds of Venery, if, hot and wild,
> He chance to get some score of maids with child,
> Chide, but forgive him, whoredom is a crime
> Which, more at this than any other time
> Calls for indulgence, and 'mongst such a race,
> To have a bastard is some sign of grace.

(649–58)

Charles Churchill, in his own lifetime, was regarded as a loose cannon, a dangerous figure whose poetic digressions were emblematic of a larger instability. His literary, political, and amorous adventures were widely seen as antipathetic to any notion of restraint or decorum. One anonymous moralist denounced Churchill with weary hyperbole:

> No language yet, in old or modern Times,
> Apt words can furnish to express thy Crimes.[37]

Churchill himself, however, cleverly forestalled serious satiric opposition with his carefully crafted persona, one that acknowledged and integrated his own worst failings. No one could better depict Churchill's physical excesses and extravagant improprieties than Churchill himself. Hogarth's ursine visual construction of Churchill is far less eloquent than Churchill's own perverse self-imagining in verse. Independence is a poem that juxtaposes his own coarse unpredictability with aristocratic insubstantiality. The following is a self-portrait:

> . . . the Second was a man
> Whom Nature built on quite a diff'rent plan;
> A Bear, whom from the moment he was born,
> His Dam despis'd, and left unlick'd in scorn;
> A Babel, which the pow'r of Art outdone,
> She could not finish when She had begun;
> An utter Chaos, out of which no might
> But that of God could strike one spark of light

(147–54)

Charles Churchill resembled a bear. He was well aware of this resemblance, and he endeavored to make a positive statement out of his own ursine substantiality. Close friends and allies, John Wilkes and Charles Churchill were two of the ugliest men in London in addition to being two of the most sexually predatory men of their generation, relishing their joint charismatic triumph on behalf of the "aesthetically challenged," and thereby transcending and yet celebrating the flesh within the same swaggering moment. Morris Golden remarked that for Churchill "Creativity means deification of an impulse (an attitude aggressively connected with sex)."[38] Impulsiveness is the stuff of freedom and *heterosexual* sex is the paradigmatic happy impulse. Churchill has no qualms about accusing his detractors of being either impotent, or sexually deviant, or both.[39]

By the 1760s, there are (according to Churchill) two versions of fantastic invention at loggerheads: the destructive version, typified by Gray, Mason, Ossian, Scottish mysticism, Bute, and anyone else Churchill has had a recent argument with, and the positive version, typified by Churchill himself, the Nonsense Club (Churchill, Lloyd, Thornton, Colman, and Cowper), Sterne, Shakespeare, and Matthew Prior. The mystics and the digressives are firmly opposed. Sane digressive freedom stands opposed to crazed quasireligious sublimity. Dunciadic vacancy is the fate of all those who parade their mystical or mystifying credentials so arrogantly. The Nonsense Club takes the view that the ode is an intrinsically "unambitious" form since its imagery and preoccupations cannot engage with the most urgent human concerns. Or rather, by affecting to be supremely ambitious, the ode *avoids* accomplishing anything real or specific. Churchill counters Gray's sublime oblivion with willful digression. Churchillian digression is vehemently opportunistic and meritocratic. *Independence* shows the poet (Churchill) and the paradigmatic aristocrat (Lord Lyttelton, or perhaps William Pitt),[40] literally weighed in the balance. The massive bearlike frame of the poet sends the insubstantial aristocrat flying. The little moral of the description is that merit is substance whereas title is air. Only solid creative accomplishment is real—everything else is mere slavish fantasy.[41]

Churchill's proud physicality is part of a rhetorical moment that celebrated blunt Englishness in opposition to all things fashionable, delicate, airy, and Italianate. Although Churchill's masculinism inhabits the same xenophobic mood-music as Brown's, the essence of Churchill's project is always *de*mystification. Churchill's masculinity is comprised of active invention, not abstracted astonishment, and his real literary achievement is accordingly an achievement of *tone*. Churchill's bantering manner *is* a libertarian statement.

The best chance of victory for patriotic English common sense concerns the *weight* (figuratively and literally) of personality, personality that uses idiosyncrasy to stave off idiocy. The Scottish villains of Churchill's *The Prophecy of Famine* are lean and haggard, ambitious yet servile, aspiring yet debased, while Churchill is Falstaffian in the enjoyment of his own substance and his own ponderously unambiguous heterosexuality. Paradoxically, Bute's heterosexuality was never placed in doubt even by his most severe and extravagant critics, since he was suspected of being the lover of the Queen Mother. This suspicion does not, however, automatically protect him from the charge of effeminacy, since evil imaginings of effeminacy in the eighteenth century could elide into either homosexuality or into an ignoble "serving" of women. For example, there appears to have been some anxiety that Italian castrati were displacing rough tuneless English husbands, serving as safe-sex toys for degenerate English gentlewomen (literally replacing substance with ingenuity). Churchill describes castrati accordingly as:

> *Half*-Men, who, dry and pithless, are debarr'd
> From Man's best jobs- no sooner made than marr'd-
> *Half*-Men, whom many a rich and noble Dame,
> To serve her lust, and yet secure her fame,
> Keeps on high diet, as We Capons feed,
> To glut our appetites at last decreed,
>
> (*The Times*, 235–40)

Churchill describes a grim state of affairs whereby a (supposedly debased) heterosexual taste can prefer "Half-Men" to whole ones. Italianate singers are therefore threats to heterosexuality while remaining heterosexually threatening. Italy is most often cited as the alien source of gender confusion. In *The Times*, Churchill refers to Italy as the nursery of every form of vice. Viral metaphors are very current: Estimate Brown has an entire chapter called "A Remark on the Unhumanity of the Italians.[42] Italy is a fifth column, a poison, and a virus. Clearly, disunited Italy formed no direct military threat to Britain in the 1750s and '60s. Italy instead functioned as the lubricant used by France to penetrate English national integrity. From Churchill's point of view it is no accident that the exiled Stuarts reside in Italy. Back home, the ruling classes have become passive and pathic, unmanned and immobile—the tool of alien interests. Unambiguous heterosexuality becomes Churchill's own contribution to vigorous national defense.

Bute (whose real name *is* Stuart) is constructed by Churchill not so much as a sexless effeminate or a homosexual, but as a *furtive* heterosexual, a creature of pious pretensions who has tutored the young George

III in the ways of hypocritically professed "virtue." King and ministry together promote a priggish and repressive rhetoric that operates in defiance of practical reality:

> A TUTOR once, more read in men than books,
> A kind of crafty knowledge in his looks,
> Demurely sly, with high preferment blest,
> His fav'rite Pupil in these words addrest:

> WOULD'ST thou, my son, be wise and virtuous deem'd.
> By all mankind a prodigy esteem'd?
> Be this thy rule; be what men *prudent* call;
> PRUDENCE, almighty PRUDENCE gives thee all.
> Keep up appearences; there lies the test,
> The World will give thee credit for the rest.
> Outward be fair, however foul within;
> Sin if thou wilt, but then in secret sin.
> This maxim's into common favour grown,
> Vice is no longer vice unless 'tis known.
> Virtue indeed may barefac'd take the field,
> But vice is virtue, when 'tis well conceal'd.
> Should raging passions drive thee to a whore,
> Let PRUDENCE lead thee to a *postern* door;
> Stay out all night, but take special care
> That PRUDENCE bring thee back to early prayer.
> As one with watching and with study faint,
> Reel in a drunkard, and reel in a saint.

> (Night, 303–24)

"Bute's speech" permits limited heterosexual expression but forbids its honest celebration. The "postern door" clearly indicates a mode of penetration designed to avoid conception and/or venereal disease. Churchill's "Bute" advocates a stunted joyless effort of sexual release, a yielding to the passions only within the context of denying their truth value. Bute is not so much a "half man" as a man of two halves.

Churchill constructs himself, by way of contrast, as a "whole man" who enjoys uninhibited success with women despite the debased tastes of "the times." His wholeness is related to his intrusive narrative "presence." The decisive literary innovation that Churchill appears to have accelerated, recognized and cherished is the creation of the character of an authorial presence that transcends (or rather "outweighs") the net effect of his or her attributed writings. Churchill's literary limitations are consciously celebrated—*by Churchill*—as a way of affirming the incapacity of form to contain the weight of his own personality.

Conclusion

Understandings of the effeminate in the eighteenth century elide into one another but cannot be said to form any logical continuum or consistently gendered mindset. I join therefore with Michèle Cohen in wishing: "to resist the attempts to make 'effeminacy' coherent and unitary by reducing it to gender, to sex or to politics. Its very ambiguity, its contradictions even, are, as Michel Foucault would say, evidence of its historicity."[43] Hyperbolic gendering does not evolve according to any predictive unidirectional trajectory, but such rhetoric does adapt to suit changing historical priorities. The progress of hyperbolic masculinity has been traced in this chapter from the medical through the social to the political, through Armstrong, Brown, and Churchill. Masculinity, constructed by Cheyne and Armstrong in terms of holistic self-maintenance and by Brown in terms of civic-minded national defense, becomes celebrated by Churchill as a paradoxical but libertarian statement of self-destructive self-sufficiency. In the 1730s a sexually ambiguous lifestyle and culture is figured as a threat to established values. By the 1760s, the triumph of the sexless is represented by Churchill as having become so complete that the poet/satirist is now the encroacher, the anachronistic heterosexual striking a blow against effeminate and sodomitical orthodoxy. The citadel has long been stormed (or rather subverted), and Churchill can only fling pebbles from outside the walls.

Churchill's "offensive" masculinity may appear with hindsight to be even more absurd than Brown's "defensive" machismo. They are both, however, innovators within a rhetorical extremity that assumes and sustains a climate of belief that treats gender as precious and insecure. A climate of sexual anxiety creates, at least for Churchill, the basis of genuinely interesting literary experiment. I should not wish to suggest for one moment that there is anything "creative" or "innovative" about homophobia in the eighteenth (or any other) century. However, the gendered context informing formal decisions made by poets and prose writers shows how productive and how intractable attempts to claim the masculine high ground could become. Within the paranoia there is creative contradiction. Sexual insecurity also becomes a defining pressure on literary form. The more urgently authors claim to know who and what they are and ought to be, the more provisional and fluid appears the whole issue of sexual identity in the eighteenth century.

Notes

1. George Cheyne, *The English Malady: Or, A Treatise of Nervous Diseases of all Kinds, As Spleen, Vapours, Lowness of Spirits, Hyponchondrical and Hysterical Distempers etc,* 3 vols. (London: Printed for G. Strahan, 1733), 14–15.

2. "Using any *Organ* frequently and forcibly, brings *Blood* and *Spirits* into it, and do makes its grow *Plump* and *Brawny*." George Cheyne, *An Essay of Health and Long Life* (London: Printed for George Strahan, 1724), 96–97.

3. Cheyne, *The English Malady*, 96.

4. Ibid., 156–57.

5. *English Poets*, ed. by Alexander Chalmers, 21 vols. (London, 1810), vol. XVI, 516.

6. *The Oeconomy of Love: A Poetical Essay*, 3ʳᵈ ed. (London: Printed for T. Cooper, 1737), 6.

7. Michel Foucault, *The History of Sexuality*, vol. I, trans. by Robert Hurley, (Harmondsworth: Penguin, 1979), 70–73. Foucault, incidentally, regards this pleasured scientism as a phenomenon that has developed since the nineteenth century.

8. Peter Wagner, "The Discourse on Sex or Sex as Discourse: Eighteenth-century Medical and Paramedical Erotica," in *Sexual Underworlds of the Enlightenment*, ed. G. S. Rousseau and Roy Porter (Chapel Hill: University of North Carolina Press, 1988), 50.

9. John Armstrong, M.D., *Miscellanies*, 2 vols. (London: Printed for T. Cadell, 1770), I, v.

10. "Of the Press," *Miscellanies*, II, 213.

11. Chalmers, *English Poets*, XVI, 517.

12. James Sambrook, *James Thomson 1700- 1748, A Life* (Oxford: Clarendon Press, 1991), 262.

13. After Thomson's death, Armstrong wrote of him, in the same choleric manner that had perversely endeared him to a number of people, in a letter to John Forbes, 3 September "If he had struggled thro' that Fever, there are many reasons to believe, that is must unavoidably have been followed by some lingering disease. . . . Besides, I think him greatly to be envied, to have got rid of this rascally world" (Sambrook, 277). The poet William Shenstone claimed that Thomson's devotion to Armstrong was the direct cause of Thomson's own death, since he delayed receiving any other doctor until Armstrong could arrive, and Armstrong arrived too late.

14. John Armstrong, *Medical Essays* (London: Printed for T. Davies, 1773), 5.

15. Ibid.

16. *English Poets*, ed. by Alexander Chalmers, 21 vols. (London, 1810), Vol. XVI, 516.

17. Judith Butler, *Bodies that Matter: On the Discursive Limits of Sex* (London: Routledge, 1993)

18. Julia Kristeva, *Revolution in Poetic Language*, trans. Margaret Waller (NewYork: Columbia University Press, 1984), 79–80.

19. John Armstrong, *The Oeconomy of Love, a New Edition, Revised and Corrected by the Author* (London: Printed for S. Bladen, 1768).

20. Andrew Kippis, *Biographica Britannica*, 6 vols. (London, 1747–66), II, 656.

21. Henry Home, Lord Kames, *Elements of Criticism*, 2 vols., 5ᵗʰ ed. (Edinburgh: Printed for A. Kinkaid, W. Creech, and J. Bell, 1774), vii.

22. John Brown, *A Dissertation on the Rise, Union, and Power, the Progressions, Separations, and Corruptions of Poetry and Music. To which is prefixed The Cure of Saul, A Sacred Ode* (London: Printed for L. Davis and C. Reymers, 1763), 135.

22. Cheyne, *The English Malady*, i–ii.

24. John Brown, *An Estimate of the Manners and Principles of the Times*, 2 vols. (Dublin: Printed for G. Faulkner, J. Hoey, and J. Exshaw, 1757), I, 30–31.

25. Ibid.

26. The most thorough treatment of the active association of homosexuality and femininity is offered in Rictor Norton, *Mother Clap's Molly House: The Gay Subculture in England, 1700–1830* (London: Gay Men's Press, 1992).

27. John Brewer, *The Pleasures of the Imagination* (London: Harper Collins: 1997), 80.

28. Brown, *A Dissertation*, 129.

29. William Roberts, *A Dawn of Imaginative Feeling: The Contribution of John Brown (1714–66) to Eighteenth-century Thought and Literature* (Carlisle: Northern Academic Press, 1996), 34.

30. John Brown, *The Mutual Connexion between Religious Truth and Civil Freedom; between Superstition, Tyranny, Irreligion, and Licentiousness: Considered in Two Sermons Preached in September 1746, at the Cathedral Church of Carlisle, during the Assizes held there for the Trial of the Rebels* (London: Printed for R. Dodsley, 1746).

31. Brown, *Estimate*, I, 34.

32. Brown, *Estimate*, II, 80–81.

33. Samuel Johnson, *The Idler and the Adventurer*, eds. W. J. Bate, John M. Bullitt and L. F. Powell (New Haven and London: Yale University Press, 1970), pp. 18–19. Carolyn Williams has also written suggestively on Brown in *Pope, Homer and Manliness: Some Aspects of Eighteenth-century Classical Learning* (London: Routledge, 1993), 192–95.

34. Brown, *Estimate*, II, 79.

35. Ibid., 97.

36. *The Poetical Works of Charles Churchill*, ed. Douglas Grant (Oxford: Clarendon Press, 1956), 398.

37. *An Epistle to the Irreverend Mr C— — C— —, In his Own Style and Manner* (London: Printed for W. Nicoll, 1764), 13.

38. Churchill, *Independence*, 147–54.

44. Morris Golden, "Sterility and Eminence in the Poetry of Charles Churchill," *Journal of English and Germanic Philology* LXVI (Urbana: University of Illinois Press, 1967), 333–46.

39. The freedom of self-luxuriance encompasses all other freedoms as far as Churchill is concerned. Servility is primarily a state of intellectual and imaginative blindness. Like Pope, Churchill defines freedom in reaction to Dunciadic absurdity. Of course, such freedom, insofar as it distinguishes itself in opposition to the Dunces, is expressively dependent on the Dunces for its expression. Without a concept of slavish stupidity there is no concept of invigorating independence. Dunciadic celebration is a moment where human detritus is reorganized by a subversive yet creative satiric vision.

40. Lance Bertelsen, *The Nonsense Club, Literature and Popular Culture, 1749–64* (Oxford: Clarendon Press, 1986), 239–41.

41. The poem is reminiscent of Johnson's caustic letter to Chesterfield. Churchill had much in common with Johnson, culturally and temperamentally. Johnson had enjoyed the "Gray and Mason" parodies of Lloyd and Thornton and had, of course, attacked the cult and the credentials of *Ossian*. Churchill, however, could only see Johnson the Tory, Johnson the Pensioner, and Johnson the Ghostbuster and mocked him accordingly. Johnson is just such another creature of pretentious wind while Churchill is, as ever, a man of substance.

42. Brown, *Estimate*, II, 41–49.

43. Michèle Cohen, *Fashioning Masculinity: National Identity and Language in the Eighteenth century* (London: Routledge, 1996), 6.

Women Behaving Well:
Early Modern Images of Female Courage

CAROLYN D. WILLIAMS

ALTHOUGH FEMALE TRANSVESTITES APPEAR FREQUENTLY IN FACTUAL and fictional writing from Shakespeare's time to the end of the eighteenth century, they cause surprisingly little disturbance to the social order. Serious challenges to traditional gender demarcation might be expected to arise from cases where women disguised themselves as men and, in order to play out their role, displayed a degree of physical courage or moral fortitude that contemporaries normally defined as "masculine." Such behavior might have been perceived as a challenge to the theory and practice of patriarchy. It might also have led to speculation about the authenticity of the femininity from which these women had supposedly deviated. Were they unnatural freaks or the product of exceptional circumstances or indications of a latent potential common to many women? In the latter case, what was to be made of the widespread belief that women were feeble creatures, helpless in any emergency and afraid of their own shadows? This investigation will reveal a fascinating variety of opinions about female nature, together with a surprising degree of complacency about the sort of lives "normal" women led.

Dianne Dugaw's invaluable insights must be the starting point for any investigation of this subject. She finds that the "Female Warrior," popular in ballads, drama, and other media, integrates three important features of early modern social history: "the physical toughness" that the age demanded from lower-class women, the frequent "participation of women in military activities," and the ways in which the Female Warrior's cross-dressing masquerades "accurately represents both the preoccupations and the experience of people living in an age obsessed at all levels with disguise and cross-dressing."[1] This study, however, extends its scope beyond military life to include female courage in general. It begins by indicating some of the anxieties and controversies that the subject aroused in early modern spectators, including those who considered courage a valuable quality in all women. The next two sections

50

show how they affected the presentation of female transvestites in factual writing and in drama. Finally, accounts of courage in early modern
women who did not attempt to pass as men raise important questions
about the authenticity of feminine "softness"—and about the failure of
most early modern writers to draw appropriate conclusions.

UNCOMELY COURAGE

The spectacle of a woman successfully filling a "masculine" role in
early modern society frequently raised the question of the respective
roles that nature and nurture played in gender differentiation. It was
often implied that it was "natural" for boys to become masculine, and
girls feminine: thus "masculine" behavior in a woman could be interpreted as the result of some drastic distortion of her innermost essence,
brought about by dire necessity or perverted upbringing. Yet the
presses were forever groaning with education tracts, sermons, conduct
literature, and other works designed to form manly men and womanly
women. To the sceptical eye, their very existence suggests that, if gender were indeed ordained by nature, it was not the sort of nature that
could be trusted to take its course unaided by years of obsessive education.[2] Although much early modern writing suggests that these awkward implications are kept in an ideological blind spot, disturbing
possibilities often ruffle the complacent surface of the text.

Another problem arising from brave female transvestites was the possibility that all gender roles were performative, that there was no true
essence of masculinity or femininity that could be securely fastened to
a male or female body. Dugaw argues that, "Commandeering masculine
gender codes as masterfully as she does her cutlass and her rigging, the
disguised heroine reaffirms these codes in her own parody of them: if
men were not recognisable as such by certain kinds of dress and behaviour and women by others, the Female Warrior of balladry could not
exist."[3]

But is the process a little too easy? Does it imply that what one sex
can put on, the other can take off? Is the man who adopts the role of
masculinity or the woman who enacts femininity any more authentic
than the effeminate male or the female transvestite? Again, literature on
the subject is rich in disquieting implications, but direct confrontation
of this hideous possibility is understandably rare.

A related topic, which occasionally received more direct treatment,
and whose complexity demands careful analysis, is the doctrine of relative virtues. Were all virtues equally suitable for either sex or were their
circumstances in which actions that would appear excellent in a person

with penis and testicles would become reprehensible if performed by a person without them? This question provoked fascinating reflections, and revealed even more fascinating assumptions, on the nature of virtue and the nature of women, not to mention that of the penis and testicles. Female reproductive organs were often described as inversions, or even negatives, of the male equivalent. *Annus Mirabilis* (1722), a hilarious prediction of a universal sex change by Dr. John Arbuthnot (1667–1735) and Alexander Pope (1688–1744), illustrates the currency of this assumption: *"Anaximander* modestly describes this Metamorphosis in Mathematical Terms: *Then,* says he, *shall the negative Quantity of the Women be turn'd into positive, their* − into +; (i.e.), their *Minus* into *Plus."*[4] Could femininity also figure as a *moral* minus sign, which not only annihilated but reversed good qualities, so that virtue itself became a perverse mirror-image of its "normal" self? The spectacle of a woman who aspired to traditionally "manly" virtues exacerbated the contradictions that arose in any female claim to virtue, when, as any schoolboy might learn from his earliest textbook, *"Virtue* derives her Name from *Vir* [man], because *Virtue* is the most manly *Ornament."*[5] Courage, in particular, was closely associated with male physiology. The *Oxford English Dictionary* offers a definition of "courage" as "sexual vigour and inclination; lust": all the examples given illustrate male desire. Thus only the slightest semantic slippage was required to make a brave woman unnatural, monstrous, and therefore repulsive.

The fiercest attacks on female courage are launched by writers who believe that it is incompatible with the life-giving, nurturing role that women ought to perform. Since the brave woman is an empowered woman, she can also be depicted as prone to insubordination. In *Doomes-Day* (1614–37), Sir William Alexander, Earl of Stirling (?1567–1640), places various kinds of female warrior among violent, perverse, ambitious, and idolatrous sinners awaiting their richly deserved damnation:

> Some women came who had (made milde, grown rude)
> A female face, too masculine a minde,
> Who though first fram'd to propagate men's brood,
> (From nature stray'd) toyl'd to destroy their kinde:
> By differing meanes both sexes grace their state,
> I scorne mens coynesse, womens stoutnesse hate.
>
> ("The Sixth Houre," stanza 86, 691–96)

They include both Amazons, who did not conceal their sex, and Semiramis, who became one of history's earliest male impersonators when she ruled Assyria disguised as her dead husband Ninus: "Ashur's empresse,

who disguis'd did raigne" (stanza 87, 697).[6] Stirling's choice of words
reinforces his argument that transference from one sex to the other
changes virtue to vice. Thus womanly modesty, in men, degenerates to
the ridiculously affected "coynesse." "Stoutnesse" is another weighted
term: according to the *Oxford English Dictionary*, it might be used simply
as a synonym for courage, but its primary meaning was "pride, haughti-
ness, arrogance." It also had connotations of "stubbornness, intractabil-
ity, rebelliousness"—all highly undesirable, not to say dangerous,
characteristics for women in the eyes of men who feared female power.

Some writers seemed incapable of separating female courage from
cruelty. In his didactic poem *The Seasons* (1726–46), James Thomson
(1700–1748) turns from a satiric condemnation of male fox hunters to
a digression on femininity; he begins by saying women should not be
fierce, then proceeds to condemn the ability to jump a fence as an inappropriate type of courage. Before we know where we are, he is recom-
mending that women should adopt an appearance of cowardice on all
occasions:

> *BUT* if the rougher Sex by this fierce Sport
> Is hurry'd wild, let not such horrid joy
> E'er stain the bosom of the *BRITISH FAIR.*
> Far be the spirit of the Chace from them!
> Uncomely Courage, unbeseeming skill,
> To spring the fence, to rein the prancing Steed,
> The Cap, the Whip, the masculine Attire,
> In which they roughen to the Sense, and all
> The winning softness of their Sex is lost.
> In them 'tis graceful to dissolve at Woe;
> With every Motion, every Word, to wave
> Quick o'er the kindling Cheek the ready Blush;
> And from the smallest Violence to shrink
> Unequal, then the loveliest in their Fears;
> And by this silent Adulation, soft,
> To their Protection more engaging Man.

(570–85)[7]

He launches into a treatise on proper feminine activities, from needle-
work and making preserves to the education of daughters; thanks to the
manner in which he has introduced it, the whole duty of woman seems
to be rooted in fear.

Jonathan Swift (1667–1745) thinks better of female potential. In *A
Letter to a Young Lady, on her Marriage. Written in the Year 1723* (1727), he
rejects the doctrine of relative virtue and deftly reverses the customary
equation of female courage with fierceness by arguing out that the com-

monly observed connection between cowardice and cruelty in men also applies to women:

> I AM ignorant of any one Quality that is amiable in a Man, which is not equally so in a Woman: I do not except even Modesty, and Gentleness of Nature. Nor do I know one Vice or Folly, which is not equally detestable in both. There is, indeed, one Infirmity which is generally allowed you, I mean that of Cowardice. Yet there should seem to be something very capricious, that when Women profess their Admiration for a Colonel or a Captain, on Account of his Valour; they should fancy it a very graceful becoming quality in themselves, to be afraid of their own Shadows; to scream in a Barge, when the Weather is calmest, or in a Coach at the Ring; to run from a Cow at an Hundred Yards Distance; to fall into Fits at the Sight of a Spider, an Ear-wig, or a Frog. At least, if Cowardice be a Sign of Cruelty, (as it is generally granted) I can hardly think it an Accomplishment so desireable, as to be thought worthy of improving by Affectation.[8]

Swift admires the fortitude of his friend Esther Johnson (1681–1728), whom he refers to as Stella in his poetry. "To Stella Visiting Me in my Sickness" (1720; first published 1727) provides the perfect context for his view that female courage can coexist with gentleness and consideration for others:

> She thinks that nature ne'er designed
> Courage to man alone confined:
> Can cowardice her sex adorn,
> Which most exposes ours to scorn?
> She wonders where the charm appears
> In Florimel's affected fears:
> For Stella never learned the art,
> At proper times to scream and start;
> Nor calls up all the house at night,
> And swears she saw a thing in white:
> Doll never flies to cut her lace,
> Or throw cold water in her face,
> Because she heard a sudden drum,
> Or found an earwig in a plum.
>
> (65–78)[9]

But it could be difficult to gain general acceptance for such a view. Even the English language worked against it. When Swift wrote his thoughts "On the Death of Mrs. Johnson" (1728; first published 1765), he declared that, "With all the softness of temper that became a lady, she had the personal courage of a hero."[10] The use of "hero" as the standard of courage shows how hard it is to break away from the notion that it is a masculine prerogative.

In *A Vindication of the Rights of Woman* (1792) Mary Wollstonecraft (1759–1797) exposed the political implications of the notion that women and men should be judged by different standards. The "virtues" deemed appropriate to women would enable them to perform only subordinate, ancillary roles, and inefficiently at that. Women who embraced this doctrine would facilitate their own oppression by appearing, or even becoming, morally, physically, and intellectually feeble:

> I wish to persuade women to endeavour to acquire strength, both of mind and body, and to convince them that the soft phrases, susceptibility of heart, delicacy of sentiment, and refinement of taste, are almost synonymous with epithets of weakness, and that those beings who are only the objects of pity and that kind of love, which has been termed its sister, will soon become objects of contempt. . . .
>
> To account for, and excuse the tyranny of man, many ingenious arguments have been brought forward to prove, that the two sexes, in the acquirement of virtue, ought to aim at attaining a very different character: or, to speak explicitly, women are not allowed [believed] to have sufficient strength of mind to acquire what really deserves the name of virtue. Yet is should seem, allowing them to have souls, that there is but one way appointed by Providence to lead *mankind* to either virtue or happiness.[11]

For Mary Wollstonecraft, courage and its kindred virtues was not the mark of masculinity, but of humanity.

"THE *MARK OF NATURE*"

We have hard evidence of women's ability to assume masculine identity, hold down a "man's" job, and even gain rewards officially reserved for good military service: "Though no woman has ever been admitted to the Royal Hospital as an In-Pensioner, two have been placed on the out-pension list."[12] Christian, Christina or Catherine Walsh, alias Welch, Ross or Davis (1667–1739), was "awarded a pension of 5d. a day in 1717 for her service in Flanders with 'the Royll Regt of North British Drags,' Royal Scots Greys, and three years later it was raised to 1s. at the instance of the Lords Justices, besides which she had £30 per annum procured for her by the Duke of Cumberland."[13] Thirty-three years later, after service in the Marquess of Frazer's Marines and Guize's Regiment, Hannah Snell (1723–1792) was "admitted to the pension list in 1750 at 5d. a day, but in 1785 was allowed 1s., 'in compassion for her infirm state of health'" (see Portrait of Hannah Snell, below).[14] Both women were best known to the public through books that added elaborate, and largely apocryphal, episodes to their life stories, but could not entirely obscure the authenticity of their military service. *The Life and Adventures of Mrs. Christian Davies, Commmonly Called Mother Ross* (1740) contains many racy stories that appear to have been attached to the heroine's name for the purpose of swelling a volume and details about the campaigns of John Churchill, Duke of Marlborough (1650–1722) that could not have lain within her immediate experience. A great deal of apparently reliable information about Hannah Snell's naval and military exploits appears in two anonymous volumes of different lengths, both entitled *The Female Soldier: Or, the Surprising Life and Adventures of Hannah Snell* (1750). To render her authentication complete, Hannah Snell even appeared on stage.[15]

The most unusual feature of their careers is probably the attention they attracted. Far more common are cases where women's naval or military careers are revealed in the course of some unrelated crisis, then swiftly forgotten. For example, the *Historical Chronicle* for 30 January 1783 reports that "A woman, in man's apparel, was charged on oath on suspicion of stealing a purse, containing 37 guineas. . . . It is said, she has been a petty-officer in the sea-service for some years."[16] A more elaborate story of crime and transvestism was revealed on Sunday 14 April 1765:

> The murder of Mrs *Ruscombe* and her maid was found out; the maid let in a female acquaintance unknown to her mistresss, and this acquaintance let in two fellows, unknown to the maid. They all three murdered the maid first, and then the mistress. This abandoned creature, having been in the marine service as a drummer, &c. has voluntarily confessed the whole; saying, that she could have no ease night nor day since she did it, but when she was drunk, and therefore made the discovery in order to ease her mind.[17]

Such women could not be used as icons of patriotism and exemplars of virtue beyond the call of feminine duty. The most celebrated eighteenth-century passing women who combined combat and crime were the pirates Mary Read and Anne Bonny. According to the *General History of the Pyrates* (1724), sometimes attributed to Daniel Defoe (1660–1731), Read was brought up as a boy from about the age of three and served with distinction in a cavalry regiment in Flanders: she "behaved so well in several Engagements, that she got the Esteem of all her Officers."[18] After becoming a pirate, she displayed equal toughness; her shipmate Anne Bonny, who passed as a boy for a brief spell in early childhood, was one of the few who could match her: "in Times of Action, no Person amongst them was more resolute, or ready to board or undertake any Thing that was hazardous, than she and *Anne Bonny*; and particularly at the time they were attack'd and taken, when they came to close Quarters, none kept the Deck except *Mary Read* and *Anne Bonny*, and one more."[19]

Authors of such narratives apparently expect incredulity, and, having removed that, wonder. An article in the *Gentleman's Magazine*, July 1750, draws attention to the amazing combination of modesty and fortitude which Hannah Snell (see Portrait of Hannah Snell) displayed at the siege of Pondicherry: "An attack was at length made, in which Hannah having fired 37 rounds, receiv'd a ball in the groin, six wounds in one leg, and five in the other."[20] With the help of a discreet woman friend, she not only recovered from her injuries, but managed to conceal her sex. An anonymous poem, "The Female Soldier," celebrates this combination of masculine and feminine virtues:

> *HANNAH* in *breeks* behav'd so well,
> That none her *softer sex* could tell:
> Nor was her *policy* confounded,
> When near the *mark of nature* wounded.
>
> (1–4)[21]

The statement that Hannah behaved "well" in these circumstances raises disquieting doubts. Good behavior in a soldier means a display of courageous aggression: by behaving well as a man, Hannah is not behaving appropriately for a woman. Although nobody could "tell" her softer sex, it was always there: Hannah, though apparently a hard warrior, was always, at some profound level, soft, because all women must be soft. Her "mark of nature" is somewhere in the vicinity of her groin: this shows what she really is, defining her in terms of her reproductive physiology. Even while this poem praises her valor, it denies its authenticity.

A similarly ambiguous response is evoked by *The Female Soldier*, which commends Hannah's "Judgment and Intrepidity" at sea and "uncommon Bravery" on land.[22] The author invites the reader to marvel at the fact that she has accomplished so much, despite being hampered by the physical and mental weaknesses natural to women:

I CANNOT help reflecting a little upon the Hardships, Fatigues and Dangers she incountered from the Time she left *Lisbon* in *Europe*, till her Arrival before *Pondicherry* in *Asia*, so many Vicissitudes, as were sufficient to damp the Spirits of an *Alexander* or a *Csar*, Storms, Hurricanes, and pinching Want, were her Concomitants, pumping an almost wrecked Vessel, was the most constant (tho laborious) Employment; seventeen Weeks short Allowance from the *Maderas* to the *Cape* of *Good Hope*, was all she had to subsist

THE
Gentleman's Magazine,
For JULY 1750.

Some account of HANNAH SNELL, *the* Female SOLDIER.

Portrait of Hannah Snell, *Gentleman's Magazine* XX (July 1750), 291.

upon; Attacks upon fortified Towns, some of which were impregnable, where Bomb-Shells and Cannons were incessantly displaying Death wherever they fell; at other Times, moving, marching, and encamping; I say such Reflections and gloomy Prospects, prove the Cause of many such Hardships and Difficulties even in the most robust of the Masculine Gender, how much more in one of the tender Sex, who are afraid of Shaddows, and shudders at the Pressage of a Dream.[23]

Instead of modifying assumptions about women in the light of Hannah's achievements, both poem and pamphlet modify Hannah herself, by setting her (presumed) essential feminine weakness against her outward seeming. Readers are not invited to draw logical inferences from her story, but to indulge in wonder: she is not only unique, but self-contradictory.

Suggesting that readers may find a story incredible is not only an effective opening for a claim of authorial reliability; it is also a good way to incite them to read on, in hope of finding an exciting story. Defoe's introduction to his account of Read and Bonny, which "some may be tempted to think . . . no better than a Novel or Romance" serves both purposes.[24] He insists that women really performed notable feats of valor, even while their own reported speeches emphasize their incredibility. When all but Read, Bonny, and one other companion responded to the threat of imminent battle by skulking below, "she, Mary Read, called to those under Deck, to come up and fight like Men, and finding they did not stir, fired her Arms down the Hold amongst them, killing one, and wounding others."[25] Would it not have made more sense, at this juncture, to ask them to fight like women? Bonny appeared equally insensitive to the implications of her own exploits when she bade farewell to her captain and lover, John Rackham: "The Day that Rackam was executed, by special Favour, he was admitted to see her; but all the Comfort she gave him, was, that she was sorry to see him there, but if he had fought like a Man, he need not have been hang'd like a Dog."[26]

The image of the fighting woman could be reconciled with the expectation that women should be gentle, affectionate, and nurturing by showing her using her skills to protect others. One appropriate role is a defender of beleaguered chastity. For example, Christian Davies challenged a sergeant who had tried to rape a virtuous girl, and wounded him severely, despite the fact that she was herself wounded and had the inferior weapon.[27] Women's combats may also be expressions of love. This happened when Mary Read fell in love with a pirate who was challenged to a duel by a formidable opponent: "she took a Resolution of quarrelling with this Fellow her self, and having challenged him shore, she appointed the Time two Hours sooner than that when he was to meet her Lover, where she fought him at Sword and Pistol, and killed him upon the Spot."[28] In these cases, Davies and Read would have shown more cruelty and hardness of heart if they had refrained from fighting.

"This Was Admirably Perform'd"

In Elizabethan and Jacobean theater, transvestite women are presented sympathetically, but seldom display much physical aggression. Since all female parts were played by boys, there may have been sound technical reasons for this. For example, if a boy in a boy's costume were to give a competent display of the manly art of swordsmanship, it would be very difficult to think of the character he was portraying as female. Some of Shakespeare's passing girls assume a certain swagger, but those who are subjected to shocks or danger reveal their fears to the audience and sometimes to other characters on stage. Jean E. Howard notes the "properly feminine subjectivity" of Viola in *Twelfth Night*.[29] When challenged to a duel, she "freely admits that she has neither the desire nor the aptitude to play the man's part in phallic swordplay. The whole thrust of the dramatic narrative is to release this woman from the prison of her masculine attire and return her to her proper and natural position in life."[30] Howard sees Portia, in *The Merchant of Venice*, as a different case:

> Her man's disguise is not a psychological refuge but a vehicle for assuming power. Unlike those cross-dressed heroines who faint at the sight of blood or who cannot wield a sword, Portia seems able to play the man's part with conviction. Her actions hardly dismantle the sex-gender system; but they do reveal that masculine prerogatives are based on custom, not nature, since a woman can indeed successfully assume masculine positions of authority.[31]

But although Portia is convincing in the courtroom, she is never called upon to display physical courage; Shakespeare never suggests that she or Nerissa would acquit themselves well in combat. Portia plans to appear as a pretentious brat, and speak of frays

> Like a fine bragging youth, and tell quaint lies,
>
> . . . .
>
> That men shall swear I have discontinu'd school
> Above a twelvemonth.
>
> (III, iv, 68–69, 75–76)[32]

Shakespeare leaves his audience secure in the knowledge that the masculinity that can be assumed by a woman is not the real thing.

After the Restoration of Charles II (1630–1685) in 1660, the arrival of actresses on the English professional stage drastically altered the sexual dynamics of female transvestite parts. They became very popular, less as an image of female empowerment than as a chance to exploit the attractions of a body stripped of the corsets, petticoats, and other impedimenta within which chaste convention sheltered the female form. Yet the fact that actresses were involved paradoxically made it easier for female characters to perform daring feats, since there was no need to suspend disbelief that a female was actually performing them. Thus post-Restoration playwrights could use transvestism to emphasize female strength or weakness. Sometimes we see both at once, as disguised female characters gamely struggle to conceal their own vulnerability. In *She Wou'd and She Wou'd Not* (1703), Colley Cibber (1671–1751) depicts the agonies suffered by Hypolita and her friend Flora when they adopt male disguise, and the demanding lifestyle that goes with it. After a day's hard riding, Flora says, "I'm sure my shoulders ache as if I had carried my horse on them." Nor is this the only damaged area. She goes on to complain, "Egad, I sha'n't be able to sit this fortnight" (I, i).[33] The girls consider the possiblity that their conduct will get them into a fight and realize that the only weapons they can use effectively are words:

> *Flora*. I can push no more than I can swim.
> *Hypolita*. But can you bully upon occasion?
> *Flora*. I can scold when my blood's up.
> *Hypolita*. That's the same thing: bullying would be scolding in petticoats.
>
> (I, i)[34]

The connection between the ability to "push" (make a thrust in fencing) with the ability to swim, a standard gendered shibboleth, highlights the fact that a woman in male disguise is out of her element.

A method of undercutting female valor that works well on stage is portraying it as a staged exhibition, a performance within a performance. A peep behind the scenes shows us that the woman we have been watching with such admiration is not nearly so brave as we thought. A prime example appears in Cibber's *The Lady's Last Stake; or, the Wife's Resentment* (1708). Mrs. Conquest, who is in love with the rakish Lord George Brilliant, loses patience with his philandering, dons male disguise, and challenges him to a duel. While Lord George is awaiting his opponent, he is set upon by four robbers. Mrs. Conquest comes to his defense with a pistol, but it misses fire. The rogues attack her with swords, then retreat, leaving her on the ground, declaring, "I am

killed—I fear the wound's quite through me" (V, iii).³⁵ A surgeon is
hastily summoned; he reveals his patient's sex, and says, " 'tis impossible she can live three hours" (V, v).³⁶ By now, the audience, like the
onstage characters, must be seriously worried. Lord George, smitten by
remorse and returning love, proposes to marry her instantly. But before
the knot is tied, Mrs. Conquest reveals that she is unwounded and that
the "robbers" and the surgeon were all part of her plot. A similar deception is carried out in *The Country Lasses: Or, The Custom of the Manor*
(1715), by Charles Johnson (1679–1748). The sprightly Aura, in male
disguise, challenges the dissolute Modely to a duel to avenge a rape attempt upon herself. She brings pistols, which she says are loaded
equally "with a Brace of Balls" (V, i).³⁷ They fire. Aura falls, and Modely runs off, afraid he will face a charge of murder. Aura's friend, the
farmer Freehold, comes in. Aura gets up and the language, as well as
her actions, makes it clear that neither pistol was loaded, and it was all
an act, which they had arranged between them:

> *Aura.* Is the stage clear?
>
> . . . .
>
> *Freehold.* This was admirably perform'd: I was afraid
> you durst not have stood the Powder.
> *Aura.* No, no—I put in but half a Charge, and no Wadding.
>
> (V, I)³⁸

Not only is Aura's apparent courage an illusion, but the illusion itself is
substandard: she cannot even fire blanks properly. Eighteenth-century
illustrations emphasize the ambiguous status of cross-dressed heroines.
Some depict them primarily as characters like any other, busily engaged
in the machinations of a complex plot, and revealing no sign of their
true sex to any viewer not already familiar with the play (See Frontispiece to Charles Johnson, *The Country Lasses: Or, the Custom of the
Manor*, and Frontispiece to Colley Cibber, *The Lady's Last Stake: Or, the
Wife's Resentment*). On the other hand, the presence of a cross-dressed
actress can afford an occasion for display of a static female form, whose
elegant, tight-fitting costume appears designed to encourage the sexual
fantasies of an aroused viewer (See "Mrs. Martyr as Aura").

The most blatant instance of a self-subverting challenge to the masculine monopoly of courage is an epilogue spoken in military dress by Peg
Woffington (?1714–1760), an actress equally famous for her feminine
allure and the flair with which she played both transvestite heroines and
attractive young heroes. Attired as a "Female Volunteer," she addressed
the audience after the British army had suffered ignominious reverses
at the hands of Charles Edward Stuart (1720–1788). At first, the epi-

Frontispiece to Charles Johnson, *The Country Lasses: Or, the Custom of the Manor*,
London: Jacob Tonson, 1735. (Designed and engraved by L. Du Guernier.)

Frontispiece to Colley Cibber, *The Lady's Last Stake: Or, the Wife's Resentment,* 3d ed., London: W. Feales, 1736. (Engraved by P. Fourdrinier.)

"Mrs. Martyr as Aura," designed by De Wilde and engraved by Leney, London: John Bell, Jan. 1792 [*sic*]. Frontispiece to Charles Johnson, *The Country Lasses: Or, the Custom of the Manor*, London: John Bell, 1791 [*sic*].

logue seems to threaten a female takeover of military power, but the racy doubles entendres quickly reassure the audience that her intended strategy depends on exploiting, rather than effacing, sexual difference:

> Well, if 'tis so, and that our *Men* can't stand,
> 'Tis Time we Women take the *Thing* in *Hand*.
>
> . . . .
>
> And really, mark some Heroes in the Nation,
> You'd think this no unnat'ral Transformation:
> For if in Valour real *Manhood* lies,
> All Cowards are but Women in Disguise.
> They cry, these Rebels are so stout and tall!
> Ah lud! *I'd lower the proudest of them all.*
> Try but my *Metal*, place me in the Van,
> And post me, if I don't—*bring down my Man*.
>
> (5–6; 9–16)[39]

The conclusion salvages male pride by pointing out that the enlistment of women into the army is, after all, a fantasy; the only practicable way for women to contribute to the defeat of the Jacobite invasion is by placing their sexual services at the disposal of courageous men:

> To no base Coward prostitute your Charms,
> Disband the Lover who deserts his Arms:
> So shall you fire each Hero to his Duty,
> And British Rights be sav'd by *British* Beauty.
>
> (45–48)

She spoke this epilogue at Drury Lane Theatre several times in the spring of 1746, generally after acting swaggering transvestite roles, including that of Mrs. Conquest.[40]

Women playwrights, particularly Aphra Behn (?1640–1689), are more likely to show a wider spectrum of behavior, within which some transvestite women display genuine courage, especially when inspired by romantic love. In Behn's *The Widdow Ranter* (1690), the Indian Queen finds her warrior garb inappropriate to her personality: "I have no *Amazonian* Fire about me, all my Artillery is sighs and Tears" (V, iii, 191–92).[41] The transvestite Ranter, on the other hand, fights *"like a Fury"* in support of her lover.[42] *The Feign'd Curtizans; or, A Night's Intrigue* (1679) has two cross-dressed heroines, Marcella and Laura, who, in two separate incidents, take on superior numbers to save the men they love. When Galliard congratulates Laura on her "wondrous" bravery, she replies calmly, " 'Twas only justice Sir you being opprest with odds" (II, i, 282–83).[43] After Marcella has rescued Fillamour in similar circumstances, he tells his unrecognised savior, "Thou'st been too kinde to give me cause to doubt thee" (III, i, 541).[44] Behn's duplication of this episode seems designed to persuade the audience that such behavior lies well within normal female parameters.

In some plays, women in breeches and petticoats display equal bravery, indicating that courage may be just as natural to women as any other virtue. In *The Maid's Tragedy* (1619) by Francis Beaumont (1584–1616) and John Fletcher (1579–1625), Amintor becomes fatally involved with two women whose unsuspected capacity for physical courage precipitates catastrophe. His bride, the glamorous Evadne, coolly tells him on the wedding night that she is the King's mistress. Amintor's passionate reproaches awaken her remorse: she stabs the King to death, and later stabs herself. Aspatia, his jilted sweetheart, is a virtuous maiden, still desperately in love with him. Unwilling either to live or to kill herself, she assumes male disguise, challenges Amintor to a duel, and allows him to kill her. Thus the girl who decorously retains her petticoats commits regicide and suicide, while the girl who usurps masculine identity does so in order to destroy herself—or, rather, to be destroyed; her valor is of an extremely passive kind. To emphasize the ironies of the situation, Evadne enters, "her hands bloudy with a knife" (V, iii), eager to boast of her treasonous revenge, at the moment when Aspatia falls with her death wound.[45]

Even more complex negotiations between sex, gender, appearance, and behavior occur in *Love's Cure or, the Martial Maid* (1647), written by Beaumont and Fletcher, with revisions by Philip Massinger (1583–1640). The basic situation is a gender exchange between brother and sister: "*LUCIO, Son to Alvarez, a brave young Gentleman in womans habit*" and "*CLARA, Daughter to Eugenia, a martial Maid, valiant and chaste.*"[46] The action concerns the restoration of Lucio and Clara to "normal" roles. But the question of courage occasions an intriguing asymmetry, since, as the list of characters indicates, Lucio gains it, but Clara does not lose it. Clara fights three times, once dressed as a man, and twice as a woman. Each time she fights in a "feminine" cause, to save someone she cares for: she protects her brother from a bully, and twice saves the life of Vitelli, her father's enemy, with whom she falls in love. Her habit of rescuing Vitelli raises awkard emotional problems: he is afraid that she will be too fierce and insubordinate to make a proper wife. So Clara renounces her inappropriate behavior:

> Clara.   from this houre
> I here abjure all actions of a man,
> And wil esteem it happinesse from you
> To suffer like a woman: love, true love

Hath made a search within me, and expel'd
All but my naturall softnesse, and made perfect
That which my parents care could not begin.

(IV, ii, 184–90)

At the play's conclusion, the interest shifts to the efforts of Eugenia, Clara, and Vitelli's sister Genevora to end the feud between Alvarez (now supported by a newly aggressive Lucio) and Vitelli. They appear together on the balcony, all modestly attired in petticoats, and appeal to their belligerent menfolk as mother, sisters, wife, daughter, and ladies who have received the vows of courtly love. Since their persuasions in all these properly feminine capacities fail to have the slightest effect, they vow to die the moment the men start to fight. Genevora and Clara hold swords to each other's breasts. Eugenia orders the steward, Bobadilla, to shoot her:

> *Eugenia*.   And rogue, looke
> You at that instant doe discharge that Pistol
> Into my breast: if you start back, or quake,
> Ile stick you like a Pigge.
>
> (V, iii, 178–81)

According to Simon Shepherd, this scene illustrates the early modern belief that

> women make their effect in male society by appeal, not by "deeds"; by using love (as with the female peace-makers here), not by the sword. This plan for social behaviour is intimately linked with woman's biological gender: just as one can't change one's genitals, so one can't change the "real" way one is meant to behave. The argument is that custom can tell lies about a person, but that underneath a woman is always a woman the way we assume women to be.[47]

Yet the words spoken by Eugenia contain as much threat as appeal, while theatrical emphasis falls heavily on weapons, actions, and body language. In order to do justice to the script, Eugenia, standing on side of the balcony, must sieze the unsuspecting Bobadilla by force and hold him close to her, with her dagger's point resting against some vital part, while the girls stand on the other side side, their swords in full view of onstage and offstage audiences. The total effect is of strength and aggression, not helpless feminine pleading.[48] Yet the most violent action is performed by Eugenia, a perfectly respectable woman, who has never been out of petticoats in her life.

The two scenes discussed above are not unusual. Most early modern dramatists who depict women in trying situations realize that, while a few timid flutters provide an agreeable frisson, the spectacle of consistent cowardice is unappealing. They work on the principle that courage is such a valuable quality that no truly virtuous character can be without it, regardless of sex or costume.

"THE BRAVERY OF A WOMAN"

There is much evidence that those dramatists who depicted courage as a quality that most women could attain, at least temporarily, gave a more accurate impression of early modern womanhood than those didactic writers who insisted on the charm of female fears. Eighteenth-century journalism gives many accounts of women who showed phenomenal courage under pressure, without needing the stimulus of male disguise. Some of them equalled or surpassed the traditional expectations indicated by the treatment of women in more "literary" genres. In August 1765, a servant's rape attempt gave one unnamed noblewoman a chance to show that she could be as handy with a blade as any tragedy queen: "a penknife lying on the dressing table before her, in the violence of her rage, she stabbed him in so dangerous a manner that his life is despaired of."[49] When the *Verelft* was wrecked on the coast of Mauritius, on April 1771, Mrs. Gruber, defying the stereotypical image of females as helpless in the water,

> was twice thrown off the raft that carried part of the crew on shore, but by an uncommon exertion of fortitude regained it again, and was then beat against the side of a ledge of rocks, where she continued near three hours, with the surf dashing on her, before she could be got on shore, which at length, with great difficulty, was happily accomplished.[50]

Women in danger strove heroically to help fellow victims. On 13 April 1799, Mrs. Creed, a tailor's wife, made the supreme sacrifice. When her house caught fire, her husband jumped out of a first floor window "in a moment," but she stayed behind in order to rescue another occupant, a blind and infirm old man. "One of the apprentices assisted in the humane attempt; but, shocking to relate! the floor suddenly fell in, and the three perished together."[51] Women who had children to protect were capable of practically anything. After an earthquake in Sicily, "One woman lived under the ruins full 11 days, and during the last 5 with a dead child, which she had taken care of, and kept alive as long as she could by her urine."[52] When the *Litchfield* was wrecked on the north African coast, many strong mariners drowned in the struggle to reach land, but the survivors included "three women, and a young child, which one of the women brought ashore in her teeth."[53] The news reports made it clear that mothers were prepared to sacrifice their lives for their children. On 23 December 1794, an inquest took place on Mrs. Katherine Chapman, who spent three bitterly cold days lost in a wood with her four-year-old daughter. They were "at last discovered by the faint cries of the poor infant, which the other had almost stripped herself to secure from the inclemency of the weather."[54] On 22 May 1772, courage and quick thinking enabled one mother to save her baby at the cost of her own life:

> Friday a poor woman of Nailsworth, picking up chips near a tree, which some men were hewing down, had laid the child at the but [*sic*] of the tree; the woman, seeing the tree falling ran to catch up her child, but before she could get clear of it the tree fell and killed her. She had the presence of mind to throw the child from her, by which means it escaped unhurt.[55]

In December 1753, mothers added themselves to the casualty list when disaster struck their sons: "A number of men and boys, . . . sliding on a mill dam, between Wigan and Chorley, the ice broke, and every soul perish'd, as also 5 or 6 women in endeavouring to save their children."[56] Even young girls might display suicidally strong protective instincts. This happened on June 1798, when a post chaise got out of control:

> a man attempted to stop the horses, as they were turning a sharp corner, which occasioned them to fly across to the opposite side of the street, where a fine girl of eight years old was playing with an infant, and perceiving their danger, instantly threw herself upon the babe, as if to save it, when the carriage passed over her, and killed her on the spot; but the infant escaped with some slight bruises.[57]

Some women might actually make use of their supposed frailty in order to survive a threatening situation. In September 1753,

> All the talk at *Florence* is of the bravery of a woman near *Sienna:* Her husband being in prison there for about 50 crowns, she made up the money and was going to discharge him. A robber came up to her, cutlass in hand, swearing he would rip her up if she did not instantly deliver her money: At first she pleaded poverty, but upon his going to strip her, she said, that indeed she had a little money, but that it was sewed up in her stays, and with his cutlass she would unrip it? [*sic*] The robber readily put his weapon into her hands, when suddenly turning upon him, she plunged it in his body, and laid him dead at her feet.[58]

This was the action of a passing woman—she coolly exploited the rob-
ber's assumption that she was a helpless little bundle of femininity, instead of a human being with a steady hand and her wits about her.

For some women, life in petticoats was so dangerous that a transvestite career in the armed forces became a soft option. Julie Wheelwright,
in *Amazons and Military Maids: Women who Dressed as Men in the Pursuit
of Life, Liberty and Happiness* (1989), describes how Marianne Rebecca
Johnson

> was raised by an abusive stepfather who bound her as an apprentice aboard
> a coal-ship. He had threatened her with murder if she revealed her identity
> to anyone. It was no idle threat, she said, and showed . . . a scar just below
> her left ear that was the result of a blow her stepfather gave her with a
> poker. Marianne worked aboard a Sutherland collier, the *Mayflower*, for four
> years without detection.[59]

This had become a hideous family tradition:

> three years before she went to sea her mother had been forced by her stepfa-
> ther aboard a man-o-war. She served seven years on different ships before
> she was mortally wounded in the British capture of Copenhagen in 1807.
> But in a letter to her daughter written just before her death, she said she
> "preferred the hardships of her situation to returning to her friends at the
> risk of meeting her unnatural husband."[60]

Even women who did not face marital or familial abuse might find
domestic life as dangerous as warfare. The Latin inscription on a memorial slab (now sadly illegible) outside the Old Church, formerly St.
Luke's, Chelsea, once told a bleakly self-explanatory story, which has
been recorded in Thomas Faulkner's *Historical and Topographical Description of Chelsea* (1829). His translation reads as follows:

> In a vault hard by, lieth Anne, sole daughter of Edward Chamberlayne,
> LL.D., born in London 20th January 1667; who long declining wedlock,
> and aspiring above her sex and age, fought under her brother, with arms
> and manly attire, in a fireship, against the French, for six hours, on the 30th
> June 1690; a maiden heroine! Had life been granted, she might have borne
> a race of naval warriors. Returning form that sea engagement, and within
> some months marrying Sir John Spragg, knight, with whom she lived very
> affectionately eighteen months, at last, giving birth to a daughter, she died
> a few days after, on the 30th October 1691. Her sorrowful husband raised
> this monument to a most chaste and much-beloved wife.[61]

Typically, Anne's exploits did nothing to change her husband's perception of women in general: her courage is "above her sex," The Latin

shows even more clearly than the English that she was not expected to set a precedent, even within her own family. It reads "Heroum poterat stirpem generare marinam" (She could have engendered a naval breed of heroes): these heroes are unequivocally masculine. Her daughter's heroic potential is swept into cultural invisibility.[62]

The weight of the preceding evidence brings us to the conclusion that courage was not a masculine prerogative in the early modern period. Nevertheless, the helpless little woman act was what most early modern men wished to see—or, at least, what they thought they wished to see. The frequency with which male readers and spectators were offered accounts of female courage suggests that they found them thoroughly delightful, so long as they could persuade themselves that the heroine of each piece was an exception to the rule. Very few were prepared to wonder whether, in the face of so many exceptions, the rule needed reformulation. As we have already seen, female courage might alarm or disgust those who needed to shore up their sense of masculine superiority with notions of gender distinctions as natural, stable, visible, and endorsed by divine law and human morality. Yet the exploits of cross-dressed women were not, ultimately, a serious threat to traditional concepts of gender in a society where, for the most part, it was believed that gender distinctions, although "natural" in origin, must be confirmed by appropriate nurture. If they had been brought up as boys, like the factual Read and Bonny and the fictitious Clara, or had grown up as "normal" women but subsequently served in the armed forces, like Davies and Snell, their conduct could be seen as a testimony to the efficiency with which manly virtue was inculcated by conventional education and military discipline. More awkward problems were raised by the conduct of women who never cross-dressed or adopted an "unfeminine" lifestyle, but who displayed equal courage in an emergency. In *An Enquiry into the Duties of the Female Sex* (1797), Thomas Gisborne (1758–1846), who considered brave women of both types, believed that Providence endowed women with large amounts of natural courage, because their lives were in general so undemanding that, unlike men, they lacked opportunities to toughen themselves by training and emulation:

> If the natural tenderness of the female mind, cherished, too, as that tenderness is in civilised nations, by the established modes of ease, indulgence, and refinement, were not balanced by an ample share of latent resolution; how would it be capable of enduring the shocks and the sorrows to which, amid the uncertainties of life, it must be exposed? Finally, whatever may be the opinion adopted as to the precise amount of female fortitude, when compared with that of men, the former, I think, must at least be allowed this relative praise: that it is less derived from the mechanical influence of habit

and example than the latter; less tinctured with ambition; less blended with insensibility; and more frequently drawn from the only source of genuine strength of mind, firm and active principles of religion.[63]

Despite his unusually generous attribution of courage to women, and his acknowledgment that it is definitely a virtue, Gisborne still displays the common, important, and fundamentally misleading assumption that women seldom need it. Even in the comparatively well-protected upper classes, early modern women, especially those who were consciously preparing themselves for the supremely "feminine" roles of marriage and motherhood, knew that they lived in a society that would often require them to lay their lives on the line. The delicate ladies who so daintily shuddered at the sound of gunfire and swooned at the sight of a spider, in the hope that they might attract a husband by these antics, might well rank among the most successful "passers" of all time.

NOTES

Illustrations courtesy of Reading University Library.

1. Dianne Dugaw, *Warrior Women and Popular Balladry, 1650–1859* (Cambridge: Cambridge University Press), 122.

2. See Vivien Jones's introduction to *The Young Lady's Pocket Library, or Parental Monitor* (Dublin: John Archer, 1790; facsimile ed., Bristol: Thoemmes Press, 1995).

3. Dugaw, *Warrior Women*, 157.

4. Dr. John Arbuthnot and Alexander Pope, *Annus Mirabilis*, in Alexander Pope and Jonathan Swift, *Miscellanies in Prose and Verse*, 4 vols. (London: B. Motte, 1727–32), Vol. III (1732), 86. The most celebrated study of sexual difference as a matter of inversion is Tom Laqueur, *Making Sex: Body and Gender from the Greeks to Freud* (Cambridge, Massachusetts and London: Harvard University Press, 1990).

5. Andrew Tooke, *The Pantheon*, 17th ed., (London: S. Birt, C. Hitch, C. Bathurst, M. Cooper, J. Ward, 1750), 342.

6. *Doomes-Day, or The great Day of the Lords Iudgment*, in *The Poetical Works of Sir William Alexander, Earl of Stirling*, ed. L. E. Kastner and H. B. Charlton, 2 vols. (Edinburgh and London: Printed by William Blackwood and Sons for the Scottish Text Society, 1921–29), vol. 2, *The Non-Dramatic Works*, 193.

7. James Thompson, *The Seasons*, ed. James Sambrook (Oxford: Clarendon, 1981), 166.

8. Jonathan Swift, *Prose Works*, ed. Herbert Davis et al., 14 vols. (Oxford: Blackwell, 1939–68), vol. 9, *Irish Tracts 1720–1723 and Sermons* (1948), ed. Louis Landa, 92–93.

9. Jonathan Swift, *The Complete Poems*, ed. Pat Rogers (Harmondsworth: Penguin, 1983), 202.

10. Swift, *Prose Works*, vol. 5, *Miscellaneous and Autobiographical Pieces, Fragments, and Marginalia*, ed. Herbert Davis (1962), 229.

11. Mary Wollstonecraft, *A Vindication of the Rights of Woman, with Strictures on Political and Moral Subjects*, ed. Ulrich H. Hardt (Troy, N.Y.: The Whitston Publish Company, 1982), 34, 54.

12. C. G. T. Dean, *The Royal Hospital, Chelsea*, with a foreword by General Sir Clive

Liddell (London: Hutchinson & Co., 1950), 222. I am indebted for this reference to a private communication from Major General P. A. Downward, CB, DSO, DFC, Lieutenant Governor, Royal Hospital, Chelsea.

13. Ibid., 222–23.

14. Ibid., 223.

15. See Anonymous, *The Female Soldier; Or, the Surprising Life and Adventures of Hannah Snell* (London: R. Walker, [1750]; ed. in facsimile by Dianne Dugaw, Los Angeles: University of California, William Andrews Clark Memorial Library, The Augustan Reprint Society, No. 257, 1989), 40. N.B. This is a reprint of a forty-six-page octavo; there is also an anonymous 187-page book with the same date, title, and publisher.

16. *The Gentleman's Magazine; or, Monthly Intelligencer* LV (January 1783), 173.

17. *The Gentlemen's Magazine* XXXV (April 1765), 196.

18. Daniel Defoe, *A General History of the Pyrates*, ed. Manuel Schonhorn (London: J.M. Dent & Sons, 1972), 154. For Mary Read's childhood, see pp. 153–54. This attribution is accepted here for the sake of convenience

19. Ibid., 154. For Anne Bonny's childhood, see pp. 163–64.

20. *Gentleman's Magazine* XX (July 1750), 292.

21. Ibid., 293.

22. Anonymous, *The Female Soldier*, 14.

23. Ibid., 14–15.

24. Defoe, *A General History of the Pyrates*, 153.

25. Ibid., 154.

26. Ibid., 165.

27. See Anonymous, *The Life and Adventures of Mrs. Christian Davies*, in *The Novels and Miscellaneous Works of Daniel De Foe. With References and Notes, Including Those Attributed to Sir Walter Scott*, 6 vols. (London: Henry G. Bohn, 1854–56), vol. 4, 379.

28. Defoe, *General History of the Pyrates*, 158.

29. Jean E. Howard, "Cross-Dressing, the Theatre, and Gender Struggle in Early Modern England," in Leslie Ferris, ed., *Crossing the Stage: Controversies on Cross-Dressing* (London and New York: Routledge, 1993), 20–46, 33.

30. Ibid.

31. Ibid., 35.

32. William Shakespeare, *Complete Works*, ed. W. J. Craig (London: Oxford University Press, 1943), 208.

33. Colley Cibber, *She Wou'd and She Wou'd Not* (London: John Bell, 1792), 10.

34. Ibid., 15.

35. Colley Cibber, *The Lady's Last Stake: Or, the Wife's Resentment* (London: John Bell, 1795), 129.

36. Ibid., 133.

37. Charles Johnson, *The Country Lasses: Or, the Custom of the Manor* (London: Jacob Tonson, 1735), 79.

38. Ibid., 81.

39. Anonymous, *The Female Volunteer; Or, an Attempt to Make our Men Stand* (London: M. Moore, 1746), broadside.

40. See W. van Lennep, E. L. Avery, A. H. Scouten, G. W. Stone, Jr., and C. B. Hogan, eds, *The London Stage, 1600–1800*, 5 parts in 11 vols. (1965–68) (Carbondale: Southern Illinois University Press, (1966), III 1227, 1231.

41. *The Works of Aphra Behn*, ed. Janet Todd, 7 vols. (London: William Pickering, 1992–96), 7, 346.

42. Ibid., 342.

43. Ibid., VI, 108.

44. Ibid., 125.

45. *The Dramatic Works of the Beaumont and Fletcher Canon*, ed. Fredson Bowers (Cambridge: Cambridge University Press, 1970), 2, 118.

46. Ibid., III, 12. All quotations are from this edition.

47. Simon Shepherd, *Amazons and Warrior Women: Varieties of Feminism in Seventeenth-Century Drama* (Brighton: The Harvester Press, 1981), 91.

48. The experiment took place at the conference on *Passing: Assumed Identities in Literature Art and Film* at King Alfred's College, Winchester, on Sunday, 14 September 1997, with the following cast: Clara: Nathalie McGrath; Genevora: Amanda Boulter; Eugenia: Tanya Cassidy; Bobadilla: Ian McCormick.

49. *Gentleman's Magazine* XXXV (August 1765), 392.

50. Ibid., XLII (January 1772), 42.

51. Ibid., LXIX (April 1799), 342.

52. Ibid., LVII (July 1787), 603.

53. Ibid., XXXI (August 1761), 362.

54. Ibid., LXV (January 1795), 73.

55. *London Evening Post*, Tuesday, 26 May to Thursday, 18 May 1772.

56. *Gentleman's Magazine* XXVIII (December 1753), 588.

57. Ibid., LXVIII (June 1798), 530.

58. Ibid., XXIII (September 1753), 443.

59. Julie Wheelwright, *Amazons and Military Maids: Women who Dressed as Men in the Pursuit of Life Liberty, and Happiness* (London: Pandora, 1989), 47.

60. Ibid.

61. Thomas Faulkner, *An Historical and Topographical Descripion of Chelsea, and Its Environs*, 2 vols. (Chelsea: T. Faulkner, Nichols and Son, and Simpkin and Marshall, 1829), I, 246–47. I am grateful to the Vicar and Verger of Chelsea Old Church, and to the staff of the Reference Section of the Public Library at the Old Town Hall, Chelsea, for their assistance in finding this reference.

62. Ibid., 246.

63. Thomas Gisborne, *An Inquiry into the Duties of the Female Sex*, 5 ed. (London: T. Cadell, Jr., and W. Davies, 1801), 31.

Voice, Gender, and the Augustan Verse Epistle

KARINA WILLIAMSON

> Blest be the man! his memory at least,
> Who found the art thus to unfold his breast,
> And taught succeeding times an easy way
> Their secret thoughts by letters to convey;
> To baffle absence and secure delight
> Which, till that time, was limited to sight. . . .
> The wings of love were tender too, till then
> No quill thence pull'd was shap'd into a pen,
> To send in paper sheets, from town to town,
> Words smooth as they, and softer than his down.
> —Anne Finch, from *To a Friend / In Praise of the Invention of Writing Letters*

THE VERSE EPISTLE ENTERED INTO ENGLISH POETIC TRADITION WITH Chaucer,[1] was immensely popular in the Renaissance and the long eighteenth century, and flourishes vigorously today in twentieth-century literatures in English. Its heyday, however, was the Augustan period—from the mid-seventeenth to the mid-eighteenth century—when it was the dominant form in English poetry. It can scarcely be a coincidence that the beginning of this period saw the foundation of the Post Office in Britain (1660), the rapid development of a nationwide network of postal services, and hence a vast increase in letter writing of all kinds. The connection between these developments and the rise of the epistolary novel is well recognized, but as Anne Finch shows, poets too were aware of the implications of a service enabling intimate messages to be conveyed "in paper sheets, from town to town." For these reasons, and because poetic conventions were so firmly encoded and widely recognized in the period, the opportunities for the play of voice and gender offered by the epistle were exploited with exceptional skill and inventiveness by Augustan poets. In particular, they fastened on the indeterminacy of gender that is central to the genre. Like the lyric, but unlike classical epic—the celebration of a masculine ethos of heroism and public *virtus*—or classical pastoral, in which gender relations and patterns of behavior are inscribed in the form of conventional

76

names and roles, the epistle as such bears no gender inscription. Unlike the lyric, however, epistolary discourse is necessarily personalized: a letter always has a writer (male or female) and an addressee. As we shall see, its peculiarly epicene nature makes it a rewarding site for exercises in gendered role-play and literary cross-dressing.

The verse epistle has hitherto been treated by scholars and critics as a poor relation in the family of literary kinds. It is not even given houseroom in M. H. Abrams's widely used *Glossary of Literary Terms*, for example, although other verse genres treated include such minor and long-dead forms as the emblem poem and the fabliau. As a subdivision of the general class of letters the verse epistle is even in danger of losing its separate identity altogether by absorption into a textual mode described by Derrida in 1980 as "not a genre but all the genres, Literature itself."[2] Since 1980, letters and letter-fiction have been the object of intensive critical and theoretical scrutiny,[3] but in spite of the close attention paid to Ovid's *Heroides* and Pope's *Eloisa to Abelard* for their narrative and psychological interest, the verse-letter genre itself has remained out in the cold. Two factors have militated against it. One is its alleged lack of formal definition. In his edition of Donne's *Satires, Epigrams and Verse Letters* (1967), Wesley Milgate remarks that the verse letter "has been little studied, probably because of its amorphousness; place into any satire, verse essay, or lyric an address to some person, and one can claim to have written a verse epistle."[4] Milgate's statement, however, is a symptom rather than an explanation of the phenomenon that he reports. He assumed, as most Anglo-American scholars and critics of the time would have done, that "address" is extrinsic to genre. Modern criticism starts from the opposite assumption: to quote Todorov's maxim, "A genre . . . is nothing other than the codification of discursive properties."[5] In terms of its discursive properties, the epistle is in fact more, not less, distinct as a kind than satire, verse essay or lyric. It appears "amorphous" only if form is defined in terms of subject matter, prosody, and the like. In other words, verse epistles have been disregarded as a genre not because they are formless but because their formal properties have not been observed closely enough.

A second factor is the divided ancestry of the genre: one line stemming from Ovid, the other from Horace. Critical attention, from the beginning, has tended to bifurcate along those lines. The pattern was set in 1714 by Ambrose Philips, who claimed to be the first person to write about "Epistolary Poetry." Although recognizing that "letters in verse" may be written on any subject, he chose to confine his discussion to "such Writings . . . as have been in Use among the Ancients, and have been copied from them by some Moderns." Philips's typology remains useful, as far as it goes. Those epistles which derive from classical models, he says, "may be reduced into two classes: in the one I shall range love-letters, letters of friendship, and letters upon mournful occasions: in the other I shall place such epistles in verse as may properly be called familiar, critical, and moral; to which may be added letters of mirth and humour. Ovid for the first, and Horace for the latter, are the best originals we have left" (*The Spectator*, No. 618).[6]

Philips's outline of the two types needs fleshing out a little. Ovid's *Heroïdes* provided the model for the "heroic epistle," normally addressed by a woman to a male lover. There is always a narrative impulse behind the letters; typically the women have been abandoned or betrayed by their lover, and their story is reflected in their letters by a passionate, high-flown rhetoric of desire, anger, grief, nostalgia, guilt, self-justification, vengefulness, and so forth. The second type of epistle, based on Horace's two books of *Epistulae* and his *Epistula ad Pisones* (better known as *Ars Poetica*), is usually addressed by the poet to a friend, enemy, patron, important personage, or to the public at large. Subject matter, mood, and style in Horatian epistles range widely, but the most common form in the Augustan period was the "familiar letter," addressed to a friend in informal, conversational language.

Modern critics, like Philips, have continued to treat the two main kinds of verse epistle separately. Two brilliant studies, by Gillian Beer and William Dowling respectively, exemplify this tendency. In " 'Our unnatural No-voice': The Heroic Epistle, Pope, and Woman's Gothic" (1982),[7] Beer discusses the poetics of the Ovidian verse-letter, drawing attention to its gendered aspects. While the nominal writer was typically a woman, the actual author, from Ovid onwards, was normally male. Thus the heroic epistle was seen in the seventeenth and eighteenth centuries as "a women's genre in its subject matter and audience, though not in its authorship." Beer comments on the paradox of men writing women's letters and its feminist implications, but she does not discuss heroic epistles actually written by women (notable examples include Aphra Behn's paraphrase of Ovid's *Oenone to Paris* and her own epistle, *Ovid to Julia*, which neatly turns the tables on the father of the heroic epistle). Dowling's book, *The Epistolary Moment: The Poetics of the Eighteenth-Century Verse Epistle* (1991), is a groundbreaking study of the Augustan epistolary mode, but despite its title it is not a study of the genre in the broadest sense. Its critical energies are concentrated almost exclusively on letters of the Horatian type because—Dowling claims—by the end of the seventeenth century the Ovidian verse epistle, "the lonely embodiment of lyric solipsism," had been "repressed in favor of a public or Horatian mode of epistolary wisdom." Gender issues are not a main interest for Dowling, though he recognizes the gendered character of his chosen form: "when we speak of the Augustan verse epistle, we are normally talking about a situation in which a male speaker, educated in classical values . . . addresses a male friend."[8] Dowling acknowledges that the Horatian epistolary mode was often adopted by women writers in the eighteenth century, but he discusses very few of the huge number of verse letters by women and denies that there is any significant difference between male- and female-authored epistles. His normative approach also entails the exclusion of poems in which male letter writers masquerade as women or female writers masquerade as men.

In short, a general typology of verse letters is conspicuously lacking. At least four kinds of inquiry would be needed for such a typology to be prepared: a conspectus of the whole range of verse letters, including of course those letter-poems that do not fit into either of the classical molds; analysis of the discursive properties of verse letters; consideration of the complex structure of "author" (actual and nominal), "reader" (actual and nominal), plus—as Dowling argues—"epistolary audience";[9] and a study of gender, race, and class orientations in verse letters. Nothing so ambitious is proposed in this essay. Nevertheless, even a brief examination of the question of gender and genre is sufficient to show why such a typology might be worth undertaking.

To begin with a fact so obvious as to be tautological, but forgotten or ignored surprisingly often in critical discussion: the verse letter is a letter. The discursive properties of letters in general are therefore of prime importance to the poetic genre. These properties have been efficiently codified by Patrizia Violi, from whose analysis I have drawn the points most relevant to the study of verse epistles:[10]

1. *The personal identity of writer and addressee, and the relationship between them*, are inscribed within the text by: use of I-you pronouns, proper names and titles; set forms of address, like "Dear X," "My Lord," etc.; signatures, such as "Your loving mother," "Your humble servant," etc.; and by personal references within the text. Violi notes the "crucial" distinction between addresser/addressee as "figures of discourse introjected into the text" and their external being. "The addresser and addressee are only made manifest through the 'traces' they leave in the text."

2. *A space-time distance between writer and addressee* is similarly inscribed by means of set formulae (address and date) and by internal references. Absence and delay are thus built into the deictic structure of letters, a fact much exploited in epistolary narrative.

3. Letters display special *"competencies"*; that is, kinds of knowledge or codes of speech that are shared by the writer and addressee but are not (or not necessarily) accessible to outside readers. By this

means, Violi comments, "compared with other texts, the letter personalizes its relationship with its own addressee to a maximum."

Verse epistles mimic private letters by exhibiting some or all of these features; but at the same time they proclaim their difference within the broad parameters of the letter form by using the artificial medium of verse. This has the paradoxical result that while the personal identity of the nominal writer—Dowling calls this the *epistoler*—is structurally prominent, his or her "natural" or "authentic" voice recedes behind the screen of meter and rhyme. In some kinds of epistle this artifice is magnified for comic or satirical purposes. Pope's *Bounce to Fop*, for example, is "An Heroick Epistle from a Dog at Twickenham to a Dog at Court." The epistoler in *The Inspir'd Quill* by Mary Leapor is the pen itself. In *Mary the Cook-Maid's Letter to Dr Sheridan* by Swift, a semi-illiterate servant supposedly writes in irregular but well-rhymed couplets.[11] In other kinds of epistle the screening effect of meter and rhyme is minimized; by force of convention, verse becomes the "natural" rhetoric of Horatian moral or critical exposition, or the "natural" rhetoric of passion in Ovidian letters.[12] Nevertheless, the overlap between the voices of author and epistoler is never complete. In "literary" letters—those written for publication—the very charade of using a private form of communication for public consumption highlights the gap, even when author and epistoler pass under the same name; as every student learns, Pope assumes an identity in his *Epistle to Arbuthnot* no less, though less obviously, than he does in the letter from *Eloisa to Abelard*.

This brings out another paradox about letters as a means of communication. All writing, we know, is subject to semantic slippage. Letters, however, seem to come closest to an ideal of direct, sincere, transparent communication by writing, an "easy way" to convey "secret thoughts," as Finch puts it; yet at the same time they are peculiarly susceptible to interference and misconstruction, owing to the hazards of transmission. Letters may be delayed, lost, stolen, erased, altered, counterfeited, smudged, burnt, torn, and so forth. In a "literary" letter (whether in prose or verse) interpretation is complicated further by the dual structure of exchange, whereby a real writer addresses a real reader in the guise of a nominal writer (*epistoler*) addressing a nominal reader (Dowling calls this the *lector*). Given also Violi's reminder that in all letters, addresser and addressee are made manifest only through the "traces" they leave in the text, the illusions of directness, sincerity and transparency become even more chimerical.[13]

Women writers from the Restoration onwards were quick to seize on the freedom the verse letter allowed them to give female subjectivity a

voice of its own. Openly feminist or at least countermisogynist letters
are common, but variations of "voice" in women's epistles are sometimes more interesting when they are less confrontational. An example
is the Horatian epistle sent on 1 July 1740 by Frances Seymour, Countess of Hertford (1699–1754), from her house in the country to her
friend the Countess of Pomfret in London.[14] Hertford's poem departs
from the Horatian epistolary standard, as defined by Dowling, not
merely by reversing the gender norms, but also by its irreverent treatment of the Augustan idealization of rural life as an embodiment of Stoi-
cal and Epicurean values—one of the Horatian themes most frequently
enshrined in seventeenth- and eighteenth-century poetry.[15] Hertford's
epistle is untitled. It is seamlessly embedded (like some of Emily Dick-
inson's poems more than a century later) within the frame of a prose
letter: "when I am writing to you," Hertford says,

> I cannot stop my pen till it has intrusted you with all the chimeras and follies
> that chance at the time to go through my brain. I am indeed very often
> ashamed, when I look back on my epistles, to find how many trifles and
> impertinences they are composed of: especially when I am in the country,
> and am compelled to furnish materials for them out of my own stock; since,
>> After the groves, the portico, and lawn,
>> Describ'd, have had their general picture drawn,
>> What can (that's new) remain for me to say—-
>> Unless I talk of poultry, farms, and hay?
>> Hay (woeful thought!) sells for three pounds each load,   5
>> Growing upon the land, before 'tis mow'd.

The iambic pentameters and down-to-earth language of the opening are
the verse equivalent of the "natural" voice of the prose letter. But this
quickly modulates into a second, more "poetic" voice:

>> Three furlongs only hence, a field is seen
>> Well sown with corn, where you scarce spy the green,
>> So many flow'rs o'errun th' ungrateful soil—-
>> The hind will reap a nosegay for his toil.   10
>> While Wiltshire swains a harder fate sustain:
>> The downs burnt up, for want of genial rain;
>> The thirsty flocks expire upon the ground;
>> And scenes of ruin fright the country round.
>> The dreadful doom which God in wrath foretold   15
>> To Israel's disobedience of old,
>> In these unhappy suff'rers comes to pass;—
>> Their earth seems iron, and their heavens brass.

This is not quite mock heroic, but close to it. The epistoler makes a
show of elevating her mundane subject matter by putting it into formal

dress: Augustan poetic diction ("ungrateful soil," "swains," "genial rain") and biblical allusion (lines 15–18, referring to Leviticus 26:19). The attempt breaks down, however, as if under the weight of its own absurdity:

> But, not to dwell on prospects such as these,
> Which eyes like yours can ne'er behold with ease,   20
> I'll try if, in a gayer style,
> Our life describ'd can make you smile;
> To see what we accept as joys,
> And what pursuits our time employs.
> We sometimes ride, and sometimes walk;   25
> We play at chess, or laugh, or talk;

The "prospects" in line 19 refer simultaneously to the real drought described in lines 12–14, and to the grandiose biblical image the writer has herself evoked. The break at line 21 into the less formal meter of octosyllabic couplets marks the entry of a third voice, a "gayer style" to match the casual, everyday character of the writer's country life, as described in the remainder of the poem. The succession of voices thus has a quasimimetic function; but more importantly it highlights the inevitable constructedness, the artificiality of even the most "natural" voice in epistolary verse.

Epistolary tradition is more radically challenged by Mary Leapor (1722–1746), a poet from the opposite end of the social scale to the Countess of Hertford. Probably her best known—certainly her funniest—verse letter is *The Epistle of Deborah Dough*, a parodic version of the Horatian familiar epistle,[16] but her letter *To Artemisia*, a self-styled "imitation" of William King's *Invitation to Bellvill*, employs more subtle forms of misprision. To appreciate fully its subversive strategies, it has to be read against its intertext. King's poem in turn is an "imitation" of Horace's well-known invitation to Torquatus.[17] It begins

> If Bellvill can his generous soul confine
> To a small room, few dishes, and some wine,
> I shall expect my happiness at nine.
> Two bottles of smooth Palm, or Anjou white,
> Shall give a welcome, and prepare delight,   5
> Then for the Bordeaux you may freely ask,
> But the Champaigne is to each man his flask.

King's poem accurately reproduces the structure and urbane manners (as English Augustans construed them) of Horace's epistle, dwelling on the plainness and modesty of the hospitality on offer, commending social intercourse as the antidote to daily work, and contrasting enjoyment of leisure to the cares and burdens of wealth. Like Horace he uses the invitation form to create an intimate world of male fellowship that, at the same time, reflects on civil society at large. The poem moves back and forth between concrete details and general sentiments, describing at one moment the "snow-white damask" of the table linen and the "glittering salvers on the side-board laid" (lines 10–11) promising at the next an atmosphere of well-bred bonhomie:

> Thus we'll disperse all busy thoughts and cares,
> The General's counsels, and the Statesman's fears (12–13)

There is a corresponding movement between private and public worlds. Topical and specific allusions anchor the poem in a life beyond the domestic scene: explicitly by reference to the battle of Blenheim (line 16), indirectly by reference to Bellvill's professional standing as a lawyer or officeholder. Like Horace, King ends by inviting his guest to choose any other friends he wishes to add to the company:

> Consult your ease,
> Write back your men, and number as you please:
> Try your back-stairs, and let the lobby wait;
> A stratagem in war is no deceit. (41–44)

The final two lines are cryptic, because King relies on his audience to remember the original, from which it appears Torquatus has clients waiting to waylay him. But even in the original the meaning is not transparent. This is one of the moments when the special *competencies* characteristic of letter discourse are brought into play. Their effect is to give the illusion that we, the external audience, are listening in on an exchange between friends whom we do not directly know, but whose larger world we inhabit, and whose social, cultural, and ethical values we are expected to endorse. King's values, like those offered by Horace, include an ideal of hospitality that is at once moderate yet well-ordered and generous (the word "generous" echoes throughout the poem); and an ideal of civil conduct that respects the active virtues of soldiers and statesmen, but keeps them in studied balance with the Epicurean values of gentlemanly ease and recreation. Entry into the society of the poem, however, is not open to everybody: gender and class barriers are clearly demarcated. The tacit embargo on women and lower-class men is common to both the original and the imitation, but it is reinforced in King's epistle by the need of a classical education to qualify for full membership. Readers unfamiliar with Horace simply will not understand the rules. Moreover King's letter-writing voice is easily recognized but hardly at all individualized. In contrast to Pope in his imitations of Horace, King is content to submerge his authorial personality entirely beneath the Horatian social type created by the original.

Leapor's invitation is addressed in the voice of "Mira" (Leapor's pseudonym for herself) to a woman friend named in Leapor's poems as "Artemisia":[18]

> *To Artemisia. Dr. King's Invitation to Bellvill: Imitated.*
>
> If Artemisia's Soul can dwell
> Four Hours in a tiny Cell,
> (To give that Space of Bliss to me)
> I wait my Happiness at three.
> Our Tommy in a Jug shall bring   5
> Clear Nectar from the bubbling Spring;
> The Cups shall on the Table stand,
> The Sugar and the Spoons at hand:
> A skilful Hand shall likewise spread
> Soft Butter on the yielding Bread;   10
> And (as you eat but mighty little,
> And seem an arrant Foe to Vittle)
> You'll cry perhaps, One Bit may do,
> But I'm resolv'd it shall be two:
> With you and your Amanda blest,   15
> Care flies away from Mira's Breast;
> O'er stubborn Flax no more I grieve,
> But stick the Needle on my Sleeve:
> For let them work on Holiday,
> Who won't be idle when they may: 20
> If I must fret and labour too,
> Like Caricus and Lumberloo;
> As well I might, like Simoneer,
> Be plagu'd with sixty Pounds a Year.
> What Nymph, that's elegant and gay,   25
> But owes it chiefly to her Tea?
> With Satire that supplies our Tongues,
> And greatly helps the failing Lungs.
> By that assisted we can spy
> A Fault with microscopick Eye;   30
> Dissect a Prude with wond'rous Art,
> And read the Care of Delia's Heart.
> Now to the Company we fall,
> 'Tis Me and Mira that is all:
> More wou'd you have—Dear Madam, then   35
> Count me and Mira o'er agen.

The lack of reference to Horace in title or text is notable. It is not at all likely that Leapor was simply unaware of King's source; if she read the poem in the source in which it first appeared she could not have helped knowing, but in any case she was certainly acquainted with Horace's epistles at second hand.[19] Hence the omission of his name has to be seen as significant: let us say provisionally that it denotes a refusal to grant Horace special authority over the epistolary form. Leapor nevertheless follows the pattern of Horatian invitation poems faithfully. Praise of the virtues of wine are represented here by praises of tea, and the poem closes with reference to the company invited, as in Horace and King, though omitting their final coda.

Leapor obviously does not "imitate" King in the same way as King imitates Horace. It is unnecessary to know who were the real Mira (a poet who worked as a kitchen-maid) and the "real" Artemisia (a gentlewoman who became the poet's friend and patron) to recognize the very different social dynamics of her text. The letter writer is clearly a woman of low class, addressing a social superior. Like King's epistoler, she offers her guest a plain menu, redeemed from austerity by its careful preparation. Both elements — the frugality of the provisions and their seemly presentation — are mockingly exaggerated. Water described as "Clear nectar from the bubbling spring" is still just water; bread and butter, however soft and yielding, is still just bread and butter, several grades below the "few dishes" promised by King. The pattern of comic bathos continues, but the point does not need laboring. One function of the humor is to provide a graceful excuse for genuinely humble hospitality without damaging the delicate fabric of intimate relations between social unequals. As an exercise in social diplomacy it is marvelously deft. But there is more to the poem than that: class and gender work together in a variety of ways to undermine the whole ethos of the Horatian epistle.

In contrast to King's invitation, *To Artemisia* is conspicuously tilted toward the concrete and particular, away from the abstract and general. "Our Tommy" stands in for the anonymous and virtually invisible servants mentioned in King's poem, while the metonymies "stubborn flax" and "the needle" (lines 17–18), representing the actualities of women's labor, contrast both with the vague "busy thoughts and cares" of King, and with his grandiose male abstractions, "The General's counsels, and the Statesman's fears," in the next line. Similarly, Mira's hospitality (lines 11–14) is geared to her guest's personal preferences, not to a civic ideal of generosity. Artemisia is said to be a small eater: perhaps by nature or ladylike restraint, perhaps out of consideration for Mira's poverty. Here, use of letter-writing "competency" leaves the text ambiguous. But either way, Mira will make sure that her guest does not go short: "One bit may do, / But I'm resolv'd it shall be two." This is generosity in its most personal and practical form.

By grounding her text so firmly in local and specific circumstance, Leapor punctures the self-complacent fiction on which—viewed from outside the Augustan club—King's epistle can be seen to rest: the fiction that allows well-educated male poets to constitute themselves as arbiters of manners and morals by virtue of their class, gender, and classical training. This is where the absence of reference to Horace becomes most significant: it denies Augustan poets the claim, based on classical authority, to speak for a supposedly timeless and universal code of values. Leapor's challenge to Augustan clubmanship is most obvious in her ending. Where King invites his friend to join a band of congenial male guests—and bring others of his own choice too—she promises a simple tête-à-tête. She makes play of Artemisia's knowledge that "Mira" both is and is not the author of the invitation. Compute it as you choose, she says, there will be just the two of us present: you and "Me" (the actual author plus the shadow-figure of Mira under whom she masquerades). Omission of the Horatian coda accentuates the difference. Where King's ending reminds the reader of a public world held at bay only for a moment, Leapor's insists on the enclosure and self-sufficiency of the private world of female friendship to which Mira and her guest belong.

The joke is set up in the preceding paragraph (lines 25–32), which envisages a very different assembly: an imagined company of "the elegant and gay" enjoying a session of spiteful gossip. These lines stand out from the rest by their distinctly Popean diction, evoking the image of female society satirized most famously in *The Rape of the Lock* and *Epistle to a Lady*. Thus the conversation à *deux* which Mira proposes, and which is to be her special "Happiness" (line 4), is pitted against two Augustan stereotypes: the convivial stag party envisaged by King, and the mannered and malicious social gathering that was supposedly the norm for women. The third option set against these, of an intimate meeting of two female friends, is offered as a more true and vital encounter, based on personal liking and respect unconstrained by predetermined social codes. It is not presented as a new social norm, however: for by emphasizing the local and personal aspects of the epistle, Leapor foregoes the opportunity that the verse epistle affords to argue general cases. The Augustan epistle was preeminently a site for ethical choice. Reading between the intertextual lines, an ethical choice does emerge clearly enough in Leapor's poem; but the choice is contingent, not universal or absolute, emanating from an epistolary self that is at once more individual, yet more solidly grounded in social context, than the ideal Horatian identity constructed by King.

To Artemisia shows the subversive potential of gender switching within the frame of classical epistolary convention: it can be used to challenge basic assumptions underlying Augustan poetic tradition as a whole. But the equivocal nature of the genre itself makes it also a fertile source of irony, satire, and pleasurable uncertainty—*jouissance*—for the reader. Consider the following short epistle:

> My Lord
> These are the Gloves that I did mention
> Last night, and t'was with the intention
> That you should give mee thankes and wear them
> For I most willingly can spare them.
> When you this Packet first doe see   5
> Dam mee, crie you shee has writ to mee
> I had better be at Bretby still
> Than troubled with love against my will
> Besides this is not all my sorrow:
> Shee writ to day, shee'l come tomorrow,   10
> Then you consider the adventure
> And think you never shall content her
> But when you doe the inside see
> You'l find things are but as they should be,
> And that tis neither love nor passion   15
> But only for your recreation.[20]

The poem is known to be the work of John Wilmot, Earl of Rochester. The words are clear, but the text is full of riddles. It displays to a baffling degree those competencies (personal and local allusions) that as we have seen characterize a letter as such. Who is the epistoler— evidently female—and what is her relationship with the addressee? Is she being ingenuous or disingenuous? What was the encounter "last night"? Is it the same as the "adventure" referred to later? If the gift is so liable to misconstruction, why send it? Why explain it in verse? In verse moreover that is technically inept: is it artless or artful? And so on. As we shall see, even when—in some ways especially when—the text is approached with traditional interpretative tools (biographical, bibliographical, literary-historical) it remains irreducibly equivocal. All interpretations are contingent on the reader's perspective; external evidence may increase the number of possible angles, but cannot foreclose on any of the options. These qualities of openness, contingency, and ambiguity, it should be reemphasized, are not peculiar to this epistle or to epistles of this period in particular; Rochester is simply exploiting to the full the properties of the genre.

The first four lines present the gloves as nothing more than a casual gift ("For I most willingly can spare them"); but the epistoler imagines the parcel being perceived by "My Lord" as an unwanted love offering and the harbinger of more persistent advances in the future; so finally she reassures him it signifies nothing indecorous, only "recreation." Is this all merely innocent flirtatiousness? Lexical and syntactic ambiguity in the last four lines are titillatingly suggestive. Is it the packet or the gloves that are being talked about? Or something else? The "it" in "'tis" is studiously vague—a whiff of fetishism is in the air. "Recreation" has a variety of meanings, but only in the most general sense of "pleasure" or "comfort" (the latter archaic even in the 1660s) is it obviously applicable to gloves. The other senses of the word—play, refreshment, reinvigoration, pleasurable activity—all carry latent sexual meanings. If lines 13–16 are read as sexual innuendo, the opposition of "recreation" to "love" or "passion" acquires a cynical force; instead of an innocent gift or simple flirtation, what is on offer becomes a (loveless, passionless) service, reducing the relationship between epistoler and lector to a negotiation between prostitute and client.

External evidence intensifies rather than reduces these ambiguities. The sole original source of the epistle is a copy in Lord Chesterfield's letterbook. It is headed, "From Mistress Price Maid of honour to her Majesty who sent mee a pair of Italian Gloves," and ends, not with the last line of the poem, but with a note by Price saying "I had a mind that you should see these inclosed papers which were writ by the Lord Rochester, and that hath occationd you this trouble from your humble servant."[21] This shows that although Rochester was the actual author, the sender was the epistoler, and that the gloves were fact, not poetic invention. Beyond that, all is inference either from the text or, if we choose, from the *hors-texte*.

One line of discussion has centered on biographical and bibliographical evidence, attempting to answer questions of meaning by reconstructing a "real" situation explaining Rochester's motives. By privileging the authorial subtext over the text, this approach asks us to look *through* the epistoler's text as if it were a semitransparent window opening on to the actual writer and her, or in this case his, intentions. It is suggested that the poem is a lampoon, a satirical attack by Rochester on Mistress Price. Thus David Vieth: "Using Miss Price as persona, the poem evidently ridicules an affair between her and Chesterfield."[22] This interpretation is very far from "evident," however, if *Letter from Mistress Price* is read with serious regard to the nuances of gender and genre. Moreover, it depends on extratextual evidence of a very dubious kind. "Miss Price" was Henrietta Maria Price, maid of honor to Catherine, queen of Charles II. So much is documented fact; evidence of her character, however, comes solely from an account given by Anthony Hamilton in his notoriously unreliable *Memoirs of Count Grammont*

(1713), which may be no more than biased hearsay or fiction. According to Hamilton, "Miss Price was witty; and as her person was not very likely to attract many admirers, which, however, she was resolved to have, she was far from being coy, when occasion offered." Hamilton goes on to say that "she was violent in her resentments, as well as in her attachments," and that in revenge for a quarrel she had with a young girl whom Rochester admired, he wrote a number of lampoons against her.[23] The lampoons are not identified by Hamilton, and it is a modern guess—no more—that *Letter from Mistress Price* was one of them. That guess itself is underpinned by gender-based assumptions (of Hamilton and critics who follow his lead) about how all the parties in this transaction would have been likely to behave. The other extratextual clue is Price's own enigmatic note, quoted above, about "this trouble" she has caused. Vieth, still confident that the epistle is an oblique attack by Rochester on Price, suggests that her note "may be an indirect appeal for some kind of retaliation against Rochester for his effrontery." The imagined sequence of events seems to be this: Price plans to send Chesterfield a gift; Rochester writes a verse letter purportedly by Price but ironically exposing her as the predatory female Hamilton alleges she was; recognizing the trick, Price nevertheless sends the gloves and the letter in the hope that Chesterfield will avenge her against Rochester in some way. It is an ingenious scenario, but it has almost nothing to do with the actual *text*; it simply piles one biographical conjecture upon another, taking us ever deeper into the murky waters of the *hors-texte*.

A reader-oriented, intertextual approach offers a way out of the quagmire of authorial intentions. The Augustan epistle relies on the reader's familiarity with well-recognized poetic codes. As we have seen, two types of epistolary verse were prevalent. Rochester himself wrote in each style, often wittily defying rather than respecting the conventions. *A very Heroicall Epistle in Answer to Ephelia*,[24] for example, proclaims itself an Ovidian letter by its title; but by assuming a male identity (not his own) and addressing a woman Rochester flouts the tradition that heroic epistles were addressed to men by female epistolers. His most famous epistle, *A Letter from Artemiza in the Towne to Chloe in the Countrey*,[25] is Horatian in manner but un-Horatian in its assumption of a female authorial identity, or rather identities. Rochester's multiple impersonations create a Chinese-box structure of voices within voices which frustrates any search for a stable and determinate meaning. *Artemiza to Chloe* takes to an extreme the game played in the *Letter from Mistress Price*. As Nicholas Fisher has shown, the latter is an Ovidian epistle in miniature both in its tripartite structure and in its motive (a rejected woman pleading with her lover).[26] But it too deviates from the Ovidian model. What English Augustan readers expected of the heroic epistle is indicated by Joseph Warton's description of it as "a passionate soliloquy; in which, the mind gives vent to the distresses and emotions under which it labours."[27] Warton's comment highlights an important point, noted later by Beer, that the heroic epistle focuses on negative aspects of women's experience: their isolation, victimization, and powerlessness. It "takes as its precondition the enforced passivity of women."[28] Rochester, by using the Horatian familiar style instead of the passionate language of Ovidian epistles, and by allowing the woman to take control of the situation, challenges these genre and gender assumptions. The epistoler here is no passive victim, taking relief from distress in passionate soliloquy; she calls all the shots. Her letter is not a soliloquy, but a dialogue in which she supplies both voices. By putting words into Chesterfield's mouth she turns defense into attack, making his complaint that she is persecuting him look merely like a conceited fantasy of his own.

The epistle thus emerges as a different kind of gambit in a different and textually more interesting game than the one Vieth imagines: played out not at the expense of the "real" Mistress Price but between epistoler and lector. Where does that leave the reader? The special pleasure offered by Ovidian texts, with their strong narrative drive, is the pleasure of pure *desire*. What has happened, is happening, is going to happen? Not only does the obliquity of epistolary discourse give the reader a crucial role in constructing the story-so-far, it is also, always, an unfinished story. Even in the classical form of heroic epistle, based on mythical or historical stories where the reader knows what happened *outside* the text, the question "What is going to happen?" is not answered by the text. The question "What if?" (What if Aeneas had not abandoned Dido? what if Paris had returned to Oenone?) lingers over the ending. In *Letter from Mistress Price*, where there is no answer even from the *hors-texte*, readerly desire is wholly unfettered.

From an intertextual angle, the question of authorial motive in the poem resurfaces in a new way. The opportunity for role reversal and literary cross-dressing provided by the epistle was evidently part of its appeal for Rochester. Cross-gendering, in verse epistles as in other literary forms, was almost a trademark of texts produced by the circle of libertine wits of which he was center. Aphra Behn, for example, adopts the voice of a male lover in several songs and in *A Voyage to the Isle of Love*, while her bawdy Horatian epistle, *A Letter to a Brother of the Pen in Tribulation*, is teasingly ambiguous. The gender of the epistoler is unspecified, but the poem was published under Behn's name in *Poems on Several Occasions* (1684); on the other hand, the brotherly tone and masculine attitude the epistoler takes toward venereal disease (the "tribulation" of the title) invites reading her/him as male.[29] The liking for gender play indicates more than merely a shared taste for witty trans-gressiveness. As the editors of *The Routledge Anthology of Cross-Gendered Verse* remark, "In crossing gender as they create their personae, poets dramatize gender itself, bringing to the fore the ways in which a society standardizes social behavior."[30] Conversely, cross-gendered verse calls into question the literary codes that reflect and reinforce those very standards. *Letter from Mistress Price* juggles gender assumptions and ste-reotypes with such adroitness and wit that it deserves to take its place alongside other poems by Rochester in which, as Edward Burns has pointed out, gender difference is itself "in play," counterbalancing the masculinist and misogynistic voices that are found elsewhere in his work.[31]

It is apparent from the examination of even a small sample of verse epistles that the genre puts a new slant on theoretical questions of gen-der and genre, authorship and readership, text and context. Above all, verse letters offer a fresh challenge to the already embattled notion of determinate meaning in literary texts. Within the confines of Augustan epistolary tradition, Dowling has traced the attempt by male writers to ground meaning in the consciousness of an "epistolary audience," that imaginary "ideal commonwealth" to which reading and classical values give access. But as we've seen, the fragile semantic stability such a com-monwealth offers is undermined when women writers or mavericks like Rochester choose to ignore its boundaries or its rules. That is not to say that the verse epistle necessarily leaves the reader adrift in an ocean of indeterminate meaning (although that may be the effect in special cases, such as the *Letter from Mistress Price*), but that readers of verse letters have to pick their way with more than ordinary circumspection through a range of alternative meanings.

NOTES

The epigraph is from *The Poems of Anne, Countess of Winchilsea*, ed. Myra Reynolds (Chi-cago: University of Chicago Press, 1903), 110–11. Text here from *Minor Poets of the Eighteenth Century*, ed. Hugh l'Anson Fausset (London: J.M. Dent & Sons, 1930), 55–56.

1. See Martin Carmargo, *The Middle English Verse Love Epistle* (Tübingen: Max Nie-meyer Verlag, 1990).

2. "La lettre, l'épître ... n'est pas un genre mais tous les genres, la littérature même." Jacques Derrida, *La Carte postale: de Socrate à Freud et au-delà* (Paris: Aubier-Flamma-rion, 1980). Text here from *The Post Card: From Socrates to Freud and Beyond*, tr. Alan Bass (Chicago and London: University of Chicago Press, 1987), 48.

3. See esp. Janet Gurkin Altman, *Epistolarity: Approaches to a Form* (Columbus: Ohio State University Press, 1982); Mary A. Favret, *Romantic Correspondence: Women, Politics and the Fiction of Letters* (Cambridge: Cambridge University Press, 1993); Elizabeth C.

Goldsmith, ed., *Writing the Female Voice: Essays on Epistolary Literature* (London: Pinter, 1989); Linda S. Kauffman, *Discourses of Desire: Gender, Genre, and Epistolary Fictions* (Ithaca: Cornell University Press, 1986), and *Special Delivery: Epistolary Modes in Modern Fiction* (Chicago: University of Chicago Press, 1992); Elizabeth J. MacArthur, *Extravagant Narratives: Closure and Dynamics in the Epistolary Form* (Princeton: Princeton University Press, 1990); Ruth Perry, *Women, Letters, and the Novel* (New York: AMS Press, 1980); Bruce Redford, *The Converse of the Pen: Acts of Intimacy in the Eighteenth-Century Familiar Letter* (Chicago: University of Chicago, 1986).

4. *John Donne: The Satires, Epigrams and Verse Letters*, ed. W. Milgate (Oxford: Clarendon Press, 1967), xxxiv.

5. Tzvetan Todorov, *Genres in Discourse*, tr. Catherine Porter (Cambridge: Cambridge University Press, 1990), 17–18.

6. *The Spectator*, ed. Donald Bond, 5 vols. (Oxford: Clarendon Press, 1965), 5: 112–13.

7. *The Yearbook of English Studies* 12 (1982), 125–51. Reprinted in *Modern Essays on Eighteenth-Century Literature*, ed. Leopold Damrosch (Oxford: Oxford University Press, 1988), 379–411.

8. William C. Dowling, *The Epistolary Moment: The Poetics of the Eighteenth-Century Verse Epistle* (Princeton: Princeton University Press, 1991), 27, and 8. It is only from the perspective of high Augustan norms that the Ovidian type can be said to have been "repressed." Its continuing popularity in the period is illustrated by the success of Martha Fowke's *Epistles of Clio and Strephon* (London, 1720), a series of love letters in prose and verse, which reached its third edition in 1732.

9. By "epistolary audience" Dowling means the ideal community of like-minded readers projected by Augustan epistolary discourse itself (*The Epistolary Moment*, 11–13).

10. Patrizia Violi, "Letters," in T. A. Van Dijk, ed., *Discourse and Literature* (Amsterdam and Philadelphia: John Benjamins, 1985), 149–67. See also Susan Wright, "Private Language Made Public: The Language of Letters as Literature," *Poetics: Journal for Empirical Research on Literature, The Media, and the Arts* 18 (December 1989): 549–78.

11. See *The Poems of Alexander Pope*, ed. John Butt (London: Methuen, 1963), 823–26; *Jonathan Swift: The Complete Poems*, ed. Pat Rogers (Harmondsworth: Penguin Books, 1983), 177–78. Mary Leapor, *Poems Upon Several Occasions* (London, 1748), 111–18.

12. For the idea of a verse style "naturally" related to its function, see Akenside's preface to *The Pleasures of Imagination* (1744): after weighing "the familiar epistolary way of Horace" against the "more open, pathetic and figur'd stile" of Virgil's *Georgics* he chose the latter because it seemed "more natural" for a work designed to change the reader's habits of mind. *The Poetical Works of Mark Akenside*, ed. Robin Dix (London: Associated University Presses, 1996), 88.

13. See Homer Obed Brown, "The Errant Letter and the Whispering Gallery," *Genre* 10 (1977), 573–99, for discussion of the "parentless drift of meaning" and "irresolvable ambiguity" of the letter genre.

14. *Correspondence between Frances, Countess of Hartford, and Henrietta Louisa, Countess of Pomfret, between the years 1738 and 1741*, 3 vols. (London, 1805), 2:37–39. The latter part of the poem, beginning at l. 25, is printed in *Eighteenth-Century Women Poets: An Oxford Anthology*, ed. Roger Lonsdale (Oxford: Oxford University Press, 1989), 109–10.

15. See Maren-Sofie Røstvig, *The Happy Man: Studies in the Metamorphoses of a Classical Idea 1600–1760*, 2 vols. (Oslo and New York: Humanities Press Inc., 1962).

16. Printed in Lonsdale, *Eighteenth-Century Women Poets*, 209–10.

17. *Epistle*. 1.5. The poem (untitled) was first published in a prefatory letter in *The*

Art of Cookery (London, 1708), in which King describes it as "an imitation of Horace's invitation of Torquatus to supper." Text here from King's *Original Works*, ed. John Nichols, 3 vols. (London, 1776), 3:52–53.

18. *Poems Upon Several Occasions* (London, 1748), 106–108. "Artemisia" has been identified by Betty Rizzo as Bridget Freemantle, daughter of a clergyman: see Richard Greene, *Mary Leapor: A Study in Eighteenth-Century Women's Poetry* (Oxford: Clarendon Press, 1993), 19.

19. King's invitation to Bellvill was often reprinted; there is no way of ascertaining where Leapor read it. For Leapor's familiarity with Horatian tradition, see Greene, *Mary Leapor*, 17.

20. *The Poems of John Wilmot Earl of Rochester*, ed. Keith Walker (Oxford: Basil Blackwell, 1984), 61–62. The poem is dated 1665–66 by Frank H. Ellis, ed., *John Wilmot, Earl of Rochester: The Complete Works* (Harmondsworth: Penguin Books, 1994), 314.

21. Walker, *The Poems of John Wilmot*, 259.

22. *The Complete Poems of John Wilmot, Earl of Rochester*, ed. David M. Vieth (New Haven and London: Yale University Press, 1968), 16. Walker quotes Vieth's comment and prints the poem under "Satires and Lampoons."

23. Extract from Hamilton's *Memoirs* in *Rochester: The Critical Heritage*, ed. David Farley-Hills (London: Routledge and Kegan Paul, 1972), 187. The editor comments, "It is impossible to decide how much of this account is fact and how much fiction."

24. Walker, *The Poems of John Wilmot*, 112–14.

25. Ibid., 83–90.

26. Nicholas Fisher, "Miss Price to Artemisia: Rochester's Debt to Ovid and Horace in his Verse Epistles," *Classical and Modern Literature* 11 (1991): 337–53.

27. Joseph Warton, *An Essay on the Writings and Genius of Pope* (London, 1756), 286.

28. Beer, 140.

29. *The Poems of Aphra Behn: A Selection*, ed. Janet Todd (London: William Pickering, 1994), 58–59. Todd's notes draw attention to the ambiguous gendering of the poem.

30. Alan Michael Parker and Mark Willhardt, *Cross-Gendered Verse* (London: Routledge, 1996), 2.

31. Edward Burns, "Absent from Home: Female Voices and Male Reading, in Aphra Behn, Rochester, and Elizabeth Malet," *The Body and the Text: Hélène Cixous, Reading and Teaching*, ed. Helen Wilcox et al. (New York and London: Harvester Wheatsheaf, 1990), 175.

The Fop, the Canting Queen, and the Deferral of Gender

THOMAS A. KING

WRITING HIS *APOLOGY* (1740) FOR AN AUDIENCE ACCUSTOMED TO Elizabeth Barry and Anne Oldfield and never having seen a boy actor himself, playwright, actor-manager, and poet laureate Colley Cibber could not believe that such boys as the Restoration player Edward Kynaston had been credible or sympathetic in female roles.[1] And so he introduced Kynaston into his memoir of the late seventeenth- and eighteenth-century theaters with a story calculated to demonstrate the lack of similitude between the boy actor and the role of Queen Gertrude in *Hamlet*:

> The King coming a little before his usual time to a Tragedy, found the Actors not ready to begin, when his Majesty not chusing to have as much Patience as his good Subjects, sent to them, to know the Meaning of it; upon which the Master of the Company came to the Box, and rightly judging, that the best Excuse for their Default, would be the true one, fairly told his Majesty, that the Queen was not *shav'd* yet: The King, whose good Humour lov'd to laugh at a Jest, as well as to make one, accepted the Excuse, which serv'd to divert him, till the male Queen cou'd be effeminated.[2]

Cibber meant his story as an example of "a ridiculous Distress that arose from these sort of Shifts, which the Stage was then put to" due to the use of men too old to play female parts during the transitional period when women actors had not yet been sufficiently trained. For Cibber, as I will suggest shortly, boyish effeminacy might have passed as femininity within an earlier (and immature) political and social economy of subjection. The theater's use of boys, paradigmatic of the hierarchical structure of super- and subordination that I will be calling "residual pederasty," indicated its failure of interest in the difference of women. Thus Cibber described the appearance of women actors in female roles after the Restoration as enabling progress toward greater realism in acting:

> And what Grace, or Master-strokes of Action can we conceive such ungain Hoydens [boy players] to have been capable of? This Defect was so well

94

consider'd by *Shakespear*, that in few of his Plays, he has any greater Dependence upon the Ladies, than in the Innocence and Simplicity of a *Desdemona*,
an *Ophelia*, or in the short Specimen of a fond and virtuous *Portia*. The additional Objects then of real, beautiful Women, could not but draw a proportion of new Admirers to the Theatre. We may imagine too, that these
Actresses were not ill chosen, when it is well known, that more than one of
them had Charms sufficient at their leisure Hours, to calm and mollify the
Cares of Empire.[3]

Erasing the sexual contract underwriting, in Carole Pateman's important formulation, the social contract, Cibber represented the theater as
having elevated women above their traditionally subjected status; the
portrayal of women by immature boys had become an insult to women's
unique difference from, and complementariness to, men.[4] Indeed, the
reciprocal constitution of privacy and publicity, in Jürgen Habermas's
treatment, within "the audience-oriented (*publikumsbezogen*) subjectivity
of the conjugal family's intimate domain (*Intimsphäre*), 'the reformation
of male manners studied at length by G. J. Barker-Benfield, the Whig
consolidation of a hegemony of politeness analyzed by Lawrence Klein,
and the representation by eighteenth-century elites of "consciousness"
and sensibility as, if not intrinsically feminine, a softening and alignment of masculinity with new heterosocial ideals all depended on the
symbolic centrality of a morally superior, classed, and heteroerotic
"femininity" located, in Pateman's and Nancy Armstrong's accounts, in
a domestic space construed as nonpolitical.[5] Cibber's ideal "of real
beautiful Women" occluded (even as it sentimentalized) the economic
and sexual vulnerability of the low or lower middling ranked actresses
who performed it.[6] Ignoring the material difference of the actresses"
bodies, even as it shifted subjection from economies of status to differences of gender, the Whig stage offered gentle femininity as the motive
for gentlemen's consent to privatizated, domestic, and heteroerotic ideals of personal and political liberty.

Privileging the difference of women from the boys who had imitated
them required an erasure of the very economy of erotic dependency in
which the boys, and their patrons, had acquired meaning—an erasure,
that is, of the embodied deference against which an increasingly privatized concept of nation was emerging. The symbolic capital made of the
"feminine" consciousness as signpost of a privatized society depended,
then, on rendering incomprehensible the boy player and the baroque
economy of imitation and decorum of which he had been a signal participant.[7] Where Renaissance and early Restoration theatricality had enabled an imitative circuit among boys and women—both subjected
sexually to their male superiors[8]—Cibber's story about shaving disal-

lowed that similitude in order to claim the incommensurableness of *adult men* and women.[9] Cibber occluded the boy as a distinct object of desire within sixteenth- and seventeenth-century courtly society, paradigmatic of a political economy in which all men, as all woman and children, ranked below the monarch had been subordinated—politically and erotically—to other men. Cibber's praise for the entrance of the actress, in short, was praise for a mature political order that had turned its boys into men.

If remembering the boy players fondly was an insult to women's authenticity, it was at the same time a derogation of men's achievement of political privacy and liberal subjectivity. That achievement had required the withdrawal of legitimacy from an earlier system of patronage and deference, studied by Alan Bray and Jonathan Goldberg, entailing what, in modern terms, would be understood as the erotic materialization of patterns of dominance and submission. Residual pederasty, however, did not derive from or originate in the sex difference of objects, nor did it reproduce gender difference as the effect of positions of desire.[10] Sexual relations with boy pages or waiting women, servants, apprentices, students, and other social or political inferiors—a status group in which women were included to the extent that their rank did not override their absorption within patriarchal sex difference—were constitutive of these performative exchanges of submission and empowerment. I use the term "pederasty" to signal the eroticization of early modern *subjection* and thus its difference from a modern economy of heterosexual, homosexual, and bisexual *subjectivities.*[11] I call the pattern of super- and subordination in seventeenth- and early eighteenth-century England *"residual* pederasty" to denote its tactical deployment as a form of counterresistance to the emergent and oppositional privacy of the men making up the liberal public sphere. I will describe sexualities within the early modern cultural formation of privacy as "emergent" in the eighteenth century, by contrast, to emphasize the cultural work they produce: the ongoing and hegemonic construction of liberal subjectivities.

At stake in the disavowal of the boy player was the assimilation of male aristocrats and private (educated, property-owning) men in the eighteenth century as a new hegemony or "political nation" recognized by their joint share in masculinity. Cibber's claim to an expanded (male, Whig) audience superseding the earlier, more courtly audience and attracted to the theaters by the spectacle of women's bodies represented such a political nation. Around the spectacle of the conscious actress, the expanding audiences of educated property owners could identify themselves, *as* men, with the "Cares of Empire" and the pleasures of the state. Such an audience would be able to represent state interests as reflecting private, gendered desires. What, then, happened to the boy player?

The year after the *Apology* appeared, William Oldys told a slightly different version of Cibber's joke in his own *History of the English Stage*, which he attributed to the actor-manager Thomas Betterton: "His Majesty being at a Representation of *Hamlet*, and thinking the Entry of the *Queen*, in that Play, a little too tedious, one of the Actors most humbly acquainted the Audience that the *QUEEN was not quite shaved.*"[12] In Oldys's version it was not the play that was delayed but Gertrude's entrance; this specification set up the comparison he (or his compositor) made between the character *Queen* (a standard italicization) and the player QUEEN (capitalized for emphasis). This slippage of type — probably mediated by the tacit homonym "quean," or strumpet[13] — made Kynaston *present*, his body foregrounded through and despite the queenly character he played, in a way that Cibber had avoided. By calling attention to the contrast between royalty and its imitation by an impudent player, Oldys's pun suggested a similitude between the former boy actress and the harlot. If this similitude was not yet "homosexuality," the pun nevertheless remembered the boy actor as whore; and it is my concern in this essay to show how the impudence of the boy player — his erotic place within a normative pederasty — became specified as the difference of a sodomitical subjectivity.

For Cibber, the differences of sex, age, and maturity between the boy player and the character Gertrude failed to produce a convincing performance of gender. Cibber's joke played on the (new) incompatibility of two innate capacities — boyishness and femininity — while nevertheless enjoying the theater's ability to play with surfaces (as in his own fop roles). For Oldys, by contrast, the similitude of Kynaston and the *player* quean, as harlots, provided a mechanism for explaining the conventional use of boys in female roles. Oldys called attention to the *subject* of the story — the boy being shaved — in a way that Cibber, with his typographical emphasis on the *shaving*, had not intended. Indeed, Cibber never clearly indicated that the specific subject of this joke was Kynaston at all. By contrast, Oldys wrote that Kynaston's playing female roles had "occasioned [the] very good Jest" he then related. This change suggests that some (here, tacit) discourse about former boy players like Kynaston had furnished, for Oldys, the key to Cibber's unidentified anecdote, rewriting the history of the boy actors as a roman à clef about sodomitical subjectivities.

This transition from a joke about the "shifts which the stage was then put to" to the shifts a particular sort of player might make was fully developed by Edmund Bellchambers in his 1822 edition of the *Apology*. Bellchambers changed the emphasis in Cibber's punch line, putting his only stress on *"Queen,"* so that the master of the company "fairly told his majesty, that the *Queen* was not shaved yet."[14] Where Cibber and the audiences he remembered had enjoyed the shaving—the process of effeminating the boy and turning him into a spectacle—and where Oldys's assertion of the gap between role and player had made Kynaston present as quean, Bellchambers's joke *identified* the boy player and the female role. His pun turning on the subjectivity of the player rather than the conventions of playing, Bellchambers construed the boy player as a theatrical subject—a prostitute quean? a drag queen?—who laid bare his "real" self to the audience's look precisely when he effeminated himself.

If Cibber refused the look's authority to determine interiority, it is clear in the *Apology* that he understood it to be his audiences' dominant mode of spectatorship. His digressions and discontinuities and his avoidance of autobiographical depth, may also be read as attempts to defend the performing agent against the spectator's "right" to witness a display of subjectivity. Known for his fops and fools, Cibber was particularly subject to hostile comparisons to the characters he played. His first major role, moreover, had been substituting for an ailing Kynaston as Lord Touchstone in William Congreve's *The Double Dealer* in 1694. What "in" Cibber made him a suitable substitute for the player quean? By considering Kynaston as agent rather than sexual subject, Cibber attempted to prevent the critical look from accruing to himself. But to see Kynaston's body we have to follow the chain of associations (the much maligned digressions) that Cibber so carefully constructed.

Measuring Masculinities

In anticipation of the restoration of monarchy, several entrepreneurs moved to open theater companies in London between May 1659 and 24 March 1659/60 (old style).[15] Along with other boy actors, Kynaston was probably performing female roles for John Rhodes by early 1660. On 21 August 1660, Thomas Killigrew and William Davenant each received patents from Charles II to form their companies and moved to suppress all other existing companies. Kynaston became a member of Killigrew's company, The King's Company, for which he continued to play female roles throughout the transition to women actors and into the second full season of the patented companies. We know, for instance, that he was still playing the title role in John Suckling's *Aglaura* as late as 28 December 1661, over a year after the production of *Othello* thought to have introduced the first woman actor (8 December 1660). Moreover, the performance of *Hamlet* at the Theatre Royal, at which

Charles II had been kept waiting while the queen was shaved, could not have occurred before 28 June 1661, when Charles made his first appearance at a public playhouse.[16] Although Cibber suggested that these youths were too old to pass as female, Kynaston, whose birth is variously dated 1643 and 1640, would have been between seventeen and twenty at this time.[17]

Cibber made Kynaston visible as a set of gestural, postural, and vocal divergences from the normative body at the center of his analyses of acting, Thomas Betterton. Betterton's body provided the field of plenitude against which Kynaston's body and gestures became visible as lacking. Betterton's normativity was not his absence in the field of vision; the norm is not disembodied. Rather Betterton's normativity for Cibber was his residual capacity to occupy the center of the field of vision, to equate his body with the seamlessness of decorum.

In late-seventeenth-century acting theory, individual differences of body and voice in theatrical characterization were achieved through proportionable, even measurable deviation from the paradigmatic body of authority—the aristocrat. Students of rhetorical training had two precedents for decorous stage action—the representation of aristocratic embodiment in painting and statuary or in the skilled performances of other actors and orators.[18] In 1710 Charles Gildon (also miming Betterton's voice) instructed the student to study the decorous and proper actions described in mythology and poetry, inscribed in "moral philosophy" (or physiognomy), and reproduced in visual representations like history painting and statuary.[19] Thomas Wright in 1604 had urged the orator to follow the actions of stage players;[20] and in the preceding decade the famous actors Richard Burbage and Edward Alleyn had been held up as patterns for courtiers.[21] That such recommendations were passed between the courtier and the actor both suggests that the imitative ideal of the stage was the courtly body and indicates that the courtly ideal taken as the norm of stage action was itself produced by imitation. Rhetorical acting in the seventeenth and early eighteenth centuries thus produced an ideal mode of gesture against which all other embodiments appeared lacking. This normative or "high" style was used to portray courtly aristocrats, primarily in the epic or tragic mode; while deviations from that norm (either lack or excess) were used to represent the lower ranks, usually in the comic mode.

The relative distance of the elbows from the body, for example, was a standard measure of the authority of a gesture from the seventeenth through the early nineteenth centuries. Gildon attributed to Betterton this observation: "The Arm extended and lifted up signifies the Power of doing and accomplishing something; and is the Gesture of Authority, Vigour, and Victory. On the contrary, the holding your Arms close is a

Sign of Bashfulness, Modesty, and Diffidence."[22] It is necessary to consider whether this normative body was a *status* body or a *male* body. To what extent was this opposition between authority and modesty, vigor and diffidence *gendered*? Are these gendered embodiments, or do these rules describe the distance between the powerful body at the center of the field of vision and the less powerful bodies who may only approach so far toward that center? Within the courtly space of the Jacobean and Caroline masques, as recorded in Inigo Jones's extant sketches, there was little slippage from status to gender; both male and female courtiers were represented, androgynously, with their arms akimbo, for example.[23] Just as courtly women could take public space as amazons, as in Ben Jonson and Jones's *Masque of Queens* (1609), so courtly men, removed from the legitimate publicity of the battlefield, could reconcile the effeminacy of courtly display and mixed-sex dancing to public virtue, as in Jonson and Jones's *Pleasure Reconcil'd to Virtue* (1618) or William Davenant and Jones's *Salmacida Spolia* (1640). But within the commercial space of the theater, the status body was becoming available as a figure for the authority of the *privatized* male body. The clarity of gender difference, and the complementariness of the sexes across those differences, provided a means for representing the emergence of class bodies over and against the traditional status bodies.

But the modeling of masculinity per se on aristocratic authority—a step in the transformation of the patriarchal power of king and father to the hegemonic power of men qua men within contract society—was far from stable or complete. Well after David Garrick had popularized Charles Macklin's innovation in "breaking the tones," the distance of the elbow from the side of the body continued to constitute a difference between "high" and "low" modes of characterization. Gilbert Austin repeated Gildon's instructions in his description of the attitude "Magnificence" in 1806:

> This consists in the ample space through which the arm and hand are made to move: and it is effected by detaching the upper arm completely from the body, and unfolding the whole oratorical weapon. The centre of its motion is the shoulder. . . . The motions of the head are free, and the inflexions of the body manly and dignified. The action of the lower limbs is decided, and a considerable space is traversed with firmness and with force.[24]

Lest Austin's gendered rhetoric should lead us to think that, by 1806, the slippage from aristocratic to male bodies was complete, or that Austin even meant to describe a "masculinity" inherent in all men regardless of age, occupation, or station (the determinants of decorous characterization), it is important to note that he still used the distance

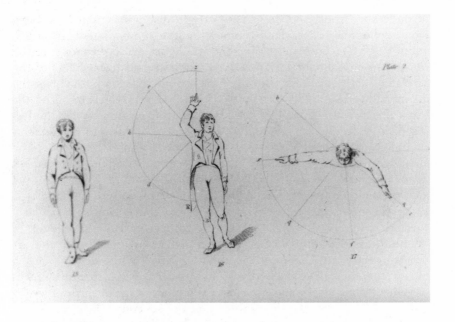

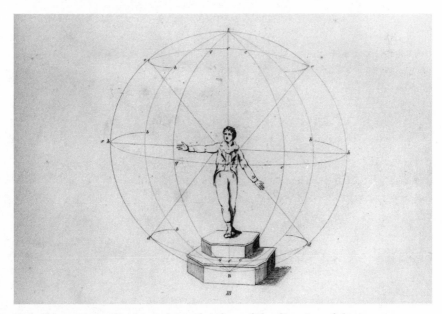

"Imaginary Circles for determining the place of the direction of the gesture [magnificent and epic gestures]." From Gilbert Austin, *Chironomia: Or, A Treatise on Rhetorical Delivery,* 1806, Plate 2, figs. 15–18. Courtesy of the Philip Mills Arnold Semeiology Collection, Special Collections, Washington University in St. Louis.

of the elbow from the side of the body to distinguish "epic" gestures from "colloquial" ones, that is, public (or state) embodiments from private ones. "Instead of unfolding the whole oratorical weapon . . . the upper arm in colloquial gesture is barely detached from the side," he directed, "and the elbow, instead of the shoulder, becomes the principal centre of motion" (458–59). Likewise, Johannes Jelgerhuis used the same measure in 1827 to distinguish tragic from comic gestures, understood in Aristotelian terms as the difference of noble and private embodiment: "For this purpose I have drawn dotted lines from the shoulder in a complete circle to indicate clearly the radius of movement of the arm and the positions of the rest of the body. . . . The circle of arm rotation from the shoulder to the finger tip shows us that tragic action must be large. In comedy, this circle of movement is particularly formed with the elbow at its center (rather than the shoulder)."[25] Within neoclassical theories of decorum, which assigned noble characters to tragedy and ordinary characters to comedy, the distance of the elbow from the side of the body would be read as producing differences of genre (tragic and comic, epic and colloquial); stage decorum thereby imitated and reinforced the authority of the sovereign gaze to give all other bodies their place in the spatial field. Reinforcing aristocratic *ap-*

"The colloquial elevations of the arms." From Gilbert Austin, *Chironomia: Or, A Treatise on Rhetorical Delivery,* 1806, Plate 4, figs. 34–36. Courtesy of the Philip Mills Arnold Semeiology Collection, Special Collections, Washington University in St. Louis.

Tragic gestures. From Johannes Jelgerhuis, *Theoretische Lessen over de Gesticulatie en Mimiek,* 1827, Plate 20. Courtesy of the Philip Mills Arnold Semeiology Collection, Special Collections, Washington University, St. Louis.

Colloquial gestures. From Johannes Jelgerhuis, *Theoretische Lessen over de Gesticulatie en Mimiek,* 1827, Plate 21. Courtesy of the Philip Mills Arnold Semeiology Collection, Special Collections, Washington University, St. Louis.

rezzatura, the normative rhetorical mode (the "high" style) demanded an absence of emotionality and gestural excess—an absence that demonstrated the superiority of the aristocrat to the ordinary, undisciplined body. The closer a character's gestures matched this ideal referent, the aristocratic body, the more power the character wielded in the social world depicted on stage. Accordingly, comic or grotesque types would be recognized by the excessiveness or awkwardness of their movements on stage.[26] Comic images—in the Aristotelian sense of nonaristocratic—were produced by a mathematically measurable deviation from the ideal represented as aristocratic style. If aristocratic stance required that the feet be placed in what later became the third position in ballet, low-ranked or comic characters simply had their feet turned parallel or inward. Differences of station, as in society at large, were bodily perversions of the imitative ideal of aristocracy.

Enacted on a commercial stage, however, the distance of the elbow from the body was at the same time producing effects of gendering *among men*, not male or female but *masculine or effeminate*. On the commercial stage the association of the low-status and the comic body meant that such registers of failed authority as "Bashfulness, Modesty, and Diffidence" could be used to portray, comically, marginalized male subjects. A plate titled "Foppery," from Henry Siddons's *Practical Illustrations of Rhetorical Gestures* (1822), illustrated the deliberate use of such confinement of gesture—the elbow held close to the side of the body—in the early nineteenth century to produce laughter. Cibber himself seems to have kept his elbows close to his body when playing Lord Foppington at the end of the seventeenth century. And the actor-manager David Garrick seems to have milked this posture to portray the effeminate Fribble in his 1747 farce *Miss in her Teens*,[27] holding his elbows close to his body in the famous duel scene with Captain Flash (he also exploited his own, very non-Bettertonian diminutiveness). For well over a hundred years, then, marginalized masculinity was produced on stage, or made visible, as a lack of fit between an actor's gestures and the rhetorical ideal of aristocratic plenitude. The titled fop was funny to aristocratic and gentle males in seventeenth- and eighteenth-century audiences because his gestural patterns were not those of aristocratic males but of low or comic characters. In the same way the fribble was funny to the *propertied* men in Garrick's mid-eighteenth century audiences because he embodied a failure of gendered sociality. The eighteenth-century fop or fribble with his elbows close to his body was not (just) a failed *man*, but a comment on the distance between residual aristocratic embodiment and emerging privatized masculinities. Failed masculinity, among private men, was fribblish aristocracy.

Foppery

"Foppery." From Henry Siddons's *Practical Illustrations of Rhetorical Gesture and Action,* 2nd ed., 1822; plate 1 (following 50). From the original in the Charles Deering McCormick Library of Special Collections, Northwestern University Library.

Colley Cibber as Lord Foppington in John Vanbrugh's play *The Relapse,* by
J. Grisoni, published in the Lowe edition of Cibber's *Apology,* 1889, vol. 2,
frontispiece. From the original in the Charles Deering McCormick Library of
Special Collections, Northwestern University Library.

"The Celebrated Fighting Scene in *Miss in her Teens.*" From *London Magazine: Or Gentleman's Monthly Intelligencer* (February 1747): facing p. 84. From the original in the Charles Deering McCormick Library of Special Collections, Northwestern University Library.

This rhetorical body—the mode of being of aristocracy as mediated by and assimilated to a commercial stage—had as its imitative center the playing of Thomas Betterton, who replaced the aristocratic body as the origin or referent of Cibber's acting theory. Cibber accordingly justified a major digression from Betterton's biography into acting theory: "As *Betterton* is the Centre to which all my Observations upon Action tend, you will give me leave, under his Character, to enlarge upon that Head."[28] Cibber's Betterton represented a seamlessness of aristocratic signification, a rhetorical plenitude toward which all other male actors tended but failed; at the same time Betterton's corporeality assimilated that authority to a *manliness* distinguished from the residually "sweet" or "curled" Cavalier:

> The Person of this excellent Actor was suitable to his Voice, more manly than sweet, not exceeding the middle Stature, inclining to the corpulent; of a serious and penetrating Aspect; his Limbs nearer the athletick, than the delicate Proportion; yet however form'd, there arose from the Harmony of the whole a commanding Mien of Majesty, which the fairer-fac'd, or (as *Shakpear* [sic] calls 'em) the *curled* Darlings of his Time, ever wanted something to be equal Masters of. (69)

If all actors tended toward the ideal plenitude presented by Betterton, it was an ideal that none of those who fashioned themselves after the courtly ideal could fully occupy: "But I am unwilling," Cibber noted, "to shew his [Betterton's] Superiority only by recounting the Errors of those, who now cannot answer to them" (61). All other male actors acquired presence on stage as types of deviation from the ideal corporeality of Betterton.

But with the increasing popularization of physiognomic theory by the time Cibber wrote his *Apology*, the failure to match Betterton's corporeality—the aristocratic body now assimilated to an incipiently capitalist political nation as the manly body—no longer directed the eye to a learned, rhetorical technique for portraying difference. Rather, as William Hogarth would write in 1753, a divergence of line indicated a difference of subjectivity: "surely no figure, be it ever so singular, can be perfectly conceived as a character, till we find it connected with some remarkable circumstance or cause, for such particularity of appearance."[29] To understand how a divergence of line could now lay bare a history, a set of external circumstances or an internal deviation that would explain visible differences, it is necessary to chart the physiognomers" treatment of male effeminacy.

QUEER HERMENEUTICS

In the early physiognomer John Bulwer's two books on oratorical gestures, bound together in one volume and published in 1644, the extended, open, or offered hand appeared frequently as a sign of good will. Bulwer described the handshake in mercantilist terms as

> the most happy point of amity, a natural form very rich in signification since they, who thus *profess communion of goods* while they WILLINGLY EMBRACE EACH OTHER'S HAND, signify that *they are both content that their works shall be common*; by this gesture speaking plainly, as if they in effect should say: *What damage happens unto thee, I shall esteem as my own loss; and thy emolument and profit I shall entertain as mine own, and thou shalt find me ready pressed with a consonant and willing mind both to yield to thee a share of my welfare* and *reciprocally to bear a part of thy* calamity.[30]

Shaking hands, men of property enacted their *identity* within the marketplace. Assimilating the Renaissance ideal of male friendship to mercantile exchange, this gesture of equality among men who shared, by virtue of their property, social status was enacted against other uses of the male body that produced distinctions among men. To the open hand, Bulwer contrasted excessive gesturing with the hands, which he described as "subtle gesticulation and toying behavior,"[31] terms generally used to describe the actions of courtiers, wanton women and boys, and boy actors—the same bodies displaying subjection that Lucy Hutchinson, describing the pederastic court of James I in her account of her husband prepared for her children (1664–71), called "fooles and bawds, mimics and Catamites."[32] Excessive gesturing, for Bulwer, was like the "sleight of hand" of magicians, pickpockets, and actors, all of whom "mock[ed] the eye."[33] Gestural excess remade the male body as spectacle, refusing the corporeal transparency of men, upon which the openness of a contract society depended. Gestural excess remembered men's submissiveness to the spectacle of sovereignty; it remade men as effeminates displaying their subjection in order to court patronage and placement.

The many gestures that Bulwer characterized as "effeminate" invariably signaled sodomy as well;[34] by this combination of terms Bulwer clearly meant to indicate and derogate men's willing display of the erotics of political super- and subordination. Thus he recounted the story of Pompey being "publicly upbraided to his face with this note of effeminacy by Clodius, the tribune, asking aloud these questions: who is the licentiousest captain in all the city? what man is he that seeks for a man? what is he that SCRATCHETH HIS HEAD WITH ONE FINGER?" (131). Scratching the head with one finger, a gesture Bulwer called "*Molliciem prodo* [I betray weakness]," was "a kind of *nice* and *effeminate* gesture bewraying a *close inclination to vice*" (131). The specific vice at stake had to do with this ambiguous seeking of one man by another, which was not (our) homosexuality but the display of a circuit of political favor achieved through dishonorable means:

> As concerning the phrase of seeking for a man, that prince of the senate of critics says that he hath read in an old manuscript of an interpreter of Lucan never published this distich:
> [What is it that you imagine "Magnus" (Pompey) means, he whom men fear when he scratches his head with one finger? A man.
> For weak men are wont to seek a strong man.][35]

It is these same "weak" men ("molles": weakness throughout Bulwer always means, not physical debilitation, but the indolent bodily style of "nice and effeminate men"), seeking reward or favor dishonorably, whom Bulwer called "womanish" in his discussion of the gesture of discoursing with the hands turned up (222). Effeminacy, that is, was not an appropriation of behaviors "properly belonging to" women, but a repetition of those eroticized modes of display through which politically subordinate males sought favor of their patrons, just as dependent females courted the favor of their male and female protectors.

At the same time that Bulwer understood a virtuosic (or "affected") gestural economy as a dissimulation and mockery of transparency, he thought affected gestures could be laid bare, seen through by the very eye that had been mocked and made to reveal themselves as natural signs of the inner disposition of the person using them. He thus followed the assumption, common in physiognomy, that the lines of the body and its movements disclosed "the present humor and state of the mind and will,"[36] claiming that gestures indicated the interior complexion of the individual and were not dependent on culture or custom.[37] Bulwer proved this hypothesis in three steps: first, he posited a difference between natural and affected gestures; next, he posited psychological differences among individuals; and finally, equating the established difference between natural and affected gestures with that between the universal and the particular, he assumed that divergences from universal gesture indicated individual psychologies and, in his words, could be used to "discern the differences of spirits."[38] Significantly Bulwer introduced the discussion of physiognomic theory in his analysis of the gesture "*Effoeminate festino* [I hasten effeminately]." Here as elsewhere he slipped from understanding effeminacy as a technique of excessive or dissimulated performance (a false use of one's body) to privileging effeminate gestures as those bodily habits that indicate particular subjectivities (a characteristic use of the body by a particular kind of person): "for as men's present passions and inclinations are brought by nature into act, so men following the vogue of nature are wrought to a reiteration of that action until the hand hath contracted a habit."[39] Earlier Bulwer had defined affected gestures as those that were not functional: "Rightly doth [his classical source] call [the slack hand] a hand of deceit because, for the most part, the lazy hand being not able to sustain itself, betakes itself to cousenage and deceit."[40] Likewise the middle finger could symbolize "sloth, effeminacy, and notorious vices" for Bulwer because it was itself lazy and unattractive, and therefore "placed in the middest, as seeming to stand in need of the defense of the other neighboring fingers." At the same time, the middle finger, being the longest, was the *most given to displaying itself*, and so "it may help to relate in a more open way of expression the notoriousness of their vices who exceed others in wildness as far as this idle finger appears eminent above the rest."[41] Because wagging the hand was not necessary to assist the body or produce work, it indicated a man's *voluntary and effeminate display* of dependency and the derivation of his social status from his placement in the field of vision. This was not yet an alternative, troubled, or marginal *male* subjectivity. Masculinity, that is, did not yet have its own inwardness; authority devolved on male and status bodies through the disciplined exercise of the passions, which, as the result of the exchange of animal spirits, were more properly located between persons than "inside" them.[42] As the failure to discipline adequately the exchange of passions and the subsequent contraction of a bodily habit, "character" itself was always suspect as effeminacy and an indication of a propensity to a range of corporeal vices grouped together as indulgence, luxury, fornication, and sodomy. Thus wagging the hand habitually indicated that "kind of *wantonness* and *effeminacy*" that should disqualify a man from military service, that is, locate him outside the public utility of male bodies.[43] Appearing during the civil wars in 1644, Bulwer's treatises challenged the celebrated sweetness of the Cavalier. Bulwer made the effeminate, subjected body the other of the useful bodies of an emergent political nation that would identify public, military strength with the expansion and protection of private, mercantile interests.

Bulwer generalized from this specific gesture to an entirely effeminate corpus: "The gate, the turning of the eye, the finger on the head, and the WAGGING OF THE HAND *show* a shameless wanton."[44] Because the passions were generated, according to Neoplatonic theory, by the exchange of spirits through the eyes, the body habitually "bewraying" its passions was a body that had given itself over to this space of ocular exchange, both showing itself as permeable to the spirits of others (women, men, and boys) and vulnerable to their dissimulated or aggressive ocular penetration. As Bulwer's use of "wanton" suggests, such a corporeal habitus indicated a sedimented, residual bodily orientation, a display of oneself as subjected within a pederastic economy, and a refusal to embody the contract among propertied men to promote each other's interests. When it became a habitual mannerism, the effeminate gesture of wagging the hand indicated an inherent effeminacy of the subject, more precisely, an effeminacy that figured sodomitical submission like that of the boy actor, a shameless wantonness of the body that declared its publicity. This wantonness that the effeminate body displays is not an appropriation of "femininity," but the redeployment of the boy's, the courtier's, and the woman's display of desirability within a pederastic economy of super- and subordination.

The increasing precision with which readings of the male body were produced suggests that there was resistance to the ideology of the liberal male self as transparently available to other men of property. In 1753 Hogarth tackled the problem of the relation of the self to self-presentation, proposing that an individual's character could be reduced to a simple line, all contradictions or excesses smoothed away. Just as a sparkler leaves a trace of its movements in the air, so one could imagine "a line formed in the air by any supposed point at the end of a limb or part that is moved."[45] The body that Hogarth envisioned had a coherent and immediate presence, such that each of its surfaces, rather than deferring to a complex history of social negotiations, referred to an innate and self-originating subjectivity. Hogarth's claim that "the motions of one part of the body may serve to explain those of the whole" marked an increasingly efficient specification of the corporeal realization of identity.[46]

But Hogarth's attempt to see psychological difference in the difference of lines foregrounds a paradox within this ideology: How to make consciousness visible on the surface of the body while at the same time understanding the body as transparent? How to display oneself as sufficiently transparent, sufficiently conscious? On the one hand, an oppositional public sphere had been enunciated against elite spectacularity; on the other, its members recognized that interiority had to be made visible if moral judgments made on the basis of character were to be legitimated. This paradox may have been aggravated by the growing awareness that the new molly identity developing after 1700 among lower- and lower-middle-class men was not always immediately recognizable in the surfaces of their bodies. The sodomite became an especially privileged case of the surveillance of male bodies—not at all surprisingly, since physiognomy had been interested (explicitly in the case of Bulwer) in generating privatized male bodies that displayed an interior difference from pederastic subjection. Somewhat more than half a century after Hogarth's *Analysis*, the anonymous *Phoenix of Sodom* noted, in a complaint that would drive sexology in the late nineteenth century: "It is a generally received opinion, and a very natural one, that the prevalency of this passion has for its object effeminate delicate beings only; but this seems to be . . . a mistaken notion; and the reverse is so palpable in many instances, that the Fanny Murry, Lucy Cooper, and Kitty Fishers, are personified by an athletic Bargeman, an Herculean Coalheaver, and a deaf tyre Smith."[47] The technique needed was one whereby the self could be made visible *despite* the body, and thus outside the agent's capacity for dissimulation and trickery—an advance in the specification of the symptomatic expressiveness of the underlying psyche.

Between Hogarth's *Analysis of Beauty* and the *Phoenix of Sodom*, John Caspar Lavater's *Essays in Physiognomy, Designed to Promote the Knowledge and the Love of Mankind* (English translation 1789) would insist on the capacity of an all-seeing but unseen look to disclose "truth": "In order to detect the imposter, it would be necessary to catch him at the moment when, imagining he is alone, he is still himself, and has not had time to dress his face in the expression which he knows how to assume."[48] The "effeminate sodomite" was problematized—given his own ideological content—in the eighteenth century through the technique of disclosing an underlying content even and precisely when the Hogarthian difference of surfaces could not be seen. But in transcoding effeminacy from a criticism of aristocratic display and subjection (a corporeal technique seen through as lacking) to a content of the sodomite's psyche (a particularized corporeal difference on its way to becoming a subjectivity), the hermeneutics of effeminacy recast the sodomite as the residually public body, a specific corporeality like that of the (lost or opposed) sovereign body. An emergent psychological discourse granted the sodomite's body what the sovereign body had lost, an innate and distinguishing content that the deliberately excessive line of the male body had reflected and reproduced.

Seeing Kynaston

Such a perversion of line—a deviation from the manly plenitude represented by Betterton—apparently characterized Kynaston's acting. In making the transition from female to male roles, the former boy actor had to adapt the span of his gestures, not just to play male but high-ranking male roles, and tragic ones at that. But Cibber wrote that Kynaston "had something of a formal Gravity in his Mien, which was attributed to the stately Step he had been so early confin'd to, in a female Decency." The habit that Kynaston apparently had to overcome in order to "execute" such roles as Henry IV "with a determin'd Manliness" and "fierce, Lion-like Majesty"[49] was an inhibition or "confinement" of the span of his gestures and gait—a mincing step, his elbows held close to his body, perhaps—that Cibber suggested had assisted his portrayal of "femininity" as a youth but was now coded as effeminate and suspect. But Cibber's slippage here is telling. Kynaston's step and mien were "formal" and "stately" because he had specialized in playing queens, royal mistresses, and ambitious or unfortunate female courtiers, in Restoration revivals of such plays as William Davenant's *Unfortunate Lovers* (Arthiope), John Fletcher's *The Mad Lover* (the Princess Calis), Francis Beaumont and Fletcher's *The Maid's Tragedy* (Evadne), and Beaumont and Fletcher's *The Loyal Subject* (the Duke's sister Olympia). Cibber's analysis collapsed the attributes of courtliness into femininity and equated the public with the masculine political nation. As divergence from the ideal of corporeal plenitude represented by Betterton, Kynaston's corporeality would lay him bare as fribblish, incapacitated, and sexually suspect; and that debilitation would itself invite interpretation. If Kynaston failed to be a Betterton, it was because he had incorporated within himself the femininity—and the courtly display suspect as "effeminacy and wantonness"—that he had portrayed as a youth. This was the charge from which Cibber set out to defend Kynaston and, by extension, himself. If marginalized masculinity was produced on stage only as deviation from the rhetorical norm, that deviation might be read, not as a "lack" expressive of subjectivity, but as theatrical technique. In defending Kynaston, Cibber worked against the description of theatricality itself as a "lack" of being or failure of self-knowledge.[50]

The rhetorical plenitude, vigor, and manliness that Cibber attributed to Betterton were not inherent in biologically male bodies but were acquired techniques for assimilating aristocratic and private men to an elite embodiment. While Gildon asserted that "the most valuable Voice" for the stage was the "grave, bass, or full," this was still a voice that required training in "right Pronunciation" including tone, tune, and cadence.[51] For example, the normative male stage voice during the period under discussion took "the Tone and Accent by which Men are known" and layered on top of it what Alfred Simeon Golding has called a "piercing" quality produced by an emphasis on head tones and the upper vocal register.[52] In his *Brief Supplement* to Cibber's *Apology* (1748), Anthony Aston noted that Betterton's "Voice was low and grumbling; yet he could Tune it by an artful *Climax*, which enforc'd universal Attention, even from the *Fops* and *Orange-girls*."[53] This elite tone, or "court tune," had been "carefully prescribed or maintained" as the rhetorical ideal of the court-sponsored Restoration theaters.[54] The tragic hero or romantic lover would not have been distinguished from the fop by a lower vocal register, but by the fop's failure to achieve, or his excessive imitation of, the piercing quality that was identified, offstage, with the court. Neither Kynaston's effeminacy nor the fop's affectation could have been read simply against a biological imperative inherent in all male bodies regardless of rank. The leveling of masculinity, rather, was an optical illusion produced by the assimilation of aristocratic to private male bodies in the commercial space of the theaters, erasing the terms of the historical opposition to pederastic display and incorporating the aristocracy into the political nation through a mutual disavowal of the subjected male body. As distinctions among men gave way to the emergent psychological identity of all men, fops were increasingly specified by their residual use of affected styles.

Despite Cibber's defense, Kynaston's vocal affectation was remembered as an inner perversion or sickness. In the last quarter of the eighteenth century, Thomas Davies recalled an anecdote about Kynaston that suggests the degree of Cibber's earlier silence about the former boy player's sexual suspectness:

Notwithstanding the high encomium, bestowed on [Kynaston] in Cibber's Apology, I have been informed, by some of the old comedians, that, from his early representation of womens characters, Kynaston had contracted some disagreeable tones in speaking, something like whining, or what we term canting. When George Powell was once discharging the intemperance of the proceeding day from his stomach, during the time of action Kynaston asked him if he was sick.—"How is it possible to be otherwise," said Powell, "when I hear you speak?"[55]

Embellishing Davies, Bellchambers emphasized that Kynaston's manner of speaking "resembled the whine or cant that genuine taste has at all times been impelled to explode."[56] It was not that Powell himself had a more essentially "masculine" voice; he also canted, or as F. Reynardson put it in *The Stage* (1713), he "twang[ed] majestically full."[57] Yet Powell's twang was distinguished from Kynaston's cant, I will argue, by the implantation of sexuality by the time Davies wrote his anecdote in the late eighteenth century.

This court tune or cant was a common attribute of the fribblish fop or petit maître during this period, marking his failure to engage the Whig project of sociable conversation. The satirical pamphlet *The Pretty Gentleman; Or, Softness of Manners Vindicated* (1747) developed this at length by making the fribble recognizable, not only through his ostentatious dress, pacifism, and fondness for occupations restricted to women, but through an extended analysis of fribblish (incapacitated) speaking and writing styles that were at once highly mannered, self-referential, and lacking in significance: "Happily freed from the Shackles of *connecting* and *restraining* Rules, the Diction roves and wanders, now here, now there; and, with a wondrous Facility, glides so imperceptibly from one Flower to another, that the most subtile Penetrator would be at a Loss to find, where *This* ends, and where *That* begins."[58] An effective account of Cibber's style in the *Apology*: indeed, Kristina Straub has made much of Cibber's "Tristram Shandy–like" narrative of nonmastery.[59] While I would agree that Cibber's textual strategies and anti-Augustan style signaled his alignment with residual economies of power, I would not agree that these strategies, in Cibber, are necessarily "homoerotic."[60] Pederasty, as I have argued, was not determined by gendered object-choice; and techniques of narrative nonmastery were used by women writers as well to register their alignment with a royalist representational economy (consider Margaret Cavendish and Aphra Behn). *The Pretty Gentleman*, by contrast, recodes this nonmastery as explicitly sodomitical by giving molly discourse an actual body.

The pamphlet's writer "Philautus" linked the fribble's discursive style to a specifically sodimitical body, imitating molly postures and gestures and transcribing the very sound of fribblish conversation—an affected but faulty tune emitted "through his half-opened Lips" and empty of any reference.[61] More precisely, this was an accent that had lost its association with the court tune and now had molly identity as its only referent. Among the several examples of molly speech reported in this pamphlet: "O! fie! ye filt-hy Creter!," "I vew, Me'me, yur'e immoderately entertaining," and "what a *Paw* Trick was that!" (16, 17, 28). It was not what the fribblish molly said, the author noted, but "the *Manner*" and "the *Accent*" of his speech that identified him.[67] The reproduction of this same speech pattern identified Fribble, in David Garrick's farce of the same year, *Miss in Her Teens*, as a molly: "As I was holding out my Hand in a threatning *Poster*, —thus; —he makes a cut at me with his Whip, and striking me over the Nail of my little Finger, it gave me such exquisite *Torter* that I fainted away."[62] The fribblish molly seems to have descended from the line of Vanbrugh's Lord Foppington, whose own speech had indicated his foppish failure to reproduce the court tune:

> Why the ladies were ready
> to puke at me, whilst I had nothing but Sir Navelty
> to recommend me to 'em. Sure, whilst I was but
> a knight, I was a very nauseous fellow. Well, 'tis
> ten thousand pawnd well given—stap my
> vitals—[63]

If the fribble's speech pattern appropriated a court tune or drawl that could no longer signify, his conversational style imitated the ironic pose of men of wit and sense, but offering no substance beneath the surface. It was mere sound without sense; or, as "Philautus" noted ironically, "the *Sound always ecchoes to the Sense*," indicating the emptiness of this speech.[64]

In his account of Kynaston's canting, Davies reduced a highly contested vocal mode to the subjectivity of a particular actor, erasing its history. In his account, "canting" and "whining," like gestural excess, had become elided with femininity, and through that elision their appearance in men had become signs of sodomitical difference. Their earlier history, however, had been of a different class. The "whine" had been associated with the romantic or heroic lover in Restoration acting,[65] and may have been used by Kynaston in such roles as Cassio in Shakespeare's *Othello* or Harcourt in William Wycherley's *The Country Wife*, which Kynaston originated. Taken to excess, the "whine" became "canting." And as the style of the whining lover quickly became trite and old-fashioned, the terms were conflated. Davies's anecdote constructed a personal and sexually suspect history for a vocal style, the lover's whine, more properly associated with the elite conventions of heroic drama and the alignment of the Restoration stage with the aristocratic circle—an alignment signaled in the stage's adoption of the nasal "court tune" imported by courtiers from France. During the fad for "Count" Heidegger's masquerades in the 1720s and 1730s, the court tune was transformed into the "masquerade squeak" or falsetto used by the maskers to disguise their voices.[66] Decades earlier, the masquerade squeak had been the property of the gentry: Snarl in Shadwell's *The Virtuoso* tells a group of masqueraders, "In sadness, you are all a company of squealing coxcombs. Would you were all eunuchs, by the mass, that you might always keep your treble voices."[67] The masquerades marked the commodification of aristocratic performance requisite to bourgeois participation.

"Canting" had a more specific history as the derogatory term applied to the particular preaching style of "enthusiastic" Puritan dissenters. In his *Characters*, Samuel Butler ridiculed the "fantastic and extravagant Tones" of the dissenters and noted that one way to be sure that a Quaker had "a Crack in his Skull" was "by the flat Twang of his Nose."[68] Aphra Behn's Lady Fancy (1678) entertained her lover Wittmore with an imitation, "through the nose," of the cant at the meeting houses to which her husband carried her.[69] In his *Life of Betterton*, Gildon criticized "a whole Discourse turning still on the same *Note* and *Tone*," by which he meant not our modern "monotone" but the overuse of the upper register and piercing tone: "you must have a Care of [raising the voice] to the highest Note it can reach," warned Gildon, for that "would be a *Bawling* or a *Monotone*, a Cant, or Identity of Sound." Gildon stressed that this overuse of the upper registers "savour[ed] of the Cant, which was formerly in some of the Dissenter's Pulpits."[70] Richard Steele, too, wrote in *Spectator* 147 that cant was like the "Improprieties" of preachers who used a false and affected "Elevation and Cadence" and did not give "due Emphasis" to the sense of the words. For Steele, cant "signifie[d] all sudden Exclamations, Whinings, unusual Tones, and in fine all Praying and Preaching like the unlearned of the Presbyterians."[71] Both Steele and Gildon placed cant, like the nasal whine, in the upper register, where we might also have heard the court tune and the treble squeak of the masqueraders. Their criticism was a way of simultaneously marking and denigrating two kinds of excesses— aristocratic affectation and Puritan enthusiasm. In neither case was the high register in men described as feminine.

Incorporating a second, more broad meaning of cant, derived from the popular stereotype of Puritan as hypocrites, Steele characterized canting as a failure of meaning, as sound without sense.[72] Just as gestures or motions were meaningful within a set of discursive conventions that had the dominant culture as its referent, so, for Oldys, quoting "an eminent writer," "every Sentence" had its "Measure, Time and Tune," rhetorical proprieties that could be notated or "pricked down as well as any musical Tune."[73] Cibber instructed the readers of his *Apology*: "The Voice of a Singer is not more strictly ty'd to Time and Tune, than that of an Actor in Theatrical Elocution: The least Syllable too long, or too slightly dwelt upon, in a Period, depreciates it to nothing." Cibber warned that the eruption of "the least syllable" against decorum would empty a speech of its meaning; by contrast, that syllable, "if rightly touch'd, shall, like the heightening Stroke of Light from a Master's Pencil, give Life and Spirit to the whole."[74] The proper pronunciation was like the caricaturing line or "heightening strokes" of Hogarth, through which, as we have seen, "the motions of one part of the body may serve to explain those of the whole." Gilbert Austin clarified this in 1806: "all the unmeaning and unmarked motions of public speakers whether on the stage or elsewhere, are attended with the same ill effect, as a mouthing and canting tone of declamation, which lays no emphasis with just discrimination, but swells and falls with a vain affectation of feeling, and with absolute deficiency both of taste and judgment."[75] Cant was most generally the eruption of sound from the grammar of rhetorical delivery, the loss of sense in speaking, and, as Bellchambers had insisted in his version of the story about Kynaston's stage voice, an affectation that threatened the community of taste. "Cant" was a residually baroque manner of speaking that called attention to itself as artifice, over and against the social contract through which language acquired reference. As Thomas Hobbes had put it in his *Leviathan* (1651), language did not consist of natural or "certain signs" but, like all other commodities, derived its value from exchange; some acts of the tongue, therefore, fell outside the social contract and "d[id] not signifie as speech."[76] For Cibber as for Hobbes, canting was an act of the tongue (an embodied practice, an exercise of the body) that could not signify. This insignificant, fribblish, or (in Cibber's protocapitalist term) *depreciated* speech marked the outside of the social symbolic, the limits of the rhetorical contract whereby the body's motions (performance) became meaningful.

Precisely because dominant culture saw its others as lacking significant discourse, these "other" discourses were able to operate at the periphery of dominant society. Indeed, Anthony Ashley Cooper, third earl of Shaftesbury recognized such alternative discourses as the product of an intolerant society: "If [Men] are forbid to speak at all upon [certain] Subjects, or if they find it really dangerous to do so; they will then redouble their Disguise, involve themselves in Mysteriousness, and talk so as hardly to be understood, or at least not plainly interpreted, by those who are dispos'd to do 'em a mischief."[77] Such discursive systems operated underground until they were discovered and appropriated, as the cant of "queer" rogues was exposed and recuperated through the commercial theatres and masquerades. A "Canting-Dictionary" included in a slim volume published in 1673, *The Canting Academy, Or, The Devils Cabinet Opened*, defined cant as a "hidden and mysterious way of speaking, which [gypsies, thieves, and other rogues] make use of to blind the eyes of those they have cheated or robb'd, and inform one another with what they have done, or designe to do."[78] Cant was the argot of "queer," in the eighteenth-century sense of suspicious or dubious, men and women.[79] It was the author's declared intent to make the secret language of these queer fellows known to the reading public—a language as counterfeit as the "queer" (forged) coins and banknotes described in thieves" cant—that the propertied might protect themselves against foul play by the canting queers they were bound to meet.

After Cibber's retirement from the stage and Garrick's debut, Davies and other popular writers collapsed the Puritan's and the thief's cant, the court tune, and the lover's whine—registers of differences among men—into a stereotype of "the affected man," a psychological subject onto whom the ambiguities of male display could be displaced following what J. C. Flügel called the "Great Masculine Renunciation" of sartorial display and more recent historians have described as the gendering of clothes, emergent in the eighteenth century.[80] Ostensibly equalizing men as a category over and against, not only women as a category, but the hierarchies that gave some men (those occupying the center of the field of vision) power over the bodies of other men, the gradual renunciation of clothing that had the court as its reference mystified the actual differences (of rank, occupation, party, franchise, and so on) among men that had emerged simultaneously with the disavowal of men's pederastic subordination. Whereas men derived their masculinity from the identification of their interests with those of other men, the "affected" man publicized his difference from the category of men. In his farcical poem "The Fribbleriad," Garrick attributed both the stage lisp and a singsong speaking style, or cant, to fribbles, along with mincing steps reminiscent of Kynaston; names like Mister Marjoram identified Garrick's fribbles as mollies.[81] As the lisp and mincing steps—like the effeminate gestures I have discussed earlier—were naturalized onto an affected body specified as the molly's body, their political history was mystified. As the whine was displaced onto the sodomite's body, the political content of cant was erased. The visibly effeminate sodomite provided the limit of the naturally manly body and confirmed the fiction equating propertied men with the authorized body, the political nation with the phallus. The sodomite could not belong to this public sphere of private men because his bodily style recalled pederastic subjection. John Dennis noted in his "Essay on the Opera's after the Italian Manner" (1706) that "an *Englishman* is deservedly scorn'd by *Englishmen*, when he descends so far beneath himself, as to sing or dance in publick; because by doing so, he practices Arts which Nature has bestow'd upon effeminate Nations."[82] Political and class divisions among men were occluded; as in Davies's anecdote about Kynaston's stage voice, a narrative of one sort of body's tendency to give itself away was superimposed over the political history of the corporeal differences among men.

If English theater in the eighteenth century was productive of cultural anxieties about sodomy, and if early theatrical memoirs, like Cibber's, disavowed the theater's own history of wanton boy player-prostitutes, since the eighteenth century remembered only through their later, burlesque traces, it is because of this process by which the theater distanced itself from its own history as a vehicle of the display of pederastic subjection. The well-known changes in acting theory in the eighteenth century can only be said to have "democratized" the stage, appealing to new republican ideals of equality among propertied men,[83] to the extent that they also collapsed the demonized referent of theatricality—the international modes of display productive of the courtly body—into a new psychic space capable of standing as an *origin* of theatricality itself: the molly's effeminacy. Within the commercial space of the theaters, the history of opposition to courtly sovereignty—the development from boys to men mapped by Dennis onto the distinction of effeminate and masculine nations—was rewritten as the difference between manliness and femininity, that is, the difference of gender among private subjects. Kynaston's effeminacy was no longer his proximity to courtly aristocracy but his proximity to femininity. Kynaston's sexual suspiciousness enabled—and mystified—the erasure of the boy as erotic object for adult men.

During the period preceding the Glorious Revolution, several satires by enemies of George Villiers, second Duke of Buckingham, denigrated him through allegations of pederastic association with Kynaston. "On the Duke of Bucks" (1678), apparently penned by John Dryden, alleged, "And Kenastons arse knows its own Buggerer."[84] Two years later, "The Litany of the Duke of Buckingham" (1680) included the following satirical prayer for relief from Buckingham:

> From transposing nature upon our *bon gars*,
> On Kynaston acting both Venus and Mars,
> From owning twenty other men's farce,
>   *Libera nos*.[85]

Buckingham is accused of taking both positions with Kynaston, an appropriation of the political rhetoric linking sovereignty and sodomy, here used against the country party.[86] The availability of accusations of sodomy and scandalous inferences about pederasty to *both* sides of the political field should not surprise us. Court and Country, Tory and Whig: both sides were constituted through appeals to a public sphere of privatized men. The political legitimacy of both would require a de-monization of residual pederasty. The accuracy of the claim is not at issue here. What is important is that the authors of these satires as-sumed that their audiences would associate a former boy actor with the politically obsolete system of pederasty. That the slur was directed against the country party, rather than the court, shows how pederasty was losing its specific meaning and being associated more generally with the political differences of "the last age" from the emerging public sphere. Unmoored from its original place in the court, sodomy became a more generalizable charge capable of floating freely across the land-scape of political representations.

Cibber on Cibber

Confronting Kynaston's suspect gender/sexual identity, Cibber re-membered Kynaston as handsome at "past sixty" as "a reigning Toast of twenty"—an expression used in every other case in the *Apology* to describe young women.[87] But Cibber deflected the sexual and gender problem of Kynaston's "formal mien" by emphasizing its centrality to a system of theatrical reference that still had the aristocratic body at its center; where others saw gender trouble, Cibber saw a technique for playing aristocratic characters. Because habitual mannerisms were in-creasingly read as an index to interiority, Cibber had to assert that the formal mien and stately step Kynaston had acquired from playing fe-male roles did not limit his ability to play the manly and majestic parts of his adult career: "But ev'n that, in Characters of Superiority had its proper Graces; it misbecame him not in the Part of *Leon*, in *Fletcher's Rule a Wife, & c.* which he executed with a determin'd Manliness, and honest Authority, well worth the best Actor's Imitation."[88] John Fletch-er's *Rule a Wife and Have a Wife* (orig. 1624) was a fitting vehicle for the adult Kynaston. This highly popular play concerned the duping of Margarita, an autonomous and wealthy woman in the market for a hus-band whom she could rule. By posing as a virgin with no will of his own—an inversion of the chaste and submissive wife of patriarchal the-ory—Leon becomes her husband. At once, he recovers his proper patri-archal authority and Margarita is forced to bend to his rule. The play presents both effeminacy and patriarchal authority as *alternative* occu-pations, by a man, of domestic space, paralleling the traditional discontinuity between boyish effeminacy and the adult male's achievement of status as the head of a household. As Leon, Kynaston could stage the transformation of his confined gait into the "determined Manliness" the end of the play required. As the "virginal" Leon developed into the dominating husband, the performance simultaneously marked Kynaston's "maturation" from boy to adult male actor.

Kynaston could enact this authority, Cibber suggested, because it was the property of "Characters of Superiority," a phrase that returns gender difference to status distinction. This authority had been the property of those *particularized*, status-bearing bodies that were being superseded in the late seventeenth and eighteenth centuries by the *collective* body of the private men making up the public sphere. As a residual performance mode that did not derive its meanings simply from gender difference, Kynaston's imitation of patriarchal authority could not guarantee him privacy—or masculinity.

If Cibber defended Kynaston from charges of effeminacy, it is because like charges were made against himself. When Thomas Davies compared Cibber and Garrick in the role of Sir John Brute in John Vanbrugh's *The Provok'd Wife*, he chose to focus, as a test of their skills, on the scene in which Sir John cross-dresses to disguise himself while, on a dare, he strikes the Constable and the Watch. Sir John had disguised himself, in the original productions of the play, as the parish parson; Cibber introduced the novelty of transvestism.[89] Because of a perceived similitude between actor and role, Cibber's cross-dressed Sir John was just not as funny as Garrick's. Cibber's performance as Sir John Brute "was justly admired," wrote Davies, but "Cibber's pale face, tame features, and weak pipe, did not present so full a contrast to female delicacy, when in women's apparel, as Garrick's stronger-marked features, manly voice, and more sturdy action."[90] As Laurence Senelick has noted, Garrick's cross-dressed Sir John depended for its comic effect on the recognizable discrepancy of the manly actor and the female clothing.[91] Where Cibber's attention to status allowed him to exploit some similitude between the sexes, Garrick made gender difference the final referent of his act.

When Cibber described his own performances in fop roles, he repeatedly asserted that he himself had no natural genius for the character type, but had imitated others as best as he could despite "the Imperfection of a feign'd, and screaming Trebble" too weak to reproduce the "clear countertenor" of the courtly mode.[92] This pointing from one actor to another established the referent of Cibber's performances as external rather than internal. When Cibber played Sparkish in William Wycherley's *The Country Wife* and Sir Courtly Nice in John Crowne's comedy of that name, he had imitated William Mountfort, who had possessed

Mr. Garrick as Sir John Brute.

David Garrick as Sir John Brute. Published in John Doran's *"Their Majesties' Servants": Annals of the English Stage from Thomas Betterton to Edmund Kean,* ed. Robert W. Lowe (London: John C. Nimmo, 1888), vol. 2, 335. From the original in the Charles Deering McCormick Library of Special Collections, Northwestern University Library.

that line: "If, some Years after the Death of *Montfort,* I my self had any Success, in either of these Characters, I must pay the Debt, I owe to his Memory, in confessing the Advantages I receiv'd from the just Idea, and strong Impression he had given me, from his acting them."[93] Cibber's foregrounding of the line of imitation allowed him to deflect the equation of his own, self-professed foppishness with a suspect subjectivity—not our "homosexuality," but an anxious, if residual pederasty.

Cibber anticipated correctly. As Straub has remarked, *The Laureat: Or, The Right Side of Colley Cibber, Esq* (London, 1740) reviewing the *Apology* "compare[d] Cibber to "Æsopus," an actor of antiquity who squeaked in a *"Eunuch's* Treble" and procured for his betters. Straub is generally correct in arguing that the slur linked Cibber to an older economy of libertinism, structured by class difference, rather than "the new emergent [construct] of the homosexual male," which she here conflates with the molly.[94] More precisely, as if anticipating this (by now familiar) alignment of the artificially high voice with a sexualized and corrupt economy of deference, Cibber insisted that his fop were imitations of theatrical convention, of a stage line formerly possessed by Mountfort. As with Mountfort, what the audience saw was a technique for entertaining his commercial audiences, and neither a vehicle of baroque power nor, the habit of a confirmed effeminate. Indeed, Cibber suggested that there was an even greater gap between his own corporeal capacities and the fops he played than was true in Mountfort's case:

> If it could be remembered how much he had the Advantage of me, in Voice and Person, I could not, here, be suspected of an affected Modesty. . . . For he sung a clear Countertenor, and had a melodious, warbling Throat, which could not but set off the last Scene of Sir *Courtly* with an uncommon Happiness; which I, alas! could only struggle thro', with the faint Excuses, and real Confidence of a fine Singer under the Imperfection of a feign'd, and screaming Trebble, which at best could only shew you what I would have done, had Nature been more favourable to me.[95]

Cibber's "feign'd Trebble" indicated that he was not an authentic effeminate, but an imitator. If not the virtuoso that Mountfort was, at least he could not be accused of being a natural. "Nature" had not given him the best of instruments, and therefore more skill in playing them was required.

Emphasizing the line of imitation, Cibber relocated stage playing as a signifier of public authority; the theater was a scene of a pederastic transmission that did not have gendered, privatized subjectivities as its origin and could not be explained in terms of subjective "desire." As Kristina Straub has argued that Cibber's "representation of himself partakes of models of difference in which sexual identity is as dependent on class as on the category of the 'third gender' of the homosexual male. . . . Resistance to the growing force of polarizing definitions of gender (male/female, 'normal'/'deviate') arises, in Cibber's case, from the implicit deployment of a sexual economy more responsive to hierarchy — especially the hierarchy of class difference — than to a system of gender that defines masculinity against femininity."[96] Cibber's strategy in his fop roles and in his autobiography was the mastery of a residual economy of display, one that he appropriated to deflect the attempt of his critics to assign him a failure of consciousness, subjectivity, and private being. Grisoni's portrait of Cibber as Lord Foppington showed him taking snuff, his hand set in a decorous posture, and his elbows held close to his body; his was an extraordinarily precise ("nice") signifying body, specifically, the would-be courtly body exposing the effort behind its imitation—a feign'd trebble, rather than sprezzatura. For this very reason, I am reluctant to describe Cibber's residual use of the erotics of hierarchy as "homoeroticism," as Straub has done, using a term that conflates status and gender, against her own stated intentions, and appears to make male-male erotic desire underwrite the contradictions of male power. Male "homoeroticism" becomes the secret rhetoric underlying the "conservative impulse" Straub has located in Cibber.[97] I have stressed, instead, the capacity of agents like Cibber and Kynaston to put competing discourses of pederasty and privacy, subjection and subjectivity, into argumentation. To describe Cibber's residual display as "self-castration" and "self-conscious nonmastery"[98]—or to equate these with "homoeroticism"—is to adopt the terms of Cibber's own critics and to reify those representational strategies whereby the aristocratic body became the fribblish and finally the sodomite's body.

PARODYING LACK: KYNASTON CAMPS

I opened this essay with an account of the discursive construction of an effeminate, sodomitical identity for Kynaston, situating Kynaston at the margins of masculinity so that his body and social space made a sort of truth claim about him. In the story with which I am now concerned, Cibber suggested that Kynaston could occupy that margin tactically, foregrounding his effeminate body space—as Cibber would foreground the stage space—as a site inscribed with competing political histories of gesture. The very attempt to read Kynaston's performances as disclosing interiority reproduced the surfaces of his body as the scene of representational struggle. I want to close this essay, then, by considering Kynaston's gestural economy (and Cibber's textual reconstruction of it) as a form of agency. Kynaston's recitation of residual gestures may be usefully read as a prototype of "camp," a gestural mode, as I have argued elsewhere, that republicizes the field of the political in which identifications are embodied and performed.[99] Any use of a gesture at once recalls the history of its uses and enables the possibility of its future uses. Despite its modern specificity, "camp" remains a useful term for that performance agency that exploits the contradictions produced by the transcodings of public gestures—from courtly to effeminate to queer, from the residual status body to the body-outside-privacy, from aristocrat to sodomite—in order to refute the naturalness, universality, and objectivity of the masculine body. If camp, today, is arguably a specifically "queer" practice, I am not so much confirming Kynaston's queerness as inquiring into those historical processes by which residually public performance modes were increasingly specified *as* queer.

Cibber expended a great deal of textual effort recording what might seem a very minor example of the difference between Kynaston's and Barton Booth's deliveries of a single speech by Morat in John Dryden's *Aureng-Zebe* (1675). Arguing that Booth took a bit too seriously the eighteenth-century imperative that men disappear within their roles, Cibber remembered how Kynaston had once played Morat:

> There are in this fierce Character so many Sentiments of avow'd Barbarity, Insolence, and Vain-Glory, that they blaze even to a ludicrous Lustre, and doubtless the Poet intended these to make the Spectators laugh, while they admir'd them. . . . For example! *Morat* having a criminal Passion for *Indamora*, promises, at her Request, for one Day, to spare the Life of her Lover *Aurenge-Zebe* [*sic*]: But not choosing to make known the real Motive of his Mercy, when *Nourmabel* says to him,
> *'Twill not be safe to let him live an Hour!*
> *Morat* silences her with this heroical *Rhodomontade*,
> *I'll do't, to shew my Arbitrary Power.*
> *Risum teneatis?* It was impossible not to laugh, and reasonably too, when this Line came out of the Mouth of *Kynaston*, with the stern, and haughty Look, that attended it.[100]

The key is Cibber's suggestion that the audience's laughter was reasonable. Kynaston's Morat called attention to his audiences' expectation that there *should be* a fit between his own allegedly ingrained effeminacy and the haughty absolutism of the character Morat. Such an equation would have been mediated at the level of characterization by the increasingly common redescription of sodomy in terms of aristocratic pride and ostentation and, at the level of the plot, by an increasingly archaic sense of effeminacy as a man's exchange of public authority for personal and erotic pleasure, as in John Dryden's *All for Love: Or, The World Well Lost* (1677), itself already anachronistic in a society that had redefined men's public interests in terms of their domestic, conjugal pleasures. Playing on these expectations, Kynaston became "present" as a player before an audience.

Along with Charlotte Charke's performances in male drag, Kynaston's pronunciation of "to show my absolute authority" may be among the first recorded instances of "camping." A theatrical eruption of the performing body from the dominant discourses that make it knowable as a subject, camp consists in a performed refusal of the social obligation to equate capacities for doing with a display of consciousness, of the coherent and unified "I" that is supposed to articulate that body space. Kynaston's "effeminacy" had once signaled aristocratic pride and narcissism, and aristocratic absolutism and male sodomy had shared the same hostile representations. "Arbitrary power" is what Whigs like Cibber feared most from monarchs, and so it is with good reason that Cibber chose this as an example of Kynaston's ability to turn his marginalization into theatrical profit. Kynaston's parodic delivery of the line signaled the history of elisions among aristocratic absolutism, spectacularity, and sodomitical excessiveness. This history had been erased as effeminacy was naturalized in the body of the sexually suspect male. "To shew my absolute authority": in throwing out this speech, Kynaston parodied his lack of phallic authority. But at the same time Kynaston indicated that authority had once been invested in performance. It had taken a great deal of representational struggle for the political nation to turn virtuosity and male display into lack (the absence of liberal subjectivity). Kynaston's vocal gesture remembered other discursive networks marginalized by the hegemonic discourse of privatized sexuality. His affectation pointed to the effeminate agent's capacity to foreground, map, and negotiate the discursive struggles that had inscribed his body.

NOTES

1. This essay expands my paper, "The Politics of Surfaces: Notes on Eighteenth-Century 'Camp,'" given at the Association for Theatre in Higher Education (ATHE), Seattle, Washington, 8 August 1991 and at Camp/Out: Symposium on Gay Theory, Performance Practice, and the Arts, Center for Interdisciplinary Research in the Arts, Northwestern University, Evanston, Illinois, 10 April 1992. I am indebted to the comments of Mary Baine Campbell, Margaret Thompson Drewal, Moe Meyer, Chris Mounsey, Susan Staves, and Randolph Trumbach.

2. Colley Cibber, *An Apology for the Life of Mr. Colley Cibber, Comedian, and Late Patentee of the Theatre-Royal. With an Historical View of the Stage during his Own Time. Written by Himself* (London: John Watts, 1740), 72. The second edition of the *Apology* duplicated this joke exactly, including the emphases, as did the fourth: 2nd ed. (London: John Watts, 1740), 100–101; 4th ed. (London: Printed for R. and J. Dodsley, 1741), 90.

3. *An Apology for the Life of Mr. Colley Cibber, Written by Himself*, 1740, ed. B. R. S. Fone (Ann Arbor: University of Michigan Press, 1968), 55.

4. Carole Pateman, *The Sexual Contract* (Stanford: Stanford University Press, 1988), 1–7, 54, and passim.

5. Jürgen Habermas, *The Structural Transformation of the Public Sphere: An Inquiry into a Category of Bourgeois Society*, trans. Thomas Burger with the assistance of Frederick Lawrence (Cambridge: MIT, 1989), 28. G. J. Barker-Benfield has argued that the re-

form of male manners in the eighteenth century followed women's demands for access to a newly heterosocial civil society: *The Culture of Sensibility: Sex and Society in Eighteenth-Century Britain*, (Chicago: University of Chicago Press, 1992), 23–24, 139–40, and passim. For Whig ideals of liberty and politeness, see Lawrence E. Klein, *Shaftesbury and the Culture of Politeness: Moral Discourse and Cultural Politics in Early Eighteenth-Century England*, (Cambridge: Cambridge University Press, 1994), esp. 124, 197–98, 210–12. Nancy Armstrong has argued that privatized subjectivity, emergent in the eighteenth-century domestic novel, was properly feminine: *Desire and Domestic Fiction: A Political History of the Novel* (New York: Oxford University Press, 1987), 4–5, 8, and passim. Emphasizing heterosexual companionship, Jean H. Hagstrum associated the late-seventeenth- and eighteenth-century ideal of "consciousness" with a range of reference including "heightened feelings, blushing sexuality, charity, subjective moral approval"; see *Sex and Sensibility: Ideal and Erotic Love from Milton to Mozart* (Chicago: University of Chicago Press, 1980), 172 n.25; see also Hagstrum's *Eros and Vision: The Restoration to Romanticism* (Evanston: Northwestern University Press, 1989), 3–27. Of particular interest is Richard Steele's suggestion, in the Preface to his comedy *The Conscious Lovers* (1722), that passions were not so easily distinguishable as the property of a specific sex: "men ought not to be laughed at for weeping till we are come to a more clear notion of what is to be imputed to the hardness of the head and the softness of the heart . . . . [It] may be a fit Entertainment for some small critics to examine whether the passion is just or the distress male or female": *Restoration and Eighteenth-Century Comedy*, ed. Scott McMillin (New York: W.W. Norton, 1973), 221. See also, Pateman, *Sexual Contract*, 12, 21, 54.

6. See my " 'As if (she) were made on purpose to put the whole world into good Humour': Reconstructing the First English Actresses," *TDR (The Drama Review)* 36 (fall 1992): 78–102.

7. Scholarly criticism of the boy actor is extensive. Especially relevant is Kathleen McLuskie's discussion of the emblematic and rhetorical quality of Renaissance acting: "The Act, the Role, and the Actor: Boy Actresses on the Elizabethan Stage," *New Theatre Quarterly* 3, 10 (May 1987): 122, 125; and Phyllis Rackin's suggestion that the boys disappeared with the "ascendancy of a literalist copy theory of language that sought to tighten the relation between word and 'thing' ": "Androgyny, Mimesis, and the Marriage of the Boy Heroine in the English Renaissance Stage," *PMLA* 102, 1 (January 1987): 32.

8. It has been argued that the boy players' apprenticeship to the adult players gendered them "feminine" by mirroring the subordinate relation of women to men in society at large: Lisa Jardine, ' "As boys and women are for the most part cattle of this colour': Female Roles and Elizabethan Eroticism," in *Still Harping on Daughters: Women and Drama in the Age of Shakespeare* (New York: Harvester Wheat Sheaf, 1983), 24; Katharine Eisaman Maus, " 'Playhouse Flesh and Blood': Sexual Ideology and the Restoration Actress," *ELH* 46, 4 (1979): 614. But the apparent traditional and juridical equation of women and boys within patriarchy does not in itself explain men's desire for either; to assume so would be to see through pederasty to an erotic structure that is always already heterosexual. Jardine, moreover, too readily defines this structure as homoerotic: "Female Roles," 31.

9. Following Stephen Greenblatt, Maus has argued that the unsuitability after the Restoration of boys in female roles was the result of the emergence of a model of incommensurableness between the sexes; see Maus, "Sexual Ideology," 597, 612; Greenblatt, "Fiction and Friction," in *Shakespearean Negotiations: The Circulation of Social Energy in Renaissance England*, The New Historicism: Studies in Cultural Poetics 4 (Berkeley: University of California Press, 1988), 66–93. But such a view suggests that Renaissance

theater allowed a similitude between *adult* men and women, ignoring the "third gender" status of male youths, that is, their effeminacy. The boys' appeal cannot be understood in terms of the similitude, or lack thereof, of (adult) men and women; at stake, instead, is the historical erasure of "effeminacy" as a distinct property of all boys and subordinated men, and the substitution of "adolescence" as the period of sexual development within an innately masculine subject.

10. Alan Bray has defined "friendship" as "that network of subtle bonds among influential patrons and their clients, suitors, and friends at court"; see "Homosexuality and the Signs of Male Friendship in Elizabethan England," in *Queering the Renaissance*, ed. Jonathan Goldberg (Durham, N.C.: Duke University Press, 1994), 42. See also Goldberg's analysis of "possibilities of identification across genders facilitated by desires that are not limited by heterosexual choice or by the regulation of gender effected by the exchange of women under patriarchy, or by the system of marriage that institutionalizes those exchanges." *Sodometries: Renaissance Texts, Modern Sexualities* (Stanford: Stanford University Press, 1992), 53.

11. For the distinction between subjection and subjectivity, see Francis Barker, *The Tremulous Private Body: Essays on Subjection* (London: Methuen, 1984), 31–32.

12. [William Oldys], Thomas Betterton, *The History of the English Stage, From the Restauration to the Present Time. Including the Lives, Characters and Amours, of the Most Eminent Actors and Actresses. With Instructions for Private Speaking; Wherein the Action and Utterance of the Bar, Stage, and Pulpit are Distinctly Considered* (London: Printed for E. Curll, 1741), 140.

13. Samuel Johnson, *A Dictionary of the English Language*, vol. 2 (London: W. Strahan, 1755; facsimile reprint, New York: AMS, 1967), s.v. "quean." *Oxford English Dictionary*, 2nd. ed., s.v. "quean"; the *OED* does not offer any examples of the use of "quean" to denote "a male homosexual of effeminate appearance" before 1935.

14. As Bellchambers's only use of emphasis in the passage, this is not an archaic italicization of a substantive: "The king coming a little before his usual time to a tragedy, found the actors not ready to begin, when his majesty, not chusing to have as much patience as his good subjects, sent to them, to know the meaning of it; upon which the master of the company came to the box, and rightly judging that the best excuse for their default, would be the true one, fairly told his majesty, that the *Queen* was not shaved yet. The king, whose good humour loved too laugh at a jest, as well as make one, accepted the excuse, which served to divert him, till the male queen could be effeminated." Colley Cibber, *An Apology for the Life of Mr. Colley Cibber, Comedian and Patentee of the Theatre Royal. Written by Himself; and Interspersed with Characters and Anecdotes of his Theatrical Contemporaries; the Whole Forming a Complete History of the Stage for the Space of Forty Years*, ed. Edmund Bellchambers, vol. 1 (London: Printed for W. Simpkin and R. Marshall, 1822), 123.

15. Allardyce Nicoll, *A History of Restoration Drama 1660–1700*, 2nd ed. (Cambridge: Cambridge University Press, 1928), 269; William Van Lennep, ed., *The London Stage, 1660–1800: A Calendar of Plays, Entertainments & Afterpieces, Together with Casts, Box-Receipts and Contemporary Comment, Compiled from the Playbills, Newspapers and Theatrical Diaries of the Period*, intro. Emmett L. Avery and Arthur H. Scouten, vol. 1 (Carbondale: Southern Illinois University Press, 1965), 5.

16. Nicoll, *A History*, 8.

17. Philip H. Highfill, Jr., Kalman A. Burnim, and Edward A. Langhans, *A Biographical Dictionary of Actors, Actresses, Musicians, Dancers, Managers, and Other Stage Personnel in London, 1660–1800* (Carbondale: Southern Illinois University Press, 1973), 9:76.

18. Alfred Simeon Golding, *Classicistic Acting: Two Centuries of a Performance Tradition at the Amsterdam Schouwburg. To which is Appended An Annotated Translation of the "Lessons*

on the Principles of Gesticulation and Mimic Expression" of *Johannes Jelgerhuis, Rz* (Lanham, Md.: University Press of America, 1984), 73.

19. [Charles Gildon], *The Life of Mr. Thomas Betterton, the Late Eminent Tragedian . . . With the Judgement of . . . Monsieur de St. Evremond, upon the Italian and French Music and Opera's; in a Letter to the Duke of Buckingham* (London: R. Gosling, 1710), 35–36.

20. Bertram Leon Joseph, *The Tragic Actor* (London: Routledge and Kegan Paul, 1959), 7.

21. Andrew Gurr, *Playgoing in Shakespeare's London* (New York: Cambridge University Press, 1987), 68–69.

22. [Gildon], *Life of Mr. Thomas Betterton*, 45–46.

23. For the significance of the elbow in the courtly pose of standing akimbo, see Joaneth Spicer, "The Renaissance Elbow," in *A Cultural History of Gesture*, eds. Jam Bremmer and Herman Roodenburg (Ithaca, N.Y.: Cornell University Press, 1991), 84–128; and my "Performing 'Akimbo': Queer Pride and Epistemological Prejudice," in *The Politics and Poetics of Camp*, ed. Moe Meyer (London: Routledge, 1994), 23–50.

24. Gilbert Austin, *Chironomia: Or, A Treatise on Rhetorical Delivery. Comprehending Many Precepts, Both Ancient and Modern, for the Proper Regulation of the Voice, the Countenance, and Gesture. . .*, eds. Mary Margaret Robb and Lester Thonssen. (Carbondale: Southern Illinois University Press, 1966), 453.

25. Johannes Jelgerhuis, *Lessons on the Theory of Gesticulation and Mimic Expression*, 1827, trans. Alfred Simeon Golding, in Golding, *Classicistic Acting*, 307.

26. See also Golding, *Classicistic Acting*, 94–99.

27. The eighteenth-century literary and theatrical figure of the "fribble" was an effeminate man who visited women, typically enjoying "feminine" occupations or ornaments more than women themselves did, but who avoided sexually or legally consummating his relations with them. Because of the common eighteenth-century association of hetero-eroticism, consciousness, and sociality per se, the fribble was described as unable to act on his feelings or even incapable of social feeling itself. In 1712, Richard Steele wrote in *The Spectator* that the fribble was "Impoten[t] of Mind," so that "those who are guilty of it [are] incapable of pursuing what they themselves approve": *The Spectator*, 288 (30 January 1712); reprinted in *The Spectator*, ed. Donald F. Bond (Oxford: Clarendon, 1965) , 3: 24. Garrick's verse satire "The Fribbleriad" (1761) described them as lacking power, unable to realize pleasure, "for ever wishing, ne'er enjoying": *The Poetical Works of David Garrick, Esq.*, vol. 1 (London: George Kearsley, 1785), 23. In *Miss in her Teens*, Garrick's Fribble tells Biddy—in verse—that in marrying him she will have "Love's better Part, / His downy Wing, but not his Dart": *Miss in her Teens: Or, The Medley of Lovers. A Farce in Two Acts* (London: J. and R. Tonson and S. Draper, 1747); facsimile reprint, *The Plays of David Garrick*, ed. and intro. Gerald M. Berkowitz, vol. 1 (New York and London: Garland, 1981), 23. Garrick's Daffodil is found to have "neither power nor spirit to enjoy" women: *The Male-Coquette*, in *The Dramatic Works of David Garrick, Esq.*, vol. 2 (London: A. Millar, 1798), 32. The word "fribble" itself connoted lack or incapacitation; a fribble was "a trifling, frivolous person, one not occupied in serious employment," and to fribble was to falter verbally (to stammer) or physically (to totter): *Oxford English Dictionary*, 2nd ed., s.v. "fribble." The idea developed, surely, from the description of the melancholic, aristocratic body as debilitated; its parts, as Robert Burton wrote, "cannot perform their functions, having the spirits drawn from them by vehement passion, but fail in sense and motion.": *The Anatomy of Melancholy. What it is, With all the kinds causes, symptoms, prognosticks, & severall cures of it*, 7th ed. (London: H. Cripps, 1660), 93. See also Laurence Senelick, "Mollies or Men of Mode? Sodomy and the Eighteenth-Century London Stage," *Journal of the History of Sexuality* 1 (July 1990): 33–67, esp. 52–55; and see my "Performing 'Akimbo.' "

28. Cibber, *Apology*, ed. Fone, 66. Unless otherwise noted all subsequent quotations from Cibber's *Apology* will be from this edition.

29. William Hogarth, *The Analysis of Beauty: Written with a View of Fixing the Fluctuating Ideas of Taste* (London: J. Reeves, 1753); facsimile reprint, ed. Richard Woodfield, (Aldershot: Scolar Press, 1971), 85.

30. John Bulwer, *Chirologia: Or, the Naturall Language of the Hand. Composed of the Speaking Motions, and Discoursing Gestures Thereof. Whereunto is Added Chironomia: Or, the Art of Manuall Rhetoricke. Consisting of the Naturall Expressions, Digested by Art in the Hand, as the Chiefest Instrument of Eloquence* . . . (London: Printed for Tho. Harper, 1644), reprinted in *Chirologia: Or, The Natural Language of the Hand; and Chironomia: Or, The Art of Manual Rhetoric*, ed. James W. Cleary (Carbondale: Southern Illinois University Press, 1974), 88. Cf. Henry Siddons: "To shake the given hand is an expression usual in friendship, benevolence, and salutation. This gesture is rich in signification, for the hand is the tongue of hearty good will. . . . the hand is the general instrument of the mind." *Practical Illustrations of Rhetorical Gesture and Action; Adapted to the English Drama: From a Work on the Subject by M. Engel* . . . (1818), 2nd ed. (London: Printed for Sherwood, Neely, and Jones, 1822; reprint, New York: Benjamin Blom, 1968), 163–64.

31. Bulwer, *Chirologia*, 229.

32. "The face of the court was much chang'd in the change of the King, for King Charles was temperate and chast and serious; so that the fooles and bawds, mimics and Catamites of the former Court grew out of fashion, and the nobility and courtiers, who did not quite abandon their debosheries, had yet that reverence to the King to retire into corners to practise them." Lucy Hutchinson, *Memoirs of the Life of Colonel Hutchinson, Governor of Nottingham, By His Widow Lucy*, ed. Julius Hutchinson, rev. ed., ed. C. H. Firth (London: George Routledge & Sons; New York: E.P. Dutton, 1906), 46.

33. Bulwer, *Chirologia*, 229.

34. As has been amply documented by Alan Bray and others, sodomy at this time was associated with the full range of sexual acts that are not procreative and was only gradually being specified as male-male anal penetration. For a summary of Bray's position, see "Homosexuality and the Signs of Male Friendship," 40–42; the argument is developed at length in Bray's indispensable *Homosexuality in Renaissance England* (London: Gay Men's Press, 1982).

After indicating the effeminacy of the gesture "putting forth of the middle finger," Bulwer discussed its use "to *brand* and *upbraid* men with *sloth, effeminacy, and notorious vices*." Bulwer analyzed the gesture as a derogatory sign for a fornicator but then assigned it, more specifically, to the pederast, to "the notorious *effeminacy* and luxurious *impudency* of that sottish emperor Heliogabulus," and to the "corrupted manners" at the court of Caligula, who used his statesmen as bawds procuring for him "Priapus or Venus." Bulwer, *Chirologia*, 132–33, 203. Likewise, Bulwer analyzed the gesture of discoursing with the hand turned up, which was "incident to nice and effeminate men," in the context of "the sins of voluptuousness, and a lascivious habit of the mind" (222). See also my discussions of the gestures of scratching the head with one finger and wagging the hand, below.

35. Bulwer, *Chirologia*, 131–32; translation is by the editor James W. Cleary. "Weak men" translates "molles."

36. Ibid., 5, 16.

37. Bulwer's manuals claimed to document "the natural language of the hand": "The intendments of which demonstrative gestures (being natural signs) have no dependence on any ordinance or statute of art which may be broken off or taken in hand, as it is either repealed or stands in force. But these, being part of the unalterable laws and institutes of nature, are by their own perpetual constitution and by a native consequence significant" (16).

38. Bulwer, *Chirologia*, 63.

39. Ibid.

40. Ibid., 38.

41. Ibid., 203.

42. See my "Gender and Modernity: Male Looks and the Performance of Public Pleasures," in *Monstrous Dreams of Reason: Writing the Body, Self, and Other in the Enlightenment*, eds. Mita Choudhury and Laura J. Rosenthal (Lewisburg, Pa.: Bucknell University Press, 1999).

43. Bulwer, *Chirologia*, 62–63.

44. Ibid., 63 (my italics).

45. Hogarth, *The Analysis of Beauty*, 140.

46. Ibid., 141.

47. *The Phoenix of Sodom: Or, The Vere Street Coterie. Being an Exhibition of the Gambols Practised by the Ancient Lechers of Sodom and Gomorrah, Embellished and Improved with the Modern Refinements in Sodomitical Practices, by the Members of the Vere Street Coterie, of Detestable Memory* (London: J. Cook, 1813); facsimile reprint in Randolph Trumbach, ed., *Sodomy Trials: Seven Documents*, Marriage, Sex, and the Family in England 1660–1800 (New York: Garland, 1986), 13.

48. John Caspar Lavater, *Essays in Physiognomy, Designed to Promote the Knowledge and the Love of Mankind*, trans. Henry Hunter, illus. Thomas Holloway, 3 vols. (London: Printed for John Murray, H. Hunter, and T. Holloway, 1789), 2: 17.

49. Cibber, *An Apology*, 72.

50. See Jonas Barish, *The Anti-Theatrical Prejudice* (Berkeley: University of California Press, 1981); and Laura Levine, "Men in Women's Clothing: Anti-theatricality and Effeminization from 1579 to 1642," *Criticism* 28, 1 (1986): 121–43.

51. [Gildon], *Life of Mr. Thomas Betterton*, 92–94.

52. Ibid., 94; Golding, *Classicistic Acting*, 126.

53. Anthony Aston, *A Brief Supplement to Colley Cibber, Esq.; His Lives of the Late Famous Actors and Actresses*, 1748, reprinted in Cibber, *An Apology for the Life of Mr. Colley Cibber Written by Himself*, ed. Robert W. Lowe, vol. 2 (London: J. C. Nimmo, 1889), 300.

54. Golding, *Classicistic Acting*, 128.

55. Thomas Davies, *Dramatic Miscellanies*, vol. 3 (London: Printed for the author, 1784), 336–37.

56. Cibber, *An Apology*, ed. Bellchambers, 2: 340.

57. Quoted in Joseph, *Tragic Actor*, 30.

58. "Philautus," *The Pretty Gentleman; Or, Softness of Manners Vindicated From the false Ridicule exhibited under the Character of William Fribble, Esq.* (London, 1747); reprinted in *Bibliotecha Curiosa*, ed. Edmund Goldsmid (Edinburgh: Privately printed, 1885), 23–24; see also 16, 17.

59. See Kristina Straub, *Sexual Suspects: Eighteenth-Century Players and Sexual Ideology* (Princeton: Princeton University Press, 1992), 68.

60. Ibid., 52–53.

61. "Philautus," *The Pretty Gentleman*, 26.

62. Garrick, *Miss in her Teens*, vol. 1, 20.

63. John Vanbrugh, *The Relapse; or, Virtue in Danger*, 1696, in *British Dramatists from Dryden to Sheridan*, eds. George H. Nettleton and Arthur E. Case; rev. ed., ed. George Winchester Stone, Jr. (Carbondale: Southern Illinois University Press, 1969), 1.3.15–20, 266.

64. "Philautus," *The Pretty Gentleman*, 20.

65. John Harold Wilson, "Rant, Cant, and Tone on the Restoration Stage," *Studies in Philology* 52 (1955): 593–94; Alan S. Downer, "Nature to Advantage Dressed: Eighteenth Century Acting," *PMLA* 58 (1943): 1024.

66. Terry Castle, *Masquerade and Civilization: The Carnivalesque in Eighteenth-Century English Culture and Fiction* (Stanford: Stanford University Press, 1986), 36.

67. Thomas Shadwell, *The Virtuoso*, 1676, eds. Marjorie Hope Nicolson and David Stuart Rodes, Regents Restoration Drama Series (Lincoln: University of Nebraska Press, 1966), 5.4.148–51, 127.

68. *Samuel Butler (1612–1680): Characters*, ed. Charles W. Daves (Cleveland, Ohio: Press of Case Western Reserve University, 1970), 50, 200; see also Joseph, *Tragic Actor*, 29.

69. Aphra Behn, *Sir Patient Fancy*, in *The Meridian Anthology of Restoration and Eighteenth-Century Plays by Women*, ed. Katharine M. Rogers (New York: Meridian-Penguin, 1994), 2.1, 41.

70. [Gildon], *Life of Mr. Thomas Betterton*, 104, 106.

71. *The Spectator* 147 (18 August 1711); reprinted in *The Spectator*, ed. Bond, 2:80.

72. Ibid.

73. [Oldys], Betterton, *The History of the English Stage*, 46.

74. Cibber, *An Apology*, 66.

75. Austin, *Chironomia*, 378.

76. Thomas Hobbes, *Leviathan*, 1651, ed. C. B. Macpherson (Middlesex: Penguin, 1971), 129.

77. Anthony Ashley Cooper, third earl of Shaftesbury, *Sensus Communis: An Essay on the Freedom of Wit and Humour* (1709), reprinted in Shaftesbury, *Characteristicks of Men, Manners, Opinions, Times* (1711), 4th ed., vol. 1 ([London], 1727), 71–72.

78. *The Canting Academy: Or, The Devils Cabinet Opened: Wherein is Shewn The Mysterious and Villainous Practices of that Wicked Crew, Commonly Known by the Names of Hectors, Trepanners, Gilts, &c. To which is Added A Compleat Canting-Dictionary, Both of Old Words, and Such as are Now Most in Use . . .* (London: Printed for Mat. Drew, 1673), 2.

79. *Canting Academy*, 43. *Oxford English Dictionary*, 2nd ed., s.v. "queer."

80. J. C. Flügel, *The Psychology of Clothes* (London: Hogarth, 1930), 117–19; Anne Hollander, *Sex and Suits* (New York: Alfred A. Knopf, 1994), 7–8, 64–65, 74–76; Elizabeth Wilson, *Adorned in Dreams: Fashion and Modernity* (Berkeley and Los Angeles: University of California Press, 1987), 22, 117.

81. Garrick, "The Fribbleriad," 1: 29, 31.

82. John Dennis, "Essay on the Opera's," in *The Critical Works of John Dennis*, ed. Edward Niles Hooker, vol. 1 (Baltimore: Johns Hopkins, 1939), 391; see also his "Essay upon Publick Spirit," in *The Critical Works*, vol. 2, 394.

83. Leigh Woods, *Garrick Claims the Stage: Acting as Social Emblem in Eighteenth-Century England*, Contributions in Drama and Theatre Studies 10 (Westport, Conn.: Greenwood, 1984), 12.

84. Quoted in Highfill, Burnim, and Langhans, *A Biographical Dictionary*, 9: 83. Elias F. Mengel, Jr., gives a slightly different version of the line: "And Keniston's A- knows the B-r"; *Poems on Affairs of State: Augustan Satirical Verse, 1660–1714* (New Haven: Yale University Press, 1965), 194, n.20.

85. Quoted in Mengel, *Poems on Affairs of State*, 194.

86. He is also criticized for "owning" the farce *The Rehearsal*, which he coauthored with several other men. This suggests why Dryden should be bitter toward Buckingham: one of the main aims of *The Rehearsal* was to parody Dryden in the character of Bayes.

87. Cibber, *An Apology*, 71, 72.

88. Ibid., 72.

89. Thomas Davies, *Dramatic Miscellanies*, 3: 455.

90. Ibid., 3: 429.

91. Senelick, "Mollies or Men of Mode?," 51.

92. Cibber, *An Apology*, 76.

93. Ibid.

94. Quoted in Straub, *Sexual Suspects*, 54.

95. Cibber, *An Apology*, 76.

96. Straub, *Sexual Suspects*, 50.

97. Ibid., 52–53, 50.

98. Ibid., 42–43.

99. See my "Performing 'Akimbo.' " For other analyses of camp, see the collection, edited by Moe Meyer, in which that essay appeared: *The Politics and Poetics of Camp* (London: Routledge, 1994).

100. Cibber, *An Apology*, 72–73.

Cross-Dressing and the Nature of Gender in Mary Robinson's *Walsingham*

Julie Shaffer

By MOST ACCOUNTS, THE TRADITION OF WOMEN DRESSING AS MEN OR presenting themselves as masculine, which had remained strong at least through the mid-eighteenth century in England, waned by the end of the century both in the arts and in reality.[1] While women might earlier be praised for choosing to cross-dress, by the end of the eighteenth century, female cross-dressing became more problematic and it was suggested that women dressing as men had been forced by others or circumstance into doing so. Women warriors lauded in ballads and fiction over the course of the century who successfully passed as men to follow lovers and fight for their country likewise diminished at this point into weak characters unconvincing as males and incapable of carrying out duties as soldiers and sailors.[2] Women in male military uniform ceased to appear in polite theater, instead being presented in burlesque and at the less highbrow pleasure gardens. Depictions of women in such garb fell from favor in portraiture as well, and stage roles for women in breeches parts likewise lapsed in popularity.[3] Men and women argued earlier in the century that women might have masculine minds and display martial courage; few, however, were willing to entertain such notions by the last two decades of the eighteenth century.[4] Even Wollstonecraft's call for women to adopt formerly masculine strengths gets downplayed by Godwin's insistence on her feminine complementarity to his masculine reason.

Dror Wahrman claims this shift arose out of what he calls the "gender panic" of the last two decades of the eighteenth century, a widely held cultural anxiety about gendered identity that caused a movement away from the "relative playfulness of former perceptions of gender" to an intolerance of the view that "gender boundaries could ultimately prove porous and inadequate; and therefore that individuals or actions were not necessarily always defined or fixed by those boundaries." By the 1780s, Wahrman asserts, "gendered behaviour was . . . made inescapably and naturally to conform to sexual bodies."[5] Thomas Laqueur argues that some time from the late seventeenth through the eighteenth century, there was a change in beliefs about the biological make-up and relation of the sexes; as a result, by the end of the eighteenth century, the sexes were considered different and incommensurable. As long as this was the case with the biology of the sexes, it would be the case for gendered behavior.[6]

As Carolyn Williams notes in "Women Behaving Well," women presenting themselves as masculine in strength of character, body, or intellect could be cast as monstrous rather than heroic earlier as well, but, as Wahrman demonstrates, such a linkage became nearly universal in the last two decades of the eighteenth century.[7] In all but the most daring works, the woman who wears male clothing and appropriates masculine behaviors and attitudes at the end of the eighteenth century and into the nineteenth fares as ill as do warrior women. Most are mocked or punished, as is the case with Miss Sparkes in Hannah More's *Coelebs in Search of a Wife* (1808) and Harriot Freke in Maria Edgeworth's *Belinda* (1801/1810).[8] Such characters' diminishment and punishment offer lessons on the unacceptability, even criminality, of severing gender roles and rights from clearly sexed bodies.

Given this situation, one need not be surprised by Chris Cullens's suggestion that Mary Robinson's *Walsingham; or, the Pupil of Nature* is perhaps unique in portraying "a male protagonist who, at the end of four volumes, is revealed to narrator and readers to be a female transvestite."[9] Cullens states that she knows of "no other eighteenth-century novel" that does so;[10] according to Dianne Dugaw and Wahrman's arguments, while such a novel might occur earlier, it should be virtually unthinkable in the last two decades of the eighteenth century. It is in fact not the only novel of the period that includes female characters who cross-dress or otherwise transgress gender roles, as Edgeworth and More's novels demonstrate. Such characters continue appearing even long after the supposed demise of the cross-dressed female, for instance with Princess Evadne in Mary Shelley's *The Last Man* (1826). It is perhaps alone, however, in sustaining its heroine's cross-dressing as long as it does.[11]

Robinson's novel, published as it was at the end of the eighteenth century, might be expected at least to contain its cross-dressing female protagonist, Sidney Aubrey, leaving her unconvincing as a male or punishing her for her transgressions, as is the case not only for the masculine Miss Sparkes and Harriot Freke, but also for the later Princess Evadne, who dies in battle as a (fe)male warrior. Sidney, however, remains convincing until her mother makes her secret public; nothing in Sidney's own deportment gives it away. Furthermore, Sidney is not particularly harshly punished by novel's end. She suffers illness and must ultimately resume her female-gendered social role, but this punishment is slight when compared to her triumph at cross-dressing and her rewards, a sizable fortune and marriage to the man she has long loved. Robinson's light treatment of this gender transgressor shows that she tolerates what Dugaw and Wahrman demonstrate was widely culturally intolerable by this point: the notion that gendered attributes, behavior, and rights need *not* be tied to sex.

Through Robinson's depiction of a female character who passes easily and for an extended time as a man, *Walsingham* addresses the nature of gender recognition and gendered identity in the late eighteenth century. Sidney's story, like others in which female characters seize male prerogative, demands that readers question late eighteenth-century economic and social limitations on women. But this novel is as much about masculinity as it is about femininity and women's rights, raising questions about the adoptability and changing definitions of masculinity, itself as constructed and shifting in this period as was femininity. Through Sidney's relationships and attractiveness to men and women who may or may not know her biological sex, the novel likewise addresses issues of intimacy and sexuality, querying limits of same-sex intimacy and the reliably natural basis of heterosexuality.

At times, *Walsingham* foresees late twentieth-century debates on sexuality and gendered identity, but the significance of Sidney's cross-dressing can best be understood by placing it in the context of late-eighteenth-century debates on sex and gender out of which it arose. At times, for instance, in questioning the constructedness of gender, the novel enters into debates on which sex may claim which (gender) attributes and privileges, a debate that at times, as Claudia Johnson argues, still insists on a binary in which one sex adopts or is defined by having qualities that complement the other's lacks.[12] In what follows, then, I will ground discussion of *Walsingham*'s gender- and sex-querying elements in debates from the period about the fixity or fluidity of gender, the linkage of gender to biological sex; and the implication of these issues for defining the limits to which interpersonal relationships between the sexes and between members of the same sex might be taken. *Walsingham* does not simply represent these debates but rather enters into them actively. Its contribution to these debates requires that we go beyond the insightful discussions provided by critics such as Wahrman and Johnson to look at the way daring writers in the era refused to be mentally cowed by mainstream responses to the era's gender panic, insisting on a fluidity and a collapse of a binary that others clearly found threatening.[13]

CROSS-DRESSING WOMEN

As Rudolf Dekker and Lotte C. van de Pol explain, many women passed as men in the eighteenth century, sometimes for extended periods of time, the trend ceasing only at that century's end. Some women cross-dressed to move about without the molestation that might come to them as women. This would be the case, for example, for laboring class women who needed to travel to find work. After reaching a place where work was available, they may have returned to wearing female clothes, or they may have continued to dress as men. Those continuing to cross-dress, along with other lower-class women who dressed as men, may have done so either to get jobs that paid men better than they paid women or to pursue activities that would not otherwise have been open to them, such as military careers.

Maria van Antwerpen, for instance, defends herself along these lines in her trial in the Netherlands in 1769 for passing as a man. She started doing so when she lost her job as a servant away from family and, she argued, "at that point in her life, what other ways were open for a destitute girl? She did not want to be a prostitute, so becoming a man was the only way to stay a pure and chaste virgin. . . . The second time she became a soldier, she did so to escape poverty."[14] Cross-dressing would likewise grant women more security from molestation in pursuing activities "on the margins of society, [such as] begging, stealing and cheating," as was the case in the early seventeenth century for Mary Frith, a.k.a. Moll Cutpurse; cross-dressing likewise allowed Mary Read to flourish as a pirate.[15]

Other women cross-dressed to become so-called female husbands, to pursue relationships with other women, as was the case with Mary Hamilton, Catherine Vizzani, Queen Christina of Sweden, and, to some extent, Charlotte Charke. Some cross-dressing women combined these reasons for their transvestism. Maria van Antwerpen, for instance, took her second stint as a cross-dressed soldier because the woman she married was pregnant and van Antwerpen "had to earn money to maintain her family."[16] Hannah Snell likewise cross-dressed to fight in wartime, and later, remaining in male garb, married a woman.[17]

Women in England and in northern continental Europe might pass as men due to a tendency in this period *not* to question the link between surface presentation and identity. They could do so in part because males were taken into the military at the age of thirteen[18] and otherwise entered the world of work as young as fourteen. Women could pass convincingly as such young men and could perform work on ship as well as these youths could.[19] Sailors' loose dress through the eighteenth century aided in women's ability to pass as males. Other elements might counteract this aid: the inability to produce male genitals when undressed or to join in "public love-making" as men, for instance. Close ranks on board ship or in military quarters led to the early discovery of some female cross-dressers for precisely these reasons, but others were discovered to be female only after death, on battlefields. Many, in military and other careers, passed for astonishingly long periods—most for up to six months and some for decades.[20]

Their ability to do so demonstrates that the English, along with the continental Europeans Dekker and van de Pol research, accepted self-representation in this period in which "people believed that one's garments unquestionably told one's sex."[21] That eighteenth-century European cultures might have held this belief more than others is demonstrated by a story involving a Frenchwoman who worked as a sailor and passed for male even in the close quarters of the explorer Bougainville until the crew arrived in Tahiti, where "she was immediately indicated as a woman by the natives [who] made no automatic assumptions related to trousers and other outward accoutrements of a European male person."[22] In Europe, not only clothes but behavior might likewise tell one's sex, and as long as a woman acted socially like a man, performing men's work well, she might be taken as a man.

Attitudes toward cross-dressing women were mixed. Emma Donoghue notes that cross-dressing in itself was not criminal in England,[23] and women caught dressing as males might or might not be punished for crimes related to their cross-dressing. Some female cross-dressers were simply required to reassume female dress and identity. On the other hand, women's passing as men was more severely punished where the women in question were suspected of having sexual relations with other women. This was most typically the case when two unrelated women lived together, with one dressing and representing herself as a man.[24] Legally, the situation was complicated because in England, unlike in America and on the continent, there were "no laws against sex between women" per se.[25] There were, however, laws against sodomy. This included penetration of a woman by another woman, which could occur if one woman had an enlarged clitoris that mimicked a penis or if the couple used a dildo.[26] Women were rarely tried for this capital offense, however. They may have escaped trials for sodomy, Donoghue surmises, because judges did not want to acknowledge that a woman could be sexually satisfied without the penis,[27] or, as Dekker and van de Pol propose, because they did not want to sentence women to death.[28] Instead, then, female cross-dressers suspected of engaging in sexual relations with other women were generally tried instead for "lewdness and fraud," the latter being the case especially when it was assumed that the female husband married a woman to get her fortune.[29]

The case of Mary Hamilton, brought to court in 1746, proves an interesting example of the difficulty the English courts had in identifying precisely what crimes might be claimed to have been committed by female cross-dressers suspected of having sexual relations with other women. Hamilton, the subject of Henry Fielding's play of that same year, *The Female Husband*, cross-dressed and married her landlady's niece (her third wife), who exposed Hamilton after two or three months of marriage.[30] Hamilton was "brought to court for a sexual offence" but was not tried for anything relating to "her gender or sexuality," suggesting that the courts found it "hard to find any legal offence that she had committed" in terms of the transgression of which she was accused.[31] She was tried and convicted, then, only for vagrancy. Despite this seemingly innocuous crime, however, she was whipped in several towns and then imprisoned, and in 1777, another such woman was exposed in the pillory and imprisoned.[32] These cases show that where cross-dressing was linked to the sexual transgression of lesbianism, it might raise "extreme societal anger,"[33] even if this anger did not lead to the death which American or continental lesbians or British male homosexuals suffered if discovered.[34]

Legal decisions do not completely reveal lay responses to possibilities that women's cross-dressing engendered. The popularity of ballads on cross-dressing women who became sailors suggests positive reception. As Dugaw makes clear throughout *Warrior Women and Popular Balladry*, females lauded in these ballads are praised for their bravery and faithfulness in love. Their positive reception did not depend on the subjects of these ballads being fictional and so nonthreatening to a system relying on male rather than female prowess; some of these songs were about real women, or were believed by contemporaries to be so. The sheer numbers of such ballads and the brave, cross-dressed women they celebrate suggest that many of their consumers did not need to see such women as exceptions to the rule, although some may have found such women worth celebrating because they saw them as comfortingly unique, as Williams suggests in "Women Behaving Well."

Tolerance is likewise demonstrated in some cases involving female-female marriages, some of which were allowed to go forward despite suspicions that the groom was a cross-dressed female. In 1737, a clergyman married John Smith to Elizabeth Huthall but his notes demonstrate his belief that both were women: "By ye opinion after matrimony my Clark judg'd they were both women, if ye person by name John Smith be a man, he's a little short fair thin man not above 5 foot. After marriage I almost co[ul]d prove [the]m both women, the one was dress'd as a man thin pale face & wrinkled chin." Despite these doubts, "the officials went ahead with the ceremony and seem to have made no attempt to have the couple punished." In another case, the groom was discovered after the ceremony to be a woman, but there is no record that efforts were made to annul the match. Newspaper items about other married female couples are "appreciative, almost approving," as in the case of a couple in which one woman was reported as having cross-dressed and wed a woman "with whom she has lived agreeably ever since,"[35] stressing the harmonious quality of the marriage rather than the illegal nature of their union. In these cases, perhaps the women were not suspected of engaging in sexual relations. Otherwise, they suggest an occasional tolerance even of suspected lesbian sex, demonstrating further the complex and inconsistent reception of sex and gender transgressing women.

Other cross-dressers were likewise tolerated. Women who cross-dressed and joined the military to fight for their country might be seen as attempting to transcend female weakness and were especially lauded for doing so in periods in which the sexes were not yet seen as incommensurable but as similar and on a hierarchical continuum, with men above women.[36] In this earlier paradigm—one widely held through the seventeenth century and into the eighteenth—women were understood to be simply undeveloped men, their genitals inverted from the male norm; women were thought to lack adequate heat for their genitals to descend so that they might become fully developed (mature) men. A woman presenting herself as a man because she wanted to be a man— even becoming a man, as was believed to have occurred in some instances[37]—was allowable because "a woman who became a man strove to become something better, higher, than she had been, and that was considered an understandable and commendable effort in itself."[38]

Even in periods in which women might be seen as trying to improve themselves by becoming male in appearance and attitude, however— well into the eighteenth century—their passing as male could equally be interpreted as damnable self-assertion instead of as a praiseworthy attempt at self-betterment. It could be read as cosmological and social insubordination and as women's refusal to contain their unruly bodies and the sexual desires considered to be innate them until late in the eighteenth century.[39] Such women did not comprise category crisis, since, existing biologically on a continuum with men, women did not cross categories in attempting to be (like) men. Such a woman, her motivations and effects nonetheless became metaphoric for category crisis, signalling and used to argue that allowing women to behave so was sign of and might lead to the overthrow of civilized people—male Britons—by ostensibly savage races and nations.[40]

While the cross-dressing woman who successfully passed as a man for any length of time might not actually constitute category crisis, her misrepresentation of self and the possibility that one might misrecognize others suggested the fragility and constructedness of identity and gender. This was especially the case when sex was held to be changeable, as it was, according to Laqueur, through most of the seventeenth century and into the eighteenth: not only could a woman become a man, but one could be born a hermaphrodite and settle into one sex or the other.[41] In such a system, that gender—femininity, at least—could be constructed was in any event clear to the extent that before 1660, when women were allowed to become actresses in England, men were considered capable of representing women accurately and recognizably on stage via a finite number of traits and gestures that show the easy assumability of culturally recognized versions of "woman."[42]

But convincing disguise is most threatening to systems based in stable identities and in which gender—attributes, roles, and social status—is tied to stable, unchangeable biological sex. In such systems, the successfully passing cross-dressed woman becomes most threatening because she foregrounds the idea that the patriarchal version of femininity—indeed any version of female identity—is a mask from which a woman might absent herself and from which that self might not in fact be identical, just as men assuming the role of women on the stage were not identical with those roles. That identity might not be delimited by sex and that gender could be constructed must prove highly troubling to any culture in which gender is tied to biologically differently sexed bodies. As Lesley Ferris notes, it "generated immense social, philosophical and existential concern in late Elizabethan and Jacobean society,"[43] when the sexes were still seen as based on one model but hierarchically ordered.

Those concerns are demonstrated by James I's 1620 edict reiterating the ban on women's dressing as men given in Deuteronomy 22:5, the first legal dictum against cross-dressing in a land in which sumptuary laws against crossing class lines had long been in place.[44] The concerns are further born out by the *Hic-Mulier, Haec-Vir* pamphlet war of 1620.[45] In the first, a woman is attacked for cross-dressing; in the second, a cross-dressed man and cross-dressed woman ultimately decide that the world would be best off if they returned to gender appropriate clothes and behavior. Given the reconception of the sexes that obtained by the end of the eighteenth century, cross-dressing would have been the more threatening then than during the Renaissance, when, as Ferris makes clear, it was clearly threatening enough.

If versions of female behavior and identity are masks that women themselves can assume or put off at will, a woman's masquerade of *any* sort must be particularly horrific, continually representing her terrible lack, not only of the phallus, the focus of Freudian-based theory, but of identity itself. Her role-play suggests that woman's identity may always be a fraud. Such a view of women underlines a belief that women are by their very lack of identity untrustworthy, which can be used to justify continued social control of them. Such views may have formed some of the basis of discourse against women's acting on stage and on their attending masquerades, although the usual reasons given against these are the sexually suspect nature of the theater and the masquerade.[46] Even when actresses played women and women attended masquerades dressed as females, their impersonation suggested that female roles could be assumed, as Joan Rivière notes much later in her well-known 1929 case study, on which Luce Irigaray also draws.[47] The assumability of all female roles could be used by women to their own advantage, as is demonstrated by Eliza Haywood's *Fantomina; or, Love in a Maze* (1724); here, a woman keeps her male lover's interest by playing different women.[48] For those concerned with stability of identity or wanting to see women as passive, subordinate, and tractable in all ways— keystones of femininity at the end of the eighteenth century—such a notion would have been hateful. However, within the temporary nature of the masquerade and the play, at least the foregrounding of women's own potentially assumed and discardable identity as females was contained. The woman who cross-dressed in real life was more threatening because she refused to contain the threat she represented.

Given that the last two decades of the eighteenth century witnessed a hardened intolerance of gender-play and fluidity, as Dugaw and Wahrman so convincingly argue it is little wonder that the masculine woman becomes by and large unthinkable and that heroism for women becomes increasingly feminized, so that any woman capable of being celebrated cannot be masculine, cannot pass for a male: the woman warrior worth lauding then can be no warrior at all, as Dugaw and Wahrman make clear. In this period in which females ceased being assumed to be sexually appetitive, the woman passing as a man or claiming male strengths and rights was frequently seen not only as improperly claiming male social, economic, and legal prerogative but as claiming male *sexual* prerogative as well. In so doing, she sinned against the entire gender system, which was increasingly based in sexed, heterosexual, and differently sexually appetitive bodies.[49] As such, it is the more startling to find not only that Sidney Aubrey passes successfully as a male but that this character is not horrifically punished for such an ostensibly unimaginable and impossible act. Through showing that the unimaginable was still imaginable in fiction at least, *Walsingham* challenges wide-reaching late-eighteenth-century intolerance of play with the nature of gender, bodies, intimacy, and sexuality.

WALSINGHAM: SIDNEY AS USURPING AND SEDUCTIVE MALE

The novel *Walsingham* concerns the relationship between Walsingham Ainsforth and his cross-dressing cousin, Sidney Aubrey. It is not well known, and as such, discussion of the implications of its use of a cross-dressing female protagonist will follow summary of Sidney's grounds for transgression and its effects. To be consistent with Sidney's social persona, I use the pronoun "he" to refer to Sidney for as long as this character passes as a man, switching to "she" when Sidney becomes known as female.

Walsingham Ainsforth is born at Glenowen, the estate owned by Sir Edward Aubrey, where Walsingham's father is curate. Walsingham's maternal aunt marries Sir Edward and the couple goes to London, returning after Walsingham's mother dies. Reverend Ainsforth leaves shortly thereafter and Sir Edward and Lady Aubrey act as loving parents to Walsingham. He therefore comes to see their estate as his, although if Sir Edward dies without a son, the estate must pass to his brother, Colonel Aubrey. Sir Edward dies while his wife is pregnant; she leaves and bears a daughter whom she passes off as a son to ensure that the estate remains within her family. She then takes her child to Nice to escape detection in the fraud. Heir as "son" to Sir Edward's estate and title, this child becomes known as Sir Sidney.

While Lady Aubrey is pregnant, everyone treats Walsingham as soon to be displaced and he therefore learns to hate his cousin as a usurper of the love and estate he had come to consider his. The two cousins meet briefly when Walsingham is seven and taken to Nice by his guardian and tutor, Mr. Hanbury. They next meet when Walsingham is about twenty-one and Sidney seventeen, at which time Lady Aubrey returns to Glenowen and Walsingham is called home from university to meet the cousin whom everyone adores as a paragon. Walsingham's predisposition to hate his cousin is exacerbated by Sidney's apparently forming intimate relationships with all the women Walsingham desires—first Isabella Hanbury, his tutor's sister, and then Lady Emily Delvin and Lady Arabella. Walsingham sees Sidney as robbing him not only of parental love and material wealth but of marital love as well. At the end, Walsingham learns that Sidney is female, loves Walsingham, and has interfered in Walsingham's relationships with other women to keep Walsingham free for *her.*

The novel proceeds in part through Walsingham's ambivalent reactions to his cousin. He is jealous of Sidney but nonetheless appreciates Sidney's kindness. When Walsingham is in Nice, his predisposition to hate his cousin is intensified by the rudeness shown to him by Lady Aubrey and her servants. Sir Sidney, however, is kind, leading Walsingham to feel grateful sympathy. Later, at Glenowen, he grows jealous when Isabella exclaims that Sidney is "a celestial being" who was "born to embellish society."[50] When Colonel Aubrey visits the estate asking to borrow money, the greedy Lady Aubrey refuses but Sidney swears that he will give Colonel Aubrey the funds he requests or serve in the military with him. Again, Walsingham admires Sidney's sympathy and generosity. Walsingham regards Sidney as his enemy when Sidney elopes with Isabella but grows ambivalent when he encounters the two later and they both help him. By this point, Walsingham has set off from Glenowen and fallen into a series of mishaps, culminating in his being accused of cheating at gambling and challenged to a duel. Walsingham finds Sidney's "easy familiarity . . . blended with good-nature" toward him a welcome change, again keeping him from hating his cousin.[51]

Furthermore, Walsingham recognizes and admires Sidney's looks and talents. Isabella describes Sidney as physically attractive and as having "manners [which] are so fascinating, so polished, so animated! He sings divinely, and plays on many instruments with skill the most enchanting!" He knows and can quote from "the Italian poets, and from Ossian; for he ha[d] been [for the previous] four years under the tuition of one of the most learned and enlightened men in Switzerland." Walsingham, despite his jealousy, admits that Sidney is "handsome, polite, accomplished, engaging, and unaffected." He acknowledges that Sidney is masterful at all the arts for which Isabella praised him and adds that "he [also] fenced like a professor of the science; painted with the correctness of an artist; was expert at all manly exercises; . . . and [was] a fascinating companion."[52]

But jealousy and anger by and large triumph when Sidney elopes with Isabella. Walsingham concludes that "Sir Sidney was the seducer of Isabella: the libertine who had robbed her of her honour." He consistently refuses to believe Sidney's claim that "by the sacred powers of truth—by all that is dear to honour! she *is* not, she never *shall* be my mistress:—I love Isabella too well to see her degraded, even were it possible that she could consider me as a lover."[53]

Walsingham cannot accept Sidney's protestations in part because no other reason for her behavior but pursuit of a sexual relation seems plausible. Sidney suggests that he retains Isabella merely because she is "a pleasant girl, who wishes to travel; I am a social being, and want a companion."[54] Isabella corroborates this when she suggests that Walsingham alone thinks her fallen. But she shows that she recognizes the implausibility of such a view by passing as Sidney's wife. She need not do so if she could travel with Sidney without doubts being cast on her purity.[55] She is also wrong that Walsingham is "the only being upon earth that suspects [her] of dishonour." Lord Kencarth, to whom Walsingham becomes tutor, sees her with Walsingham, recognizes her as "Sir Sidney's mistress," and assumes that if she is out of Sidney's protection, she is literally up for grabs, "[catching] her in his arms" and nearly "forc[ing] a kiss from her." Walsingham claims that "this lady is my property," but when Isabella denies this, Lord Kencarth assumes she can become anyone's "property." Refusing to give her up to either Lady Aubrey or Walsingham, he proclaims she must become his: "Return to Lady Aubrey she *shan't*—stay with you she *won't*—and therefore go with me she *must*." Walsingham and Lord Kencarth's shared assumption that the two can settle "ownership" of another man's cast-off mistress constitutes a shared male view that a woman who has traveled alone with a man is free goods because already (as good as) fallen.[56]

Furthermore, other women in the novel recognize that if they travel or fraternize alone with men, their reputations will be compromised. So thinks Lady Arabella, for instance, who travels alone with Lord Kencarth to Walsingham at Glenowen, noting that if Walsingham does not marry her, she is ruined because her traveling alone with one man to go to another "expose[s] her to the censure of the world" and so compromises her that she "cannot return to [her] home." Walsingham has no other model for interpreting a woman's close relationship with a man, following the cultural model that virtually all other characters also accept to be the rule. But because he does not know that Sidney is female, he has no means of recognizing that Sidney's relationship to Isabella is a bond between two *women*, one formed because one of them — Isabella — admires the other and gives up whatever maritally directed love she may have had for Walsingham so as not to impede her friend's chance to win him.

Unmasking would seem the most likely way to forward Sidney's desires for Walsingham. Once Walsingham discovers that Sidney is female, after all, he falls instantly in love with her, exclaiming, "How unworthily, how barbarously have I repaid this heroic attachment!" and recognizing that "all the trifling crowds of women appear as shadows of the sex, when compared with this transcendent, this unequalled Sidney."[57] But she could not unmask earlier. She had promised her mother that she would never unmask, as unmasking would expose her mother's greed and fraud, and Lady Aubrey is kept from releasing Sidney from this promise by her evil maid, Mrs. Judith Blagden, who originally suggested that Sidney be passed off as a son and depends on the secret for her own gain.

Lady Aubrey only allows the truth to be known after she has been almost fatally poisoned by Mrs. Blagden's son, whom she has recently married. Not realizing she has been given poison and so not able to retaliate against her husband and maid, Lady Aubrey nonetheless casts their influence aside. She gives up her greed and, feeling Mrs. Blagden can hardly bring her closer to death than she already is, she loses her fear of telling her secret. Walsingham appears at this juncture and Mrs. Blagden, fearing discovery, jumps from a window when Walsingham is about to burst into the room where she is scheming with her son. With Mrs. Blagden's death, Lady Aubrey's fears of retribution for telling the secret disappear entirely. Sidney, after recovering from a long illness due in part to the strains of hiding her feelings and sex, becomes publicly a woman.

An Education in (Human) Nature

Each character's grounds for beginning and perpetuating fraud are different, ranging from Mrs. Blagden's and Lady Aubrey's greed to Sidney's filial duty and love. But the original motivation for the fraud is the conventional proviso in Sir Edward's will that passes his estate to a son but not to a daughter. As such, the protracted masquerade works as an indictment of a patrilineal passage of property and an exposure of the cost to women of accepting their cultural role. As Cullens argues, not just Sidney's but other characters' identities as well are mistaken as characters double for one another; through these mirrorings, doublings, and mistaken identities, the novel questions the linkage between signifiers, such as "heir" or even "man/woman," and bodies, playing with a carnivalesque crisis in the readability of signs, in which bodies are included. By the end, however, when Sidney reverts to being a woman, Cullens sees Robinson as capitulating to a cultural imperative to accept one "natural" identity for each individual, which for women—certainly for the women in this novel—entails "a string of accepted losses (of title, fortune, and, nearly, life)." According to Cullens, Robinson treats this "situation as a necessary precondition for the restabilization of an epistemological order based, in the first instance, on binary sexual difference."[58] Even while accepting this binary, *Walsingham* "makes clear that the biology of incommensurability . . . remains intimately tied up with material inequality, and testifies to the high price exacted, in the form of psychic trauma and residual melancholy [Sidney's illness], by the cultural mandate to produce sexed bodies."[59]

But the novel, even its resolution, works in more complex ways, and Robinson does not simply capitulate. The complexity derives in part through the novel's destabilizing the term "nature," a word that first appears in its subtitle and that locates Walsingham as the novel's "pupil of nature." And that he is: he must learn that Sidney is "naturally" (biologically) female. He is also given the opportunity to learn that Sidney's female nature in no way reduces her. Whether he learns from Sidney's masquerade that female nature cannot be easily identified or defined is unclear, but that lesson is certainly offered for readers.

That there is something Walsingham must learn is first hinted when he goes to Nice to meet Sidney. Lady Aubrey's servant tells Walsingham and Hanbury that they may learn "a secret of the most important nature" by eavesdropping on Lady Aubrey; he tells them tantalizingly that "Sir Sidney is not—," at which Lady Aubrey enters the room and the conversation is interrupted. That Lady Aubrey is hiding something of note is further suggested in a discussion she has with Hanbury in which Hanbury argues that "sincerity cannot be incomprehensible. . . . It is only deception that is mysterious." Lady Aubrey disagrees, saying that "one likes sometimes to be agreeably deceived."[60]

If *Walsingham* followed the model taken by other late eighteenth- and early-nineteenth-century depictions of cross-dressed women, the real sex of the male-masquerading Sidney would be apparent to Walsingham and, indeed, to everyone else. As Dugaw asserts, warrior women in ballads from this point on are depicted as weak, passive, and delicate, more the "suffering helpmate" than self-reliant.[61] Wahrman likewise asserts out that when late eighteenth-century fictional women pass as men, they do so as particularly effeminate, sexless men, and Williams notes that depictions from this period of real cross-dressing women who lived earlier in the century cease highlighting the strength for which these women were earlier celebrating, stressing instead their femininity, their "properly maternal and domestic" attitudes.[62] By conforming to late eighteenth-century rules on feminine behavior, the laudable cross-dressing female protagonist gives herself away by her overriding femininity.

Sidney, however, does not function thus: his admirable qualities include, after all, expertise in manly exercises, making him not effeminate but androgynous—having both male and female strengths. When Walsingham is told that Sidney is female, he exclaims, "what a blind, thoughtless fool have I been!"[63] but his blindness, at least regarding Sidney's sex, is not unique: the only ones who know that Sidney is biologically female are her mother, Mrs. Blagden, and a few others who have been told the secret or learned it by eavesdropping. Anyone might take Sidney for male, given Sidney's failure to follow late eighteenth-century representations of real-life and fictional cross-dressing women as overwhelmingly feminine.

The novel's subtitle, along with Walsingham's assertions and some of his actions, suggest, however, that Walsingham is a good enough pupil of nature to discover Sidney's secret. He claims to be a pupil of nature from having received a Rousseauian education at Hanbury's hands and from having been raised in nature, at Glenowen, rather than in the artifice of cosmopolitan and court life. In Rousseauian (and Romantic) terms, this education should lead its recipient to draw on natural benevolence and to respond to the benevolence of others. When seven years old, Walsingham demonstrates his sensibility by rescuing a horse and a dog slated for immediate death; to signal the sentimental weight of Walsingham's first rescue, Robinson even has the horse shed a reciprocally sentimental tear. More importantly, Walsingham shows his sensibility whenever he responds positively to Sidney. When Sidney is kind to Walsingham in Nice, for instance, Walsingham exclaims, "Oh! how vivifying! how grateful to the heart are the sympathies of benevolent minds!" His benevolence toward others manifests itself when he frees a man he perceives to be unfairly arrested for debt, even though it leads to his being arrested for his interference; as he here explains in the conventional language of sensibility, "the fibres of my heart quivered with that emotion which never failed to wring them when I beheld a weaker object in the power of a stronger."[64] He shows beneficent sensibility as well when he liberates the jailed Julie de Beaumont, a young woman who has been seduced and abandoned, left to make her livelihood from prostitution.[65]

Were Walsingham presented as truly rooted in sensibility, Robinson might be seen as suggesting, along with Wollstonecraft, for instance, that as long as men are thus ruled by sensibility and are emasculated by it, women must become men. If Robinson were participating in this discussion, one traced by Claudia Johnson, she might seem to be accepting the complementarity of the sexes, continuing to express a binary, oppositional sex-gender system.[66] But Walsingham, despite occasional responsive sympathetic feeling and the benevolence rooted in it, is neither truly a man of sensibility nor emasculated. His status as a man of sensibility is compromised in part because he frequently cannot act on his beneficent wishes. After he liberates Julie, for instance, he finds a note that suggests she has committed suicide; because he is immediately arrested as responsible for the death she is assumed to have met, however, he can neither discover that she remains alive nor help her. While a failed ability to act on one's feelings need not prove one lacks true sensibility, Walsingham's inadequacies as a man of sensibility are highlighted throughout by his contrast to the one truly benevolent character in the novel, Mr. Optic, who saves Julie and others whom Walsingham is unable to succor.

Worse, however, Walsingham actively wrongs others and refuses to take responsibility for doing so. He claims to love Isabella, for instance, yet his behavior to her seems driven not by love but by desire for vengeance. He pretends to have an attachment to Lady Emily because getting Isabella jealous thereby "would gratify my self-love, and humble my exulting rival."[67] His most serious sin against her fails, but only because he mistakes another woman for her when he sees a woman at a masquerade who is wearing the same costume Isabella had at a previous masquerade. He whisks the woman into his carriage, takes her home, and rapes her. This woman, Amelia Woodford, resembles Isabella even when not in costume, and Walsingham's raping her is both a symbolic rape of Isabella and an actual rape of Amelia. He palliates his guilt by blaming "intoxication" and Amelia's curiosity, calling her "the victim of her own susceptibility"[68] and himself "an involuntary criminal."[69] According to his logic, if she had not chosen to dress as Isabella had at a previous masquerade, the mistake never would have occurred; her choice of a costume thus leaves her at fault. When Optic then insists that Walsingham marry the girl, Walsingham employs a double standard to refuse to do so, saying that "The frailty which had rendered her my victim, made me suspect that she would scarcely fulfil [sic], with honour, the duties of a wife . . . it is the reasoning of nature."[70] His logic is specious and his refusal to wed her shows hard-hearted selfishness.

Walsingham's sensibility is at times like that modeled by Goethe's *Werther,* but as such, it is self-centered and self-indulgent rather than based on feeling or concern for others.[71] He blames his lack of remorse on discovering the identity of his victim on the fact that he was then "too wretched to know pity, too distracted to feel the throb of commiseration." But through such responses, through their negation or "Wertherization" of Walsingham's sensibility, with sensibility ostensibly developing best in those with a "natural" education, the novel redefines both human nature and the external nature that forms it. Human nature is revealed as *not* benevolent, not rational, not based in emotions that connect humans to one another, but based instead in self-centered pity and in querulous and harmful passions.

Walsingham's education close to nature clearly has not led him to the better human nature adherents of sensibility think it should. He asserts at one point that "Nature is a liberal parent; and were not her children the slaves of prejudice, or the dupes of their own passions, the circle of enlightened humanity would enlarge, till vice and folly would be extinguished in its lustre." He seems to refer to himself when asserting that "the child of nature" acts on sensibility,[72] making the same link when he asserts that "Sir Sidney . . . would have been the delight of my bosom, had nature been permitted to take the place of compulsion" when he is called on to love his cousin.[73] Hanbury makes the same connection in instructing Walsingham early on that "it is in our power to assume such greatness of mind as becomes wise and virtuous men . . . [if we] conform ourselves to the order of Nature"; he clearly does not have selfish passions in mind as part of the order of Nature. To him, nature must lead us to truth about ourselves and others, as he suggests when he tells Walsingham that as "the student of nature," he cannot be mistaken about others and their feelings.[74]

Walsingham later asserts, however, that "the natural passions implanted in the breast of man were too often terribly triumphant over the sober dictates of reason and reflection" and that he, at least, "had not strength of mind to vanquish the strong hand of Nature"—here, apparently, "Nature" means the passions, rather than the soberer qualities of reason, reflection, sensibility, those qualities to which Hanbury clearly refers in advocating "conform[ing] ourselves to the order of Nature." When Walsingham says that he is "the pupil of resistless nature," he means that he is "the dupe of [his] own passions, an alien from reason, the slave of early impressions" rather than one who can find truth. Nature becomes highly individual, rather than universal or trustworthy; Walsingham learns that his is "perverse."[75] By the time he asserts that he has "outraged the very laws of Nature" and become "[Nature's] victim," it is impossible to know what nature means.[76]

That nature is not trustworthy and that individual nature can mislead from the truth is demonstrated by Walsingham's consistent mistakes about others and himself. These are, of course, exacerbated by the disguises in which others dress—not just Sidney, but Miss Woodford as well, at the masquerade ball at which he mistakes her for Isabella. That scene is perhaps predictable in the way it draws on discourse in the period that sexualizes masquerade, seeing it as allowing both men and women to indulge sexual license with impunity because the individuals behind the masks might not be easily identified. In such discourse, Walsingham is right to assume that the woman he pursues is as interested in sex as is he. In these terms, she is at fault not only for dressing as the woman he loves dressed at a previous masquerade, but for appearing at a masquerade at all.

However predictable in its sexualization of masquerade, the scene is remarkable for its revealing ugly truths about Walsingham's faults in perception about women and the nature of his emotions toward them. It acts thereby both to prove Walsingham no real man of sensibility and to problematize the view of women as lacking both individuality and moral lives. This occurs first by Walsingham's belief that Amelia "resembled, fatally, strikingly resembled, Isabella." This resemblance is intensified in her dress for the first masquerade they attend together;

knowing that he is Welsh, she dresses as "a Welsh peasant girl," and when he sees her in this garb, he claims "she was the exact counterpart of Isabella" and his "whole soul was absorbed in contemplating the perfect resemblance of that divinity whose fascinations were not yet unbroken." By the time she appears at the second masquerade in the same outfit that Isabella had worn at the previous masquerade, Walsingham is ready to see them as identical. In fact, however, his great desire at this point to find Isabella makes him susceptible to seeing any woman as identical with Isabella; at this second masquerade, he explains, "I fancied that I saw and heard, at least, a dozen Isabellas. Every pretty figure, every soft voice, seemed to mark the object of my search." If not seeing every woman around him as Isabella, he sees them as all equally able to satisfy his desire by serving as "the object of [his] search."[77]

His conflation of all women is furthered by his description of his feelings toward Isabella and Amelia. Late in the novel, when he still wants to marry Isabella—before he discovers that Sidney is female—he claims that "I love [Isabella] as I should love a sister."[78] He uses similar vocabulary to characterize his feelings toward Amelia. After he has effected Amelia's ruin, since she feels she cannot return home, he places her in lodgings as his sister and "visit[s] Miss Woodford as [his] sister." When she begs him to retain her, he tells her to "consider me henceforth as a dear brother."[79] By describing his relationship to both women in terms of sibling love, he shows sexual and sibling love slide overly easily into one another for him, or that he is unable to recognize his emotions and desires for what they are.[80]

The identical nature of his (mis)representation of his feelings for these two women, along with his mistaking one for the other, suggests not only Walsingham's lack of real honor but his refusal to see women as at all differentiated, as though they are all at base identical ciphers with "no Characters at all."[81] Using the scene of the masquerade in this book about disguises to highlight Walsingham's conflation of Amelia and Isabella points us to beliefs that women's social personae are always masks, with nothing but a lack behind those masks. By showing the extent to which Walsingham draws on such views and the harmfulness of his doing so, *Walsingham* asks us to reject this formulation of female (non)identity. Because Walsingham's views and treatment of women are here especially shown to be both misguided and deleterious, and because these errors are linked to Walsingham's misperception of Sidney, the novel insists that while masks misguide, women must be individuated, and their individuation should not be based solely— primarily—on gender.

But any ability to recognize how individuals should be individuated—how their actual identities should be perceived—is made difficult. *Walsingham* makes this point by showing that while Walsingham misperceives Sidney's identity, motivations, and love, it is perhaps un- derstandable that he should be thus mistaken. His confusion about Sid- ney, after all, is exacerbated in part because Isabella and everyone else intimately connected with Sidney do little to help Walsingham recog- nize the truth behind Sidney's appearance. Without the trustworthy guidance of those who know Sidney's secrets or of what Hanbury might mean by a natural understanding —which Walsingham clearly lacks—it is hard to discern either Sidney's sex or the nature of Sidney's desire.

It is easy to disbelieve Sir Sidney, for instance, when he claims that it is impossible that "[Isabella] could consider me as a lover" because Sidney does not explain what prevents Isabella from considering Sid- ney thus. Such equivocation reinforces the jealousy to which Walsin- gham is prone by his personal nature. But Walsingham's mistakes about Sidney are justified by their being so widely shared, which demon- strates how difficult it is to identify one's true "nature." No one recog- nizes Sidney as female, after all, until s/he shares her secret. But Sidney does not simply *appear* to be male; she has been constructed *as* male by her education. As such, Walsingham cannot sense that the person be- fore him is a woman; Sidney is not simply female except biologically. Nature again proves untrustworthy, or less important than other fac- tors. The biological *nature* of Sidney's sex is displaced, socially, by edu- cation. Sidney must be reeducated or shed her male-gendered education to be reconnected with her biological nature.

Such seems to be the argument when Lady Aubrey announces that Sidney is female and Walsingham wants to rush to her and declare his love; Hanbury explains that "the amiable Sidney has been educated in masculine habits; but every affection of her heart is beautifully femi- nine; heroic though tender; and constant, though almost hopeless. She will, nevertheless, demand some time to fashion her manners to the graces of her sex." Once the change has taken place and Walsingham is reunited with her, he asserts that "the transcendent Sidney" has "heroic virtues," continuing, "so completely is she changed, so purely gentle, so feminine in manners; while her mind still retains the energy of that richly-treasured dignity of feeling which are the effects of a masculine education, that I do not lament past sorrows, while my heart triumphs, nobly triumphs in the felicity of present moments."[82]

It is hard to know, however, in what Sidney's transformation in- heres—what constitutes Sidney's new femininity, her "manners" and "graces" rooted in her biology, however much newly fashioned—in part because we never see her again. We read only Walsingham's assertion that she has changed, and that assertion contains no specifics. Further-

more, most of the qualities that made Sidney marvelous as a man make
a woman of this era particularly admirable too: singing, dancing, playing instruments, knowledge of and ability to emulate poets, and painting. Isabella's initial description of Sidney, before she knows Sidney is
female, seems to fit a woman more than it would a man, calling Sidney
"an angel . . . born to embellish society" with "a form moulded by the
Graces, and fashioned by a studious desire to please." Sidney's "studious desire to please," after all, matches the ostensibly "feminine . . .
manners" that she gains after her transformation. Virtually all that is
masculine in Sidney is that Sidney "fenced like a professor of the science . . . [and] was expert at all manly exercises," along, perhaps, with
his "easy familiarity."[83] Sidney as a woman no doubt gives up easy familiarity and fencing, although when this novel was written, the Chevalier d'Eon, whose female sex at this point had been established, fenced
in exhibitions. The combination of Sidney's androgynous appeal and
his fencing might in fact be a gesture to d'Eon, who was himself never
hyperfeminine, even when cross-dressed and passing as a woman.[84]

Even if we accept that Sidney had to learn greater modesty (perhaps
learning to wait for Walsingham's courting rather than pursuing others,
as Sidney appears to do in running off with every woman threatening
to come between Sidney and Walsingham), Walsingham admits that
Sidney is the more lovable precisely *because* she leaves all other women
behind as "shadows." Does Sidney's "transcend[ing]" other women
stem from some hyperfeminine quality she has possessed all along?
After all, Walsingham exclaims that Sidney is transcendent when he
learns that Sidney is female but before Sidney undergoes gender transformation. Or are the "heroic virtues" she retains after her gender
change due to her having been formed by education as *male*? Sidney's
attachment to Walsingham, proven by his pursuit of the women whom
Walsingham might have married, is treated by Walsingham as a "heroic
attachment," which, when echoed by the "heroic virtue" she exhibits
after her gender change, becomes admirable, even in a female. The reiteration of the term "heroic" suggests that Sidney's active courtship may
not have harmed what was admirable in her as a woman. Taken together with the increased ambiguity of what "nature" means in this
novel, that which constitutes Sidney's admirable femininity likewise becomes ambiguous, and as it is linked to Sidney's initial (mis)education
and then to Sidney's reeducation, that femininity, along with Sidney's
admirable masculinity, are suggested to be constructs. Traits rooted in
nature become increasingly hard to identify, and, as a result, gender
itself becomes detached from nature, connected more thoroughly with
education. Far from capitulating to a system of "natural" identities that

reiterate a binary sex-gender system, then, Robinson leaves the issue muddied and indeterminable.

In so doing, Robinson also raises the question of whether desire is naturally, unproblematically heterosexual. When Walsingham first meets and grows jealous of Sidney, after all, he sees Sidney as "too generous, too exquisitely worthy, not to impress the female heart with admiration bordering on idolatry" and likely to fill women with "sentiments with which the liberal Sir Sidney inspired every bosom"— sentiments that would make women love Sir Sidney rather than Walsingham. Isabella responds precisely so: her encomiums on Sidney before she knows that Sidney is female and her claim that "Every spot which Sir Sidney inhabits must be a terrestrial paradise!" suggest that she can imagine few men more lovable than Sidney.[85]

That Sidney is a woman, however, and that we can never be certain which of Sidney's attributes are due to education, which due to "natural" feminine ideality, suggests that women might prefer women to men. As Cullens points out, those readers who guess Sidney's true sex have "[a] field of potentially transgressive speculation opened up, namely, the nature of the attachment between her and her 'companion,' Isabella, and whether Isabella herself is a dupe, accomplice or lover."[86] Given that two women living together with one of them cross-dressing were taken by eighteenth-century Britons to be lesbians, once we realize that Sidney is female, we are invited to see their relationship as sexual. In her vow to "mock the world's surmises, and, by the zeal and fidelity of my attachment, [to] deprecate its scorn,"[87] Isabella may be referring to scorn that she would receive not as a man's mistress but as the feminine partner in a lesbian relationship.[88]

To complicate the issue further, Robinson presents Isabella as trying to convince Walsingham to stay at Glenowen when he returns from university to meet his cousin by telling him that "with such a companion, you cannot fail to be happy."[89] Walsingham is more concerned with winning Isabella as a lover, and given her refusal to acknowledge this desire along with her offering Sidney (in her place?) as a companion who ensures "felicity," she seems to offer a same-sex relationship, sexual or otherwise, in place of the heterosexual relationship that would be formed by *her* union with Walsingham. Sidney's behavior toward Walsingham and Walsingham's reactions to Sidney suggest that the two are drawn to such a union as well. As Cullens suggests, as long as we consider Sidney as male, we might "ponder the motivations for the mixed signals sent by 'his' alternately kind and cruel, but clearly obsessive behavior toward his cousin; the two 'men's' tormented pattern of flight from/pursuit of each other lends an implicitly eroticized impetus to their relationship, suggesting the classic uncanny configuration of homosocially bonded doubles."[90]

Given that it is difficult to decide which qualities make Sidney admirable and desirable derive from the education that prepared Sidney to be male and which qualities are "natural" and based in Sidney's female sex, it is unclear whether Isabella suggests that a male is more likely to make Walsingham happy than a female could—than Isabella could, for instance. The issue is made more complex by Walsingham's instant adoration of Sidney when discovering that Sidney is (biologically) female. Is an admirable man who happens to have female genitals a man's best mate? What sort of eroticism is offered here? The answer is the harder to establish because of the difficulty in establishing exactly what kind of creature Sidney is. As Debra Bronstein provocatively explains, we need not see Sidney as a (cross-dressed) heterosexual woman who longs for a heterosexual relationship with Walsingham. The story equally invites us to see Sidney as wishing to become a man either to pursue a heterosexual relationship with Isabella or to pursue a homosexual relationship with Walsingham. She may thus be either a heterosexual or homosexual man in a woman's body. She can equally be seen as a cross-dressed lesbian wishing for a homosexual relationship with Isabella, however much Sidney believes it is impossible for Isabella to return her desire.[91]

The confusion about Sidney's sex, sexual identity, and habits on the one hand and the confusion about the nature of Sidney's relationship with Walsingham and Isabella on the other blurs lines among heterosexual, homosocial, and homoerotic/sexual relationships in ways that may be seen as treating as positive forms of intimacy elsewhere treated as unnatural.[92] That Sidney's qualities make Sidney equally admirable as a man or a woman suggests that as far as internal, intangible qualities go, it may be appropriate to fall in love with someone of one's own sex. If this is true, any system that insists on heterosexuality must place all its weight on biological sex because Sidney's case suggests that it is misguided to gender the sexes as absolutely different, albeit complementary, by any other means.

The ambiguity about Sidney's sex, sexual desires, and sexual appeal should be the more threatening, culturally, because it makes the homosexual man, by most accounts the period's worst sexual criminal, harder to identify, punish, and eradicate, unsettling in a period in which the male homosexual was easier to convict than rapists, more vilified than prostitutes, and more liable to capital punishment than lesbians.[93] According to Randolph Trumbach, such ambiguity should not be possible by the end of the eighteenth century, given that the male homosexual becomes defined at the beginning of the century, according to Trumbach, by his effeminacy and exclusive homosexuality, along with his aristocratic class status.[94] It was precisely the male homosexual's effeminacy, Trumbach argues, that made him most problematic; he departed from a masculinity that increasingly foregrounded dominance. That effeminacy likewise worked to the male homosexual's detriment because it made him an easy mark of hatred and punishment. Trumbach then argues that the fop, effeminate both in the sense of liking women's company and of modeling (negative) female behaviors, such as narcissism and too great an interest in clothing, becomes identified and used as the male homosexual type.

The identification of the fop or otherwise effeminate male as homosexual and of the male homosexual as the biggest deviant from the sanctioned version of masculinity in this period is highly problematic. As Laurence Senelick points out, "most of the sodomites arrested and tried were indistinguishable from the rest of the population: solid fathers of families, hitherto respectable tradesmen, schoolmasters, and clerics, generally mature in age" although given the strong popular view of the male homosexual as effeminate, "it became hard to conceive that a 'manly'-looking man should share his same tastes."[95] As Philip Carter explains, the (certainly heterosocial) fop was problematic for his *antisocial* behaviors of all sorts, such as his disruptive exhibitionism, for sinning against emergent versions of masculinity that required complaisance and "genuine fellow-feeling and a desire to please."[96] All the same, the fop might be used to stand in not only for social deviance but for sexual deviance as well—on stage, as Laurence Senelick argues—in a way that reassured audiences intolerant of homosexuality that its practitioners were easy to identify.[97] The effeminate male, fop or not, was certainly a social deviant; he might also be taken for or represent a sexual deviant; in either case, he sinned against acceptable masculinities as they evolved over the course of the eighteenth century.[98]

But Sidney is neither an effeminate nor a socially deviant male in the way that those writing on fops and homosexuals suggest. He appears desirable as a male, however, for precisely those reasons that also apparently make him desirable as a woman. To the extent that these qualities are not effeminate, the novel suggests that femininity too in this period is in some ways defined along the same lines as is masculinity, including complaisance—"studiously desiring to please." In this way, the novel suggests that lines between acceptable gendered behaviors are not particularly divergent. Sidney may therefore have attributes equally admirable in a man or a woman without being effeminate. But Sidney's lack of effeminacy problematizes views of the male homosexual as easily spotted because effeminate; as long as Sidney is thought to be a man, he may be read as providing Walsingham with a male—that is, homosexual—love object. Sidney's lack of effeminacy and the fascination he provides to the equally non-effeminate Walsingham argue, along with the trials noted by Senelick, that the male homosexual may not be so easy to spot after all. Sidney's attractiveness to Walsingham suggests, further, that a man's lack of effeminacy is no protection against feeling attraction to another man.

Given the accepted criminality of the male homosexual along with the possibility that Sidney might be a male homosexual who becomes the object of homosexual desire in a noneffeminate man, it is the more interesting that Sidney's punishment is mild. Hanbury suggests that Sidney need not be particularly punished because even if "the fastidious will say [that] she violated the laws of strict propriety, . . . her virtues, her sensibility, were her own; her crime, if the concealment of her sex can be considered criminal, was Lady Aubrey's."[99] It is hard to understand how concealing her sex might *not* be considered criminal, given that it involves usurping what is not hers, apparently sexually attracting others of the same sex, and challenging views that behaviors, attributes, roles, and rights were absolutely gendered, specific to each sex.

Sidney is symbolically punished through her long illness, through losing "title, fortune, and, nearly, life," and through her transformation; the "transvestite Sidney must 'die' as a male, or at least be confined to the passivity of unconscious immobility, in order to be reborn female."[100] Yet that symbolic death occurs offstage, effectively downplaying it as punishment. Furthermore, neither the title nor the entire fortune Sidney held were hers, since she was not a son. Had Lady Aubrey born Sir Edward a son, he would have inherited sixty thousand pounds and his father's estates, and Walsingham would have received eight thousand pounds, plus funds for his education. As a daughter, however, Sidney is entitled to thirty thousand pounds plus funds for her support while a minor, and Walsingham is entitled to twenty thousand pounds.[101] He inherits an additional ten thousand pounds from Isabella's early guardian, Randolph. Together they have sixty thousand pounds rather than sixty-eight thousand pounds plus an estate: meaning they end up with nearly as much of a fortune as she would have if the masquerade had been successful. What underlines the mildness of Sidney's punishment is the much worse end that comes to Mrs. Blagden. Once she jumps out a window to escape discovery by Walsingham, "she . . . expired in agonies which mocked the powers of description; every feature was distorted, every limb lacerated and broken," "her skull fractured, and her flesh bruised," and she is left a "blackening corpse."[102] That Mrs. Blagden gets all the highly visible, tangible punishment that *Walsingham* doles out suggests that she is the most guilty character in the novel.[103]

Through leaving Sidney so much more lightly punished despite her transgression of sartorial and behavioral gender codes, Robinson disavows Sidney's guilt, confirming that Walsingham is right finally to accept Isabella's assertion about Sidney that "never did nature form so wonderful a creature!"[104] But Sidney is an indeterminate "creature," neither clearly masculine nor feminine. As such, she challenges clear differential gendering, natural or triumphant heterosexuality, and easily identified homosexual types and desires. Others' responses to Sidney, along with the plot movement and its dispensation and withholding of punishment, suggest that this indeterminacy is not monstrous, however, and that the challenge Sidney presents to the late-eighteenth-century sex-gender system need not be seen as negative.

Robinson reinscribes her characters as heterosexual and bases the gender behavior and attitudes with which they end in biological sex, but she nonetheless leaves us with a vision in which both gender and sexuality are greatly destabilized, unraveling the certainties that continue to be reasserted with every insistence that the sexes are different not only in biology, but in behavior, rights, and roles. She also unravels the idea that we are all innately, unproblematically heterosexual and that the sexual deviant is easy to identify, leaving us uncertain about the nature of sex, desire, and gender and suggesting that unnatural affections are not so unnatural after all.

NOTES

1. See Rudolf M. Dekker and Lotte C. van de Pol, *The Tradition of Female Transvestism in Early Modern Europe* (New York: St. Martin's, 1989); Dianne Dugaw, *Warrior Women and Popular Balladry, 1650–1850* (Cambridge: University of Cambridge Press, 1989); and Dror Wahrman, "*Percy*'s Prologue: Gender Panic and Cultural Change in Late-Eighteenth-Century England," *Past and Present* 159 (1998): 113–60. Dekker and van de Pol situate the start of this tradition at the end of the sixteenth century (2); they concentrate on the tradition in the Netherlands but note numerous cases in England and argue that the tradition there paralleled what occurred in the Netherlands (1).

2. Dugaw discusses this movement throughout *Warrior Women and Popular Balladry*. Wahrman, in "*Percy*'s Prologue," notes their diminishment in balladry and fiction at the end of the eighteenth century (127–29, 157–59).

3. See Dugaw, *Warrior Women*, 179–89; Wahrman, "*Percy*'s Prologue," 132. See also Randolph Trumbach, "London's Sapphists: From Three Sexes to Four Genders in the Making of Modern Culture," *Body Guards: The Cultural Politics of Gender Ambiguity*, eds. Julia Epstein and Kristina Straub (New York: Routledge, 1991), 134; Pat Rogers, "The Breeches Part," *Sexuality in Eighteenth-Century Britain*, ed. Paul-Gabriel Boucé (Totowa, N.J.: Barnes, 1982), 244–58; and Kristina Straub, *Sexual Suspects: Eighteenth-Century Players and Sexual Ideology* (Princeton: Princeton University Press, 1992), 127–50.

4. On portrayals of women as brave in the seventeenth century and through much

of the eighteenth, see also Carolyn Williams, "Women Behaving Well," in this volume. Late-eighteenth-century writers stressing qualities in women not ordinarily thought to be theirs—courage, for instance—usually based those qualities in more acceptable versions of femininity. Late-eighteenth-century examples that Williams uses base courage in maternal love, merging it with discourses naturalizing women's selfless maternal drives.

5. Wahrman, "*Percy*'s Prologue," 115, 135, 177, 126.

6. Thomas Laqueur makes this argument throughout *Making Sex: Body and Gender from the Greeks to Freud* (Cambridge: Harvard University Press, 1990).

7. The mixed response to masculine women that Williams finds, rather than their outright rejection, may derive from the fact that the texts she cites predate the last two decades of the eighteenth century and the gender panic that then takes over.

8. On Miss Sparkes, see Wahrman, "*Percy*'s Prologue," 146; on Freke, see Emma Donoghue, *Passions Between Women: British Lesbian Culture, 1668–1801* (New York: Scarlet, 1993), 100–103.

9. Chris Cullens, "Mrs. Robinson and the Masquerade of Womanliness," *Body and Text in the Eighteenth Century*, eds. Veronica Kelly and Dorothea von Mücke (Stanford: Stanford University Press, 1994), 267–68. Cullens mistakenly cites the original publication date of *Walsingham* as 1796. The edition I use is Mary Robinson, *Walsingham; or, the Pupil of Nature*, 4 vols. (London: Longman, 1797).

10. Cullens, "Mrs. Robinson and the Masquerade," 267.

11. The other examples I provide here, along with *Walsingham*, suggest that what had elsewhere become unimaginable remained alive in female-penned fiction. Although the sex/gender-transgressive female characters in *Belinda*, *The Last Man*, and *Coelebs in Search of a Wife* are ultimately contained, they too, I would argue, challenge a sex-gender system based on an oppositional or hierarchical, mutually exclusive binary of male/female. So too do those in yet other female-penned British novels at the end of the eighteenth and into the nineteenth century. Portrayals and treatments of female characters who transgress sex-gender norms in novels of this period are too varied and address issues too numerous to examine in adequate depth in this essay, however. My focus on *Walsingham*, with its extensive treatment of a female cross-dresser, suggests some of the ways other women writers of the period too challenged the sex/gender system through their treatment of female characters with masculine characteristics.

12. Claudia Johnson, *Equivocal Beings: Politics, Gender, and Sentimentality in the 1790s: Wollstonecraft, Radcliffe, Burney, Austen* (Chicago: University of Chicago Press, 1995).

13. Debra Bronstein argues, however, that Robinson may also buy into this binary, as in insisting that women have "masculine" strength of mind, especially in her treatises on women's rights. Bronstein makes this point in her "Whose Gender? Which Gender?" presented at the Seventh Annual Conference on Eighteenth- and Nineteenth-Century British Women Writers; Chapel Hill, North Carolina, 27 March 1998.

14. Dekker and van de Pol, *The Tradition of Female Transvestism*, 10–11, 126.

15. Ibid., 10, 38, 40; see also 9–10, 30–33; Dugaw, *Warrior Women*, 121–42; and Lynne Friedli, " 'Passing Women'—A Study of Gender Boundaries in the Eighteenth Century," *Sexual Underworlds of the Enlightenment*, eds. G. S. Rousseau and Roy Porter (Chapel Hill: University of North Carolina Press, 1988), 242–43.

16. Dekker and van de Pol, *The Tradition of Female Transvestism*, 26.

17. On Hamilton, see Donoghue, *Passion Between Women*, 73–80; Friedli, " 'Passing Women,' " 239–40; Sheridan Baker, "Henry Fielding's *The Female Husband*: Fact and Fiction," *PMLA* 74 (1959): 213–24; Terry Castle, " 'Matters Not Fit to be Mentioned': Fielding's *The Female Husband*," *ELH* 49 (1982): 602–22; and Lillian Faderman, *Surpassing the Love of Men: Romantic Friendship and Love Between Women from the Renaissance to the*

Present (New York: Morrow, 1981), 52. On Vizzani, see Donoghue, *Passion Between Women*, 80–86 and Friedli, " 'Passing Women,' " 249. On Queen Christina, see Faderman, *Surpassing the Love of Men*, 55. Erin Mackie notes the complexity of Charke's cross-dressing from childhood on in "Desperate Measures: The Narratives of the Life of Mrs. Charlotte Charke," *ELH* 58 (1991): 841–65. On Charke, see also Castle, " 'Matters Not Fit,' " 607, 617); Faderman, *Surpassing the Love of Men*, 57–58; Friedli, " 'Passing Women,' " 240–42; Donoghue, *Passions Between Women*, 97–100, 164–67); Straub, *Sexual Suspects*, 127–50; and Felicity Nussbaum, "Heteroclites: The Gender of Character in the Scandalous Memoirs," *The New Eighteenth Century*, eds. Felicity Nussbaum and Laura Brown (New York: Methuen, 1987): 163–66. On van Antwerpen, see Dekker and van de Pol, *The Tradition of Female Transvestism*, 1, 63–69. Snell's story appears in *The Female Soldier; or, the Surprising Life and Adventures of Hannah Snell*, 1750 (Los Angeles: UCLA-Augustan Reprint Society, 1989). For discussions of that story, see Donoghue, *Passions Between Women*, 91–94; Friedli, " 'Passing Women,' " 242; Wahrman, "*Percy*'s Prologue," 130–31; and Dugaw, *Warrior Women*, 184. Other early modern women, Susanna Centlivre for example, cross-dressed for ease in carrying on sexual affairs with men (Faderman, *Surpassing the Love of Men*, 57).

18. Dugaw, *Warrior Women*, 131.

19. Dekker and van de Pol, *Tradition of Female Transvestism*, 15, 18; Dugaw, *Warrior Women*, 131.

20. Dekker and van de Pol, *Tradition of Female Transvestism*, 15, 22, 19.

21. Ibid., 23. Faderman, *Surpassing the Love of Men*, argues that this was also true for the Renaissance (48).

22. Dekker and van de Pol, *Tradition of Female Transvestism*, 23.

23. Donoghue, *Passions Between Women*, 61.

24. As Faderman notes throughout *Surpassing the Love of Men*, if neither woman dressed as a man or took a culturally masculine role, they may not have been suspected of having sexual relations, being instead possibly simply romantic friends. Donoghue, *Passions Between Women*, too notes that where women's friendship was concerned, a number of different details had to coalesce, including one friend's taking a masculine role and the other a feminine role, before that friendship became suspected as sexual (11). See also Dekker and van de Pol, *Tradition of Female Transvestism*, 74–75.

25. Donoghue, *Passions Between Women*, 60.

26. Faderman, *Surpassing the Love of Men*, 47–61; Dekker and van de Pol, *Tradition of Female Transvestism*, 77–80.

27. Donoghue, *Passions Between Women*, 18.

28. Dekker and van de Pol, *Tradition of Female Transvestism*, 80.

29. Donoghue, *Passions Between Women*, 18.

30. Donoghue, ibid., gives the time elapsed as two months (73, 79); Castle, " 'Matters Not Fit,' " identifies it as three months (604).

31. Ann Rosalind Jones and Peter Stallybrass, "Fetishizing Gender: Constructing the Hermaphrodite in Renaissance Europe," in Epstein and Straub, *Body Guards*, 89.

32. Faderman, *Surpassing the Love of Men*, says that Hamilton was whipped in three towns and then imprisoned (52), while Donoghue, *Passions Between Women*, identifies the number of towns in which Hamilton was whipped as four (79). Faderman discusses the other case mentioned here (52–53).

33. Faderman, *Surpassing the Love of Men*, 52.

34. Donoghue, *Passions Between Women*, points out that the term lesbian did exist in the eighteenth century (2). On the harsher reception of cross-dressing women judged to be in lesbian relationships on the continent or in America, see Jones and Stallybrass, "Fetishizing Gender," (88) and Faderman, *Surpassing the Love of Men*, (50–52). On the

more extreme punishment of male homosexuals, see Dekker and van de Pol, *Tradition of Female Transvestism*, 78; Faderman, *Surpassing the Love of Men*, (51); and Randolph Trumbach, "Sex, Gender, and Sexual Identity in Modern Culture: Male Sodomy and Female Prostitution in Enlightenment London," *Journal of the History of Sexuality* 2.2 (1991): 186–87; 190.

35. Donoghue, *Passions Between Women*, 66, 67.

36. They might equally be lauded later, despite a shift in the understanding of the physical relation between the sexes. Dekker and van de Pol, *Tradition of Female Transvestism*, note that British female soldiers were granted favors and incomes from nobles and royalty at both ends of the eighteenth century (96). According to Dugaw, *Warrior Women*, women who served on board ships as gunpowder carriers during the 1798 Battle of the Nile afterwards received honors. She points out too that Victoria proclaimed in 1847 that medals should be awarded "without reservation to sex" for those who served in battle. These were ultimately not awarded because it was feared that "multitudes" of women might claim them (128–29). Dugaw does not specify whether these women fought dressed as men or as women. Dekker and van de Pol explain this late lauding of female warriors by suggesting that in periods of national military crisis, normal rules constraining women's behavior are suspended, an intriguing but questionable formulation, given the greater constraints placed on most women in both Great Britain and France at the turbulent end of the eighteenth century.

37. Laqueur, *Making Sex*, 127.

38. Dekker and van de Pol, *Tradition of Female Transvestism*, 74. Women's adoption of male-gendered strengths was considered laudable at least through the late seventeenth century. Such was the case in late antiquity, as Mary Castelli notes in " 'I Will Make Mary Male': Pieties of the Body and Gender Transformation of Christian Women in Late Antiquity" in Epstein and Straub, *Body Guards*, 29–49); in the sixteenth and seventeenth centuries, as Dugaw, *Warrior Women*, explains (172–74); and in the late seventeenth century, as Janet Todd points out in *Gender, Art and Death* (New York: Continuum, 1993).

39. Castelli, " 'I Will Make Mary Male,' " 46. See also Jean Howard, "Crossdressing, the Theatre, and Gender Struggle in Early Modern England," *Shakespeare Quarterly* 39 (winter 1988): 421–25. For a discussion of debate on when women became seen as passionless rather than sexually voracious, see my "Not Subordinate: Empowering Women in the Marriage-Plot—the Novels of Frances Burney, Maria Edgeworth, and Jane Austen," *Criticism* 34, 1 (winter 1992): 51–73. See also Nancy Cott, "Passionlessness: An Interpretation of Victorian Sexual Ideology, 1790–1850," *Signs* 4, 2 (1979): 219–36.

40. Howard, "Crossdressing," 425.

41. For varied views on when this change occurred and the new paradigm on the sexes' nature and relation was accepted, see Dekker and van de Pol, *Tradition of Female Transvestism*, 49–53; Donoghue, *Passion Between Women*, 25–58; Friedli, " 'Passing Women,' " 235, 246–49; Laqueur, *Making Sex*, (135–42); Trumbach, "London's Sapphists," 115–21; and Jones and Stallybrass, "Fetishizing Gender," (80–111). Although such a change occurs gradually and at different rates in different places and classes, most agree that by the end of the eighteenth century, the change had occurred and the new paradigm was virtually universally accepted.

42. Ferris, Lesley *Acting Women: Images of Women in Theatre* (New York: New York University Press, 1989) 60–64.

43. Ibid., 4.

44. Jones and Stallybrass, "Fetishizing Gender," 89. Given Donoghue's assertion, in *Passions Between Women*, that cross-dressing was not illegal in eighteenth-century En-

gland (61), James's dictum must have lapsed into disuse with other sumptuary laws in the 1690s. Deuteronomy 22:5 likewise forbids male cross-dressing, but James did not deploy this element of biblical law in his own anti–cross-dressing edict.

45. For discussion of these pamphlets, see Jones and Stallybrass, "Fetishizing Gender," 104; Dugaw, *Warrior Women*, 163–89; and Howard, "Crossdressing," 424–28.

46. On these views of masquerades, see Terry Castle's "The Culture of Travesty: Sexuality and Masquerade in Eighteenth-Century England," in Rousseau and Porter, *Sexual Underworlds*, 156–80, and her *Masquerade and Civilization* (Stanford: Stanford University Press, 1986). On these views of the theater, see Straub, *Sexual Suspects*. On the variety of objections to the theater, see Jonas Barish, *The Anti-Theatrical Prejudice* (Berkeley: University of California Press, 1981).

47. Joan Rivière, "Womanliness as Masquerade," *Formations of Fantasy*, eds. Victor Burgin, James Donald, and Cora Kaplan (London: Methuen, 1986), 35–44; and Luce Irigaray, *This Sex Which is Not One*, trans. Catherine Porter (Ithaca: Cornell University Press, 1985), 76.

48. Catherine Craft-Fairchild discusses Haywood's use of masquerade in *Fantomina* in *Masquerade and Gender: Disguise and Female Identity in eighteenth-Century Fictions by Women* (University Park: Pennsylvania State University Press, 1992), 51–72. See also Mary Anne Schofield, *Masking and Unmasking the Female Mind: Disguising Romances in Feminine Fiction, 1713–1799* (Newark: University of Delaware Press, 1990).

49. On increased calls for men to be exclusively heterosexual, see Randolph Trumbach, "Sex, Gender, and Sexual Identity in Modern Culture," and "The Birth of the Queen: Sodomy and the Emergence of Gender Equality in Modern Culture, 1660–1750," *Hidden from History: Reclaiming the Gay and Lesbian Past*, eds. Martin Bauml Duberman, Martha Vicinus, and George Chauncey, Jr. (New York: Penguin–New American, 1989), 129–40.

50. *Walsingham*, I: 267–28.

51. Ibid., II: 126.

52. Ibid., I: 267, 269.

53. Ibid., II: 38, 40; III: 86.

54. Ibid., III: 86, 83.

55. Ibid., III: 137. She in fact does so "for private reasons," which may have as much to do with convincing Walsingham that she is unavailable as with concern for her reputation.

56. Ibid., IV: 136, 76.

57. Ibid., 297, 387, 390.

58. Cullens, "Mrs. Robinson," 268.

59. Ibid., 269.

60. *Walsingham*, I: 173–74, 149.

61. Dugaw, *Warrior Women*, 67.

62. Wahrman, "*Percy*'s Prologue," 131.

63. *Walsingham*, IV: 387.

64. Ibid., II: 167–69.

65. Ibid., II: 178–79. That he is perceived by others to have sensibility is demonstrated by Sidney's assertion that Walsingham should believe that Sidney does not mean to persecute Walsingham in eloping with Isabella, saying, "you have sense, discernment, feeling!—you have faculties of mind that should place it above prejudice" (III: 81). Isabella too, despite all Walsingham's cruelty, refers to him obliquely as the object of Sidney's love, and, as such, as "the most deserving, the most enlightened of men" (IV: 132). Given his callous, self-centered behavior, such assertions reveal their bad judgment rather than his true nature.

My treatment of Walsingham's sensibility here diverges from Eleanor Ty's argument in *Empowering the Feminine* (Toronto: University of Toronto Press, 1998), 51. Ty does not address the possibility that Robinson presents Walsingham's sensibility as negative or incomplete. She stresses that Walsingham helps others without including discussion of his *not* doing so in key instances, and in harming those he ostensibly loves through his self-centered sensibility.

66. In *Equivocal Beings*, Johnson argues that this was the case with Wollstonecraft, for instance, who continued claiming in this time of gender panic that women needed to model what was elsewhere defined as masculine strength.

67. *Walsingham*, II: 134.

68. Ibid., III: 99, 97.

69. Ibid., IV: 195.

70. Ibid., III: 125–26.

71. Peter Garside argues that *Walsingham* follows models of the sentimental novel provided by Goethe and Rousseau and that his sensibility at times draws on nature but at other times is more "morbid" in his Introduction to his edition of *Walsingham* (London: Routledge-Thoemmes, 1992), ix–x. The assertion that the morbid side of Walsingham's sensibility is Wertherian is mine.

72. *Walsingham*, I: 84–85, 201.

73. Ibid., II: 211.

74. Ibid., I: 163, 319.

75. Ibid., III: 271, 338.

76. Ibid., IV: 192. The novel plays throughout with varied views on nature and on the genius, benevolence, or ignorance that belongs to one raised in nature, for instance identifying Shakespeare as an example of a natural genius that might as easily be found in laborers as is in the well-born (II: 270–71). Elsewhere, the notion of the natural man is used in a manner challenging Hanbury's and Walsingham's use of it as guarantee of truth and benevolence to suggest that the person raised in nature will be an ignorant boor, not skilled in fashionable behaviors (III: 228–30). At times, Walsingham seems to differentiate between external nature, capitalizing "Nature" when referring to it, and human nature. This typographical differentiation is inconsistent, however, allowing for the conflation between the two.

Ty, *Empowering the Feminine*, likewise focuses on nature and the construction of gender (45–46, 52). She does not treat the novel as dislocating or relativizing nature to the extent that I outline here, however. She nevertheless quite usefully examines the permeability of gender lines in ways that augment my discussion of the issue.

77. *Walsingham*, III: 2, 29, 30, 74.

78. Ibid., IV: 162.

79. Ibid., III: 96, 112, 117.

80. Walsingham could also simply be lying, or otherwise reconstructing his version of the past from his aim to exculpate his behavior without recognizing his inconsistencies—or, to put the case more accurately, his telling consistencies. His blurred boundary between sexual and sibling love is otherwise in keeping with the relation between these two sorts of love elsewhere in the period. For a discussion of ways in which sibling love both properly and improperly merges with sexual love elsewhere, see my "Familial Love, Incest, and Female Desire in late Eighteenth- and Early Nineteenth-Century British Women's Novels," in *Criticism* 41 (1999): 67–99.

81. Alexander Pope, "Epistle II. To a Lady. Of the Characters of Women." 1743.

82. *Walsingham*, IV: 388, 398.

83. Ibid., I: 267–69; II: 126.

84. Bronstein likewise links Sidney and d'Eon in "Whose Gender? Which Gender?"

See also Peter Ackroyd, *Dressing Up: Transvestism and Drag* (New York: Simon & Schuster, 1979): 81.

85. *Walsingham*, I: 304, 305, 318.

86. Cullens, "Mrs. Robinson," 339 n.15.

87. *Walsingham*, II: 38.

88. I do not mean to suggest that one partner's taking a masculine role and the other's taking a feminine role was not the only model for lesbian relationships in the eighteenth century. Donoghue's *Passions Between Women* explores different kinds of lesbian desires, relationships, and models that women who loved other women might follow.

89. *Walsingham*, I: 317.

90. Cullens, "Mrs. Robinson," 339 n.15.

91. Bronstein makes these points in "Whose Gender? Which Gender?"

92. For another discussion of the valorization of forms of relationships normally considered deviant and unnatural, see George Haggerty, *Unnatural Affections: Women and Fiction in the later 18th Century* (Bloomington: Indiana University Press, 1998).

93. See page 000 of this essay for comparison to punishment meted out to lesbians. Randolph Trumbach, throughout "Sex, Gender, and Sexual Identity in Modern Culture," points out that prostitutes could be more gently dealt with because they, unlike male homosexuals, were seen as socially redeemable and because they were held as necessary to keep men from turning to sodomy. On chances of convicting rapists, see Antony Simpson's "Vulnerability and the Age of Consent," in Rousseau and Porter, *Sexual Underworlds*, 181–205).

94. Trumbach makes this argument in "The Birth of the Queen," "London's Sapphists," and "Sex, Gender, and Sexual Identity in Modern Culture."

95. See Laurence Senelick, "Mollies or Men of Mode? Sodomy and the Eighteenth-Century London Stage," *Journal of the History of Sexuality* 1 (1990): 51.

96. Philip Carter, "Men about Town: Representations of Foppery and Masculinity in Early Eighteenth-Century Urban Society," *Gender in Eighteenth-Century England: Roles, Representations and Responsibilities*, eds. Hannah Barker and Elaine Chalus (New York: Longmans, 1997), 49. Susan Staves also argues that the fop is heterosexual in her "A Few Kind Words for the Fop," *SEL* 22 (1982): 413–28. Carter foregrounds the fop's social rather than sexual deviance by pointing out that given that male homosexuality was a capital offense, the male homosexual or molly is necessarily "clandestine in practice [while] the fop is social, flamboyant, vigorously heterosocial, and, above all, conspicuous" (39). Were a molly to be so flamboyant and conspicuous, he would be arrested, pilloried, and possibly stoned to death (Trumbach, "Sex, Gender," 190). Carter notes too that given the scandalous nature of the molly, works on him—specifically on his dangerous sexuality—might have been received as pornographic and so would have been less prevalent and public than those on the fop, who was "regularly featured in the more 'respectable' format of essay periodicals, serious or satirical social commentaries, courtesy books and conduct guides." (40).

97. Senelick, "Mollies or Men of Mode?," argues that the fop was used thus to stand in for the male homosexual without his sexuality's being specifically addressed (43).

98. Pertinent discussions of such shifts include Anna Clark's "The Chevalier d'Eon and Wilkes: Masculinity and Politics in the Eighteenth Century," *Eighteenth-Century Studies* 32, 1 (1998): 19–48, and Gary Kates's "D'Eon Returns to France: Gender and Power in 1777," in Epstein and Straub, *Body Guards*, 167–94.

99. *Walsingham*, IV: 388.

100. Cullens, "Mrs. Robinson," 272.

101. *Walsingham*, IV: 383–84.

102. Ibid., IV: 366, 359–60.

103. Bronstein presents Mrs. Blagden's punishments in similar terms, in part because she, like Cullens, "Mrs. Robinson," sees Sidney as returning to proper femininity. The detailed delineation of Mrs. Blagden's and literary precedents for it deserve exploration, but providing it lies beyond the purvue of this essay.

104. *Walsingham*, I: 266.

2
Passing Politics

The Metamorphosis of Sex(uality): Ovid's "Iphis and Ianthe" in the Seventeenth and Eighteenth Centuries

David Michael Robinson

I

Some Binarisms: Discontinuity/Continuity — Dissimilarity/Similarity — Difference/Sameness

IF I COULD CHANGE ONE ASPECT OF THE FIELD OF LESBIAN/GAY/QUEER/ Sexuality Studies, it would be the privileging of dissimilarity over similarity, discontinuity over continuity, that has prevailed among practitioners for the past decade or two. It is my firm conviction that, both in our scholarship and our pedagogy, we ought to resist reinforcing this either/or tendency, which has arguably become the central theoretical divide structuring, and assigning value to, our work. Both from the standpoint of historical truth and from the standpoint of political efficacy, the current dogma prescribing defamiliarization of the past — enforced especially through more or less contemptuous dismissal of work that renders the past, or elements of it, familiar, as well as through omission of such familiarizing work from anthologies and course syllabi — is a costly mistake.[1] A both/and approach would be far more useful, given that, as far as I can see, past concepts, categories, ideologies, and (to the extent they are recoverable) experiences of sex, sexuality, and gender have been both like and unlike present ones.[2] Eve Kosofsky Sedgwick makes this point brilliantly in *Epistemology of the Closet*, in the section headed, "Axiom 5: The historical search for a Great Paradigm Shift may obscure the present conditions of sexual identity" (44–48). She argues that in "radically defamiliarizing and denaturalizing the past," in asserting that past same-sex practices are fundamentally different from "the homosexuality 'we know today', . . . such an analysis . . . has tended inadvertently to *re*familiarize, *re*naturalize, damagingly reify an entity that it could be doing much more to subject to analysis . . . [,]

counterposing against the alterity of the past a relatively unified homo-sexuality that 'we' *do* 'know today' " (44–45).[3] In contrast, Sedgwick proposes a different approach: "to show how issues of modern homo/heterosexual definition are structured, not by the supersession of one model and the consequent withering way of another, but instead by the relations enabled by the unrationalized coexistence of different models during the times they do coexist" (47).

But whereas Sedgwick defamiliarizes the present, in this paper I aim to refamiliarize the past, both classical and early modern. My conten-tion is simple: 1) An examination of, on the one hand, Ovid's tale of Iphis and Ianthe, and, on the other hand, two seventeenth-century dra-matizations of this tale reveals strikingly similar ideologies of sexuality and gender, impressed upon readers/viewers through the invocation and linkage of a common set of simultaneously repellent and attractive topics—lesbianism, sex-changing, effeminacy, excessive female desire, misogyny, paternal tyranny—that together delineate the boundaries of the normal, the natural, the approved; and 2) these boundaries, while different in significant ways from those that are dominant today, are nonetheless also rather familiar, certainly far more so than recent his-tories of sexuality would have us believe.[4] My aim is perhaps best ex-pressed by quoting Margaret Anne Doody's eloquent declaration of purpose in *The True Story of the Novel:* "It is my purpose in *this* book to deal with continuities and to make a point of connectedness. Such an interest does not preclude a respect for difference. It is simply that dif-ference is not my subject here; I write because I feel our comments on some kinds of differences have recently tended to obfuscate connections and to blot out continuities. There are continuities and connections in the Western world, after all."[5] The rest of this essay explores some of these continuities and connections, involving sex, gender, and sexuality.

II

To conclude Book IX of the *Metamorphoses* (2 B.C.–8 A.D.) Ovid re-lates a story (ll. 666–797) in which lesbian desire—the sexual and ro-mantic love of one woman for another—is the central problem, the issue that results in the metamorphosis. The story goes as follows: Ligdus, a poor but upright man of Crete, tearfully tells his pregnant wife Tele-thusa that, because of their poverty, if their child is a girl, it will regret-tably have to be killed. As Telethusa is about to give birth, the goddess Isis appears and instructs her to care for the child whatever its sex—even if this means disobeying her husband—and trust that she, Isis, will take care of everything. With only a nurse as witness, Telethusa gives birth to a girl, but passes her off as a boy. As luck, or Fate, would have it, Ligdus, naming the child after its grandfather, gives it a gender-neutral name: Iphis. The girl is then raised as a boy (without difficulty it would seem) until she reaches the age of thirteen, when her father betrothes her to her childhood play- and schoolmate, Ianthe. The two girls, we learn, have fallen in love, Ianthe not suspecting her beloved's true sex. Telethusa postpones the wedding as long as she can, but eventually the day is immovably set. The night before it is to take place, the disguised girl and her mother shut themselves in Isis's temple and pray for help. The goddess transforms Iphis into a boy. The next morning the now heterosexual couple is married.

The centerpiece as well as longest section of "Iphis and Ianthe" (taking up almost a quarter of its length) is Iphis's lament, the three interconnected themes of which are the utter uniqueness of her desires, their unnaturalness, and the impossibility of fulfilling them.[6] Iphis believes she is not only the sole woman but also the sole living creature ever to experience these 'new, unknowne, prodigious loves' (*cognita . . . nulli, . . . prodigiosa novaeque / cura . . . Vereris* [IX.727–28]):

> No Cow a Cow, no Mare a Mare pursues:
> But Harts their gentle Hindes, and Rammes their Ewes.
> So Birds together paire. Of all that move,
> No Female suffers for a Female love.[7]

William S. Anderson is probably correct to read this mistaken belief as an indication of Iphis's innocence, and to assert that "all this emphasis on novelty must have amused [Ovid's] Roman audience."[8] For as Bernadette Brooten demonstrates in *Love Between Women*, "Whereas pre-Roman-period Greek and Latin literature contains very few references to female homoeroticism, the awareness of sexual relations between women increases dramatically in the Roman period, as a detailed study of astrological texts, Greek love spells, Greek medical writings, ancient dream interpretation, and other sources reveals."[9]

Yet by leaving undisputed, both in this story and elsewhere in the *Metamorphoses*, Iphis's belief that her desires are entirely unprecedented, entirely new, Ovid's text colludes in what will become a staple trope of antilesbian Western discourse: newness. For example, in William Walsh's *A Dialogue Concerning Women, Being a Defence Of the Sex. Written to Eugenia* (1691), Misogynes (Woman-hater) informs Philogynes (Woman-lover) that "*Sappho*, as she was one of the wittiest Women that ever the World bred, so she thought with Reason it wou'd be expected she shou'd make some additions to a Science in which all Womankind had been so successful: What does she do then? Not content with our

Sex, she begins Amours with her own, and teaches us a new sort of Sin" (34). Such crediting of Sappho with the "invention" of lesbianism, a recurring theme in seventeenth- and eighteenth-century British writing (as Emma Donoghue discusses in *Passions Between Women*),[10] does not preclude—indeed goes hand in hand with—the simultaneous ascription of newness to lesbianism in the writer's own time and place. Thus in his *Vies des dames galantes*, after remarking that "It is said that Sappho of Lesbos was a very good mistress of this trade, indeed, they say, that she invented it, and that (ever) since the lesbian ladies have imitated her in it, and continued to this day; just as Lucian says: that such women are the women of Lesbos, who do not want to endure men, but approach other women just as men themselves (do)," Brantôme still feels compelled to account for lesbianism's existence among his contemporaries, and therefore soon adds, "In our France, such women are quite common, and yet it is said that they have not long been mixed up in it, even that the practice of it was brought from Italy by a lady of quality whom I will not name."[11]

According to Iphis, however, lesbian desire is not only new, it is also unprecedentedly strange and unnatural—even bestiality seems normal to her in comparison. The latter, she asserts, is still always heterosexual: Pasiphæ fell in love with a bull, but at least "They [were] male and female" (*femina nempe marem* [IX.737]). Her feelings for Ianthe, a female human being's love for another female human being, are "farre more full / Of uncouth fury!" (*meus est furiosior illo . . . amor* [IX.737–38]).

Above all, Iphis and Ovid treat her love as hopeless, her desires as impossible to fulfill. Not for the typical reasons, such as a watchful guardian, a jealous husband, a strict father, an unloving beloved. No, she and Ianthe are both unmarried, both in love, their fathers both approve, indeed are hurrying on, the match. The very gods have done all in their power to bring it about: "What they can give, the easie Gods afford" (*dique mihi faciles, quicquid valuere, dederunt* [IX.756]). But an unconquerable, unbending opponent makes this match impossible: "What me, my father, hers, her selfe, would please, / Displeaseth Nature; stronger then all these. / Shee, shee forbids" (*quodque ego, vult genitor, vult ipsa, socerque futurus. / at non vult natura, potentior omnibus istis, / quae mihi sola nocet* [IX.757–59]). Other characters in *The Metamorphoses* are willing, even able, to brave Nature. Iphis, however, seems not even to consider the possibility. She, and the story as a whole, ultimately treats lesbian sex as unnatural not merely in the sense of going against what Nature intended, but in a far more absolute sense as well: lesbian sex is an oxymoron, it cannot happen, it is literally, physically impossible.

Yet in a text premised upon the impossible happening—upon miraculous metamorphoses—an assertion of impossibility bears scrutiny. In this case, we are supposed to find believable or plausible (at least within the fictional realm of the poem) a goddess's transformation of a girl into a boy, but not two girls having sex. It's not hard to see that this assertion of lesbianism's impossibility is meant to conceal a rather glaring ideological faultline, or set of frequently overlapping, multiply intersecting faultlines, involving sex, gender, and sexuality.[12]

In a fundamentally patriarchal society such as Ovid's Rome, a society in which no binarism seems more fundamental and pervasive than man/woman, or masculine/feminine, love between men and women is inherently capable (although by no means assured) of adhering to the strictures imposed by dominant ideology, since clearly marked, hierarchical difference is built right in. Female masculinity violates this natural hierarchy, and so must be found out, fought, fixed.

Still, if lesbianism is so threatening, why is it treated so lightly by Ovid? For Anderson is right to argue for a humorous reading of "Iphis and Ianthe." He points out that the story's beginning, "The decision of the poor man that a female child must be exposed[,] constitutes one of the stock motifs of New Comedy" (466). And his characterization of Iphis's complaint as her "tearful, but untragic, soliloquy" is apt (469). As mentioned earlier, her belief in the utter uniqueness of her desires surely amused Ovid's original readers. And what Anderson calls her "argument from animals to men"—*nec vaccam vaccae, nec equas amor urit equarum: / urit oves aries, sequitur sua femina cervum. / sic et aves coeunt, interque animalia cuncia / femina femineo conrepta cupidine nulla est*—"[makes her] appear more witty than pathetic, so that we may enjoy this speech without engaging our emotions in this pseudo problem. The word order of 731 and 732, the five quick dactyls of 732, and the alliteration of 734 keep the tone light" (470). And, of course, all ends happily for her.

This happy ending unmistakably highlights the penis that is the focal point of "Iphis and Ianthe": the one Iphis lacks and eventually gains. Of course, this penis is never directly spoken of, not even at the moment of Iphis's transformation from girl to boy: "the mother left the temple; and Iphis walked beside her as she went, but with a longer stride than was her wont. Her face seemed of a darker hue, her strength seemed greater, her very features sharper, and her locks, all unadorned, were shorter than before. She seemed more vigorous than was her girlish wont. In fact, you who but lately were a girl are now a boy!"[13] Anderson asks us to "Note how Ovid delicately slides over the chief change by which Iphis became a man ready for marriage," contrasting this Ovidian delicacy with an earlier rendering of this scene: "Nicander was only interested in the miraculous new genitals" (473).[14] But delicate sliding notwithstanding, Ovid's version is no less genitalia-obsessed. The longer stride, the darker hue, the greater strength, the shorter hair

all serve as unmistakable signs of the all-important change that has occurred in Iphis's breeches (or the Cretan equivalent), the only change
that could fit her for marriage to Ianthe.[15]

This elaborate, tongue-in-cheek indirection—in which dirtiness is
twice as much fun for masquerading as delicacy—was to become, like
the tropes of invention and newness, a staple of Western homophobic
discourses. With its highly self-conscious, self-congratulatory pose of
knowingness—"You and I, dear Reader, are so worldly, so sophisti-
cated, we don't need these things spelled out. That would only rob us
of the fun of pretending to be naive!"—this is a particularly wily finish
for a story that has been premised upon and dedicated to *not* facing
facts, to preserving/constructing ignorance, to *unknowing*.[16] By simultaneously mocking and unknowing lesbianism, by treating it as both a
joke and an impossibility, "Iphis and Ianthe" does its part to seal over
the faultlines in the conservative sex/gender/sexuality ideology producing and being produced by *The Metamorphoses*. In other words (to answer the question I posed a few paragraphs above), it is *precisely because*
it is so threatening that lesbianism is treated lightly by Ovid, so lightly
that it seems not even to exist, or to exist only as impossible desire. For
if lesbianism is possible, if it's true, if it's real, then it erases, displaces,
dethrones the phallus. Even to acknowledge such a threat is to give it
power, to show that our account of "the way things are" is really an
account of "the way things ought to be," which is barely a step away
from "the way *we* think things ought to be," by which point the towering
absolute has shrunk to the merely relative, dwindled to an opinion, with
no greater claim to authority than anyone else's. Better far to unknow
such threats; after all, what we don't know can't hurt us.

III

Sometime in the early 1620s or 1630s, Henry Bellamy, a student at
Oxford, dramatized "Iphis and Ianthe," most likely for performance at
his college, St. John's.[17] Bellamy relies on Ovid's original story for the
basic plot of his play, *Iphis*, as well as for some of his language, but he
introduces innovations. Some are merely dramatic amplifications of the
Ovidian material: Ianthe becomes a full character, as does her father,
Telestes, who is only mentioned in "Iphis and Ianthe"; another passing
mention, Iphis's nurse, becomes a minor character, along with a mere
implication, Iphis and Ianthe's teacher. But as Freyman et al. point out,
"It is . . . in his creation of Nisus, would-be suitor to Ianthe and ultimate
comic villain, that Bellamy makes his most profound departure from
Ovid" (5). Nisus courts Ianthe, with Telethusa's encouragement, but

Ianthe rejects him. Telethusa then reveals the secret of Iphis's sex to Nisus and attempts to persuade him to transfer his love from Ianthe to Iphis. Her efforts backfire: he tries to stop the marriage by, as it were, "outing" Iphis at the altar. He is too late, however: the metamorphosis has already taken place. The laugh is on Nisus, the marriage proceeds, the play ends.

Bellamy's treatment of lesbianism sticks very close to Ovid's. He thus suggests, like Ovid, that Iphis and Ianthe are like twins. Telethusa, plotting to dupe Nisus into transferring his affections from Ianthe to Iphis, predicts that "Ianthe's faithful suitor, who just now raised her to heaven with deserved praise, deceived by my fraud, will seize Iphis with tender arms. Because a like blush adorns their cheeks and a like beauty brightens their eyes, an alluring grace smiles from the face of each; . . . the fool will think that she is his and will rush headlong upon the false Ianthe. Who cannot fool the eyes of the gullible?" (93).[18] The plan works momentarily: Nisus at first mistakes Iphis for Ianthe, at least until he gets close enough to kiss her.

Bellamy also repeats much of Iphis's lament, altering it mainly by giving a few of the lines to Iphis's mother:

Iphis.   Harsh divinity! I live in misery, destined not to die a common death. A strange end awaits me, a strange fate. Never does a woman set passion aflame in another woman, except in my case. Phoebus, although a prophet, has never known such a thing.

Telethusa.   Illustrious Pasiphae, daughter of the knowing Sun, desired a bull, a female desiring a male. But, unhappy one, your love is more outrageous. She acquired what she sought; she obtained her wishes.

Iphis: Even if Daedalus should fly back on his wings, could he change me or delicate Ianthe by his arts?
                (97)[19]

Because of the assignment of some of the lines to Telethusa, the presentation of lesbian desire as completely unprecedented, as well as impossible to fulfill, reads less clearly than in Ovid as a humorous comment on Iphis's innocence/ignorance (although it's possible both mother and daughter are being presented here as naive and sheltered). In any case, in *Iphis*, even more so than in "Iphis and Ianthe," the lament's construction of lesbianism ought not to be understood as evidence of the author or the text's inability to imagine lesbian sex as possible. In "Iphis and Ianthe" the lament's assertions are contradicted by numerous other texts of Ovid's time; in *Iphis* they are contradicted by evidence from within the text itself. In the final scene, Nisus condemns rather than unknows lesbianism, declaring, "Iphis is a woman! Does any god join tender women on the same marriage bed? You are deceived. The gods greatly fear this unspeakable evil" (109).[20] Forbiddenness, rather than impossibility, is the key concept here. ("Unspeakability" is the transla-tors' not inappropriate addition: although literally claiming impossibil-ity—such and such *cannot* be named or put into words—in practice "unspeakable" underlines forbiddenness—such and such *ought not* to be spoken.) The fact that the desperate, spurned comic villain utters these words does not invalidate them. They are humorous, but their humor derives from Nisus's ignorance of Iphis's sex-change. His declaration that Iphis is a woman is now untrue. His characterization of lesbianism, however, although irrelevant in the new circumstances, is accurate ac-cording to the play's ethos. He is clearly voicing its dominant ideology. Nothing in the play suggests that were Iphis revealed to be still a girl, the other characters would react with anything but horror and condem-nation—it is this fact that is the sine qua non of the scene's humor.

Another Ovidian element repeated in *Iphis* is its deceptive critique of paternal tyranny. As Freyman et al. observe, Bellamy uses Ianthe's father Telestes "as a foil to Lygdus . . . [,] contrast[ing] the extreme reaction of Lygdus to the possible birth of a daughter to the loving re-sponse of Telestes to the actual birth of a daughter, and . . . counter-point[ing] the insistence of Telestes that Ianthe must approve of her future husband with the demand of Lygdus that Iphis must marry whether or not he [Iphis] approves" (4). Yet despite this apparent cri-tique, piety rather than paternal authority is the issue in Bellamy's de-piction of Lygdus. He is "a pious man of modest means" (Freyman, et a., 4) tortured by the prospect of financial ruin and familial suffering should his child turn out to be a girl. His opening soliloquy invites com-passion, as he struggles to figure out what to do: "But, behold, my mind swells; I am drawn this way and that. Burning pain orders that a female child be destroyed, although piety forbids this. Pain sets piety to flight and piety drives out pain. Thus I am borne upon a rising sea, and I, fool that I am, do not know what I shall do" (64).[21] Certainly, once Lygdus has decided that his child, if female, must die, and once we see him per-sisting in this decision despite his wife's fervent supplications, we feel increasingly less sympathy for him.[22] Yet the play soon lets him off the hook. As Freyman et al. point out, "the emergence of Nisus as comic villain . . . softens the unpleasant side of Lygdus's nature and gives the characters, and the audience, someone other than Lygdus to reject" (6). In the end, it is Nisus, not Lygdus, who gets a comeuppance.

There is one moment, though, when Lygdus feels he is being pun-ished, and it centers upon *Iphis*'s most important thematic deviation from "Iphis and Ianthe," although not from *The Metamorphoses* as a whole: Iphis's effeminacy. From the first moment Iphis appears on-stage, "his" failure to behave like a man is emphasized. "You know nothing manly, nothing strong," his Teacher scolds. "The things which you can do are unbecoming to men. You should be running over rocks and coursing over the sea. Why are you amazed at the thought of these things?" (83; *Quod nil viril, nil sapis validum. Viris / Sunt indecora quae potes: rupes, fretum / Superare cursu te decet. Cur haec stupes?* [III.iv.498–500]). Yet the Teacher is actually quite tolerant, defending Iphis against his father's angry disapproval by characterizing the effeminate boy as a mistake of nature, and hence beyond human power to change: "Lygdus," he explains, "nature sins, not they themselves. Iphis, although not taught, sings. His spirit, although worked on, shudders at manly arts; and he pursues soft trifles although the arms of Achilles are given to him" (84; *Natura peccat Lygde, non ipsi. Cani / Non doctus Iphis: horret, excultus licet, / Artes viriles animus; et molles tricas, / Quamvis Achillis arma tradantur petit* [III.v.516–19]). Lygdus is not calmed by this reasoning. On the contrary, he bewails his misfortune: "O just punishment from heaven! The evil answers the fault, and the punishment fits the crime in every way. My mind impudently wished for a male child, almost demanding it. It has what it wishes (o sorrow!), but it is a male heart filled with a female spirit. Will Crete, already known for such things, always bring forth new monstrosities?" (85)[23] At this moment at least, Lygdus seems to be punished for his impiety. Even more importantly, his refusal to accept any deviation from the norms of masculinity seems implicitly to be criticized. The text, like the Teacher, appears to defend effeminacy, using arguments that, interestingly, would come to be used as "defenses" of male homosexuality in the mid-nineteenth to mid-twentieth century: However strange, even freakish, the fact seems, and indeed is, Nature sometimes puts a female soul in a male body; when this is the case, we must let things be (of course, we can only determine that this is the case by repeatedly attempting, and failing, to masculinize the boy).

Yet this (pathologizing) tolerance for gender deviance is not, in fact, ultimately supported by the text. Bellamy makes the plot-resolving metamorphosis at the play's end as much a gender-change as a sex-change, with Iphis commenting at least as much upon his mental and emotional as upon his physical transformation:

What new strength wanders through my awestruck breast? What blood flows in my heart? Scarcely am I in possession of myself! A great seething boils within me. My strong feet are eager to trample troops slain by swords in warfare; my hand desires to brandish torches and fierce swords. My eyes dart fire; my hair flows loosely down. . . .

And I am changing totally. Does someone order unwilling hands to destroy the cowardly form of this face? Goodbye to the tricks of my former countenance. Put on virile wrinkles, a shaggy visage; be a Cretan man! What my former spirit shuddered at my bold spirit now encourages. Nothing does it fear, except fear. (106)[24]

In "Iphis and Ianthe," gender is assumed to follow sex. Consequently, Iphis's initial lack and then possession of a penis is the focus of textual interest. Concern that a person fully equipped with a penis might nonetheless *not* behave in a properly masculine fashion (might, for instance, choose to put an orifice rather than the appendage to use) is repressed and displaced, expressed only obliquely, through other tales in the *Metamorphoses*. But in Bellamy's play, such anxieties are made explicit. Not just the person, but the person's body must be shown to have the properly gendered emotions: "My strong feet are eager . . . ; my hand desires. . . ." Sex and gender must be shown to be indivisible. "I am changing totally," Iphis announces.

One might argue, of course, that this focus on mental and emotional metamorphosis is simply a practical dramatic expedient: a change in the character's internal state requires no change in the actor's costume or makeup, much less in his actual physical body.[25] But up until this moment, the audience knew it was watching a male actor portray a female character. Why would such an audience nevertheless demand realistic, visible evidence of the character's physical sex-change? It wouldn't. The metamorphosis passage addresses a problem in ideology, not stagecraft. It attempts to shore up a dominant sex/gender/sexuality construct, all the while refusing to admit the construct needs any such support.

I should be more precise, however, when I speak of a dominant sex/gender/sexuality construct, because *Iphis* is not concerned with sex, gender, and sexuality in general, but only with masculinity. Despite the supposedly monstrous possibility that one woman might love and desire, let alone have sex with, another, the textual attention Bellamy devotes to this frightening prospect is relatively minimal and derived wholly from Ovid—in other words, it is perfunctory. In contrast, he lavishes creative energy on the subject of masculinity and effeminacy. Indeed, effeminacy effectively replaces lesbianism as the wrong that must be set right during the course of the play, as when, in the passage quoted above, Lygdus rhetorically asks, "Will Crete, already known for such things, always bring forth new monstrosities?" (*Nova / Semperne monstra nota iam Crete feret?*) The wording—the use of *monstra*, the focus on Cretan tales—obviously recalls the opening lines of "Iphis and Ianthe"—"The story of this unnatural passion would, perhaps, have been the talk of Crete's hundred towns, if Crete had not lately had a wonder of its own in the changed form of Iphis" (*Fama novi centum Creteas Forsitan urbes / implesset monstri, si non miracula nuper / Iphide mutata Crete propiora tulisset* [ll. 666–68]) — except with effeminacy as the wonder/monstrosity in question.

In another work, such a substitution might reasonably be read as evidence that lesbianism is *more* threatening, ideologically speaking, than effeminacy, the obvious fear of the latter masking a deeper, unacknowledgeable fear of the former, a thematic ruse James Creech neatly characterizes (in a discussion of male homosexuality vs. incest as the unnameable subject of Melville's *Pierre*) when he writes, "we might do well to recall the warning that the French post next to the trickiest railroad crossings: 'One train can hide another' " (85). And yet, if this were the case in *Iphis*, how would we explain Nisus's explicit acknowledgment of lesbianism in the final scene, his condemnation of it as forbidden? Unlike its Ovidian source, Bellamy's play, rather than camouflaging a deeply panicked reaction to lesbianism with a more manageable concern about effeminacy, does seem to be more genuinely worried about the latter than the former, more concerned about men's behavior than women's — which really isn't all that surprising, considering that *Iphis* was written by an Oxford student to be performed by and for other members of his college. In such an all-male setting, devoted to the formation of ruling-class men, the question of the proper way to be a man finds its way to the center of a great many endeavors. And considering that in *The Metamorphoses* masculinity and effeminacy are implicitly linked, through related stories, to "Iphis and Ianthe," Bellamy's foregrounding of it is as much an imitation of as a departure from his Ovidian model.

Not that Bellamy could prevent his play from affording unsanctioned pleasures and meanings to dissident performers, audience members, and readers.[26] For instance, the fact that the actors playing Iphis and Ianthe kiss during the marriage ceremony at the end of *Iphis* certainly offered the possibility of transgressive pleasure for them and/or for homoerotically inclined audience members, as did, for boys or men attracted to effeminacy or femininity, the spectacle of male actors performing effeminate/feminine characters throughout the play. Yet any such homoerotic or gender-transgressive pleasure is clearly marked by the text as illicit. The play's insistence on the horrors of effeminacy and the glories of a decidedly bloodthirsty masculinity (think of Iphis's metamorphosis speech) may or may not read as a rather panicked defense against precisely such pleasures, pleasures well-nigh inseparable from all-male theatrics; I'd read it this way. But panicked or not, the text is clearly defensive.[27]

IV

In Charles Hopkins's *Friendship Improv'd; Or, The Female Warriour. A Tragedy* (perf. 1699; pub. 1700), a man in love with a woman passing as a man wishes aloud that his beloved be transformed into a woman. But here the beloved responds, "Those Metamorphoses, alas! are past" (I, 10).[28] The line seems to explain the genesis of the play, as if Hopkins's reworking of Ovid's tale derives from the question, "If a metamorphosis, a sex-change, is no longer a possibility, how can the story of Iphis and Ianthe still be told?"[29] The answer (at least for Hopkins) is to make Iphis fall in love with a man rather than a woman. The obstacle to their love will therefore be removed, rather than revealed, once her true sex is made known. No physical transformation will be needed. But as we shall see, if Hopkins all but banishes physical impossibility from his play, he more than makes up for the loss by a marked increase in ideological impossibility.[30]

Hopkins's alterations of "Iphis and Ianthe" are far more drastic than Bellamy's. The story is now set in Sicily. The Ligdus character is called Zoilus, and he is the country's usurper, having killed its rightful ruler, Orontes, twenty years earlier. His wife is named Semanthe, and his daughter, secretly raised as a boy, Locris. Locris is in love with her father's general, Maherbal, who, unbeknownst to everyone, including himself, is Orontes's son Araxes. Maherbal clearly loves Locris, and wishes they could somehow be more than just "friends" (hence the play's title, *Friendship Improv'd*). At Zoilus's command, Locris is soon to be married to Orontes's daughter, Orythia, and Maherbal to Locris's older sister, Cyllene. Both Orythia and Cyllene love their husbands-to-be.

Friendship Improv'd focuses upon and condemns the abuse of paternal authority. Zoilus, the tyrant, is both a bad *pater familias* and a bad *pater patris*. His vaunting ambition—his refusal to accept the existing dispositions of power in the world, to accept his place in the divinely ordained hierarchy, to submit to the paternal authority of his rightful king—is the ultimate cause of all the plot conflicts: it leads him to usurp the kingship of Sicily, thus disordering the political realm, and to value a male heir so highly he threatens to kill his own child if it's a girl, thus disordering the familial realm. (That Maherbal and Locris eventually fall in love only reinforces this complete blending of the political and familial.) His tyrannical behavior also precipitates the play's immediate action, as he attempts to force Locris and Maherbal to marry the women he has chosen for them.

And yet, like Bellamy's version, Hopkins's retelling reproduces rather than resists the ideology of the Ovidian original. As the play progresses, Zoilus is supplanted as chief villain by his daughter Cyllene, her villainy the direct result of her active female heterosexual desire. Rather than wait for Maherbal to speak first, she has already confessed her passionate feelings to him (II, 18). Even worse, despite rejection, she proceeds to woo him ever more fiercely, her resolve neatly summed up in the words, "Down then the strugling [*sic*] Woman in my Breast, / I'll forfeit Modesty to purchase Rest" (II, 22). A woman without modesty is no longer a woman, she is a monster. Cyllene accordingly becomes monstrous. Turned down yet again by Maherbal, she resolves to make him fear "the Revenge of a rejected Maid" (III, 31) and instigates his arrest. Although she then balks at the prospect of his death, and helps Locris engineer his escape (pointing out to the latter, and to the audience, "The mad Effects of Women's Passion . . . , / How they can Love and Hate at once" [IV, 36]), when she learns that Locris is really a girl, and that Maherbal and this girl are in love, Cyllene gives herself over entirely to hatred, imagining herself, and prompting us to imagine her, a veritable demon, as in the following soliloquy:

> Now leap my ravish'd Heart, now mount my Soul,
> And each extended Arm grasp either Pole.
> Reach yonder Starry roof, and Chrystal Spheres,
> And shew the Gods a Genius great as theirs.
> Then downwards drive, search the deep Plots of Hell,
> And learn if Women, or if Feinds excel.
> Make Fate with industry thy task pursue,
> For thou hast set it work enough to do.
> If half tir'd Furies at their toyl repine,
> Give them new Fury; Woman, give them thine.
>
> (V, 50)

She is the living embodiment of the saying "Hell hath no fury like a woman scorned."[31] Sexual desire, it is clear, is the root of all female evil.[32]

The play's misogyny extends further, however. Not only does Cyllene replace Zoilus as the chief villain, she is made responsible for his worst crimes. When he becomes truly tyrannical toward Locris and Maherbal, Cyllene turns out to be responsible, having stirring up "his Passion" against them (IV, 34). When he later kills Semanthe, Cyllene drives him to it (V, 49), after boasting of her matricidal (and sororicidal) intentions: "Fly all respect of Nature and her Laws, / 'Tis Nature bids Revenge in such a Cause. / Mother, and Sister shall my Victims fall, / And universal Ruine swallow all" (V, 48). Moreover Zoilus, bad as he is, eventually begins to feel remorse for his deeds (v, 48). Indeed, after killing his wife, he kills himself, unable to bear "the sting / Of Conscience giv[ing] at last the secret Wound" (V, 52). In contrast, Cyllene hasn't a shred of humanity left by this point; she has become entirely evil and remains so to the extravagantly bitter end. When her attempt to stab Locris fails, she turns the dagger on herself, and dies cursing her sister:

> Gods! tho' on him [Maherbal] your Blessings you conferr,
> Be Just by halves—heap Plagues—heap Hell on her.
> Soon may she Die—shall that poor Curse suffice?—
> Long may she Live, long slighted, e're she dies.
> May she most Vertuous be, most chastly good,
> But he believe her most abandon'd lewd!
> Then may this flourishing, yet happy she
> Die thus Desdain'd, thus in Dispair like me.   [*Dies.*]
>
> (V, 55)

The substance of the curse is significant. The worst thing a woman can be believed to be is "most abandon'd lewd," a fact of which Cyllene herself is dying proof: Her uncontrollable desire for Maherbal makes her the text's arch-villain, eclipsing her murderous tyrant of a father.

As often happens, the play attempts to disavow its ideological nastiness; in fact, it would have us believe it an *anti*misogynist text. It does so by first depicting both Zoilus and Maherbal as blatant misogynists, then condemning the former and reforming the latter. Thus Zoilus at one point philosophizes, "In vain with life-long Trouble we contend, / Where women are concern'd, it cannot end. / On them we lavish our unhappy Life, / The Mistress plagues us first, and then the Wife" (II, 13). He later communicates his views on women more succinctly, calling Semanthe "Traytress, Viper, Monster, Woman, Wife!" (V, 51; see also I, 8). For his part, Maherbal focuses upon women's voracious and duplicitous sexuality, advising his "friend" Locris:

> Believe me, Youth, who know what Women are,
> The Sex was never worth a Soldier's Care.
> Hard to be won, inconstant when obtain'd,
> Like new forc'd Towns, lost with more Ease than gain'd.
> The foolish Bridegroom makes the Nuptial Feast,
> But he that gives the Banquet shares the least.
> Safe in that State, to worst Extreams they fall,
> They wed but one, their Wishes are for all.
>
> (I, 11)

Zoilus is a villain, and the woman he derides, Semanthe, a loving mother. His words are thus to be understood as further evidence of his evil-mindedness. Maherbal, however, is a hero. He must therefore be made to recant his misogyny. The eventual sight of Locris's bared breast, which reveals her true sex to him, elicits this recantation, in the form of an extravagant, fourteen-line paean to Woman, source of the soldier's courage, theme of the poets' words and prophets' dreams (V, 47). The play, we are meant to conclude, opposes misogyny.

Yet Maherbal's new sentiments prove to be the flip side of the same old sexist coin. Women—at least good ones—are mere objects in his enlightened view of the sexes: women inspire, men act (which means that active women, like Cyllene, are bad). As the play concludes, Maherbal, now identified as Araxes, proceeds to treat them accordingly. Although he had once declared, "He tyrannizes most o're human Life, / Who would, against our Will, impose a Wife" (III, 28), Araxes, at the end of the play, orders Orythia to marry a young man he wishes to reward, telling her, "On that brave Youth you must your Love bestow, / For you can Rival me no longer now" (V, 55). He does not give her the option of remaining single now that her beloved Locris is unattainable, nor even allow her to voice her reaction to the news that her husband-to-be is actually a woman and is about to be married to someone else. Orythia's wishes and feelings are irrelevant to him. And to the text: she has no more lines in the play. Araxes, meanwhile, appears to have forgotten his recent conversion to philogyny, for he sums up Cyllene's horrifying end with the following observation:

> What sad extreams make most of Women's Fate,
> Raging with love, relentless in their hate:
> Successive passions in their turns prevail,
> Less fair their Person's [*sic*], than their tempers frail.
>
> (V, 55)

Only a short while ago he had declared to Locris that "The gods for your Creation we adore / But still we Worship you their Creatures more" (V, 47). Now, in one of the oldest ideological oscillations known to man—Woman is Angel, Woman is Devil—he paints Cyllene as the rule rather than the exception where females are concerned.

Araxes oscillates once again a few minutes later, and in this final reversal displays the literally stupefying ability of dominant ideology to unknow whatever might contradict it. When Locris momentarily swoons at the sight of her parents' dead bodies, Araxes comforts her with the assurance, "You shall not grieve alone, my Charming Fair, / Give me your Sorrows, or at least my share; / Too soon your Sex is with your woes opprest, / Which would sit better in a manly Breast" (V, 56). He and the text have forgotten, have unknown, that throughout the play, up until the moment Locris revealed her true sex to him, she too was a soldier, a "fearless Hero in the Field," and "tho' a Maid, [had] a Manly Heart" (I, 5). Nurture had triumphed over Nature (Locris was "bred up to wield / The Shining Sword, to lift the pondrous Shield" [5]). The text seemed to approve of this gender reversal, to take pleasure in it and to invite the audience to do the same. Indeed, the play's subtitle, *The Female Warriour*, advertises female manliness as one of its main attractions.

But everything changes when Locris bares her breast. As if magically—or rather, as if naturally—Maherbal converts from misogyny to philogyny, delivering his panegyric on womanhood. And as if with equal inevitability, as if hailed irresistably by sexist ideology, Locris accepts normative femininity. "Here all the Warfare of my life is o'er," she declares, "And I must play the Man's great part no more" (V, 47). In addition to the double meaning of "the Man's great part" (both the masculine role and the anatomical equipment needed for playing it, both of which together equal the phallus), the ambiguity of "must" in this sentence—does Locris mean "I no longer have to" or "I no longer am allowed to"?—is fitting. Locris loved warfare and bids it a very fond, almost regretful, extended farewell (thirteen lines long, with nine repetitions of "Farewel"). As she does so, the text itself renounces the pleasures of gender-transgression. From here on in, what was wrong will be made right, what was crooked will be made straight. And lest the text's earlier enjoyment of female masculinity provoke guilt, now that such pleasures have been renounced, Cyllene will be scapegoated for this sin as well. Standing by the newly dead body of her father, she says, "Farewel, great soul; and now farewel all Fear, / I am thy Offspring, and thy Spirit's heir" (v, 53). The repetitions of 'Farewel' draw attention to the substitution occurring: Locris has just bid a lengthy farewell to gender-transgression; Cyllene now embraces it, usurping a son's place as heir. As a sexually aggressive woman, Cyllene was already masculinized. In case we didn't get the point, we now learn she's a woman with a man's spirit. She thus takes the rap for gender-transgression, as she earlier took it for paternal tyranny.

By killing off Cyllene, turning "The Female Warriour" into a fainting woman, and silencing Orythia, Hopkins expunges any remaining traces of female masculinity from the play. My inclusion of Orythia as an example of female masculinity may seem strange, but she has after all been passionately in love with another woman. Of course, Orythia didn't know Locris was a woman.[33] Nor is there reason to believe she would have continued to love Locris once the latter's true sex had been revealed. On the contrary, Locris earlier reassures herself, and us, "[Orythia's Passion] will be cur'd as soon as I am known" (II, 16). Hopkins will not admit the merest trace of the possibility of a woman loving another woman. In his play, lesbian desire, let alone lesbian sex, doesn't even exist. It is at most an illusion, and thus likened (in a soliloquy by Locris), not to Iphis's passion for Ianthe, but to Narcissus's self-love:

> —What an odd fortune must I hourly prove,
> A Woman still prest with a Woman's Love;
> *Narcissus* like, the Love-sick Nymph betray'd,
> Pursues, and woes [*sic*] her own deceitful Shade;
> She Follows that in following of a Maid.

(II, 14)

A love so insubstantial—an unknown love, actively imagined as insubstantial—poses no risk to dominant practices or ideologies. And yet the play's final, bizarrely harsh treatment of Orythia perhaps registers the very fear about lesbianism it otherwise seeks to unknow: that love between women could indeed rival love between women and men.

The play has not been concerned solely with sex/gender/sexuality transgression in women, however. It devotes equal, and equally schizoid, attention to, flirts with and then recoils from, male homosexuality. But not just any male homosexuality. The text constructs, and then cures, a hypermasculine, misogynist male homosexuality.

The issue is raised in the first exchange between Maherbal and Locris, when their weddings have been indefinitely postponed because of the outbreak of war (I have provided an unusually lengthy excerpt, since the play is little known and the passage so surprising):

> *Ma.* . . . The Clash and din of War your Soul delight,
> And you love Glory gain'd in open Fight,
> More than the secret Pleasures of the Night.
> By Heav'n, I swear, when *Hymen*'s sacred Tye
> Was broke abruptly off; a suddain Joy
> Sprung in my Soul, and yet I knew not why.
>   *Lo.* My Thoughts no other End but Fame pursue,
> To fight, to conquer, or to dye with you.
> Young as I am, I love a glorious Field,
> More than the Bliss my charming Bride could yeild.
> Thou art the Center where my Wishes joyn,
> My Fame, my Friendship, and my Soul is thine.
> Your very Sight transports me, for I see
> My Champion and my Genius move in thee.
>   *Ma.* I love you with a Fondness far above
> All that was ever known in Woman's love.
> My Friend—Oh! whither would my Transport tend?
> Can I say more than what I say? my Friend!
> Something there is beyond that very Name,

Something that sets my Spirits in a Flame,
I wish I were a Maid of Form divine,
To make your Soul and Body ever mine.
Rather I wish that you, dear Youth, could be
That charming Maid to be belov'd by me.
Friendship alone to wond'rous Heights may soar,
The change of one of us would make it more.
    Lo. Those Metamorphoses, alas! are past,
Could Wishes do, mine should not be the last.
But from our Theme our Thoughts are wander'd far,
We talk of Love, when we were bent for War.
And yet your Words such tender Passion move,
That I could ever talk with you of Love.
    Ma. Had not your Arms establish'd your Renown,
Were not your vast Exploits and Valour known,
By those sweet Looks, that charming Face betray'd,
My sight would all my other Sence invade,
And make me think you, what I wish, a Maid.
Oft have I entertain'd that pleasing Thought,
Till my Mistake your manly Actions taught,
And spight of them destroy'd the hopes I sought.
    Lo. Were I that Maid, already so intire,
My Love is grown, it never could aspire,
To a more Sacred or Cœlestial Fire.
My Friendship has attain'd to that Excess,
Fond as she is, my Sister loves you less.
But hark, . . . Trumpets and Drums summon their Chiefs away,
Who want *Maherball* [*sic*] to begin the day.
    Ma. Then farewell Love, leave all those empty Joys,
To longing Maids, and to deluded Boys.

                          (I, 9–11)

Maherbal is, and Locris is pretending to be, the man of war, intensely
bonded to other men, contemptuous of women (Maherbal's misogynist
remarks, discussed earlier, conclude the exchange). Locris's feelings are
perfectly acceptable: she knows she is a woman in love with a man.
Maherbal's feelings are decidedly problematic: His feelings are identical
to Locris's, yet he believes they are directed toward a man (or at least a
youth). How does the text handle this danger?

Above all, by unknowing. Maherbal and the text stress his inability
to articulate or even to imagine the precise implications of his love for
Locris. Joy sprang into his soul when the weddings were postponed,
"yet [he] knew not why." He wonders "whither . . . [his] Transport[s]
tend?" He senses that "Something there is beyond" friendship, but
doesn't name that "Something." Or rather he names it — "To make [Lo-

cris's] Soul and Body ever his," to share sex as well as feelings with his friend—only when he imagines one of them transformed into a woman. "Friendship Improv'd" is friendship with sex, which the text would have us believe necessarily requires a man and a woman. What it steadfastly refuses even to consider is the possibility the same result could be achieved between two men.

Sex between men, with or without friendship, would be sodomy. And sodomy, which ever since the medieval Church "invented" the concept had been conceived of as a malignancy requiring extirpation, was, with the growth of and reaction to molly-house culture in late-seventeenth-century northwestern Europe, becoming inextricably associated with effeminacy.[34] Maherbal, at the turn of the eighteenth century, immediately runs that risk, even though he is a triumphantly heroic soldier whose masculinity ought to be beyond question.

Not that all effeminacy was equally negative. In the Renaissance, the man considered effeminate because of homosexual activity was despised, even hated. But the man considered effeminate because of excessive heterosexual activity was as likely to be admired as criticized. Being a man's man may have been a cultural ideal, but being a ladies' man came in for its share of praise. This tolerance and even admiration for heterosexual effeminacy continued into the Restoration. Thus Maherbal can indulge in the startling fantasy of being a woman ("I wish I were a Maid of Form divine"), because it's in the service of heterosexual love and sex ("To make your Soul and Body ever mine"). His momentary, fantasmatic gender-transgression is excused by heterosexual desire, as is the equally fantasmatic gender-transgression of any men in the audience identifying with him.

The exculpatory powers of heterosexual desire extend even further here, for such desire is used to explain—to explain *away*—not only an imaginary sex-change, but also what would otherwise have to be recognized as sodomitical desire. Maherbal is not a sodomite because we know, intuitively, that he knows, intuitively, that Locris is really a girl. We're sure he wouldn't feel these desires for an actual man, only for a woman disguised as a man. (Whether he would have felt them for a woman *not* disguised as a man is a question we'll consider in a moment.) One might say that he, or rather his heart/penis, has X-ray vision, a special heterosexual power to penetrate disguise to the true sex underneath. To be even more precise, perhaps this is not just a heterosexual power but a hetero*male* power, as my use of the word "penetrate" suggests, since Orythia doesn't seem to possess it. If she did, we would have to perceive her as a tribade, since we would know, intuitively, that she knows, intuitively, that her beloved is really a girl. Instead, whereas Locris's concealed sex excuses Maherbal's desire, her displayed gender excuses Orythia's. Despite her silencing at the play's end, she is not portrayed as a tribade.[35]

As for whether Maherbal would have fallen in love with a woman not disguised as a man, the passage we've been examining would have us believe so. Maherbal says he was attracted "By those sweet Looks, that charming Face," the sight of which "would make [him] think [her], what [he] wish[ed], a Maid." These fancies, these "hopes," are then habitually "destroy'd" by Locris's "manly Actions." Yet a later passage suggests otherwise. There, Maherbal, once again rejecting Cyllene's advances, describes the only relationship that attracts him: soldierly comradeship. With feigned regret he declares:

> Would you were a Man to make a Friend. . . .
> Then should we never part, but side by side,
> Thro' broken Ranks in batter'd Armour ride.
> Urge on our foaming Horses o're the slain,
> And pant with noble Toyl along the Plain.
> Our chief Concern should for each other be,
> I guarding you, and you defending me.
> Shielding from either's Head the falling Blow,
> So should we live, —*Locris* and I live so.
>
> (II, 21)

Granted, Maherbal is playing up the manly-man-who-doesn't-like-women act in order to let Cyllene down more easily, let her save face. But his description of battle seems unduly erotic, with its riding, panting, and foaming side by side, never to part. And it recalls the opening of his exchange with Locris, his praising the latter's preference for soldiery over "the secret Pleasures of the Night" (with women, that is). I would thus argue that, his remarks about Locris's prettiness notwithstanding, Maherbal is attracted as well by the latter's valiant masculinity, displayed in wartime male friendship. Officially, of course, there's nothing wrong with men enjoying battle together; on the contrary, it's the most "natural" thing in the world. But in this ideologically conservative play, any homoeroticism is potentially perilous, likely to cause anxiety, and thus necessitate counterbalancing by further "proofs" of the characters' heteromasculinity.

Which is why, only a few pages later, we learn that Maherbal was warned against marriage by his foster-father Archias, against the "Charms" of "Syren Women" in general and those of Cyllene in particular (III, 24). His coldness, even antipathy, toward women is thus not innate. Indeed, blocked by paternal command from their normal target, his sexual desires have nevertheless located a woman he can love, even if he doesn't know it.

Yet even this reassuring bit of information seems insufficient to guard against homophobic anxiety, and so the text labors on, trying to banish the notion that Maherbal's desires for Locris are sodomitical. It does so by excessively proliferating the obstacles to the confession, let alone fulfilment, of Maherbal and Locris's love. Already, from the start, Hopkins has overdone things in this respect, as when he has Locris lament:

> I love a Man, from whom I hide my Fires,
> And with my Sex conceal my fond Desires.
> A Man, a Stranger, whom no Kindred claim,
> Of Parentage obscure, tho' known to Fame.

(II, 16–17)

In most plays, the heroine's need to conceal her true sex would suffice as the obstacle in the path of true love that must and will be overcome by-story's end. Here though, an additional impediment, inequality of birth, is immediately added. Although Locris resolves never to let this second obstacle stand in her way (since by marrying Maherbal she can raise him to her level, or indeed above it, making him "[her] . . . and [her] Empire's Lord" [17]), it eventually becomes a nonissue when Maherbal's royal parentage is revealed. Locris's sex-disguise ought then to be the sole barrier to her love's fulfillment. But it is not: the revelation that Maherbal is Araxes turns Locris and her beloved into mortal enemies, since she is heir to the usurper who murdered his father. "Is he I Love *Araxes*? — " Locris cries. "Ah! since he is, he never can be mine" (V, 42). In the space of a single soliloquy, however, Locris overcomes this obstacle as well, vowing to resign her crown and empire to Maherbal, as she has already resigned her heart. Once again, we seem back to a single, easily removable obstruction. And once again, the text introduces another.

Or rather, the text reintroduces the obstruction we thought had just been banished: the hatred between the houses of Orontes and Zoilus. For although Locris is willing to sacrifice family loyalty to love, Maherbal is not. His honor, he believes, demands that he henceforth treat his dearest friend as his bitterest foe. Introduction or reintroduction, the effect is the same: the protagonists' love remains doubly impeded.

This time, however, the implausibility—worse, the injustice—of Maherbal's attitude and behavior makes the impediment's superfluity rather glaring. At worst, Maherbal ought to be struggling between conflicting claims on his honor: family loyalty versus loyalty to a friend. But despite his protestations that Locris has "wrong'd [his] Honour" (V, 43), he seems motivated by something else in his implacable determination to cast off his beloved companion in arms (who, moreover, has just betrayed his/her own father by rescuing their "Houses mortal Foe" from prison [V, 42]). Even when, in response to Maherbal's objection that "A Crown divides us," Locris asserts, "Here our diff'rence ends, / Divide the Crown; that should not sep'rate Friends," Maherbal refuses to make peace: "Crowns will admit no Rivals," he retorts, "I'll resign / Not the least Jewel that enriches mine" (V, 45). We therefore agree with Locris when s/he accuses the "Poor man" of being "with Frenzy, and Ambition lost" (45). He seems not only ready but almost eager for the two of them to cross swords in a battle to the death.

Taking the excessive impediment of Locris and Maherbal's love to new, almost fatal lengths — the two actually draw their swords — this last barrier, so unnecessary, so unbelievable, seems to cry out, "Ideological Faultline!" The text's production of obstacles seems compulsive, hysterical, as if serving some purpose other than the ostensible, rather ordinary one of keeping the hero and heroine apart until the end of the story. This other purpose, I would argue, is to defend against the horror the text has come too close to representing: sodomitical love. The overabundance of obstacles, of forbiddenness factors, substitutes for this unmentioned, unknown one, itself a substitution for the female homosexuality at the center of "Iphis and Ianthe," which Hopkins has rewritten.[36]

In the end, the long-delayed moment when all obstacles to Locris and Maherbal's love are removed, combined with the additional contradictions and incoherences this moment immediately produces, furthers the sense of unacknowledged ideological strain. Letting his "Rage . . . have its course," Maherbal is ready to battle Locris. Then she offers him her "bare Breast" to strike with his sword. In an instant, his rage vanishes, replaced by love, repentance, and forgiveness. Prepared to kill Locris for being Zoilus's son, he now not only absolves the daughter of responsibility for the father's crimes ("Thou wert not guilty of my Father's blood"), but even feels capable of forgiving the father for the daughter's sake ("for thy sake I could, I doubt, forgive / His woeful Fate, and let thy Father live" [V, 46]). Rather than reproach Maherbal for not having chosen love over vengeance when he thought her male, Locris actually takes responsibility for his murderous fury, claiming, "I wrought your rage, high as I could to see / That if (when known) I might forgiven be, / And then concluded you could Love like me" (46). Even worse, although Maherbal earlier made clear his "friendship" for Locris was actually romantic love, identical to her feelings for him, Locris — and through her the text — rewrites their earlier exchanges by declaring, "*Maherbal* was my Friend, *Araxes* loves" (47).

It is tempting to try to smooth out these contradictions. One might thus recall/imagine that even when Maherbal and Locris were companions in arms, their relationship was an unequal one: his having been older, the commanding officer, and (if he is to be believed) having "more oft preserv'd [Locris's] Life . . . / And Sheilded [him/her] in a more dang'rous strife" (44) might explain his inability to continue their friendship after s/he reverses or negates its power differential by rescuing him from Zoilus's dungeon. Before, what must have felt to him (consciously or unconsciously) like homoerotic desires, were nonetheless tolerable (if uneasily so), since they were directed, in time-honored, semiapproved fashion, toward a pretty, androgynous, subordinate youth; now, when this youth turns the tables, or at least becomes his equal, he has no choice but to fight his former comrade. Indeed, given his sudden eagerness to cross swords with Locris, he seems more than ever to be a repressed *erastes*, suddenly directing against his *eromenos*, now that the latter has challenged his superiority (or illusion of superiority), the aggression through which he has always channeled his homoerotic desire. As for Locris, one could say that, like the properly feminine woman she really is, she fell in love with and subordinated herself to a properly masculine man. Justified in upsetting this hierarchy in order to save his life, she of course wishes to restore the former, natural power differential between them as quickly as possible. Hence the extravagance of her submission once she has revealed her true sex, as when she tells him, "Our [hers and her father's] Fates to thee, as to a God we trust, / Mild amidst Wrongs, more Merciful than Just" (46).

And yet, such attempts to make the text ideologically coherent and psychologically plausible seem forced. Having eliminated Iphis's physically impossible sex-change, it's as if Hopkins feels no further need to attend to questions of plausibility. One might even say that his elimination of the physically unbelievable is meant to distract attention away from the psychologically and ideologically unbelievable. In any case, the play is riddled with ideological holes so big you could drive a deus ex machina through them. These culminate, as we have seen, in the replacement of Iphis's spontaneous sex-change with a spontaneous gender-change—Locris gives up warfare forever and becomes a conventional, submissive woman—and a spontaneous sexuality-change—Maherbal, once attracted to a sword-wielding pretty-boy buddy (whom he sometimes fantasized to be a woman), is now attracted to a fainting *femme* female. Indeed, the text pretends to subject Maherbal to a gender-change, to turn him effeminate (in the ladies' man sense), as well: he responds to Locris's "Farewel to Warfare" speech with a matching, although shorter, renunciation of soldiery ("Hear me, My *Locris*, take my Farewel too, / Ye sevenfold Sheilds, and shiv'ring Spears adieu, / Farewel to War—to all the World—but you" [V, 47]). He never follows through on these words, however. The next we hear of him—"Romans and Rebels ravage all the Town, / *Araxes* marches on to Snatch the Crown. / *Archias* Proclaims him at his Army's head, / And the War done, he and . . . *Locris* wed" (53)—he has assumed the normative masculine role: aggressively manly and exclusively heterosexual. All that remains is to complete the scapegoating and then purging of Cyllene for her father's tyranny, for the play's misogyny, and for its gender-transgression, and then to silence and punish the unwittingly woman-loving Orythia for having rivaled, however ridiculously, the now heterosexual hero, leaving us, at play's end, exactly as do Ovid and Bellamy: with a sex/gender/sexuality–conforming male-female couple.

CONCLUSION

Ever since Foucault's *History of Sexuality*, volume 1, most practitioners of Lesbian/Gay/Queer/Sexuality Studies have treated present-day constructions of sex/gender/sexuality normativity and deviance as relatively new, "inventions" of the modern or early modern age. To some extent, they may be correct. The waning of the active/passive divide and waxing of the homo/hetero one; the disappearance of the "ladies' man" sense of effeminacy; the exaltation of heterosexual marriage bonds over male friendship—these are just a few of the changes to which one could point in asserting difference, and indeed they merit continued investigation and consideration. By no means do I wish to suggest that Ovid's Rome is the same as Bellamy's England and Hopkins's England and my (or your) late-twentieth-century West. I simply wish to offer my readings of Ovid's "Iphis and Ianthe" and of the seventeenth- and turn-of-the-eighteenth-century dramatizations of it as evidence that there are also strong continuities and connections between these different places and times, and to suggest that, despite significant and often striking variation and change, over the past two thousand years dominant ideology in the West regarding sex, gender, and sexuality has remained strikingly consistent in some key respects: demonizing female sexual desire, stigmatizing effeminacy, rejecting and/or unknowing female homosexuality, rejecting and/or unknowing most forms of male homosexuality, exalting hierarchical heterosexual bonds between sharply differentiated men and women, and associating these topics with sex-changing, paternal authority/tyranny, and the breakdown or safeguarding of fundamental societal distinctions and divisions more generally. By recognizing and exploring such continuities and similarities over time and place, without ignoring or denying discontinuities and differences, we will hopefully gain a better understanding not only of the past, but also of the present, and perhaps have a better chance of denaturalizing, of loosening the grip of, these highly resilient, destructive ideologies of sex, gender, and sexuality.

NOTES

"Some Binarisms (I)" and "Some Binarisms (II)" are, of course, the titles of two chapters of Eve Kosofsky Sedgwick's landmark book, *Epistemology of the Closet* (Berkeley: University of California Press, 1990), a work I find continually instructive, not least because, despite its near iconic status in Lesbian/Gay/Queer/Sexuality Studies, some of its most perceptive insights have been routinely ignored by her admirers (see below).

1. By "historical truth," I mean the sort of "provisional accuracy" that Joyce Appleby, Lynn Hunt, and Margaret Jacob propose as the object of historical inquiry in *Telling the Truth About History* (New York: W.W. Norton, 1994), 290 (see especially chapter 7, "Truth and Objectivity," and chapter 8, 'The Future of History'). As for the omission of some scholars' work, I am still shocked by the absence from the *Lesbian and Gay Studies Reader*, eds. Henry Abelove, Michèle Aina Barale, and David M. Halperin (New York: Routledge, 1993), of any work representing the so-called essentialist side of the essentialist-constructionist controversy, an absence repeated in several of the syllabi of lesbian/gay/queer history courses I have either seen or been told of over the years.

2. I am far from the first writer on the history of sexuality (although not, perhaps, of "sexuality") to make such a critique. See, for example, the concluding section, entitled "The Half-Empty Glass," of Amy Richlin's "Not Before Homosexuality: The Materiality of the *Cinaedus* and the Roman Law against Love between Men," in the *Journal of the History of Sexuality* 3, 4 (April 1993): 571–73; John Boswell's "Categories, Experience, and Sexuality" (or "Concepts, Experience, and Sexuality"), in Edward Stein, ed., *Forms of Desire: Sexual Orientation and the Social Constructionist Controversy* (New York: Routledge, 1992), 149 (the title appears as "Categories" in the body of the text, as "Concepts" in the table of contents); and the first two chapters and the afterword of James Creech's *Closet Writing/Gay Reading: The Case of Melville's* Pierre (Chicago: University of Chicago Press, 1993). Regarding the term "sexuality," as Bruce Thornton points out (in an otherwise largely regressive, conservative, anti-"p.c." review of Halperin's *One Hundred Years of Homosexuality and Other Essays on Greek Love* [New York: Routledge, 1990] and John J. Winkler's *The Constraints of Desire: The Anthropology of Sex and Gender in Ancient Greece* [New York: Routledge, 1990]): "Foucault used the word 'sexuality' mainly in a narrow sense—'scientific discourse about sex.' . . . In English translation 'sexuality' implies a whole range of meanings different from the French 'sexualité.' . . . Thus to say in English that 'sexuality' is a modern construct is a more radical and paradoxical statement than it is in French, where 'sexualité' has more scientific connotations." (Thornton, "Constructionism and Ancient Greek Sex," *Helios* 18, 2 [1991]: 182; 192, n.8). Throughout this essay, I use 'sexuality' in the colloquial or English, rather than scientific or French, sense.

3. She demonstrates her argument by "juxtapos[ing] two programmatic statements of what seem to be intended as parallel and congruent projects" (45): Foucault's "hermaphrodism of the soul" passage from the *History of Sexuality*, Volume I, trans. Robert Hurley (New York: Pantheon, 1978), 43, and a passage from *One Hundred Years of Homosexuality* in which Halperin asserts that the 'highest expression' of modern homosexuality is the 'straight-acting and -appearing gay male,' a man distinct from other men in absolutely no other respect besides that of his 'sexuality,' " (8–9), a passage in which

Halperin therefore treats "sexual inversion," gender deviance, as merely a "stage" that preceded "homosexuality." As Sedgwick astutely points out, the two views are presented by their authors "*as if [they] were the same [narrative]*." Their form is identical: "Each is a unidirectional narrative of supersession. Each one makes an overarching point about the complete conceptual alterity of earlier models of same-sex relations. In each history one model of same-sex relations is superseded by another, which may again be superseded by another. In each case the superseded model then drops out of the frame of analysis" (46–47). Yet the content of the two views is decidedly different.

4. In a longer version of this essay, which will find a more spacious if not more gracious home in my first book, I place "Iphis and Ianthe" in the context of related tales from *The Metamorphoses*, among others the tales of Narcissus and of Orpheus, which foreground same-sex desire.

5. Margaret Anne Doody, *The True Story of the Novel* (New Brunswick, N.J.: Rutgers University Press, 1996), 9.

6. I shall refer to particular tales in *The Metamorphoses* by the names of their protagonist(s), within quotation marks, so as to avoid having to repeat "the story of . . . ," "the tale of . . . ," etc. Unless otherwise noted, English quotations from "Iphis and Ianthe" are taken from George Sandys's 1626 translation, *Ovid's Metamorphosis Englished, Mythologized, and Represented in Figures*, ed. Karl K. Hulley and Stanley T. Vandersall (Lincoln: University of Nebraska Press, 1970), chosen for its contemporaneity with one of the dramatizations of "Iphis and Ianthe" I will be examining (see pp. xvii–xviii on the various editions of Sandys's translation). English quotations from the rest of the *Metamorphoses* are taken from Frank Miller's Loeb Classical Library text (Cambridge: Harvard University Press; London: William Heinemann Ltd.; 1916), v. 2 (the Loeb Classical Library, v. 43), unless otherwise noted. All Latin quotations are from Miller.

7.   nec vaccam vaccae, nec equas amor urit equarum:
       urit oves aries, sequitur sua femina cervum.
       sic et aves coeunt, interque animalia cuncta
       femina femineo conrepta cupidine nulla est.

(IX.731–34)

8. *Ovid's* Metamorphoses *Books 6–10*, ed., with introduction and commentary, by William S. Anderson (Norman: University of Oklahoma Press, 1972), 469.

9. Bernadette Brooten, *Love Between Women: Early Christian Responses to Female Homoeroticism* (Chicago: University of Chicago Press, 1996), 1.

10. Emma Donoghue, *Passions Between Women: British Lesbian Culture 1668–1801* (London: Scarlet Press, 1993), 253–68.

11. Pierre de Bourdeille, Seigneur de Brantôme, *Vies des dames galantes* (written late 1500s and/or early 1600s, pub. 1665–1666), repr. as *Les Dames galantes*, texte établi sur l'édition originale par Jacques Haumont (Paris: Jean de Bonnot, 1972). The first quotation is my translation of: "On dit que Sapho de Lesbos a été une fort bonne maistresse en ce mestier, voire, dit-on, qu'elle l'a inventé, et que depuis les dames lesbiennes l'ont imitée en cela, et continué jusques aujourd'huy; ainsi que dit Lucian: que telles femmes sont les femmes de Lesbos, qui ne veulent pas souffrir les hommes, mais s'approchent des autres femmes ainsi que les hommes mesmes" (121). The second quotation is my translation of: "En nostre France, telles femmes sont assez communes; et si dit-on pourtant qu'il n'y a pas longtemps qu'elles s'en sont meslées, mesmes que la

façon en a esté portée d'Italie par une dame de qualité que je ne nommeray point" (122). As I discuss in the longer version of this essay, when examining Ovid's "Orpheus," male homosexuality is also represented as an "invention."

12. I take the term "faultline" from Alan Sinfield's discussion of cultural materialism's approach to ideology in *Faultlines: Cultural Materialism and the Politics of Dissident Reading* (Berkeley: University of California Press, 1992). As Sinfield explains, people produce ideologies in order to perpetuate the social systems in which they are dominant. These ideologies are attempts to create a plausible explanation of "who we are, who the others are, how the world works. . . . The strength of ideology derives from the way it gets to be common sense; it 'goes without saying' " (32). Yet such strength is always in peril. "Despite their power, dominant ideological formations are always, in practice, under pressure, striving to substantiate their claim to superior plausibility in the face of diverse disturbances. . . . Conflict and contradiction stem from the very strategies through which ideologies strive to contain the expectations that they need to generate" (41). Such conflicts and contradictions can be usefully viewed as "faultlines" in the would-be seamlessly plausible explanations of the world offered by dominant ideology, spaces or moments "through which [the social order's] own criteria of plausibility fall into contest and disarray" (45).

13.   mater abita templo. sequitur comes Iphis euntem,
        quam solita est, maiore gradu, nec candor in ore
        permanet, et vires augentur, et acrior ipse est
        vultus, et incomptis brevior mensura capillis,
        plusque vigoris adest, habuit quam femina. nam quae
        femina nuper eras, puer es!

                                                              (IX.786–91)

14. Interestingly, Nicander's version of the story in his *On Changes of Shape* (*Heteroioumena*) did not include the lesbian love element, which seems to be Ovid's own invention (see Anderson, *Ovid's Metamorphoses*, 464–65).

15. Indeed, earlier the text prompts readers to imagine not only actual penises but also fake ones—dildos. In her lament, after remarking that Pasiphæ fooled the bull into fulfilling her desires by counterfeiting a cow, Iphis asks, "Though all the ingenuity in the world should be collected here, though Daedalus himself should fly back on waxen wings, what could he do? With all his learned arts could he make me into a boy from a girl? or could he change you, Ianthe?" (*huc licet ex toto sollertia confluat orbe, / ipse licet revolet ceratis Daedalus alis, / quid faciet? num me puerum de virgine doctis / artibus efficiet? num te mutabit, Ianthe?* [IX.741–44]). Some readers will surely imagine an artificial supplement Daedalus the inventor might attach to a girl presumptuous enough to try to soar above her sexual station.

16. I take the verb "unknow" from Sedgwick's "Privilege of Unknowing: Diderot's *The Nun*," in *Tendencies* (Durham, NC: Duke University Press, 1993), 23–51.

17. See Jay M. Freyman, William E. Mahaney, and Walter K. Sherwin, *Iphis: Text, Translation, Notes*, Salzburg Studies in English Literature, Elizabethan & Renaissance Studies (Salzburg: Institut Für Anglistik Und Amerikani-

stik, Universität Salzburg, 1986) [Cited as Freyman et al]. The play is in Latin. According to Freyman et al., it does not seem to have been translated or printed until recently. Regarding its dating, they argue (1–2) that 1622–24 is most likely, although 1622–26 or even 1628–32 are possible.

18.   . . . Qui modo constans procus
            Meritis Ianthen laudibus caelo tulit,
            Iphida tenellis (fraude deceptus mea)
            Captabit ulnis. Quod genas similes rosae
            Ornant, quod oculos similis accendit decor,
            Utriusque fronte blandiens ridet Charis:
            Stultus suam putabit, et praeceps ruet
            In fictam Ianthen. Credulis quis non potest
            Oculis abuti?

                                                    (IV.iii.713–22)

19.   *Iphis.* Immite numen! vivo, communi nece
            Ne misera peream: me novus finis manet,
            Nova sors. Adurit feminam mulier (nisi
            Me) nulla: tale Phoebus, augur sit licet,
            Nit novit unquam. Tel: Nota Pasiphae omnibus
            Solis nata conscii, petiit bovem:
            Femina, marem. Sed vester, infelix, magis
            Furiosus amor est: illa, quod petiit, tulit;
            Fruiturque votis. Iph: Huc revolet alis licet
            Daedalus, an ipsam possit, an teneram artibus
            Mutare Ianthen?

                                                    (IV.v.805–15)

20.   . . . Iphis femina est.
            An quis ceoru,m feminas iungit thoro
            Molles, eodem? falleris. Divi nefas
            Hoc pertimescunt.

                                                    (V.vi.1099–02)

21.   Sed en; tumescit animus, in varium trahor;
            Iubet necari feminam fervens dolor,
            Vetante pietate: ille pietatem fugat,
            Illumque pietas. Sic mari in tumido feror,
            Quidque ipse faciam stultus ignoro.

                                                    (I.i.34–38)

22. In a nice Ovidian touch, Bellamy has Lygdus justify his impious decision using divine precedent, as both Byblis and Myrrha do in the *Metamorphoses*. Arguing with Telethusa, Lygdus chillingly says, "This degeneracy has frequently polluted the gods themselves; Saturn himself devoured his own children. Do you think that it is not permitted for me to do what such a fearsome and sacred divine power does? He did it and, by his doing, has ordered that I do it. Kill her" (69; . . . *Haec frequens labes deos / Maculavit ipsos: ipse Saturnus suos / Natos vorabat.Facere non licitum putas, / Quod tam verendum, tam sacrum numen facit. / Fecit: et agendo iussit ut faciam. Nece* [I.iv.170–74]).

23.   O iusta poena numinis! culpae, malum;
             Scelerique cunctis poena respondet. Marem
             Animus volebat impudens, pene iubens:
             Habet quod optat (proh dolor!) sed masculum
             Pectus repletum mente feminea. Nova
             Semperne monstra nota iam Crete feret?

                                                      (III.v.547–52)

24.   . . . Quis novus stupidum vigor
             Pectus pererrat? corde quis sanguis fluit?
             Vix capio memet. Fervet immensus calor:
             Et per cohortes gestiunt validi pedes
             Calcare caesas ensibus turmas: manus
             Flammas vibrandas optat, et gladios truces.
             Ardescit oculus, defluunt lapsae comae. . . .
             Et tota mutor. Ecquis invitas manus
             Abolere formam frontis ignavam iubet?
             Valeatis ergo pristini vultus tricae:
             Rugas viriles, hispidam frontem cape,
             Cretensis esto. Quicquid horrebat prius,
             Irritat audax animus; haud quicquam timet,
             Praeter timorem.

                                                      (V.iv.1027–34, 1036–42)

25. The odd remark about Iphis's hair flowing loosely down — in Ovid's version Iphis's hair grows *shorter* when she becomes a he — makes more sense in this light: it makes possible a simple, easily manageable physical alteration — letting the actor's hair (or wig) down — that can stand in for more extensive bodily changes that would require a bit more ingenuity in the use of costumes and makeup. This detail might also reflect Bellamy's knowledge or beliefs about ancient Cretan hairstyles.

26. I share Alan Sinfield's preference for the term "dissident" over "subversive," in order, as he explains, "to circumvent the entrapment model [of New Historicism], since ['subversive'] may seem to imply achievement — that something *was subverted* — and hence (since mostly the government did not fall, patriarchy did not crumble) that containment must have occurred. 'Dissidence' [implies] refusal of an aspect of the dominant, without prejudging an outcome" (49).

27. In the longer version of this essay, I next examine a dramatization of "Iphis and Ianthe" in which lesbianism remains the central ideological concern, Isaac de Benserade's *Iphis et Iante* (perf. 1634; pub. 1637). In comparison to Bellamy's *Iphis*, Benserade's work is relaxed and playful. While ultimately attempting to bolster dominant ideology regarding sex, gender, and sexuality, *Iphis et Iante* is far more willing to admit not only that an ideological faultline exists, but also that exploiting it can be quite pleasurable.

28. The play is divided into acts, but not scenes; lines are not numbered. I have therefore cited the play as Hopkins, the act number, followed by the page number, for all quotations.

29. John Dennis, in the preface to his translation of Ovid's *Byblis*, entitled "The Passion of Byblis, Made English" (1692), explains that he has changed

the ending of the tale (Byblis goes mad and then dies, instead of being trans-formed into a fountain) for precisely this reason: '*The Transformations of* Byblis *might do very well in the time of* Augustus Cæsar . . . *but those transubstantiating Doctrines . . . would look as absurdly to us as the Chimerical Metamorphosis, which is pretended to be acted at the very time it is sung in our modern* Roman *Churches.*' (Any excuse for an anti-Catholic swipe.)

30. I say "all but banishes" because we are told of a ghost having delivered a warning to one of the characters years earlier.

31. The sentiment had recently been expressed in Cibber's *Love's Last Shift* (1696) and Congreve's *Mourning Bride* (1697), as cited by Burton Stevenson, ed., *The Macmillan Book of Proverbs, Maxims, and Famous Phrases* (New York: The Macmillan Co., 1948), 2566–67. Cibber's play contains the lines "We shall find no fiend in hell can match the fury of a disappointed woman, — scorned, slighted, dismissed without a parting pang" (IV.i), while Congreve's contains "Heav'n has no rage, like love to hatred turn'd / Nor Hell a fury like a woman scorn'd" (III.viii.42–43).

32. In the longer version of this essay, three of the Ovidian tales I discuss, "Byblis," "Myrrha," and "Salmacis and Hermaphroditus," also represent fe-male sexual desire as villainous, as monstrous even.

33. Indeed, when Orythia voices her suspicion that Locris doesn't recipro-cate her feelings, "he" deceives her with deliberately misleading replies, such as, "What shall I say to make you think me true, / By Heav'n, I never lov'd a Maid like you. / You reign sole Mistress of my faithful Heart, / No other Fair can claim the smallest Part" (II, 16). The joke, of course, is on Orythia: Locris never loved a Maid like her, s/he loves a Man.

34. On the coining of the word and the idea(s) "sodomy," see Mark D. Jor-dan, *The Invention of Sodomy in Christian Theology* (Chicago: University of Chi-cago Press, 1997); see 43 for the notion of sodomy as "malignant." On the representation of sodomites and sodomy in the Restoration and eighteenth cen-tury, see Alan Bray, *Homosexuality in Renaissance England* (London: Gay Men's Press, 1982), and "Homosexuality and the Signs of Male Friendship in Eliza-bethan England," *History Workshop Journal* 29 (spring 1990): 1–19; Rictor Nor-ton, *Mother Clap's Molly House: The Gay Subculture in England 1700–1830* (London: GMP Publishers, 1992); and Cameron McFarlane, *The Sodomite in Fiction & Satire 1660–1750* (New York: Columbia University Press, 1997), as well as essays in Gerard and Hekma, eds., *The Pursuit of Sodomy*. On the chang-ing conceptions of sexuality and gender in this period, see Randolph Trum-bach, *Sex and the Gender Revolution* (Chicago: University of Chicago Press, 1998), as well as his earlier essays (cited and incorporated in his book). But also see my master's thesis, "Mollies Are Not the Only Fruit: being comprised of an Exploration of Male Homosexuality in some Eighteenth-Century British and French Fiction with a Testy and Querulous Analysis of Recent Gay Histo-riography" (University of California at Berkeley, 1993), for a much needed critique of Bray's and especially Trumbach's work.

35. An alternative hypothesis is that this special X-ray vision operates only when ideologically convenient.

36. The text's repetition of the word "unnatural" reinforces this impression. Semanthe refers to Zoilus, twice, as an "unnatural" father (III, 23; V, 51); Zoilus calls Locris an "unnatural Son" (V, 48). Given the millennia-old condemnation of homosexuality (or forms of homosexuality) as unnatural, the adjective's repeated usage here, in a text that flirts with both male and female same-sex desire, cannot help but intensify the simultaneous gesturing toward and away from the taboo topic.

Enigmatic Gender in Delarivier Manley's *New Atalantis*

RUTH HERMAN

W HEN THE SECOND VOLUME OF DELARIVIER MANLEY'S *THE NEW Atalantis*[1] appeared in October 1709, it caused a sensation. It was perhaps to be expected that a Tory *roman à clef* that made risqué suggestions about the intimate affairs of the Whig ministers and their families would have made a stir. However, it is not immediately apparent why this text created such a furore. As one modern critic has remarked, it was "no worse" than other contemporary satire.[2] It was, rather, the arrest of the author that was remarkable.[3] In this essay I shall examine the idea that the Whig ministry's alarm at this text was not at the salacious gossip overtly retailed in Manley's "memoirs," but in the way that she embedded within this hackneyed scandal hints of a Whig culture tainted with male homosexuality. I shall demonstrate how these hints, targeted at a minister open to such suggestions, gave her free reign to illustrate Whig "perversion" of accepted male and female roles. I shall also suggest that Manley's complex scandal strategy, whereby she invented, altered, and subsequently re-gendered stories, enabled her to attack a vulnerable Whig ministry while remaining just within the boundaries of libel, and it is only by addressing this aspect of the text that we can understand *New Atalantis*'s full political significance.

Certainly the Earl of Sunderland, Secretary of State with responsibility for controlling sedition and libel, saw the text as dangerous. He wrote to his mother-in-law, Sarah Churchill, the Duchess of Marlborough, "I believe Mr. Manwaring [*sic*] has given you an account of the Lady, I have in Custody for the New Atlantis [*sic*] & of the noble worthy Persons, she corresponds with, I [verso] shall spoil their writing, at least for some time for I promise them, I will push it, as far as I can by law."[4]

It is curious that Sunderland took so much notice of *New Atalantis*. He seems to have been unconcerned at the other defamatory material circulating at the time, and there is no mention of any similar texts in his correspondence to Sarah Churchill at this date.[5] If we turn briefly to the reaction of nonministerial contemporary readers, it is apparent, from the evidence available, that, whatever Sunderland's reaction, they perceived nothing particularly incendiary in the endless tales of seduction and betrayal or in the titillating snippets of gossip. On hearing of Manley's arrest, Lady Mary Wortley Montague commented, "[I] have five hundred arguments at my fingers' ends to prove the ridiculousnes [*sic*] of these creatures that think it worth while to take notice of what is designed only for diversion."[6] Even Arthur Maynwaring, Sarah Churchill's secretary did not react particularly strongly to the *New Atalantis*. He wrote to his patron, "I desire you not to trouble or concern yourself of what is said of [the Duchess], 'tis all old and incredible stuff of extortion and affairs with [Godolphin] and [the Duke of Shrewsbury], which not a soul living believes a word of."[7]

So we must ask ourselves, why Sunderland found it necessary to imprison the author. After all, the age was one of ad hominem satire, and by her own later admission, Manley had concentrated on stories that had been current long ago.[8] This is the thorny question I will address in this essay, and in doing so will examine the subtle ways in which Manley directs her readers' attention away from the superficial tales of maidens and aristocratic lovers toward issues of more political importance. Careful contextualisation of *New Atalantis* suggests that we should seek a radical rereading and reassessment of the novel's role in the onslaught of propaganda directed at the crumbling Whig ministry by the Tories.

First, it is necessary to set the scene of Manley's most notorious work. The framework of the *New Atalantis* is formed by a tour of England by Astrea, the Goddess of Justice, and Virtue, her mother, at the moment of Anne's accession. They are conducted on their tour by the gossipy figure of Intelligence, out and about on her investigative travels in the service of the Princess Fame. The deities are deliberately distanced from the main narrative in order to demonstrate how far the qualities they represent are alien to the Whig ministry and to the real politik that provides the ammunition for the Tory text. Perhaps Sunderland considered Manley's positioning of the goddesses as particularly insulting. He may have recognized in their invisibility and alienation a deliberate comment on the licentiousness, which the novel claimed was rife in the Whig-ruled world. But, as I have already noted, *New Atalantis* was by no means unusual in advertising sexual irregularity among the political elite. *The Benefits of a Theatre*, for instance, suggests that the theater is a useful institution since it provided whores for Lords. The Duke of Devonshire, the poem claims, had found his mistress in the theater and was paying her "soundly" for her favors.[9]

Therefore, it could not have been the suggestion of extramarital ac-

tivity in *New Atalantis* that upset Sunderland. Nor could it have been
the eminence of the individuals targeted, such as the Marlboroughs,
that caused Sunderland's reaction. The Duke and Duchess, above all
other Whig notables, were considered fair game for Tory pamphleteers.
We need only look at the number of volumes of satire on the Duke and
Duchess that still remain.[10] Indeed, the Whigs were acutely aware of
the volume of invective heaped upon the Marlboroughs, particularly
Sarah, by the Tories:

> His Duchess shall have all the Spite
> That Fools can put upon her.

ran one Whig reaction to the opposition pamphleteers.[11]

Neither the individual tales within *The New Atalantis*, nor the huge
range of characters makes the task of identifying Sunderland's motive
in arresting Manley any easier. Even with detailed knowledge of the
period, it is difficult to ascertain the political significance of the protagonists, even when they can be identified. There are, indeed, some individuals whose presence is puzzling, with the result that the *New Atalantis*
presents itself as a hodgepodge of stories, apparently without a single
identifiable target, resulting, it has been suggested, in a loss of textual
unity.[12]

Manley herself appears to acknowledge the shapelessness of her
work by admitting that it "seems . . . to be written like Varronian satires,
on different subjects, tales, stories and characters of invention."[13] The
definition of Varronian, or Menippean, satire is "a rag-bag of prose and
verse loosely relating to some topic, but making use of all kinds of literary modes, including conversations, digressions, lists and so on."[14] Hollis Berry has attempted to explain this "shapelessness" by quoting
Northrop Frye's definition of Menippean satire as "intellectual exuber-
ance and expansion," explaining that the "appearance of carelessness .
. . is a reflection of the reader's own carelessness."[15]

I must agree that Berry's idea of the reader's carelessness is the best
way to unravel the complexities of *New Atalantis*. The text depends for
its impact on the reader's ability to pick up resonances of truly outrageous Whig behavior among the plethora of old or fanciful scandals. To
understand Manley's "rag-bag" it is necessary to decode contemporary
political messages reworked within the text from "old Stories that all
the World had long since reported."[16] Essentially, the text relies on the
reader's ability to distinguish those stories that may simply be camouflage items, from the political explosive hidden beneath textual wadding.

The most obvious map through the minefield of deliberately misleading invective would appear to be the textual keys. In these keys real and fictional names are printed side by side in two columns. They were published separately, but simultaneously, with the novel itself. In the keys to Manley's *New Atalantis*, however, we find that some of the fictional characters are missing and many of the real names given are unlikely models. Even at the time of publication, the puzzling editorial strategy of *The New Atalantis* was questioned. When the text first appeared *The Tatler* pointed out that the author of *New Atalantis* had "brought many Persons of both sexes to an untimely Fate, and, what is more surprising, has, contrary to her profession . . . reviv'd others who had long since drown'd in the Whirlpools of Lethe."[17]

We must ask ourselves why Manley included in a piece of propaganda so many people who were either politically inactive or irrelevant, or sometimes, even, deceased. Careful examination of the keys reveals that clear-cut cross-referencing to specific contemporary individuals is not always possible, and the political purpose behind the inclusion of some characters is difficult to ascertain. For instance, there are no identifiable originals for Elonora and Don Antonio.[18] Yet their story of passionate seduction and abandonment occupies fifty pages in the original edition.

In the same way the keys give an unreliable identification of the incestuous Polydore and Urania as the children of Lord Haversham, which both Ballaster and Koster, Manley's most recent editors, query.[19] Manley claims that the two children were orphaned young and, as they became adolescents, carried on an incestuous relationship. When their guilty secret was discovered, the brother went to sea and died in heroic circumstances, while the sister perished giving birth to the product of their illegal union. The reported facts about the real young Havershams bears no resemblance at all to this story. Both children, Maurice and Altharna, were still alive in 1711, two years after the publication of *The New Atalantis*. Maurice had married the daughter of a Mr. Smith of Hertfordshire, while his sister had remained unmarried, but certainly living.[20] Even if Haversham was intended as the dead parent of the orphaned pair (and he was still alive in 1709), to target him in such a convoluted way is curious, even if we take into account his previous Whiggishness and his connection with the unpopular High Tory, the Earl of Nottingham.[21] The invention of an incestuous liaison between Haversham's offspring would be unnecessary if Manley simply wished to embarrass him. She could surely have found (or invented) something that implicated Haversham himself, as she did with other Whig targets. Of course, identification of some figures may have been incorrect by accident. But it is equally possible that it was Manley's deliberate act to make use of out-of-date, problematic, or fictional tales as "insurance"

against the accusation of seditious writing.[22] But we know that the rai-
son d'être of *The New Atalantis* was parliamentary political propaganda.
Manley confirmed her purpose in a letter to a Tory minister, the Earl
of Oxford, "I had the fortune two years ago to publish some pieces for
which I suffered imprisonments injured my health and prejudiced my
little fortune. Tho the performances were very indifferent yet they were
reckoned to do some service having been the publick attempt made
against those designs and that ministry which have been since so happily changed."[23] The paradox thus set up by the inclusion of the Haversham story is that propaganda, even in the eighteenth century,
needed to be timely. The usefulness of propaganda as a parliamentary-
political tool is severely limited if the targets are unrecognizable.

The supply of information (and the speed with which this can be
achieved) is perceived as crucial in *The New Atalantis*, but Intelligence
will not allow a lack of a firm foundation of facts to impede her in her
duties. It appears that quantity and expedition are of far more importance than veracity. She says, "My business is indeed to give intelligence of all things, but I take Truth with me when I can get her.
Sometimes, indeed she's so hard to recover that Fame grows impatient
and will not suffer me to wait for her slow approach."[24]

If we follow this reasoning through and accept that *The New Atalantis*
is primarily a vehicle for Tory propaganda, then we must also accept
that its effectiveness as a political scandal sheet must depend on the immediate relevance of what it says. However, it is nevertheless the case
that much of Intelligence's information is politically obscure or old, and
therefore would be discounted by the "knowing" reader. From this, we
should deduce that the stories Intelligence relates to the Goddesses fall
into varying grades of "newsworthiness." Princess Fame, and, through
her, the political world, has already heard them, and their value is at
the level of entertaining gossip to be told to visiting dignitaries, or, for
Manley's purposes, textual wadding.

We might conclude from this, that while the bulk of *The New Atalantis*
provides fascinating real or invented gossip about the sexual habits of
the gentry and aristocracy of early eighteenth century England, they
carry little political weight simply as stories. And since the purpose of
the text was political propaganda, we must assume that they were specifically encoded to engage with issues that were important in 1709.

This encoding becomes increasingly clear if we look in more detail at
the individuals named. The political message delivered through Manley's "secret memoirs" immediately becomes more complex. It is not
simply Whig versus Tory. For example there is the personally, not politically, motivated attack on her "husband," the Tory MP, John Manley.[25] His inclusion in the text is clearly a matter of personal spite.

Again, it may have been Catherine Trotter's association with the wife of the Whig Bishop of Salisbury, Gilbert Burnet, that invoked Manley's wrath against her, but it seems more likely to have been some now long-forgotten personal affront. Certainly Sarah Fyge Egerton had been guilty of giving evidence against Manley in a court case a few years earlier, and it is undoubtedly this misdemeanor that prompted Manley's unkind attack on her.[26] The second wife of Manley's lover, John Tilly, may equally have had little political significance, but is also a victim of Manley's ascerbic pen.

I have taken some time to look in detail at the political irrelevancies to establish the amount of textual wadding Manley used, and under which she hid the subjects Lord Sunderland found so worrying in the second volume of *New Atalantis*. The references to topical issues of the day, such as peculation in the navy, or fraud in the formation of mining companies, would not have caused the Secretary of State too much anxiety.[27] They were topics well aired in newspapers, pamphlets, and broadsides.[28] It would also have been no surprise to Sunderland that the disreputable and staunchly Whig Junto member, Earl Wharton, is described as "one of the most artificial men of the age . . . all must be intrigue and management where he is concerned" (85). Tory pamphleteers had been churning out this kind of invective for years. Manley is hardly less complimentary than a poem that claims

> This W[harton] has by great Example shown
> How he another's wife has made his own
> Only by keeping 'till the Husband's dead
> Then taking the chaste Spouse to his own bed.[29]

Again Sunderland can hardly have been upset at the unflattering description of the High Tory, Henry St. John, or Manley's omission of St. John as a Tory hero in the second volume. Indeed, Sunderland would surely have positively welcomed other targets, such as the High Tory MP, Anthony Hammond. Another pamphleteer, Joseph Browne describes his wife as a "coquet," [31] while Manley goes further, and accuses the husband of being "as great a libertine as her self."[30]

As these few examples make apparent, Manley's text is far more complex than any direct attack on the Whigs, targeting, as she does, senior Tories and troublesome back benchers like Charles Caesar. As we have seen, in so far as gossiping about real people is concerned, Manley is merely following a contemporary trend in circulating snippets of salacious gossip. For example, in a manuscript poem, *The Assembly at Kensington*, the anonymous author reveals that

> Whils't innocent Lady Essex at Basset play'd
> Violent Love her Lord to St. Albans made,

'Tis time for Grafton to give place,
Since she appears with fading Face.[31]

On the printed page, Joseph Browne's various satirical pieces were equally suggestive.

Thus Manwering's the Vanity to boast
Of what he ought to be asham'd of most.
One that deserves no better Name than W[hor]e [Anne Oldfield?]
Tho' many a P[ee]r had had her before.[32]

Revealing the extramarital sexual activities of one's political opponents was not uncommon. Perhaps, therefore, to find a reason for Sunderland's reaction to *New Atalantis*, we should not look for the obvious scandal, but scrutinize the text for the hints and rumors that may have been more shocking to Manley's readers than hackneyed tales of seduction. We must try to judge whether the kind of scandal Manley was peddling was as overt as it appears. Sunderland may perhaps have reacted so strongly (and quickly) to the second volume, because there were resonances in it of Whig sexual deviancy, rather than an excess of Whig promiscuity. An investigation of contemporary rumor shows Manley is hinting not at Whig sexual profligacy, but at Whig perversity, and this would have been regarded as far more dangerous. It would also have provided Sunderland personal cause for imprisoning the author, since, in the light of recent scholarship, he was himself open to the accusation of sodomy, a criminal practice. Manley, presumably, would not dare to accuse the Secretary of State of such activities outright, and therefore had to resort to innuendo and code. However, if she had wished to be more specific, she would not have been the first. In 1704, William Shippen described Sunderland as the husband of the beautiful Anne Churchill, who, unable to appreciate her, is pictured as her

Dull husband, sensless [*sic*] of her Charms
Lies lumpish in her soft encircling Arms.[33]

This is a circumspect hint at Sunderland's homosexuality, but taken with other persistent rumors that circulated throughout the period, it becomes decodable as an accusation of homosexuality. But this was a complex and contentious subject to broach in 1709 and one that required considerable caution. Therefore, before dealing with Sunderland himself, we must see how Manley laid a trail of clues, and how she treated the clique with which he was associated.

The suggestion of Whig homosexuality in the context of *New Atalantis* becomes more apparent when viewed in the context of the rumors that abounded in late Stuart England. To understand this aspect of the text, reference must be made to the Tory smear campaign, which suggested that the last Stuart king was well known for his homosexual activities.[34] The Whigs are therefore tarred through their strong association with the supposedly sexually deviant William III. For instance, one poet, with remarkable economy, managed to target both the Whig, Sarah Churchill, and William III in the following few lines.

> Mother Jenning's Race
> And the Spawn of her Grace,
> Shall hold Nanny [Queen Anne] fast in their Clutches.
> It is not the same Thing,
> As when I was King,
> Albemarle was as good as the Dutchess.[35]

The association of Sarah Churchill (the daughter of Mother Jennings), Anne's favorite, with Arnold Keppel, Earl of Albermarle, William III's favorite, is significant. As we shall see, the link indicates that the Whigs of Anne's reign were regarded as the inheritors of the traditions of the Whigs of William's reign, and of all the sexual practices that that entailed. It should therefore be taken as deliberate that one of the first tales that Manley includes in *New Atalantis* is a story about William Bentinck, Duke of Portland, Albermarle's predecessor for the favors of William III. It is equally significant that it is a story of Portland's passionate love for a young female ward, named in the keys as Stuarta Howard.

Since no records appear to survive in Portland's estate papers of any legal wardships Manley's claims cannot be checked for authenticity.[36] But perhaps the story was intentionally misleading. This tale, as Manley tells it, is superficially a simple story of seduction and violation of a young and vulnerable girl by an older man. She comes to him as a child and as she reaches a marriageable age he begins to fall in love with her. He systematically corrupts her with pornographic literature and finally, unable to restrain his lust any longer, rapes her. She is abandoned by her guardian, who marries her closest confidante, and she dies in "horror, sorrow and repentance."[37] Internal evidence within Manley's text suggest that the story, if it is true, must have taken place in 1699–1700 and must end in 1700, when Portland married his second wife. This dating renders the keys useless as aids to identification. Stuarta's father died in 1668. In 1700 she would have been a minimum age of thirty-two. She would have long reached her majority by this time and been far too old to act as a model for the innocent adolescent depicted in Manley's story.

This analysis indicates that we must look at other issues if we are to find the true contemporary political significance of this story. That it was intended to have political significance is unquestionable, since Portland was a key Whig statesman and had, as we shall see, been closely connected with the powerful clique of Whig statesmen known as the Junto. Moreover, although we can have no real knowledge of the story's immediate reception, a closer look at Portland's personal history suggests that Manley's inclusion of him, so early on, and in such a clearly contrived and deliberately heterosexual story is a signal that in specific instances within this text, sexual orientation may need to be decoded to be read as exactly opposite to the way in which it is portrayed.[38]

Manley no doubt uses Portland in her story because he had been the favorite of William III. Since it was also openly reported that he was the preferred sexual partner of his king, a story detailing Portland's all-consuming and uncontrollable lust for a young girl may have seemed laughably ironic to the "knowing" eighteenth-century reader.[39] They would certainly have picked up the curiously masculine spelling of the young female ward's name, Charlot, a common French diminutive for "Charles."[40] In the same way, Manley's suggestions that Portland's ministrations to the king during his bout of smallpox, which involved sharing a bed, along with the rumor of William's habit of sleeping between Portland and his wife, would have been believed by very few cognoscente as being "all very innocent."[41] They may well have been aware that William and his favorites, Portland and then Albermarl, enjoyed specially designed adjoining bedrooms.[42]

Indeed, those readers who were aware of the rumors (and there could have been few who were not) would not wonder at the real object of the king's attention in the bedroom—it was undoubtedly Portland and not his Duchess. As someone who had spent time in the household of the Duchess of Cleveland, one of Charles II's mistresses, Manley cannot have been unaware of William's alleged homosexuality. It was common gossip in such circles. James II's court at St. Germain referred to William's Court of St. James as the *"château de derrière,"* while King William was identified as belonging "to that brotherhood."[43] The lampoons current at the end of the seventeenth century were explicit about William's proclivities, suggesting that if the "secrets of the Cabinet" were exposed, one could

> . . . tell how they their Looser Minutes spend,
> That guilty Scene would all Chaste Eyes offend,
> For should you pry into the close Alcove
> And draw the Exercise of Royal Love
> K[e]ppell and he [William] are *Ganimede* and *Jove.*[46]

As we have already noted, Albermarle was the favorite who super-seded Portland in William's affections. Archly, Manley suggests that Albermarle "was a favourite not at all interfering with the Duke, who was ever trusted and esteemed. By this means he oftener found a recess from court; his great master would sometimes in goodness dismiss him to his villa, to take a rest from power, a calm of greatness, a suspense of business, a respiration of glory."[45]

The supplanting of Portland by Albermarle, however, was not simply sexual tittle-tattle. It had political ramifications. It was the Whig Junto who had been determined to replace Portland with a more amenable favorite. By the Easter of 1699, "Portland, jealous of Albermarle, had resigned his Court appointments, and was publicly sulking."[46] William, meanwhile, was sending Portland distraught letters, begging him to re-turn to court.[47] Even without the information she may have gained from Peterborough, Harley, and Masham, her "noble patrons," Manley had no doubt gained inside information on these affairs during her brief stay with Barbara Villiers. That sodomy was supposedly common at court is evident from one contemporary poem that, leaving nothing to the imagi-nation, describes courtiers' efforts to curry favor with the King.

> Thinking they must be mimicks to the Crown
> They to each other put their Breeches down.[48]

Manley's story of Charlot and the Duke is, therefore, one of "disin-formation," a story of heterosexual seduction set around a character whose notoriety was centered on his homosexuality. The openness with which William courted his male favorites, and the seemingly casual re-mark that Portland had, before he gained political power, been the fa-vorite "of his pleasures," indicates that we should look much more closely at Manley's insistence on the "innocence" of their activities as bedfellows.[49] It can only be taken as an ironic warning for the reader to be aware of inconsistencies in her stories, and to read between the lines for the Truth which the news gatherer, Intelligence, insists that she takes with when she "can get her."[50]

The political impact of this as damaging innuendo becomes more evi-dent if we review the political connections of the Duke of Portland. Only nine years earlier he had faced impeachment in the Tory domi-nated House of Commons alongside Somers, Halifax, and Orford, all members of the Whig Junto, and all, in 1709, still powerful men. Port-land's sexuality and his close political association with the Junto inevi-tably brought their moral principles into sharp Tory focus. By implication, they could be shown to be men who would willingly coun-tenance anything if it kept them in power.

Furthermore, for the writer, however morally reprehensible their eighteenth-century heterosexual readers may have regarded the seduction of young females, and however much the most prudish may have disapproved of laying bare such scandal, it was far less dangerous a subject for a novel than explicit descriptions of sodomitical behavior at Court. It was a safer strategy to use an elaborate, but easily decipherable "fiction" to remind readers of William III's and Portland's relationship. The Whigs' tacit acceptance of the King and his favorite, and their subsequent efforts to supplant one male favorite with another for their own benefit was not ancient history. Tories would not have forgotten the dominant sexuality of William's Whiggish court, so that Manley's focus in these memoirs highlighted homosexuality as the dominant Whig preference. Using the technique of deliberate gender reversal, Manley was able to manipulate and thereby reveal sexual orientation. For instance, the undoubtedly heterosexual James II becomes Princess Ormia in the second volume of *The New Atalantis*. Likewise, in *Memoirs of Europe* (1710) Queen Anne becomes Emperor Constantine VI, while her husband, George of Denmark was Mary the Armenian. To expose the queen's suspected homosexuality, Abigail Masham appears as Theodecta the second wife of Constantine, in volume 1; and as Leonidas the male favorite of Constantine in volume 2. Such sleight of hand enabled her to destabilize sexuality in the entire novel, and, by association, cast a shadow of doubt on an entire Whig political regime, enabling her, obliquely, to smear figures not even featured in the text.

The technique of deliberately destabilizing the gender of her targets, which becomes more developed in the second volume of *New Atalantis* had been devised some two years earlier, in her 1707 epistolary work, *The Lady's Pacquet Broke Open*.[51] It is here that we may find the clue to the underlying reasons for Sunderland's reaction to the publication of the second volume of *New Atalantis*.

In this earlier work Manley refers to an incident that had taken place some thirteen years earlier. A young man named Beau Wilson, almost overnight, achieves fabulous wealth from near destitution. The mystery surrounding his sudden good fortune was never discovered and remains a mystery today. Beau Wilson's story ended tragically, however, when he met an untimely death in what appeared to be a rigged duel. His murderer somehow escaped punishment and fled the country. The case was a sensational one and was the subject of intense speculation. Manley attributes the source of his wealth to a wealthy, but mysterious, woman, which in the light of the evidence available, is a deliberate falsification. Several theories have been put forward as to the actual identity of Wilson's benefactor, but it appears most likely that it was a man, rather than a woman, to whom he was indebted for both his sudden wealth and his equally sudden death.[52] The two most likely candidates for the role of lover appear to be either the Duke of Portland, or the Earl of Sunderland who fifteen years later was determined to "push" Manley's prosecution as far as he could "by law." Sunderland would have been twenty years old at the time of the scandal, and as heir to his father's earldom, still a private individual (he did not enter the House of Commons until the next year, 1695). Nevertheless, he was sufficiently wealthy to bring about Wilson's change in fortune. We shall examine *The Lady's Pacquet of Letters* in some detail shortly, but it appears to serve as evidence that before she came to write *The New Atalantis*, Manley had already tried her hand at the deliberate manipulation of gender to publish politically sensitive material. Perhaps it was while preparing *The Lady's Pacquet* that she realized that this technique could be used on a larger scale to undermine confidence in the entire Whig leadership, rather than simply spreading coded rumours about one of them. Of course, in trying to understand why Sunderland felt driven to pursue Manley and her noble friends, his identification as the lover becomes crucial. It explains why curtailing Manley's writing career became important to him, particularly if he suspected that she had the backing of parties powerful enough to protect her if she became too bold. It also indicates why it was sufficiently important to him to mention it to his mother-in-law in the midst of letters dealing with far more "important" political affairs.[53] There is also a suggestion that he may have been particularly sensitive in 1709, the year *The New Atalantis* was published, when nine sodomites were apprehended at a brandy house in Jermyn Street a few minutes from Sunderland's home. It has been suggested that Sunderland set this establishment up as a "molly house" for his own purposes.[54]

Whatever the background, it is clear that Sunderland regarded Manley as some kind of threat, and that he felt it necessary to stop her. We can only speculate that he was frightened in case she enlarged and elaborated upon a story of which she had already demonstrated some intimate knowledge in *The Lady's Pacquet Book*. Therefore when the second, more explicit, volume of *The New Atalantis* appeared, any anxiety he may have experienced before was inevitably exacerbated. There was now a very real threat that, with her powerful patrons, she could afford to be bolder in her narrative. If this narrative now threatened to expose his sexuality and his attempt to cover up the disposal of Wilson, it was something that needed to be stopped.

It will be useful now to make a closer examination of *The Lady's Pacquet* and see how Manley's gender swapping technique had already enabled her to document, without the risk of a libel action, the scandal of 1694. And we should particularly note that it is not simply a moral lapse that is detailed in *The Lady's Pacquet Book*. It is also explicit about Wilson's murder. The noble lover declares, "W[ilson] shall never see me more, that Vainglorious Fool . . . the Wretch must die, that's certain."[55] Identification of the lover could lead to an embarrassing court case, at the very least.

However, more central to my argument is the fact that *The Lady's Pacquet* deliberately confuses the lover's gender. Throughout the episode in *The Lady's Pacquet*, it is stated that Beau Wilson's lover was a Lady ——. Uncharacteristically for the period, there are no initials included that might identify her as a specific woman. Moreover, twice during the text, Manley deliberately casts doubt upon "her" sex. Wilson was, she says, *"not known to be an admirer of Ladies*; for amidst all his Diversions, we (that way) hear no news of his Pleasures" [my italics], and furthermore "if they would say he deriv'd his good fortune from the Ladies, there was scarce any rich enough to support him, neither did he bestow any of his Time unaccounted for; and 'tis not to be believ'd that the fair Sex, being such rigid Creditors in Love, would not at least, expect Use-fruit for their Money, especially for such considerable Sums."[56] In this way Manley herself suggests a note of caution when assigning a definitive gender to this unknown lover, while retaining "her" title.

It only serves to reinforce the argument that Manley means us to take the lover as male when we note that the only woman who has ever been put forward as the possible original for Lady ——, is the Duchess of Cleveland. But, the author of *The Plot Discover'd* commented at that time that many believed he was maintained by a woman, but "there is only one Dutchess [of Cleveland?] in the kingdom able to support a Gallant in the expensive Grandeur of his Living," and nothing linked Wilson to her.[57] It seems particularly unlikely, if the story involved the Duchess, that Manley should be at all reticent about being more specific. She had after all described Cleveland's amatory escapades with the Duke of Marlborough in considerable detail only two years before in her previous political text, *The Secret History of Queen Zarah*.[58] Moreover, unlike Marlborough, Wilson was both dead and a political nonentity. There was considerably less necessity to be circumspect about his secret affairs than about those of the hero of Blenheim.

Even at the time of the original incident, the world at large was curious of Wilson's lifestyle. The following entry in John Evelyn's diary illustrates this curiosity:

A very young gentleman named Wilson, the younger son of one who had not above £200-a-year estate lived in the garb and equipage of the richest nobleman . . . was killed in a duel, not fairly. . . . The mystery is how this so young a gentleman . . . could live in such an expensive manner, it could not be discovered by all possible industry, entreating his friends to reveal it. It did not appear that he was kept by women, play, coining, padding [highway robbery] or dealing in chemistry.[59]

The story, therefore, was not a new one, but undoubtedly Sunderland, if he were the unknown lover, would wish it to remain a mystery. So while, Manley had chosen to remain circumspect in the earlier text, with her newfound influential friends, she could threaten to become more explicit. Her endless reworking of the old stories about the Marlboroughs in *Queen Zarah* and *The New Atalantis* indicated that her authorial strategy was one of repetition. Sunderland's anxiety is made clearer if we move forward several years to his death in 1722, when stories about his private life became more current. He is thought by some historians to have committed suicide in 1722 after the collapse of the South Sea Company in 1721, for which he was blamed. Before his sudden death, by suicide or not, he had already come under attack for his rumored sexual preferences. A particularly vicious and explicit pamphlet appeared, and while it specifically attacked him for his role in the collapse of the South Sea Company, it also made full use of rumors about his sexuality.

He married several times, but chiefly as people suspected by the Convenience of strengthening himself by *Alliances* with *Great Men*, rather than out of any affection for the Ladies, For if we may believe some Authors, he had a most *unnatural* Tast in his Gallantries. And in these Hours when he gave a Loose to Love, the Women were wholly excluded from his Embraces. . . . Tis certain, however, odd and unnatural his Lewdness was (yet it was a notorious Practice among some great Men of that Age) and some of his Ganymedes were pamper'd and supported at a high Rate at his Expence.[60]

After Sunderland's death in 1722, the full text of a correspondence, alleged to be between Wilson and Sunderland, appeared. The story told through these letters replicates Manley's relation of it with a few salacious details such as transvestism added, and the sex of the "Lady" changed to that of "Lord." The letters chart the sudden attraction of the nobleman for an impecunious but good-looking young man and the clandestine physical relationship that follows. There are details of the money that the Lord lavishes on his lover. The tragic end of the young man is also given. The letters themselves do not detail the end of the affair, but the anonymous author makes it clear that the Lord, frightened of the consequences of his former passion, organizes the murder of the young man, hiring a ruffian to do the deed.

One near contemporary commented on Sunderland that

Profaneness never abounded more at London and through England than now. The abomination of sodomy is too publick . . . it was a story of his enemies, of whom he had many, that the Earl of Sunderland was the first who set up houses for that vile sin, and when this was like to break out, poisoned himself to prevent the discovery. This is so horrid that it's not to be believed till vouched.[61]

Clearly, if anxiety had prompted Sunderland to commit suicide in 1722, it had been with him for many years.[62] And while it can only remain speculation, it seems likely that the fear of being openly exposed in a further volume of *New Atalantis*, prompted him to react very quickly against it.

When we consider this gender destabilization in the context of Portland's story and Beau Wilson's mysterious lover, we can begin to see why Sunderland should become anxious to prevent further volumes of *New Atalantis* being written. The second volume moves from simple gender swapping to a semiserious discussion of female sexuality and homosocial behavior in the New Cabal. Sunderland may well have asked himself if Manley's next volume would contain far more damaging details of male homosexuality, and the reintroduction of the story of Wilson and the unknown lover. Therefore when Sunderland saw that Manley was becoming increasingly bold in her discussion of sexuality, it is not inconceivable that he began to worry that she would quickly progress from arch discussions of quasilesbian cabals to a full-blown exposé of his activities.

An obvious caveat to this is the unarguable fact that Sunderland does not feature at all in *New Atalantis*.[63] As Whig Secretary of State, responsible for the prosecution of seditious libel, he would have been one of the main targets of a Tory work of propaganda. But it is likely, that given the dangers of saying what she intended to say about Sunderland too openly, Manley chose to leave hints within the text for those who could pick up them up. For those who were aware of the rumors about Sunderland the reference to the Earl "amusing" himself with the "politeness of the Turin court" can be taken as a subtle hint of "Italian" practices, that is to say, buggery. Again, knowledgeable readers would know that Sunderland's diplomatic service was situated in Vienna rather than in Italy.

It is equally remarkable that in *New Atalantis* Manley suggests that the Earl's wife is having an affair with one of Sunderland's political enemies, Ross, a man also accused of being part of William III's sodomitical circle. Inconsistencies such as these inevitably color any assumptions about *New Atalantis*. However, such hints of "unnatural" sexual orientation within the text would, we must assume, have been clear to contemporary readers, making Sunderland's attempt to silence Manley entirely understandable.

In the light of the *New Atalantis*'s heavily encrypted references to male homosexuality, it might seem puzzling that her references to the quasi-lesbian New Cabal are so extraordinarily explicit. An examination of the most virulent Whig pamphlets helps explain Manley's tactics. The Whig propagandists directed much of their venom at Abigail Masham, the woman who had supplanted Sarah Churchill in Anne's affections. Much of their invective openly accused her of lesbianism.

When compared to these texts, Manley's description of the New Cabal is not particularly original, although the direction it took was. A Whig pamphlet had appeared in the year before *New Atalantis* which made very specific claims about the "Female Vice" at the English court, which had reached a "great perfection in sinning," and included a story about an attempted rape by a Lady of an innocent young girl on her way home from the theater.[64] The pamphlet, which Sarah Churchill mistakenly seems to have believed constituted part of *New Atalantis*, takes the form of a conversation between Madam Maintenon, in the French court, and Abigail Masham, in England.[65] Here, Masham is made to confess her lesbianism,

> At Court I was taken for a more Modish Lady, but was rather addicted to another Sort of Passion, of having too great a Regard for my own Sex, insomuch that few people thought I would ever have Married, but to free myself from that Aspersion some of our Sex labour under, for being too fond of one another, I was resolved to marry as soon as I could fix to my Advantage or Inclination.[66]

Better known perhaps is the poem which accuses Masham of "pierc[ing] this Royal heart" and "dark Deeds at night."[70] There is also, of course, Sarah Churchill's accusation of Queen Anne that she had "noe inclination for any but one's own sex."[68] At first sight, it seems incongruous for Manley to have made so much of the rumors of lesbianism that for the most part were directed at Tory Masham, the woman whom the Whigs suspected of being her patron. Her motive must have been to direct the accusations *away* from Tory to Whig women, given the persistent discussion of homosexuality at William's (Whiggish) court. For this reason, it is particularly important not to miss the reference to Socrates at the center of the section on the New Cabal with its reiteration of the theme of male homosexuality,

> There are, who will not allow of innocency in any intimacies, detestable censurers who after the manner of the Athenians, will not believe so great a man as Socrates (him whom the oracle delivered to the wisest of all men)

could see every hour the beauty of an Alcibiades without taxing his sensibility. How did they recriminate for his affection, for his cares, his tenderness to the lovely youth? How have they delivered him down to posterity as blameable for too guilty a passion for his beautiful pupil? — Since then it is not in the fact of even so wise a man to avoid the censure of the busy and the bold, care ought to be taken by others (less fortified against occasion of detraction, in declining such unaccountable intimacies) to prevent the ill-natured world's refining upon their mysterious innocence. (155)

Something that may have disturbed Sunderland even more in Manley's treatment of homosexuality is her treatment of cross-dressing practices in her discussion of the New Cabal. In the *Love Letters Between a Certain Late Nobleman and the Famous Mr Wilson*, there is a passage in which Sunderland requests that Wilson wear the female clothes that he has bought him, and another in which Wilson refers to his female clothing.[69] If, as is apparent from this, Sunderland's tastes also ran to transvestism, he would have been even more alarmed to read Manley discussing this "this irregularity of taste" so openly (235). She continues,

> They [the women of the Cabal] do not in reality love men, but dote on the representation of men in women. Hence it is those ladies are so fond of the dress en cavaliere, though it is extremely against my liking, *I would have the sex distinguished as well by their garb as by their manner* [italics added]. That bewitching modesty which is so becoming to the opening veil is against kind in the confirmed, bold and agreeable air of the hat, feather and peruke. If in this dress you retain the shamefacedness of the other, you lose the native charm that recommends it.

If we replace female cross-dressing with male cross-dressing, the encrypted message becomes clear, and Sunderland could well have suspected that he was the actual target of this slander, since he is accused of having an interest in Wilson's cross-dressing in *Love Letters Between a Certain Late Nobleman and the Famous Mr. Wilson*. The point of the Cabal, in this reading, is that the deviant practices of the Whigs (following the example of their hero, William III) force Whig women to turn to one another for sexual satisfaction. Manley's Tory readership would have recognized it as a reenactment of rumors of lesbianism that had been rife ten years earlier. For, while the identification of the women of the Cabal is problematic now, it was clear to contemporary readers to whom Manley was referring. For instance, while Hearne identified the Marchioness of Sandomire as Lady Sandwich, Ballaster and Koster query this.[70] However, stories about Lady Sandwich's lesbianism can be seen in such poems as the *Assembly at Kensington*, to which I have already referred,

> In Sandwich, Rochester is still alive,
> His leud wit, the daily does survive
> It must be allowed she does Excel
> Him on Earth, and all the Devils in Hell.
> Fitzharding and she are new Recreation
> Such as afford but dull diversion
> Their velvet Rubsters can faintly please,
> And only free them from the French disease.[71]

Lady Fitzharding, too, appears in this poem as Sandwich's partner and was also considered a lesbian, although not accused of being of the Cabal in *New Atalantis*. In another poem of the same period, however, she was accused of "Play[ing] the Man's Part / You are for no Masculine Lover."[72] By associating Whig women with such well-known lesbians, Manley makes it plain that they have been forced to adopt the unnatural practices of the Whig men to gain sexual satisfaction.

Once we assume that this is the point of the episode, we can begin to distinguish Manley's strategy. Some women are included out of personal spite, such as Lady Sarah Piers, the amateur poet who was closely associated with Catharine Trotter for whom Manley reserved particular antagonism.[73] However, other women, such as the Countess of Macclesfield and Lucy Wharton were included not only because of their Whig connections, but for the very fact that their heterosexual activities were notorious. To associate Whig ladies, whose appetites were "normal," if reputedly voracious, with the Lesbian coterie suggests that given the parlous state of Whig manhood, this is their only chance for any sexual activity.

By this means Manley effects a polarization of Whig and Tory sexuality. For Manley is careful to stress throughout *New Atalantis*, that Tory gentlemen, whatever other vices they exhibit, are never "unnatural" in the objects of their desire. They are rather typified by St. John and his aggressively heterosexual rakishness, Anthony Hammond's promiscuity, and Nottingham's passion for a female Italian opera singer. Even John Manley, her own husband, ridiculous as he is portrayed to be, is distinguished by his lust for women. It is as though Manley is demonstrating, even through her satire on her own party, that Tory men, while often far from virtuous, are at least recognizably masculine, while Whigs offer only the "representation of men." In the same way readers with sufficient knowledge of Portland's relationship with William III would be aware that the story of his seduction of a young female virgin could only be a "representation" of his sexuality. If we look at this from an early eighteenth-century viewpoint, Manley is indicating that the Whigs are a political party whose equivocal masculinity leads their women into seeking the "representation" of men among themselves. Whig men are, by implication, incapable of the inherently male duties of leadership and government. The Tory gentleman might ask, how a party that sheltered the likes of Sunderland, William III, and Portland could be entrusted with the guardianship of the nation. Such men, who wished male lovers to represent women, and even forced their own wives into "unnatural practices'" would surely have been tainted. The followers of William III, who preferred criminal "Italian" joys to good English heterosexual practices, must therefore be considered inherently vicious and unfit to govern.

J. G. A. Pocock discusses at length the Whiggish movement to reassert the "ideal of the citizen, virtuous in his devotion to public good" and "virtuous . . . in his independence of any relation that might render him corrupt."[74] In the light of Pocock's argument on the importance of virtue, which is conspicuously absent in Manley's depiction of the Whigs, we might argue that it is valid to suggest that Sunderland attempted to suppress the second volume of New Atalantis because it reiterated and amplified much more confidently those suggestions of "deviant" practices that had been subtly suggested in the first volume. By stopping Manley's pen, he hoped he would need not live in fear of what might appear in her next publication.

NOTES

I am grateful to W. R. Owens for his helpful comments upon the initial drafts of this essay.

1. Delariviere Manley, Secret Memoirs and Manners of Several Persons of Quality, of both Sexes. From the New Atalantis, an Island in the Mediteranean [sic]. Written originally in Italian, and translated from the third edition of the French. (London: John Morphew, 1709). For convenience of citation, the edition used is Delarivier Manley, New Atalantis, ed. Ros Ballaster, (London: Penguin, 1992).

2. J. A. Downie, Robert Harley and the Press (Cambridge: Cambridge University Press, 1979), 115.

3. Narcissus Luttrell, A Brief Relation of State Affairs from September 1678 to April 1714, 6 vols., (Oxford: 1857) vi, 505, 506, 508.

4. Charles Spencer, 3rd Earl of Sunderland to Sarah, Duchess of Marlborough, 4 November 1709. BL Add. Ms. 61443 f.35. The "noble persons" were Robert Harley, erstwhile Secretary of State who would, within the year form a government, and Abigail Masham, Anne's new favorite, and Harley's assiduous supporter with the Queen.

5. See for instance, William Shippen's Duke Humphrey's Answer (London: 1708).

6. Lady Mary Wortley Montague to Mrs. Frances Hewet, 12 November [1709],

The Complete Letters of Lady Mary Wortley Montague, ed. by Robert Halsband, 3 vols. (Oxford: Clarendon Press, 1965), vol. 1, 18.

7. Mainwaring to Duchess of Marlborough, undated, 1709, *Correspondence of Duchess of Marlborough*, 228.

8. Delarivier Manley, *The Adventures of Rivella* (London: 1714), 110.

9. "The Benefits of a Theatre," in *A New Collection Poems Relating to State Affairs from Oliver Cromwell to this Present Time by the Greatest Wits of the Age* (London: 1705) 588, or Joseph Browne's *St. James's Park* (London: John Morphew, 1708), which satirizes many of the same Whigs (and some Tories) as Manley.

10. The list of anti-Marlborough (and particularly anti-Sarah) satires and lampoons is too long to quote. They probably run into the hundreds, and many are along the lines of Joseph Browne's *Fox Set to Watch the Geese* (London: 1705), which repeats the rumor of Godolphin's affair with Sarah. Others concentrate on her fiery temper and her avarice.

11. *The Age of Wonders* (London: 1710).

12. John Richetti, *Popular Fiction before Richardson: Narrative Patterns 1700–1739* (Oxford: Clarendon Press, 1969), 132.

13. Manley, *New Atalantis*, 132.

14. Martin Gray, *A Dictionary of Literary Terms* (Beirut: York Press, 1992), 256.

15. Elizabeth Hollis Berry, *Sexual Politics in Delarivier Manley's Secret Histories* (unpublished Ph.D. diss., University of Alberta, 1993), 7.

16. Delarivier Manley. *The Adventures of Rivella* (London: E. Curll, 1714), 110.

17. *The Tatler* No. 63, 3 September 1709.

18. Manley, *New Atalantis*, 162–86.

19. For a discussion of this see Ballaster's *New Atalantis*, 291–92, and Patricia Köster, ed., *The Novels of Delariviere Manley*, 2 vols. (Gainsville, Fla.: Scholars Facsimiles and Reprints, 1971), 909.

20. *Some Memoirs Relating to the Life of the Right Honourable John Lord Haversham from the Year 1640 to 1710* (London: J. Baker, 1711), iv.

21. Haversham had orchestrated this "grave Seignior's" invitation to Sophia, the Electress of Hanover to England, in her capacity as heir to the English throne, an act that won Anne's lasting disapproval of the Earl. See Keith Feiling, *A History of the Tory Party 1640–1714* (Oxford: Clarendon Press, 1924), 390.

22. For the boundaries to which the careful author could write, but never cross without fear of prosecution, see C. R. Kropf, "Libel and Satire in the Eighteenth Century," *Eighteenth Century Studies* 8 (1974–75): 153–68.

23. BL Add Mss 70028. Letter dated 19 July, 1711.

24. Manley, *New Atalantis*, 162.

25. To explain Manley's attack on her cousin, who married her bigamously, many critics have taken the view that he must have been a Whig. As he was an active member of Parliament for many years, and Tory agent in Cornwall, it is difficult to see how they have come to this conclusion. There is no evidence that John Manley ever had Whig sympathies. See Dolores Duff, *Materials Towards a Biography of Mary Delariviere Manley* (unpublished Ph.D. diss., University of Indiana, 1965) 62; Ballaster, *Seductive Forms*, 119; Paula McDowell, *Women of Grub Street* (Oxford: Claredndon, 1998), 225.

26. *The Epistolary Correspondence of Sir Richard Steele*, ed. John Nichols, 2 vols., (London, 1787) vol. 1, 455.

27. Manley, *New Atalantis*, 12, 60.

28. For a discussion of Naval propaganda see Peter LeFevre's "To Save Some Guesses": The Later Seventeenth-Century Navy, Information and Propaganda From Rupert to Rooke," in William B Cogar, ed., *New Interpretations in Naval History: Selected*

Papers from the Twelfth Naval History Symposium (Annapolis, Md.: Naval Institute Press, 1997), 79–92, and various pamphlets, including spoof ones, such as *The Case of Sir Humphrey Mackworth, and the Mine Adventurers, with respect to the Extraordinary Proceedings of the Agents, Servants and Dependents, of the Right Honourable Sir Thomas Mansell, Bar* (London, 1707), or [Sir Humphrey Mackworth] *A Familiar Discourse, or Dialogue concerning the Mine-Adventure. Or, a vindication of the proceedings of the Governour and Company of the Mine-Adventurers of England . . . demonstrating the reasonableness and necessity of a call, and of complying with the resolutions of the General Court. By William Shiers* (London, 1709).

29. Anonymous, *Almonds for Parrots: or, A soft answer to a scurrilous satyr, call'd St. James's Park* (London: 1708), 7.

30. . Joseph Browne, *St. James's Park: A Satyr* (London: John Morphew, 1708), 16.

31. Nottingham University Library, Portland Collection, PwV44, "The Assembly at Kensington," dated 1699, in *A Collection of Poems and Lampoons & co. Not yet Printed*, 263.

32. Browne, *St. James's Park, A Satyr*, 11.

33. "Moderation Display'd," in G. de F. Lord, ed., *Poems On Affairs of State*, 7 vols. (New Haven: Yale University Press, 1975), vol. 7, 41.

34. A fuller discussion of this can be found in Dennis Rubini, "Sexuality and Augustan England: Sodomy, Politics, Elite Circles and Society," in Kent Gerard and Gert Hekma, eds., *The Pursuit of Sodomy: Male Homosexuality in Renaissance and Enlightenment Europe* (London: Harington Park Press Inc., 1989), 351.

35. Anonymous, "A New Ballad Writ by Jacob Tonson and Sung at the Kit Kat Clubb on the 8th March 170   ," in G. de F. Lord, ed., *Poems on Affairs of State*, vol. 7, 57. Jennings was Sarah Churchill's maiden name. See discussion below for the rumours of homosexuality at William's court.

36. I am grateful to the Manuscripts Department of Nottingham University Library and the Library Services of Nottingham County Council for their assistance in trying to trace details of Portland's activities as a guardian.

37. Manley, *The New Atalantis*, 45.

38. There were rumors of a Mistress Howard having an affair with Portland, but at least one correspondent put these rumors down to malicious gossip aimed at destroying Howard's "more than ordinary reputation." The same correspondent quotes Portland as saying that this Mistress Howard was "the last woman in the world that he would marry." See University of Nottingham, Portland Collection PwA 2798. Anonymous to William Bentinck, 1ˢᵗ Earl of Portland, 26 June 1699.

39. Rictor Norton, *Mother Clap's Molly House* (London: GMP, 1992), 35.

40. See, for instance, *Charlot. Eglogue pastorelle sur les miseres de la France, & sur la tresheureuse & miraculeuse deliurance de . . . Prince Monseigneur le Duc de Guyse, etc.* (Troyes : I. Moreau, 1592); *Les Amours de Charlot [Charles, Count d'Artois] et Toinette [Mary Antoinette]. Pièce dérobée à V* (Paris, 1789).

41. Manley, *New Atalantis*, 29.

42. Rubini, "Sexuality and Augustan England," in *The Pursuit of Sodomy*, Hekma, 361.

43. See Elisabeth Charlotte, Princess Palatine, and Duchess of Orleans, *Letters from Liselotte*, trans. and ed. Maria Kroll (London: Victor Gollancz, 1970), 70.

44. *A New Collection of Poems Relating to State Affairs, from Oliver Cromwell to this Present Time by the Greatest Wits of the Age* (London, 1705), 502.

45. Manley, *New Atalantis*, 32.

46. Feiling, *A History of the Tory Party*, 327, 332.

47. Marion Sharpe Grew, *William III and William Bentinck: The Life of Bentinck, Earl of Portland, from the Wellbeck correspondence* (London: John Murray, 1924).

48. Quoted in Rubini, "Sexuality and Augustan England," in Gerand and Hekma, eds., *The Pursuit of Sodomy*, 367.

49. Manley, *New Atalantis*, 29.

50. Ibid., 162.

51. [Madame d'Aulnoy], *Memoirs of the Court of England* . . . [Delarivier Manley], *To Which is Added The Lady's Pacquet of Letters* . . . (London: B. Bragg, 1707), 523–24.

52. For a discussion of these theories see Michael Kimmel, ed., *Love Letters Between a Certain Late Nobleman and the Famous Mr. Wilson* (London: Haworth Press, 1990).

53. I am not suggesting that Sarah Churchill was in any way aware of her son-in-law's personal anxiety.

54. Norton, *Mother Clap's Molly House*, 51.

55. [d'Aulnoy], *Memoirs of the Court of England*, 541.

56. Ibid., 523–24.

57. Quoted in Norton, *Mother Clap's Molly House*, 36.

58. There were several other pamphlets which detailed Barbara Palmer, Duchess of Cleveland's scandalous love life. See *The Duchess of C— —s Memorial (General Fielding's answer to the Duchess of C— —'s Memorial* [London, 1707?]; *A faithful account of the examination of R. Feilding, . . . before . . . Ld. Chief Justice Holt, and his commitment to Newgate* (London: [1706.]; Sebastien Bremond, *Hattige: or, the Amours of the King of Tamaran.* (Amsterdam, 1680).

59. *Diary of John Evelyn*, ed. Austin Dobson, 3 vols. (London: Routledge/Thoermes Press), vol. 3, 307–8.

60. *The Conspirators; or the Case of Catiline. As collected from the best Historians impartially examined* . . . (London: 1721), 24.

61. For a discussion of Sunderland's suicide, see Norton, *Mother Clap's Molly House*, 35–42. Ms. note on flyleaf, British Library copy, C.115.d.15, *Love Letters Between a Certain Late Nobleman and the famous Mr. Wilson: discovering The True History of the Rise and surprising Grandeur of the Celebrated Beau* quoting Rev. Robert Woodrow Analect; Anecdotes, 20 September 1727 (Maitland Club, 1842–1843), vol. III, 443.

62. Beau Wilson's murderer, John Law, was pardoned in 1719, and returned to England in October 1721. He was presented to George I on 22 October. The reappearance in England of a man on whose absent silence Sunderland's place in polite society may have depended, can only have added to his anxiety, and may have been a contributory factor to his putative suicide.

63. In her next secret history, *Memoirs of Europe*, Manley complains that she was prosecuted for "glancing" at Sunderland's errors in the *New Atalantis*. In the present argument, the "glance" is read as being so oblique that it required prior knowledge to be recognized as an attack.

64. *The Rival Dutchess: or Court Incendiary. In a Dialogue between Madam Maintenon and Madam M[Masham]* (London: 1708).

65. Churchill to Queen Anne (undated 1709), 235.

66. *The Rival Dutchess*, 4.

67. G. de F. Lord, ed., *Poems on Affairs of State*, vol. 7, 309.

68. Quoted in Norton, *Mother Clap's Molly House*, 48.

69. Kimmel, *Love Letters*, 4, 7.

70. Ballaster, ed. *New Atalantis*, 293, n.357, and Köster, *The Novels of Delariviere Manley*, 910.

71. *Assembly at Kensington*, 263–64.

72. Nottingham University, Portland Collection, PwV 44, *Venus's Answer*, 246.

73. Manley had had cordial dealings with Lady Sarah Piers during the preparation of *The Nine Muses*, published in 1700. By 1709, however, she was no doubt doubly guilty in Manley's eyes, being both a Whig and a friend of Catharine Trotter. See letters to Trotter from Piers, 28 October 1700, BL Birch Collection, Add. Ms. 4264, f. 291v and

Add. Ms. 4264, f. 324–324v. I am grateful to Anne Kelley for suggesting that Lady Sarah Piers is the most likely original of Zarah, the wife of Chevalier Pierro.

74. J. G. A. Pocock, *Virtue, Commerce and History: Essays on Political Thought and History, Chiefly in the Eighteenth Century* (Cambridge: Cambridge University Press, 1985), 48.

The Key to Stowe: Toward a Patriot Whig Reading of Eliza Haywood's *Eovaai*

ELIZABETH KUBEK

Such were the difficulties and dangers which encompassed this princess
—Bolingbroke, on Queen Elizabeth I

ELIZA HAYWOOD'S 1736 *ADVENTURES OF EOVAAI, PRINCESS OF IJAVEO* is often described as resistant to classification, "a wild blend of genres" further confused by participation in "an uneasy piecemeal alliance of otherwise contradictory [political] positions."[1] Certainly *Eovaai* is a hybrid of various forms, although it most closely resembles the popular class of roman a cléf commonly referred to in early modern England as the scandalous chronicle, two examples of which had already procured Haywood some notoriety. However, the assertion that *Eovaai* lacks coherence is based in misinterpretation of the fiction's specific political context and goals. Constructing the adventures of her "pre-Adamitical" princess, Haywood combines scandal narrative, anti-Walpole satire, fairy tale, and erotic bildungsroman in an act of overdetermination, since all of these genres are employed to demonstrate the same master trope: the conflict between the desire for power and the "Spirit of Patriotism." This last phrase, spoken in *Eovaai* by the virtuous Alhahuza, is a clear indicator of the fiction's political allegiance. The identification of Alhahuza as Henry St. John, Viscount Bolingbroke, is an obvious one, but what remains to be noted is the degree to which this statesman's ideas and goals inform the entire work. Read in the context of Bolingbroke's writings[2] and the situation and actions of his supporters in the 1730s, *Eovaai* emerges not merely as a novel *with* a key, but as a fiction that *is* a key. *Eovaai* deliberately fictionalizes and popularizes the political writings and theories of the exiled Bolingbroke, and also functions as a guidebook to another political text: Stowe, the estate of Bolingbroke's ally Richard Temple, viscount Cobham, and the gathering-place of the so-called "Patriot Whigs." During the 1730s Cobham commissioned for Stowe's gardens and park a series of structures honoring the allies and heroes of the Patriot Whigs, making the estate a vast allegory of partisan politics. At the center of *Eovaai*'s main narrative is a thinly disguised description of some of Stowe's political icons, and a guide to their proper interpretation in terms of Bolingbroke's writings. Haywood's fiction and its embellishments (including a dedication, introduction, mock commentary, setting, and interpolated tales), form a coherent whole in the light of this metatextual function, which ties together seemingly disparate textual and generic elements.

The identification of *Eovaai* as a contribution to patriot Whig political theory has been hampered by a tendency to define Haywood as a Tory feminist, largely because of her previous political writings. The last of three political satires by Haywood, *Eovaai* appeared eight years after the *Dunciad*, in which Pope attacked her specifically for "profligate licentiousness" in writing "those most scandalous books, called the Court of Carimania [*sic*], and the New Utopia"—her first two works in the genre—and four years after Savage accused her in *An Author to be Let* of "scandalizing Persons of the highest Worth and Distinction."[3] In these texts, Haywood attacks the Hanoverian monarchy and its supporters for opportunism, both sexual and economic; however, similar criticisms of George II and his circle were voiced by both Whigs and Tories, party labels that in the 1720s and 1730s were in any case highly fluid. *Utopia* and *Caramania* simply demonstrate that Haywood was an effective political writer in a mode traditionally used by women.

While her specific allegiances can be determined only by careful historical analysis, rather than by generic tendencies, Haywood's protofeminism emerges more clearly in her satires. This is evinced not only by her concern for women's sexual commodification but also by the very boldness of her choice to engage in political discourse. Pope no doubt spoke for many of his peers in the 1720s when he denounced the chronicles" mixture of erotic gossip and politics as especially unsuitable for "that sex, which ought least to be capable of such malice and impudence." Haywood's use of a male "Translator" in the anonymously published *Eovaai* is widely recognized as a device for avoiding the appearance of gender transgression while continuing to focus on women's sexuality, in ways that her admirers find pleasingly subversive of authority.[4] Here again, however, general tenets must be balanced with detailed historical analysis. Certainly *Eovaai* is "about" gender and authority, but its partisan politics informs the specific functioning of difference within the narrative and its textual apparatus as more than a simple binary. Described on the title page as "the son of a MANDARIN, residing in *London*," Haywood's Translator is not simply "feminized," as Wilputte states, but rather marked as male Other by his status as "Oriental" exile, and by his deference to the "cabal" of seventy

Chinese "Commentators" identified as the initial translators of the text from "the Language of Nature." Moreover, the claim made in the Preface that the main text of *Eovaai* originates from "before the Reign of Adam" places the story as a prepatriarchal myth.[5] The exiled narrator and the mythopoetic use of history both point the reader to Bolingbroke, who by 1736 had taken refuge in France but remained determined, in his own words, "to revive the spirit of the Constitution in Britain."[6] Bolingbroke's mythic history of British constitutional politics, as outlined in his 1730–31 *Remarks on the History of England*, in fact informs the whole of *Eovaai*, just as the "Chinese" history and scholarship constructed to justify the "translation" dominates and overwrites the main narrative. This parallel suggests that Haywood's use of a male narrative persona may be intended not simply to disguise her "real" gender but rather to situate the speaker as a philosopher and historian, an alternative-universe Bolingbroke.

Within this context, female figures and voices in *Eovaai* point to specific historical and political referents that promote a Patriot Whig agenda. Femininity in *Eovaai* is hardly a simple binary device, the equivalent of a standpoint "liminal . . . in society and politics";[7] for example, the piece is dedicated to Sarah, the Dowager Duchess of Marlborough, one of the most powerful and visible Whigs of her day. However, difference does function as a device in *Eovaai*: as a sign of political "otherness," or, to use a word that for Haywood and her circle in the 1730s had specific meaning, "opposition." In the early decades of the eighteenth century, gender opposition was emerging as a key structuring trope of social consciousness, the "natural" sign of difference. Simultaneously, the development of constitutional monarchy had led to the emergence of Opposition as a viable political position, envisioned by Whig theorists such as Bolingbroke as having a legitimate function within the semimythic "ancient constitution." The legitimization of political opposition as a necessary component of civil liberty is a central tenet of "Patriot Whig" political discourse, which drew upon traditional conceptions of "mixed government" as antidote to the individual leader's natural love of power. Opposition in this naturalistic system arises when an imbalance occurs (usually in the person of corrupt ministers or a bad king) and reintegrates with the system when the imbalance has been corrected.[8]

Attempting to legitimize opposition by investing it with a jingoistic prehistory, Bolingbroke in his *Remarks* identifies "a perpetual jealousy" of "liberty" as the "true old English spirit."[9] *Eovaai* goes further back into time, outstripping even the "Chinese" history Haywood invokes and representing the text as belonging to an age before "the narrow Chronology" of the Christian calendar, when people traveled between the planets and spoke "the Language of Nature."[10] This pretense allows "the Cabal" and "the learned Commentator on the *Chinese* Translation" to stage elaborate arguments in terms of various types of difference: appropriate "feminine" behavior, historical change versus "human nature," and so on. These exchanges between authorities grow more intense during erotic scenes and political discourses, and often take on a tone of extreme irony, as when the Chinese "Cabal" is "assured" by "the Ladies" that, unlike the "pre-Adamitical" Eovaai, the daughters of Eve are "wholly free from any Inquietudes" caused by desire.[11] Opposition and difference thus begin to emerge as necessary correctives to the "prejudices of education" and the hypocrisy of a culture that has lost "the language of nature."

As an alien observer who is nevertheless aristocratic, scholarly and male, the "son of a Mandarin," who assembles the disparate pieces of *Eovaai* privileges his Otherness as making him an ideal observer, capable of judging a culture less ancient and (his introduction implies) less literate than his own. From this standpoint, he can challenge "the *Reader* [to] divest himself of the Prejudice of Education, and consider it as no Impossibility, that our Calculation should be more just than that he has been instructed in"—and even demand that the reader who persists in doubt "take at least a trip to *Nanquin*" and view the "authentic Testimonials" there.[12] Opposition, this standpoint implies, comes from superior wisdom and pedigree—an implication typically made in Bolingbroke's writings through his use of a "venerable" speaker. Moreover, the figure of China, as a trope for "otherness," is employed by Bolingbroke to illustrate his own discussion of historical and political "prejudice" in his *Letters on the Study and Use of History* (begun in 1735):

> There is scarce any folly or vice more epidemical among the sons of men, than that ridiculous and hurtful vanity by which the people of each country are apt to prefer themselves to those of every other, and to make their own customs, and manners, and opinions, the standards of right and wrong, of true and false. The Chinese mandarins were strangely surprised, and almost incredulous, to when the Jesuits showed them how small a figure their empire made in the general map of the world.[13]

While the "Oriental" narrator was a trope of early modern satire, the figure of the Mandarin in *Eovaai* and its connection with the critique of epistemic "vanity" reflects Bolingbroke's train of thought with startling directness. Moreover, the two scenarios have similar ironies: *Eovaai's* translator, faced with an alien text from a culture identified as prelapsarian, and thus to the "Western" reader superior to his own, struggles with issues of interpretation and "truth," just as Bolingbroke's Mandarin confronts not only the colonial "truth" of the Jesuit's map, but the motives of the priest himself—a figure that elsewhere in Bolingbroke's work stands for the "fanatical" distortion of history.[14] The standpoint of the racial Other in both texts becomes sympathetic precisely because of its ability to undercut the stance of authoritarian objectivity, forcing the reader instead to rely on individual ethical judgment.

Haywood further destabilizes the problem of truth by introducing that quality as a character, the goddess Halafamai, who saves Eovaai from becoming corrupted by her own vanity and lust. This figure's name is glossed as "signif[ying] *Truth*, according to the Cabal," with the caveat that "both the Commentator, and *Hahehihotu* are of opinion, that *Mercy* is more agreeable to the Original."[15] Halafamai, who unlike other divinities in *Eovaai* intervenes directly and physically to assist the motherless heroine, introduces a veritable cascade of ambiguities centered on the issues of perception and judgment. Perhaps more importantly, this invocation of a goddess provides a specific link between Eovaai's dual role as desiring individual and political ideal, situating this connection within a specifically feminine identity previously Other to English political consciousness. Halafamai's protection of Eovaai reflects the emergence of a feminine national "genius" that consecrates the political by referring it to an atemporal sacred order (Truth). This order, however, is based not in monarchical patriarchy but in maternal tenderness and compassion (Mercy); the danger that Eovaai will transgress calls forth a spirit of (m)Otherness capable of redeeming rather than judging. The female-oriented space briefly shared by Halafamai and Eovaai allows the latter to progress by training her "feminine" epistemophilia toward the Good. Moreover, the dyad of Mother/nation and daughter/ruler is effective specifically as Whig political mythology because it functions as a replacement for both the affective and the transhistorical (dynastic) registers of Tory iconography's martyred Father/king. Eovaai, whose royal father has died and left her unprotected, participates in a new family dynamic in which legitimacy is based on tested worth rather than patrilineage. Halafamai's intervention intertwines the psychological and the political, suggesting that the interpersonal reality associated with the feminine is the womb of those acquired virtues that serve the state. That transgression and opposition are employed as structural and theoretical elements of *Eovaai* is thus not a result of political or generic confusion, or simply a gesture toward gender subversion, but a deliberate device employed for specific political reasons.

While *Eovaai*'s various levels of commentary enact the ahistorical necessity of opposition, Haywood combines narrative elements freely in the service of her specific political goal. The representation of Robert Walpole as an evil magician follows a contemporary trope of Opposition allegory.[16] Simultaneously, Haywood's use of a heroine rather than a hero allows her erotic scenes to represent ministerial influence as seduction, connecting a critique of desire found in her earlier scandalous chronicles with Machiavellian conceptions of power politics similar to those of Bolingbroke. The fairy-tale plot of *Eovaai*, with its central heroine, allies it with the mythopoetic and heroic structures of Bolingbroke's published political writings, especially the *Remarks on the History of England*. Meanwhile, apparently minor but meaningful details of the narrative provide evidence that Haywood paid minute attention to Bolingbroke's goals and circumstances in 1735–36, suggesting that she may have been in contact with him and/or his circle of intimates. Certain details indicate that she also either visited Stowe (as did many other Opposition writers, including Pope and Swift) or was privy to Cobham's current and projected additions to the park. Many of *Eovaai*'s seemingly random features are actually meant to be read metatextually in this way, rather than as fragments of unrelated genres.

The scandalous chronicles often begin with the conceit that their purpose was to record current affairs for the education of a future King; see for example the most famous example of the genre, Delarivier Manley's *Atalantis*. However, these works typically are represented, as part of this trope, as substitutes for direct experience on the prince's part.[17] *Eovaai*, however, insists on the inadequacy of precepts, a countertrope that in the scandalous chronicles is often limited to observations on erotic knowledge. The adventures forced upon Eovaai, the hereditary queen of Ijaveo, reflect Bolingbroke's theory (stated most directly in *The Idea of a Patriot King*) that a virtuous monarch should suffer with his people: "He would be formed in that school out of which the greatest and best of monarchs have come, the school of affliction."[18] Eovaai's afflictions begin when she loses a magic jewel left her by her father, and with it the protection of a guardian spirit. Her people fall prey to disorder and faction, while she herself is carried off by the lustful enchanter Ochihatou (Walpole), who controls an adjacent kingdom, Hypotosa, through his magical influence over King Oeros (George II). Eovaai's wanderings lead to her political enlightenment; but while her resistance contributes to Ochihatou's defeat, she must ultimately be rescued by Oeros's son Adelhu. Oeros himself is restored to power by the "virtuous Patriot" Alhahuza, who leads a popular uprising against Ochihatou and "boldly" plucks from the King's crown the feather that represents Ochihatou's magic.[19] The fairy-tale quality of *Eovaai*'s conclusion, which leaves the heroine and her prince uniting their kingdoms into "the most powerful, most opulent, and happiest Monarchies in the World,"[20] reflects what Bolingbroke's critics call his "high-flown metapolitics": the Patriot King effortlessly restores his country to happiness and peace.[21]

This ending reflects Bolingbroke's conviction that a monarch merited only that power s/he attained and kept with the help of the people, and stages the exiled patriot's triumphant return as the only hope for England. The heroic ending of *Eovaai*, therefore, closely follows Bolingbroke's political mythologies.

While ensuring that these myths would continue to flourish in Bolingbroke's absence, *Eovaai* also functions as a combination of propaganda and patronage-seeking, denouncing Bolingbroke's enemies and praising those whose influence the Patriot Whigs most sought to engage. Even apparently minor details reflect this agenda; witness this footnote on Alhahuza: "this great Patriot never ask'd any thing for himself, and was so strictly just to his Country, that he gave up his own Brother, finding he had been corrupted by *Ochihatou*."[22] The "brother," previously unidentified, must represent William Pulteney, afterwards Earl of Bath, and in the early 1730s Bolingbroke's partner in *The Craftsman*. Bolingbroke for some time had suspected Pulteney (rightly, as it turned out) of making separate alliances in pursuit of his own interests. By 1736, Pulteney, in his new alliance with the Carteret "bloc," was in direct competition with Bolingbroke's "broad bottom" allies for the patronage of Frederick, Prince of Wales, represented in *Eovaai* as the heroic Adelhu.[23] Central to the continued unity of Bolingbroke's supporters were their hopes for the Prince on the one hand, and on the other, in Archibald Foord's words, "the influence and pugnacity of the septuagenarian Sarah, dowager Duchess of Marlborough." Thus while Bolingbroke's desire to engage Frederick informs *Eovaai*'s conclusion, Haywood's Dedication bids for the support of a fairy godmother in the form of the formidable Sarah Churchill, who loathed Walpole, and whose oncesour relations with Bolingbroke had recently been sweetened by the latter's offer of a panegyric for the dead Duke's monument at Blenheim.[24] Invoked by Haywood as the wife of "that Godlike Man" and the mother of "Generations of Heroes and Heroines," Sarah, so perfect as to risk being thought "an *imaginary* Heroine," is praised for her ability "to undergo, with the same Sweetness, the *severest* Trials: — Trials! to which no other Woman was ever liable, because no other Woman ever *possess'd*, and *lost* such Treasures" — a reference followed by the list of Sarah's dead children.[25] The Whig heroine is praised, like the Roman matron, as the reproducer and underwriter of civic virtue; yet Haywood's reader would be aware also of Sarah's own powerful career as Queen Anne's "favorite," and of her fall from the Queen's grace, an image with great resonance for those who wished to see Walpole undergo a similar fate. Sarah's image thus provides *Eovaai* with a typically multivalent set of associations: current political connections, the cautionary tale of royal infidelity, and the reminder that women's political influence was not to be despised. The inclusion of the dowager Duchess of Marlborough also reminds the reader that political ambition is a form of desire experienced by women as well as men, expanding upon Bolingbroke's contention that "the love of power is natural" to all "men."[26]

Yet this "love of power," and its corollary, the desire for sexual power, are precisely the traits that in Eovaai must be exposed and rejected for her to become a virtuous ruler. Far from endorsing "divine-right monarchist sentiments," as Ballaster claims,[27] *Eovaai* follows Bolingbroke in depicting all forms of monarchy as making a dangerous appeal to the "natural" desire for power. This conviction causes the narrative to appear inconsistent in both its politics and its attitude toward Eovaai herself, unless the story is read through the lens of Bolingbroke's conception of constitutional monarchy, as described by the "ancient venerable gentleman" who is Bolingbroke's "translator" in *Remarks on the History of England*. According to this narrative persona, who engages to defend the previous writings of "Caleb D'Anvers," the pen name used by the writers of *The Craftsman*, "liberty cannot be long secure, in any country, unless a perpetual jealousy watches over it. . . . The hundred eyes of Argus were not always kept open; but they were never all closed. The whole body of a nation may be as jealous of their liberties, as a private man of his honour."[28] The metaphor of sexual jealousy embedded in this passage becomes a dominant conceit in *Eovaai*. Haywood's Translator and Commentators reenact this Argus-eyed watchfulness over the actions of Eovaai by depicting the constant examination and control of her political and erotic desires as essential to her virtue and happiness, and thus to the nation. Haywood does not simply depict active sexual/political desire as immoral and dangerous; instead she attempts to demonstrate, through Eovaai's erotic adventures as well as her education in leadership and self-control, the role "natural" desire plays in the development of an autonomous and mature self. The narrative represents the transition from a blindly desirous self to an enlightened one through Eovaai's use of two significant objects: a magic carcanet, the gift of her father, the loss of whose central jewel requires her to undergo a political education; and a telescope, the gift of a maternal goddess, which allows her to control her newly awakened libido by correctly valuing its objects. Together, these two symbolic objects represent the "masculine" issue of political power and the "feminine" issue of sexual control, but their physical images (a circle reduced to "the exterior Ornament, which had encompass'd" the missing stone, and a phallic instrument) reverse the traditional gendering of the political and the sexual, and remind us that the goal of this fairy-tale quest is the creation of a unified, virtuous being—Haywood's political goal as well.

Following the tenets of Bolingbroke, *Eovaai* begins by dramatizing the profound and ambiguous effect the character of the monarch has upon the public sphere. The Translator praises the virtuous Chinese Emperor who ordered the translation of *Eovaai* into Chinese in order to promote "*Virtue,* and a *Desire of Knowledge*," as well as "the *Opulence* and *Welfare* of his Subjects," and whose "Glory was to be at the head of a *brave*, a *wise*, and a *free* People." This theme is developed further with the portrayal of Eovaai's royal father, Eojaeu, or "Father of the People," who "represented to her, that the greatest Glory of a Monarch was the Liberty of the People, his most valuable Treasures in *their* crowded Coffers, and his securest Guard in their *sincere Affection*," to which a footnote adds, "This implies, that the *Ijaveans* were a free People, tho' under Monarchical Government." Eojaeu also warns his daughter that she will not be accessible to her people "if you suffer yourself to be engrossed by any *one Man, or Set of Men;* above all things, therefore, beware of *Favourites,* for Favour naturally implies *Partiality,* and *Partiality* is but another Name for *Injustice.* All Passions deceive us, but none more than the Goodwill we bear to such whose Sentiments seem to fall in with our own."[29] However, as Eovaai's adventures demonstrate, precepts alone are not sufficient to protect us from our own desires. The deceptive power of passion must be combated with the "jealous" vision of the true patriot.

Scopophilia, epistemophilia, and sexual objectification are thus among both the vices opposed by the narrative and the devices it employs to engage its readers—one of the traits that ally *Eovaai* with the scandalous chronicle and its maxims on sexuality. Significantly, Eovaai's name means "The Delight of Eyes," although her father makes sure she receives an education in "the Virtues of the *Mind*," rather than the traditional feminine arts of "Singing, Dancing, [and] Playing on the Musick," and forbids praise from either sex of her "Beauty, or any Endowment of the *Body*." Virtuous masculine authority thus represents Eovaai as highly desirable but controls both her status as object and her awareness of that status. This "double standard" is at the heart of the scandalous chronicles" cynicism about traditional images of female virtue; the classic example, upon which *Eovaai* repeatedly draws, is the history of the naïve but passionate Charlot in Delarivier Manley's *Atalantis.* "Curiosity," Manley opines, discussing Charlot's interest in erotic books, "is an early and dangerous enemy to virtue."[30] In *Eovaai* as in the *Atalantis,* epistemophilia is represented as inherent in "human Nature"; Eovaai's "Curiosity," and her having "flatter'd [herself] with the Imagination, that her own Ingenuity" might decipher the mysterious words engraved inside the magic carcanet, lead to her loss of the protective jewel. This catastrophe not only leaves Eovaai vulnerable to being carried off to Hypotosa by Ochihatou but also deprives her of a previous immunity to his ability "to transform himself into the reverse of what he was" by "cast[ing] . . . a Delusion before the Eyes of all who saw him." Deprived of this protection, Eovaai sees Hypotosa as "delightful as the Dwellings of the Blessed," while Ochihatou, whom she once found repulsive, now appears "one of the most lovely" of men.[31]

Instantly attracted to both the seemingly transformed Ochihatou and his palace, a "gorgeous Magazine" of luxurious goods and services, Eovaai is far from being a passive victim. Just as she was initially betrayed by curiosity and intellectual vanity, in Hypotosa she is seduced through her own scopophilia, especially in the form of the very narcissism her father's edict forbade. Walpole was frequently represented by his Opposition as a monster of lust and materialism; here Haywood, drawing on the scandalous genre, depicts the two forms of desire as intimately related. The palace functions as an erotic cabinet, a sexually charged "Magazine" of desirable objects wherein "Court-Bauds" entice Eovaai with "gross Flattery":

> laying her on the Bed, the Canopy of which was lined with Looking-Glass: Cast up your Eyes, most lovely Princess, said one of them, and behold a Sight more worthy the Admiration, even of yourself, than anything this sumptuous Palace, or the whole World can shew. — Your own heavenly Person. — Ah, what a ravishing Proportion! — What fine-turned Limbs! — How formed for Love is every Part! — What Legs! — What Arms! — What Breasts! — What —[32]

The mirror is often used in early-modern satires as a device to represent the ability of the text to reflect "truth" and disclose the spectator's own vanity, performing an epistemic switch not unlike that enacted by the figure of the Mandarin. But here the glass and the Bauds" accompanying narration, like the Jesuit's map, manipulate the image to establish control. Eovaai responds to deception by becoming deceptive herself; she interrupts the "Bawds" at a crucial point, "desir[ing] to be cover'd," for her "Modesty would not allow her to *seem* pleased with Discourses of this nature" (emphasis added). Yet in fact Eovaai is pleased, both by the fetishization of her body through its conventional breakdown into "Charms," and by the elaborate clothing with which her nakedness is adorned: "she now, for the first time, considered the Perfections of her Person: She view'd herself with pleasure."[33] Becoming her own object, Eovaai simultaneously attempts to limit the ability of others to objectify her, refusing to let her body be fully described or displayed. However, the description stops at the precise point of "lack," the point at which the female body becomes threateningly (rather than pleasingly) "different"; the blank in the list of "Charms," like the heroine's resistance to seduction, simply perpetuates (narrative) desire through *differance*, fragmentation, scotomization, and displacement.

Indeed, while the "Pride" aroused in this scene initially helps Eovaai resist Ochihatou's initial sexual advances, it also increases his desire, in another erotic truism borrowed from the scandalous chronicles. Meanwhile, Translator and Commentator also seem aroused by Eovaai's resistance, engaging in a conventionally ironic debate about feminine vanity, which proves "of more service to her than all the grave Lessons of Virtue and Philosophy." Eovaai's sudden awareness of her own "innate Vanity, . . . to which she had hitherto been a perfect Stranger"[34] is treated as a natural consequence of her sexual awakening under these circumstances. Yet the narrative's invasion by opposing voices at this point reminds the reader that the body the Bauds lay before the Princess as mirror-generated ego-ideal and object of visual pleasure is a controlled, censored one—fragmented and scotomized by the interested discourse of others. She in effect becomes a display in his "Magazine" of objects.

Ochihatou continues this distortion of Eovaai's self-image by promising her perfect unaccountability to "the People," which awakens in her an inner demon of desire: "That *Ypre*, which inspires the Lust of arbitrary Sway, now twisted its envenom'd tail round the Heart of *Eovaai*" (74). Ochihatou then engages her in "a kind of antick Dance" with his fawning courtiers, which quickly becomes an orgy: "not a Man but discovered himself ready to ravish what his kind Partner shewed an equal Propensity to grant; they ran, they flew into each other's Arms, and exchanged such Kisses, as the chaste Reader can have no Idea of" (75–76). Aroused by the dance, Eovaai allows herself to be drawn into a grotto in a "Garden behind the Palace," a traditional erotic site in the scandalous genre.[35] Ochihatou's promise that Eovaai "shall reign sole and absolute Queen of my Soul, and all its Faculties, as well as of the adoring Nations," looses in her a "Torrent of Libertinism," for "there is no Sentiment more flattering to human Nature, than that of being above Controul." Eovaai swears that "from henceforth I renounce all Rules but those prescribed by my own Will—all Law, but Inclination." But this declaration of selfish autonomy in fact places her further in Ochihatou's power: "he saw the melting Passion display itself a thousand different ways; . . . Beauties which till then he knew but in Idea, her treacherous Robes too loosly girt revealed." Believing herself liberated, Eovaai is reduced to a passive, fetishized object, as Ochihatou "feast[s] his Eyes upon her yielding Charms" and makes "his eager Hands . . . Seconds to his Sight."[36] The language of the scene is conventional, making Eovaai's surrender seem typically feminine and "natural," but the allegorical subtext transforms the seduction into a scene of political, as well as sexual, seduction and corruption.

At the critical moment when Eovaai's ruin "was not quite completed," the erotic scene is interrupted by news of a political crisis: the minister of Habul (Austria) is about to leave Hypotosa in disgust, since Hypotosa's ally Oudescar, King of Habul "think[s] himself trifled with." This forces Ochihatou to leave the garden, allowing an explanation of "what Miseries were occasioned . . . by the Wickedness of ambitious and unsatiable [*sic*] Man" in "Countries far distant from" Hypotosa, in the form of the interpolated tale of Queen Yximilla of Ginksy. The image of Eovaai, half-naked and lost in "a Pleasure not inferior to that she gave," is frozen in the narrative's "eye" for the duration of this story, a seeming failure of narrative coherence that in fact serves Haywood's political and satiric goals. Caught once again seeking the final, unrepresented "Charm," we as readers are reminded of the true nature of Ochihatou's desires, and those of other "ambitious and unsatiable" men; and we face the reality of desire in ourselves.[37]

"The History of Yximilla," which to a casual reader might seem merely a confusing intrusion into Eovaai's adventures, is significant both in terms of the political context it invokes—the War of the Polish Succession—and because it uses an unfortunate heroine to represent the state of a nation. Yximilla, who represents the electoral monarchy of Poland, has chosen a husband, the virtuous Prince Yamatalallabec, "but the Laws of *Ginksy* not permitting the Heir of the Crown, much less the Person in actual Possession of it, to marry without the Consent of the People, cast an Impediment in their way to Happiness." While Yamatalallabec is widely beloved, "Avarice and Ambition" lead some of the Ginksyans to oppose the marriage, creating an opening for an attack from "Broscomin, the Sovereign of a petty Principality," "*Oudescar*, King of *Habul*," and "*Tygrinonniple*, Queen of the *Icinda*'s." During the siege of Ginksy, Oudescar is forced to withdraw his forces to fend off an attack on his borders by Yamatalallabec's ally Osiphronoropho, King of Fayoul. Tygrinonniple's army takes Ginksy; Yamatalallabec is exiled and Yximilla taken captive. Haywood then spends several pages dramatizing Yximilla's imprisonment, and her forced marriage to Broscomin, whose power corrupts even "the Chief Priest" of her country.[38]

Yximilla's tale, with its dramatic conflation of erotic and political action, is a microcosm of *Eovaai* and supports its methodology and goals by allegorizing a recent breakdown of limited monarchy, caused, as Haywood's version would have it, by the electorate's neglect of virtuous princes and vulnerability to foreign interests. The story also allows Haywood to suggest that "a Woman and a Queen [should have] that

Liberty of chusing a Husband for herself, which the meanest of her Subjects enjoyed" (81), thus referring to a domestic history of royal and ministerial opposition to the Prince of Wales's marriage; and to attack the clergy for political corruption, a favorite theme of Bolingbroke and his supporters. Ochihatou's refusal to assist Oudescar against the kings of Fayoul and Narzada, who "had laid a Scheme for engrossing universal Monarchy between them," reflects traditional Opposition representations of Walpole: "Ochihatou, knowing the universal Hatred his Measures had incurred, wou'd not suffer the Army he so long had kept in Pay to depart; and thought it a less Evil to expose his King and Country to the violence of a rapacious Conqueror and ancient Enemy, than himself to the just Resentment of a People he had injured." While historians disagree as to whether Walpole's treatment of Austria stemmed entirely from reluctance to intervene in European wars or from desire to propitiate France, "the standard view is clear—George II was keen to aid the Emperor but was persuaded by the contrary views of Walpole."[39] This anti-Walpole rhetoric is intensified by the location of the tale at Eovaai's moment of greatest moral peril: the near-seduction of Eovaai reenacts, and reinvests with erotic affect, Ochihatou's earlier political seduction of his king. This scenario is in turn given an ominous "double" in the rape of Yximilla by Broscomin, whose "whole Conduct testified it was not the Woman, but the Crown she wore, with which he was enamoured."[40] Haywood's female monarchs, as subjects and objects of both political and erotic desire, demonstrate the interested motives of those who court royal favor, as well as emphasizing the monarch's humanness and vulnerability. Haywood's solution to this problem, like Bolingbroke's, combines experience and intervention: not masculine *a priori* control and education (which have already failed her heroine), but rather the influence of feminine virtue, in the form of a "spirit" capable of employing "masculine" vision as instrument.

Left in the "agreeable Solitude" of the "Grot," Eovaai enters the realm of sexual fantasy: "[a] Thousand rapturous Ideas did her perverted Fancy . . . excite in her; . . . Those warm Inclinations which the Behavior of *Ochihatou* had raised, demanded Gratification; she . . . was beginning to feel Emotions, as might very well deserve the Name of painful." Here the "Cabal" of Commentators intercedes to insist, on behalf of "the Ladies," "that the Sex is wholly free from any Inquietudes of that nature," an assertion "it would be unmannerly to doubt"; Eovaai's condition reflects either "Malice in the Historian" or a pre-Adamitical stage of women's "Constitutions."[41] The debate reenacts a crisis in the representation of (female) desire. Is it a perverse, multiform rapture or a natural, prelapsarian state? Are women, as representatives of virtue, "wholly free" from desire, and only the victims of masculine

"Malice" when desire is attributed to them? Or are they forced to be pious hypocrites, their masquerade of chastity sustained by masculine "manners"? Again, the question carries over to the political plot, becoming a neo-Machivellian discourse on the problematic nature of desire in the powerful, whose choices impact entire nations. But *Eovaai* resists a simple resolution of this question; conflicting representations and ironies are allowed to stand, while the reader is left to recollect his/her own "painful" suspense concerning Eovaai's fate during the interpolated tale. Instead of moralizing, Haywood stresses the developmental structure of her narrative by returning to the fairy-tale plot, introducing the "Genii" Halafamai (glossed as "truth and mercy") to rescue Eovaai from her desires. The feminine thus emerges here under another aspect, one signaled by the earlier invocation of Sarah Churchill: the Good Mother, underwriter of civic and personal virtue.

Halafamai's appearance to Eovaai in the grotto is preceded by "a sudden Gloom," followed by "a Stream of Light" that reveals, hovering five feet above the ground, "a Woman, . . . of a Stature far exceeding every thing in human Nature: She was neither so naked as to offend Decency, nor so habited as to conceal the fine Proportion of her Legs, her Arms, or Breast." Halafamai's flowing golden hair conceals "Eyes whose Lustre would else have been too divinely bright for *Eovaai* to have safely seen." Telling the "unhappy happy" Eovaai that she has been sent by Aiou "to save you from yourself" and from the evil spirits "who have ensnared your Virtue," Halafamai "stoop[s] to take her in her Arms," and carries her in "a Chariot drawn by Doves" to a vantage point from which she, with the help of a "sacred Telescope," can see Ochihatou in his true and shocking deformity.[42]

The figure of Halafamai carries multiple significations: she reflects certain traditions of Patriot Whig iconography (see below); she allegorizes Bolingbroke's tendency toward mythologizing "the spirit of liberty" that "like the divine rod of Aaron, will devour all the serpents of the magicians";[43] she embodies the emerging early modern "progressive" image of woman as protector of virtue; and she expresses a proto-feminist psychological impulse toward an alternative to the power of the Father. With her conflicting attributes of darkness and light, nakedness and "Decency," Cytherian doves and Palladian truth, Halafamai unites dual representations of the feminine as erotic and virtuous. Possessed solely of "charming" body parts in "fine Proportion," her dangerous gaze controlled by fetishistic hair, she is scotomized according to the cultural values ("Decency") that textually fill in and cover her sexuality, even as she promotes the true vision of Ochihatou's vice. As she towers over Eovaai and lifts her in her arms, Halafamai represents the good mother, purifying the daughter's vision and freeing her from

narcissism and objectification. Where the "bawds" attempt to fixate Eovaai at the mirror-stage, Halafamai redirects her away from a false
image of her own greatness. Like the magical mothers in fairy-tales, she
helps the heroine to take control of her life and her own psychic development.

This reading exposes *Eovaai* as problematic if read simply in terms of
modern feminist consciousness. The scotomization of Halafamai's body
reminds us uncomfortably of Eovaai's earlier containment within the
narcissistic discourse of Hypotosa, while the rebuke to narcissism offered by the goddess seems to force the heroine back to her original
posture of sexual ignorance. Yet Eovaai's further adventures show that
she does not "unlearn" the lessons of Hypotosa. Moreover, the text's
engagement with "masculine" political discourses, the challenges it
poses to the representation of female narcissism and desire, the invocation of powerful women, all mark *Eovaai* as a "feminine" fiction critical
of patriarchal epistemologies. In terms of epistemologies, Halafamai's
role is a crucial one: the Jungian critic Marie-Louise von Franz suggests that the recurrence of fairy godmothers in fairy tales represents
the return of the neglected mother goddess to the Western psyche.[44]
The goddess's "decency" in this light indicates self-knowledge and self-
control, leads to a refusal to be reduced to a sexualized body-object, and
reflects positively on Eovaai's attempt at maintaining decency before
the "Court-Bauds." Finally, Halafamai's balanced nature, which recon-
ciles opposites, suggests the ideal image of organic closure at the heart
of Bolingbroke's fantasy of Opposition: forces seemingly at odds in fact
support the integrity of the whole.

The fact that this scene is set in the garden is an important indicator
of its dual significance. On the psychological level, the garden setting is
transformed from "natural" erotic zone to site of ethical rebirth. Eovaai,
unlike other female characters in the scandalous chronicles who enter
erotic gardens, escapes unseduced and unraped; the intervention of Halafamai suggests that the garden scene can represent a feminine desire
for a "space" wherein a maternal, sheltering love can be experienced.

> To establish and maintain relations with oneself and with the other, space is
> essential. Often women are confined to the inner spaces of their womb or
> their sex insofar as they serve procreation and male desire. It's important
> for them to have their own outer space, enabling them to go from the inside
> to the outside of themselves, to experience themselves as autonomous and
> free subjects. How can the creation of this space between mothers and
> daughters be given a chance?[45]

Eovaai's flight from Hypotosa, now revealed to her corrected vision as
"[a] Scene of Desolation," is a passage to maturity which leaves her

with bleeding feet but allows her to continue her political education as an "autonomous and free subject"—a phrase that resonates with the Patriot Whig focus on the freedom of the British subject under the "ancient constitution."[46]

The beautiful but maternal Halafamai is thus the miraculous "mother" who restores the heroic princess to virtuous self-control, substituting for the false mirror of interested flattery the divine glass of truth. However, she also functions as a political symbol in a very direct and specific way: as a reference to the images of Venus that in the 1730s were among the allegorical constructions in the gardens of Stowe, the estate of Bolingbroke's supporter Cobham. Removed from office by Walpole in 1733, Cobham promptly became the mentor and patron of a group of opposition Whigs, the "young Patriots" (several, including the Pitts, were his nephews), who took Stowe as their meeting place. During the 1720s and '30s, Cobham commissioned for Stowe a series of "overtly political" architectural allegories. These included a "Sylvan Temple" dedicated to "Saxon Gods," a "Temple of British Worthies" and a "Temple of Ancient Virtue," and two buildings dedicated to Venus. One of the latter, a Vanbrugh Rotondo, contained a gilt replica of Praxiteles' statue of the goddess; the other, dedicated to "the Venus of the Garden," was decorated with paintings based on *The Fairie Queene*.[47] Inspired perhaps by this design, or perhaps by the image of Friga, one of the "Saxon Gods" contained in Stowe's "Sylvan Temple," Pope in his 1731 "Epistle to Burlington" connects Stowe with the image of a "decent" goddess:

> In all, let Nature never be forgot.
> But treat the Goddess like a modest fair,
> Nor over-dress, nor leave her wholly bare;
> Let not each beauty ev'ry where be spy'd,
> Where half the skill is decently to hide.
>
> ("Epistle to Burlington," 50–54)

The wealthy man who follows this advice, Pope concludes, will create a harmonious estate: "A Work to wonder at—perhaps a STOW [*sic*]." In similar language, Cobham's nephew Gilbert West in 1732 describes "fair Friga": "Array'd in female Stole and manly Arms. / Expressive image of that Double Soul, / Prolifick Spirit that informs the Whole."[48] Halafamai, with her balance of attributes, reflects the symbolic economy advocated in these literary descriptions, as well as directly resembling Stowe's iconic female deities. Haywood's goddess thus points the reader to both Stowe and its literary/political representations, consciously linking *Eovaai* to a body of contemporary works that extol Cobhan's patriotism and taste.

Fittingly, it is through Halafamai's truth-discerning telescope that Eovaai sights her next destination, the castle of the patriot Alhahuza. In describing her heroine's tour of Alhahuza's "Hall of Patriots" and "Theatre of the Gods," Haywood provides an explicit guide to Stowe's Opposition iconography. Eovaai first visits the "Hall of Patriots," in which are enshrined the images of "those illustrious Persons, who, in Times of Tyranny and Oppression, had happily been the Deliverers of their Country, or bravely perished in the great Attempt, immortal Men, true Sons of Fame, and worthy of the Name of Heroes!" Inquiring about the absence of crowned heads, Eovaai is told "that it was the Business of *True Patriots to humble* the Pride of *Crowns*, not wear them." When Eovaai, conscious of her own status, objects "that a good Prince was the first of Patriots," she is assured that such a monarch "merits . . . to have his Image placed in the Theatre of the Gods." In this separate structure Eovaai is shown statues of the virtuous conquerors Glaza and Ibla, King and Queen of Hypotosa, and of another Hypotosan King, Amezulto.[49]

By 1735, Walpole's influence over the press was dangerously strong; Haywood deliberately juggles details, making it difficult for those not her contemporaries to identify the figures in the Theatre. Glaza, who successfully defended Hypotosa against the King of Tolzag, has been correctly identified by Wilputte as William of Orange, although Tolzag here probably represents not France, as Wilputte suggests, but rather Scotland and Ireland. Ibla, Glaza's Queen, who "throwing off all the Delicacies of her Sex and Rank, went at the head" of an army to fight off a simultaneous invasion from "Bitza"[50] represents not Anne or Mary, but a key progressive image of feminine political power: Bolingbroke's ultimate ideal, Queen Elizabeth. The image is almost certainly that of the armor-clad Elizabeth at Tilbury: "I know I have the body of a weak, feeble woman," the Queen assured her "loving people," "but I have the heart and stomach of a king—and of a King of England too, and think foul scorn that Parma or Spain, or any prince of Europe, should dare to invade the borders of my realm; to which, rather than any dishonour should grow by me, I will myself take up arms."[51] In his *Remarks on the History of England*, Bolingbroke praises Elizabeth for (among many other things) her clever and cautious handling of foreign affairs: "She managed France, until she had taken such measures, as left her less to fear from Scotland; and she managed Spain, until she had nothing left to fear from France."[52] He interprets her foreign policies as wisely isolationist: "An island under one government, advantageously situated, rich in itself, richer in its commerce, can have no necessity, in the ordinary course of affairs, to take up the policies of the continent." Perhaps most importantly, according to Bolingbroke, the feminine Elizabeth used "her head and her heart" to gain the affections of her people, proving herself both "wise" and "alluring."[53] Elizabeth/Ibla thus represents the human embodiment of affective and virtuous monarchy.

The marrying of Glaza/William to Ibla/Elizabeth not only excises the intervening years of Stuart monarchy, but also mirrors jingoistic Whig rhetoric; the heterosexual couple becomes an emblem of political "union," concealing ongoing tensions and injustices. Glaza's defense of England's "North side" in this reading fuses Ireland and Scotland under the heading of William's triumphs in the latter. In just this manner, Bolingbroke unites the images of William and Elizabeth by deliberately contrasting the problem of Scotland during Elizabeth's reign with "that happy change which the union of the two kingdoms has brought," the ideal security of the island as "one nation under one government."[54] Haywood's image of Hypotosa simultaneously "*invaded* on the North and South sides" (emphasis mine), an image that ends with "entire Victory" for both Glaza and Ibla, depicts William not as an aggressor but rather as an Elizabeth-like defender of England's borders. This coupling, and the resultant disappearance of conflict, foreshadow the novel's end, where the need for opposition is obviated by the marriage of Eovaai and Adelhu; a similar rhetoric is found in Gilbert West's depiction of Friga, the goddess of love and marriage, who like Elizabeth is both armed and feminine, and who also "informs the Whole;/Whose Genial Power throughout exerts its Sway,/And Earth, and Sea, and Air, its Laws obey." The ultimate goal of Whig political theory, these texts subtly claim, is a "natural" peace and reconciliation.

While the pairing of William and Elizabeth lacks historical "realism," it reproduces a Whig iconography found not only in Bolingbroke's writings but, significantly, at Stowe. In the early 1730s, Cobham commissioned William Kent to construct, in the central section of the grounds known as "the Elysian Fields," a "Temple of British Worthies." Into this semicircular structure were moved eight busts, created "by Michael Rysbrack in about 1729," and originally placed around an earlier building by Gibbs, also known as "the Temple of the Worthies." Stowe is now a school, with an exceptional website that provides detailed descriptions and illustrations of the gardens and park, down to the very inscriptions on the busts. Photographs of the Temple of British Worthies show the busts of Elizabeth and William placed side by side on one wing of the Temple; their inscriptions are tentatively attributed to "George Littleton, perhaps with help from Alexander Pope and others."[55] The classically draped William, according to the inscription, "by his virtue and constancy having saved his country form a foreign master by a bold and generous enterprise preserved the liberty and religion of Great Britain." Elizabeth, depicted as a young woman in a ruff collar and armored corselet, "confounded the projects, and destroy'd the power that threatened to oppress the liberties of Europe; took off the yoke of ecclesiastical tyranny."[56] While *Eovaai* describes Glaza and Ibla's statues as full-length "Figures," the "blended Dignity and Sweetness" of their faces[57] certainly fits Rysbrack's busts.

Assuming, then, that Glaza and Ibla refer both to Bolingbroke's *Remarks* and to the statuary of the Temple of the Worthies, one is justified in looking to these sources for the identity of the third figure Eovaai is led to admire, that of "another scepter'd Hero," Amazulto. Identification of this image has led to problematic readings of Haywood's politics; Wilputte follows Ballaster in assuming that Amazulto represents James II, partly because Eovaai's guide gives this ruler a reigning period of "fifty moons," which Wilputte reads as fifty months and thus four years, and partly because both critics seem to assume that the layout of the Theatre of the Gods is chronological. This interpretation leads to the theory that Haywood had "Jacobite sympathies," or at least suffered from political nostalgia.[58] However, there are several reasons for setting this interpretation aside. First of all, by 1736 the Jacobite party had little real power in England—certainly not enough for Haywood to risk so much for a mere sentimental gesture. Bolingbroke had publicly fallen out with the Jacobites;[59] Sarah Churchill had always detested them, and James by this point was a stock figure for both "ecclesiastical tyranny" and absolute monarchy, two of *Eovaai*'s main targets. Moreover, Bolingbroke's *Remarks* offer another perfect candidate for Amazulto: Edward III, who next to Elizabeth was Bolingbroke's ideal.

Amazulto is depicted in terms of a reconciliation of oppositions already seen in Halafamai:

> He seem'd in that Bloom of Life, which, one may say, is but just arrived at Maturity; yet, with the Fire of Youth, was mingled all the Wisdom of Old-Age; fierce, but yet sweet; . . . commanding and beseeching . . . awefully lovely, and delightfully austere. As scorning Ease he stood, not sat upon a Throne: In one extended Hand he held a Sword of more than common Size; in the other, a Scepter ornamented with Doves, the Emblems of soft Peace.[60]

To finish off this image of perfection, Amazulto's statue is placed between two "Adamantine Pillar[s]" bearing a long list of his heroic deeds of war. This alone should show that James II is not here represented; Edward III, on the other hand, is praised by Bolingbroke for his balanced nature, as well as his aggression: "Few and short were the struggles between him and his people; for as he was fierce and terrible to his enemies, he was amiable and indulgent to his subjects. . . . No man contrived, prepared, resolved with more phlegm, or acted with greater fire." Bolingbroke credits Edward not only with having suppressed "popery" and improved parliament but also with having undone the evils inflicted on the country by his father:

> Edward the Second lost his crown and his life, in the most miserable manner, by allowing himself to be governed by his ministers, and protecting them from the resentments of his people; so his son very early exerted his own authority, and freed himself from the guardianship, or rather subjection, of the queen and Mortimer, who had long oppressed the nation, and dishonored the young king by their scandalous conduct.[61]

This passage, which was inevitably read in the 1730s as a reference to Walpole's alleged affair with Queen Caroline, drew a parallel made more dangerous by the fact, obliquely alluded to here, that Edward II in 1327 "was made to renounce the throne in favor of his son."[62] Not surprisingly, the publisher of *The Craftsman*, in whose pages the *Remarks* first appeared, was arrested for the publication of the two Letters on Edward III.[63] Presumably in order to mitigate the dangers of invoking Edward II, Haywood in her narrative includes the accusation of "scandalous conduct" in the paragraph immediately following the description of Amazulto, placing the scandal in the later reign of a king from "a different Branch of the Royal Family," who "was weak, wholly ruled by his Queen and Minister, who regarded more their private Interest than the Publick-Good, and were suspected to live in a more than becoming Intimacy." But the connection to Edward III, as described by Bolingbroke, is still clear, driven home by the closing details of Amazulto's heroic history: "with a Handful of Men, . . . he over-run one of the most potent Empires of the Earth, annex'd the Crown thereof to that of Hypotosa"[64]—a reference that has no parallel in the life of James II but fits perfectly with Edward's victories over France and his claiming the French throne during the Hundred Years' War. Even the mysterious "fifty moons" can be explained as a simple "alteration of circumstances," as Swift in 1710 had recommended for satirists making historical parallels:[65] Edward III reigned from 1327–77, or exactly fifty years.

Turning back, then, to Stowe, we might expect to find Edward III sharing the Temple of Worthies with Elizabeth and William. We do not; Cobham like Haywood may have thought this direct a gesture too risky. Instead we find, flanking Elizabeth, a surrogate: Edward III's son, also Edward, the Black Prince. This figure, sculpted by Peter Scheemakers between 1734 and 1738, and wearing a medieval helmet and corselet, is described in the accompanying inscription as: "The terror of Europe[,] the delight of England[,] who preserved unaltered in the height of glory and fortune his natural gentleness and modesty." It was the Black

Prince, Stowe's webmasters remind us, who captured the French King at Poitiers. "Amazulto" may or may not predate the addition of this figure to the Temple; but this monarch, with his conflicting attributes of age and youth, could represent both father and son.

Eovaai's tour is interrupted by the entrance of Alhahuza before she can "examin[e] some other Images of Monarchs who had reigned in *Hypotoſa*, before and after *Glaza* and *Ibla*" —another hint that the images are not to be read chronologically. Her conversation with "this truly great Man" restores Eovaai to her "Principles" of virtue and modesty, and the next morning she witnesses Alhahuza's impassioned speech to "the distressed and discontented Citizens of *Hypotoſa*," whom he exhorts to attack Ochihatou: "remove the Enchanter from before the Throne,—drive him from those Pleasure-Houses, those Palaces, erected on the Ruin of your Fellow-Citizens, those Gardens water'd with the Widow and the Orphans Tears, and, with his Blood, wash away the Barriers which divide you from your King!"[66] But although they are moved by this speech, the citizens of Hypotosa are too enervated by luxury to act, a representation that again reflects Bolingbroke's political theories in the 1730s.[67] All hope must rest on Eovaai and Adelhu, whose wanderings (especially their respective encounters with Alhahuza) will inspire the love of a supine people. The gender balance that will accompany Eovaai's eventual marriage to Adelhu is foreshadowed by the heroine's two mentors: as "mother," Halafamai has laid the groundwork for an ethical vision based on self-restraint; Alhahuza, instructing Eovaai in patriot rhetoric, acts as "father" to her political virtue.

At Alhahuza's recommendation, Eovaai next travels to the neighboring republic of Oozoff ("impartiality"), a perfectly balanced country protected by "a Genius" able to withstand all evil powers. Here the influence of Bolingbroke again makes itself known, as Eovaai encounters "an antient Man, . . . infinitely less venerable for his length of Days, than Extent of Knowledge."[68] This figure in some ways resembles the spokesman of the *Remarks*, "an ancient venerable gentleman" who impatiently defends "Caleb D'Anvers" from charges of sedition by discoursing on the history of "the true old English spirit" of liberty. The Republican of Oozoff repeats many of the most cynical points made by the spokesman of the *Remarks*. Thus where Bolingbroke writes, famously, that "liberty is a tender plant" and "the love of power is natural."[69] *Eovaai*'s Republican observes that "Humane Nature is not to be trusted with itself: all Men have in them the Seeds of Tyranny, which want but the warm Sun of Power to be enabled to shoot forth in proud and undisguised Oppression." The Republican also criticizes constitutional monarchies in which "the Power of conferring all Titles, Honours, and Badges of Distinction, [is] entirely lodged in one of those limited Monarchs, as you call them."[70] This refers to Opposition support for various attempts to limit the Crown's control over Parliamentary seats (for example, the Peerage Bill of 1719 and the Place Bill, presented by Sandys in 1734, 1735, and 1736).[71] Like Bolingbroke's spokesman, the Republican describes virtuous citizens as "very jealous of their Liberties";[72] but the Republican describes monarchy as perpetually lacking in "Balance" because of this jealousy —"balance," of course, being a key characteristic of Bolingbroke's ideal constitution.[73] Finally, the Republican concludes that a virtuous monarch, if s/he existed, "certainly would merit and possess a Throne in every honest Heart," but would not deserve either "*divine* Honours" or "a Sacrifice of those dear Rights given us by Heaven and Nature"[74] —a statement that resembles Bolingbroke's emphasis on the "hearts" of the people, and his insistence that "a free, a generous, a virtuous people, . . . will sacrifice everything, except liberty, to a prince like Edward the Third."[75] A key difference between Bolingbroke's spokesman and the Republican is the latter's inability to believe that "a prince like Edward the Third" could exist—a difference hammered home by the insistence of the "Republican Commentator" Hahehihotu that the Republican's statement "many Kings have been bad" should have been translated as "*all Kings*, instead of *many Kings*."[76]

Certainly, as Kramnick points out, these ideas were not unique to Bolingbroke;[77] but that Haywood derived them from this source is suggested not only by the parallels above, but also by Eovaai's reaction to the Republican's speech. She is sufficiently convinced of the justice of his arguments to consider adopting some of his "Republican Principles" as "Part of the Constitution" if she should return to power. Yet the narrator is critical of Eovaai for her change of heart: "She who, by the Insinuations of *Ochihatou*, had imagin'd Princes might exalt themselves to Gods, . . .was now, by this Republican, brought into as great an Extreme of Humiliation, and ready to resign even that decent Homage and respectful Awe which were the Requisites of her Place." The narrative attributes the change to Eovaai's "fluctuating . . . Human Nature," so susceptible to "the Force of Persuasion and Example," a comment that provokes another debate between authorities over Eovaai's motives and self-control. However, this discussion is in part a smokescreen for the dangerous political point being made: that the appointment of "great Officers" by a "despotick" Prince leads inevitably either to absolutism or, if the placemen are virtuous and oppose the ruler, to the abolition of monarchy (an observation cautiously located in a footnote and attributed to "Tatragraoutho the Rabbin").[78]

Haywood's deliberately overextensive use of her "scholarly" apparatus at this stage of Eovaai's political education makes it clear that the "multivocal" and oppositional structure of the narrative is also meant to provide a palimpsest effect, blurring as well as balancing certain elements of its political arguments. By this point Haywood's narrative has partly deconstructed the image of discursive authority through its continual quibbles, thus creating in the reader a skepticism about the exclusive value of any one standpoint—a lack of conclusion that again resembles Bolingbroke's statement in the *Remarks* that "Every system of human intervention must be liable to some objections; and it would be chimerical in us to expect a form of government liable to none." For this reason, his venerable gentleman argues, the "spirit of jealousy and watchfulness" must be "always alive" to protect the nation from "greater evil": "We must be content therefore to bear the disorder I apprehend from that ferment, which a perpetual jealousy of the governors in the governed will keep up, rather than abandon that spirit, the life of which is liberty."[79] The reader must remember that the old gentleman's speech begins as a defense of *The Craftsman*; Haywood's narrative participates in a "disorder" and opposition of the press essential to the watchful and critical spirit of Whig patriotism. The reader, struggling to reconcile conflicting representations of political power, reenacts the duties of the citizen. However, Eovaai, excluded from the complex debate raging around her, instead must gain the firsthand experience that, rather than "Pageantry" and "Arrogance," is appropriate to "her Place."

Before entering Oozoff, as Alhahuza's guest, Eovaai has had time, "left to herself" in "an Apartment neat, but not curious, . . . to ruminate on the Wonders of the Day." This image of a feminine but decorous retirement is set in deliberate contrast to the luxury with which Ochihatou deceives and entices her. Under Alhahuza's influence, Eovaai is able to learn from her adventures: "[she felt] the Shame of having abandon'd herself, tho' but for a few moments, to Pleasures so contrary to the Modesty of her Sex, and so much beneath the Dignity both of her Birth and Understanding: but . . . cou'd not think how close she was to being lost, without remembering she was not wholly so."[80] The austere beauty of the castle, like Stowe with its powerful images of Queen Elizabeth, encourages feminine wisdom and virtue. However, in order to complete her development, Eovaai must revisit Hypotosa and successfully resist the erotic blandishments of power. After a brief sojourn in Oozoff, she is recaptured by Ochihatou, whom she now sees in his hideous true form. The attention of the narrative turns again from ways of knowing the monarch to the monarch's ways of knowing, and addresses the problem of epistemophilia—the desire for knowledge—in this context.

Imprisoned in Ochihatou's castle, Eovaai receives an education in the price of unreasoning lust from Atamadoul, a lovesick elderly woman whom Ochihatou has turned into a monkey to "deter all Woman-kind from aiming at Delights they are past the power of giving" (131). Atamadoul is forced to watch his "Raptures" with other women, so that she suffers from "wild Desires": "I still languish in the most consuming Fires for my inhumane Persecutor." Having shown Eovaai how to transform her from monkey to human and back again, Atamadoul volunteers to take the Princess's destined place in Ochihatou's bed. Eovaai now becomes an unwilling witness to "the tumultuous Pleasures" of Atamadoul and the deceived Ochihatou, and she finds her "Nature" aroused by "the Fierceness of their Bliss" until she uses Halafamai's "Perspective." This device reveals the lovers to be surrounded with evil spirits whose "obscene and antick Postures animated their polluted Joys": "Sick to the Soul, and quite confounded with the horrid Prospect, she put her Glass again into her Pocket, and bless'd the Darkness which defended her from so shocking a Scene."[81]

This episode, which ends with Atamadoul's transformation into a rat by an enraged Ochihatou, rebukes women for both desire and scopophilic "Curiosity," a note informing us that "the Commentator employs no less than three whole Pages in the most bitter Invectives on this Propensity, which, he will have it, is only natural to Woman-kind." As "bad" parents/mentors, Ochihatou and Atamadoul reenact a primal scene that parodies the idea of gender balance, making Eovaai wish to be defended from erotic knowledge; her "feminine" curiosity and desire become their own punishment. Yet the premises of the epistemophilic bildungsroman require that she observe this "shocking" manifestation of desire, while the Perspective of Halafamai, representing an intervention divinely inspired, is necessary to ensure that "Nature" is not deceived. Vice, especially in its ability to mimic the good and arouse "nature," must be witnessed by, and glossed for, the prince who wishes to become truly virtuous.

Like the rest of *Eovaai*, the story of Atamadoul begs to be read in a specific political frame of reference. Atamadoul confesses that she first encountered Ochihatou when she was "Woman of the Bedchamber" to Princess Syllalippe of Assadid, whence she tricked the enchanter into carrying her off in the place of her royal mistress. Atamadoul has never previously been identified with any historical figure, but it is tempting, especially given the dedication of *Eovaai* to the dowager Duchess of Marlborough, to see the unfortunate monkey-woman as representing Abigail Hill, later Mrs. Masham. A relative of Sarah Churchill, Abigail supplanted Sarah in Queen Anne's favor, after the Duchess had helped her gain the post of "Bed-Chamber Woman" to Anne, then Princess of

Denmark. Sarah, indignant at finding herself put aside for "a Woman whom I had raised out of the Dust," had gone so far as to hire a hack writer to help her compose an anonymous letter to her rival. Moreover, Mrs. Masham was an ally of the Marlboroughs" enemy Robert Harley; thus, as one 1708 ballad will have it, "Abigail" became "A Minister of State," charged with "the Conduct and the Care/ Of some dark Deeds at Night" (that is, admitting Harley to the royal bedchamber). Sarah's angry description of Harley in a manuscript of her memoirs resembles Haywood's portrayal of Ochihatou: "This mischievous darkness of his soul was written in his countenance & plainly legible in a very odd look, disagreeable to every body at first sight, which being joined with a constant awkward motion or other agitation of his head & body betrayed a turbulent dishonesty within."[82] The resurrection of this previous scandal involving the influence of a "Favorite" and the "dark deeds" of a scheming minister serves two of Haywood's agendas in *Eovaai*: Atamadoul's mating with Ochihatou, which paints both in the most grotesque colors, might appeal to the Duchess of Marlborough's famed spite, while to a more general audience, it would be a reminder of the fleeting quality of "favor," and the tendency of Ministers towards dark deeds and unworthy tools.

The encounter with Atamadoul is Eovaai's final lesson in self-control and caution. Taught both to feel and to control desire, Eovaai upon meeting the virtuous Prince Adelhu glosses "the Passion she was enflamed with for him" as gratitude for his rescue of her and her people. Eovaai is uncertain for some time as to whether Adelhu is indeed worthy, or whether he has usurped her kingdom; only when she has heard Adelhu's history from his own lips, and discovers that he has found her missing jewel and is destined to marry its owner, does she offer herself to him in marriage. Significantly, Adelhu's narrative establishes their mutual destiny by providing proof of divine intervention: the Prince has been given Eovaai's missing jewel by a "Celestial Conqueror," who with the aid of "a mighty Comet" thrown by "a superior, but unseen Hand" has defeated a gigantic rival in battle. The titanic struggle witnessed by Adelhu reflects the reconciliation of opposing forces that was ostensibly the goal of Bolingbroke's theory of Opposition; the marriage of Eovaai and Adelhu is the natural manifestation of a divine will that mandates overall equilibrium. Yet politic skepticism has the last word; in a final footnote the cynical Commentator suggests that it was in Eovaai's "Interest" to conceal from Adelhu "that Part of her Behavior with *Ochihatou* in the Gardens of *Hypotosa*." The "Historian" must have heard the episode from "others on the same Errand, in some adjacent Grove or Arbour," or from Ochihatou himself.[83] "Interest" and desire continue to be manifested in terms of conflicting political representations. The final implication seems to be that even the triumphant patriot prince must be examined with the eternally "jealous" eyes of the immortal "spirit of liberty."

In his *Letters on the Study and Use of History*, written during his self-imposed exile in France, Bolingbroke delineates a distinction between useful history and "ingenious fable": "When imagination grows lawless and wild, rambles out of the precincts of nature, and tells of heroes and giants, fairies and enchanters . . . reason does not connive a moment.'. Bolingbroke's aristocratic addressee, Baron Hyde, being properly "fraught with knowledge, and void of superstition," will reject these texts, except "as fables" suitable for "imagination" rather than rational thought. However, Bolingbroke's comments, explicitly addressed to one "by . . . birth, by the nature of our government, and by the talents God has given you, attached for life to the service of your country,"[84] are not meant to apply to the audience who would devour the work of a woman novelist. Bolingbroke and his followers, attempting to reach all classes in order to gain popular support for their Patriot King, made use of such disparate discourses as the emerging medium of journalism and the ancient hegemonic device of estate building (the latter, as the Duchess of Marlborough's defiant efforts at Blenheim attest, itself evolving into a form capable of carrying Opposition discourse).[85] As "fabulous" text, moreover, *Eovaai* could be represented, when the Patriot triumph was complete, as prophesy: its ending, with the death of Ochihatou and the return of Alhahuza, could be recast as prescient, a sign of Bolingbroke's genius. Indeed, *Eovaai*'s republication, as *The Unfortunate Princess; or, The Ambitious Statesman*, during the 1741 decline of Walpole's ministry, was followed by Bolingbroke's return to England and his continued efforts to engage the Prince of Wales.[86] The Patriot Whigs hesitated to advertise their use of a popular woman writer, especially while their leader continued to write as the scholar-advisor to princes and lords; but the effectiveness of her fiction is attested by its repackaging and reuse during a potential crisis.

As a contribution to opposition discourse, *Eovaai* at least complicates the image of the female novelist in flight from powerful male peers. Pope and Savage attacked Haywood not merely for her gender, but specifically for writing about politics. Analysis of *Eovaai* reveals that, far from being "silenced" by this criticism, as conventional wisdom on Haywood has long suggested,[87] she became more closely involved in political discourse, even to the extent of joining or seeking to join Bolingbroke's circle. Describing the political education of a princess, invoking the power of women like Queen Elizabeth and Sarah Churchill, Haywood was claiming a place for women in the public sphere. Yet describing this place required Haywood to conceal her gender and her name; nor does that name appear in published accounts of the distinguished visitors to Stowe. If indeed she entered its gates, she did so unheralded. Still, to Haywood's politically informed contemporaries *Eovaai*'s metatextual frame of reference would have been clear. Now that *Eovaai* is at last back in print, perhaps its author can be recanonized among the shades of Stowe.

NOTES

1. Earla Wilputte, introduction to *The Adventures of Eovaai*, by Eliza Haywood (Ontario: Broadview Press, 1999), 9; Ros Ballaster, *Seductive Forms: Women's Amatory Fictions from 1684 to 1740* (Oxford: Clarendon Press, 1992), 157.

2. All references to Bolingbroke's *Remarks on the History of England* and *Letters on the Study and Use of History* are from *Lord Bolingbroke: Historical Writings*, ed. Isaac Kramnick (Chicago and London: University of Chicago Press, 1972). References will be cited within the essay text.

3. Alexander Pope, *The Dunciad Variorum*, in *The Poems of Alexander Pope*, ed. John Butt (New Haven: Yale University Press, 1963), 385; Mary Anne Schofield, *Eliza Haywood* (Boston: Twayne Publishers, 1985), 83.

4. Wilputte, *Eovaai*, 27–30.

5. Eliza Haywood, *Adventures of EOVAAI, Princess of Ijaveo. A Pre-Adamitical HISTORY*, ed. Earla Wilputte (Ontario: Broadview Press, 1999), 48. All references to *Eovaai* are to this edition.

6. Letter of December 1735, quoted in Isaac Kramnick, *Bolingbroke and His Circle: The Politics of Nostalgia in the Age of Walpole* (Cambridge: Harvard University Press, 1968), 30.

7. Wilputte, *Eovaai*, 28.

8. Archibald S. Foord, *His Majesty's Opposition, 1714–1830* (Oxford: Clarendon Press, 1964), 154; Kramnick, *Bolingbroke and His Circle*, 160–63; 137–52; Foord, *His Majesty's Opposition*, 150.

9. Bolingbroke, *Letters*, Letter 1, 156–57.

10. *Eovaai*, 48–51.

11. Ibid., 92 n. 1.

12. Ibid., 48

13. Bolingbroke, *Letters*, Letter 2, 14.

14. See *Letters on the Study and Use of History*, especially Letter 3, 35–48; Letter 5, 72–77; and Letter 6, 83–6.

15. *Eovaai*, 93 n.

16. Christine Gerrard, *The Patriot Opposition to Walpole: Politics, Poetry, and National Myth, 1725–1742* (Oxford: Clarendon Press, 1994), 176.

17. Delarivier Manley, *Secret Memoirs and Manners of Several Persons of Quality, of Both Sexes. From the New Atalantis, an Island in the Mediterranean*, ed. Ros Ballaster (New York and London: Penguin Books, 1992), 7–8.

18. Quoted in Foord, *His Majesty's Opposition*, 149.

19. While the feather is often interpreted as signaling Oeros's "feminine" vanity, here again gender binaries oversimplify the allegory. Although vanity is certainly appealed to here, the feather probably represents empty military honors, one of the famous Hanoverian weaknesses.

20. *Eovaai*, 166.

21. Foord, *His Majesty's Opposition*, 142.

22. *Eovaai*, 144 n. 1.

23. Foord, *His Majesty's Opposition*, 145.

24. Ibid., 141–42; David Green, *Sarah, Duchess of Marlborough* (New York: Scribner's, 1967), 45–46; Frances Harris, *A Passion for Government* (Oxford: Clarendon, 1991), 262–77.

25. *Eovaai*, 45–6.

26. Bolingbroke, *Remarks*, Letter 1, 158.

27. Ballaster, *Seductive Forms*, 157. Pursuing the argument that Haywood is a "conflicted" Jacobite, Ballaster also identifies Adelhu as the Pretender, but as Wilputte points out (64 n.1) Frederick is a much more likely candidate. When Bolingbroke's influence on *Eovaai* is factored in, there can no longer be any doubt about the identification.

28. Bolingbroke, *Remarks*, Letter 1, 157.

29. *Eovaai*, 57, 50, 53, 54.

30. Manley, *Atalantis*, 35.

31. *Eovaai*, 57, 62, 69–70

32. Ibid., 72.

33. Ibid.

34. Ibid., 73.

35. See April London, "Placing the Female: The Metonymic Garden in Amatory and Pious Literature, 1700–1740," in *Fetter'd or Free?: British Women Novelists, 1670–1815*, ed. Mary Anne Schofield and Cecilia Macheski (London and Athens: Ohio University Press, 1986), 101–23.

36. *Eovaai*, 77–78, 78–79.

37. Ibid., 91, 79.

38. Ibid., 80, 80–81, 87.

39. Foord, *His Majesty's Opposition*, 127; Jeremy Black, *The Politics of Britain, 1688–1800* (Manchester: Manchester University Press, 1993), 152.

40. *Eovaai*, 80.

41. Ibid., 92–93.

42. Ibid., 93–94.

43. Bolingbroke, *Remarks*, Letter 2, 175.

44. Marie-Louise von Franz, *Problems of the Feminine in Fairytales* (Zurich: Spring Publications, 1972), 25–26.

45. Luce Irigaray, *je, tu, nous: Toward a Culture of Difference*, trans. Alison Martin (New York and London: Routledge, 1993), 48–49.

46. *Eovaai*, 96.

47. Gerrard, *Patriot Opposition*, 36; website *Stowe School: Historic Stowe*. Accessed 15 May 1999. http://www.stowe.co.uk/historic/index.html. See also John Tatter's very useful Stowe website at http://panther.bsc.edu/jtatter/stowe.html. This site includes several examples of poetry from the 1730' about Stowe, evidence that the estate was actively promoted during that period as political and economic "text."

48. Alexander Pope, "Epistle to Cobham" and "Epistle to Burlington," in *The Poems of Alexander Pope*, ed. John Butt (New Haven: Yale University Press, 1963), 549–59, 586–95; Gilbert West, "Stowe, the Gardens of the Right Honourable Richard Viscount Cobham," on John Tatter's Stowe website, http://panther.bsc.edu/jtatter/west. html. Pope's praise of Cobham, begun in this Epistle, continues in the 1734 "Epistle to Cobham," which addresses not that nobleman's estate but his "ruling passion," love of his country. In other words, Pope clearly signals Cobham's "Patriot" credentials in his

"Epistles." The Earl of Burlington had gone into Opposition in 1733 after a falling-out with the King (Foord, *His Majesty's Opposition*, 126); Haywood may also be fishing for a political alliance, at least in the minds of readers.

49. *Eovaai*, 97, 98–100.

50. Ibid., 98.

51. Queen Elizabeth, "On the Eve of the Spanish Armada, 1588," on "Monarchy Through the Ages: The History of the Crown." *The British Monarchy: The Official Web Site.* Accessed 15 May 1999. http: //www.royal.gov.uk/history/crown.htm.

52. Bolingbroke, *Remarks*, Letter 15, 258.

53. Bolingbroke, *Remarks*, Letter 16, 266; Letter 13, 243–44.

54. Ibid., 269.

55. The figures in the Temple include "On the left . . . the men of letters, thought and architecture (Alexander Pope, Sir Thomas Gresham, Inigo Jones, John Milton, William Shakespeare, John Locke, Sir Isaac Newton, and Sir Francis Bacon), while on the right are those famous for their actions in political and military service to their country (King Alfred, the Black Prince, Queen Elizabeth I, King William III, Sir Walter Raleigh, Sir Francis Drake, John Hampden, and Sir John Barnard) . . . the two on the sides, Pope's and Barnard's, were not added until 1763, since they were both alive when the Temple was built." During the 1730s Cobham also had built a "Temple of Friendship," which contained images of his intimates; among them was an image of the Prince of Wales (Stowe website).

56. Although the paintings in the Temple of Venus of the Garden, dating from 1735, have mostly vanished, the fact that they represented scenes from Spenser makes it likely that Queen Elizabeth was the "Venus of the Garden" as well.

57. *Eovaai*, 98.

58. Wilputte, *Eovaai*, 99 n.2.

59. Foord, *His Majesty's Opposition*, 117; see also Bolingbroke's *Remarks*, Letter 2, 171–72, where his spokesman describes "the spirit of jacobitism" as not only dead but without hope for a revival "at home."

60. *Eovaai*, 99.

61. Bolingbroke, *Remarks*, Letter 5, 183–86.

62. *British Monarchy: Official Web Site*.

63. Bolingbroke, *Remarks*, Letter 6, 188 n.

64. *Eovaai*, 100.

65. Quoted in Kramnick, *Bolingbroke and His Circle*, 22.

66. *Eovaai*, 100, 95, 106.

67. Ibid., 32–35.

68. Ibid., 110.

69. Bolingbroke, *Remarks*, Letter 1, 155–56; 157–58.

70. *Eovaai*, 114, 115.

71. Foord, *His Majesty's Opposition*, 184.

72. *Eovaai*, 116.

73. See Bolingbroke, *Remarks*, Letter 2, also Letter 7, 197–98.

74. *Eovaai*, 114.

75. Bolingbroke, *Remarks*, Letter 5, 184.

76. *Eovaai*, 113 n. 1.

77. For discussion of Bolingbroke's influences and overall place in English constitutional theory, see Kramnick, *Bolingbroke and His Circle*, 137–87, passim.

78. *Eovaai*, 127, 119, 116 n. 1.

79. Bolingbroke, *Remarks*, Letter 2, 163.

80. *Eovaai*, 102–103.

81. Ibid., 135 n. 1, 131–32, 135. Perhaps coincidentally, one of William Kent's 1736 additions to Stowe's grounds, the Congreve Monument, is topped by the image of a monkey looking into a mirror.

82. Green, *Sarah*, 119–24, 315, 322, 117; Harris, *Passion*, 121–62.

83. *Eovaai*, 154–65, 163–64, 165 n. 1.

84. Bolingbroke, *Letters on the Study and Use of History*, Letter 4, 50; Letter 6, 81.

85. For the Duchess's use of the Marlborough estates to signify her husband's power and her political convictions, see Green, *Sarah*, 248; Harris, *Passion* 212–14, 221, 238, 253.

86. Foord, *His Majesty's Opposition*, 219–79.

87. See for example Schofield, *Eliza Haywood*, 82–83.

The Very Scandal of Her Tea Table: Eliza Haywood's Response to the Whig Public Sphere

Rachel K. Carnell

It seems reasonable to suggest that the gendered separate spheres, so familiar to twentieth-century academics through poetry and art from the Victorian period, arose in Britain in their modern form during the eighteenth century. The increased distinction between male and female spheres of duty might be ascribed to the increased leisure of middle- and upper-class women who were able to enter into what Lawrence Stone terms "companionate" marriages, rather than unions based on an ability to share equally in business duties.[1] It is thus tempting to describe a trajectory from Richard Allestree's *Whole Duty of Man* (1658), in which woman's general subordination to her husband is set out within a rubric of High-Church patriarchy, to mid-nineteenth-century conduct books such as Sarah Stickney Ellis's *The Wives of England* (1843), which describe in minute detail the ways in which women might best perform their duties within the domestic sphere. However, as is the case with most teleological narratives of history, the linear trajectory from Allestree to Ellis is complicated by particular anomalies along the way. For example, the eighteenth-century novelist Eliza Haywood advised women, in her conduct books, to keep silent about their political opinions in the household even as she protested, in her periodical writings, women's exclusion from the political debates of the public sphere.[2]

The apparent contradiction in Haywood's different narrative strategies points us to the overlap that Jürgen Habermas observes between the literary and the political public spheres in eighteenth-century Britain. Habermas describes the private citizens who publicly exchanged ideas about the political realm as bonding through an affective humanism that derived from "the world of letters."[3] This realm of letters was marked by an "ambivalence" between individuals referring to themselves on the one hand as property owners concerned with their political rights and on the other as simply human beings. In other words, the

255

public sphere fostered a slippage between the idea of man as *bourgeois* and man simply as man. Habermas suggests that this slippage was maintained because the "educated classes" assumed an exact identity between *bourgeois* and *homme*, and despite the fact that women and dependents were legally excluded from the political public sphere but often took a more active part in the literary public sphere than property owners themselves. For Habermas, "the humanity of the literary public sphere served to increase the effectiveness of the public sphere in the political realm" insofar as "political emancipation" was understood as "human emancipation."[4] Such an assertion about the liberating effects of the bourgeois public sphere's humanist claims is complicated, however, by the example of educated women writers, such as Haywood, who demanded a voice in the political public sphere but never claimed to be writing from the supposedly "universal" position of the Whig bourgeois male.

Haywood's narrative response to the increasing hegemony of bourgeois and Whig public sphere derived from her doubly marginalized political position of woman writer and probable Jacobite sympathizer,[5] during an era (1719 to 1756) in which anti-Jacobite discourse frequently equated the Jacobite cause with Amazonian, or "unnatural," femininity.[6] As I will show, Haywood modified her narrative persona from that of a fictional group of four women in her first periodical, to that of an androgynously gendered, Jacobite parrot in her second periodical, to that of a paragon of wifely virtue in the conduct books she wrote at the end of her career. Haywood's strategy involved challenging the exclusively male (and frequently Whig) preserve of coffee-house conversation by contrasting it with the more civilized conversation of women's tea tables (frequently slandered as cabals of Jacobite sympathizers), during a period before drinking tea became an established facet of British cultural identity.

Murray Pittock has recently argued that many protofeminist writers in late-seventeenth- and early-eighteenth-century Britain "leant towards a Jacobite perspective, with its distrustful and rebellious attitude to the new property rights and laws."[7] I would add that the very definition of "natural" femininity that became familiar through eighteenth-century texts—political, domestic, and fictional—was necessarily informed by the increasingly misogynistic discourses of Whig hegemony. The trajectory from Allestree's *Whole Duty of Man* to Ellis's *Wives of England* thus inscribes not only the increasing rigidity of the gendered separate spheres but also a second strand of history evident in the very titles of the two works: Allestree's reference to *man* indicates all of humankind while Ellis describes a wife's duties to the particular nation of *England*.

Consistent with the hypothesis that the evolution of gender norms cannot be separated from the evolution of Whig hegemony in Britain is Ros Ballaster's observation that the nature of periodical literature written for women evolved from having a definite political content in the early decades of the eighteenth century to demonstrating an entirely apolitical focus by the century's end.[8] However, we should observe that within the increasingly rigid discourses of separate spheres existed the subversive articulations of writers such as Eliza Haywood who simultaneously protested both the anti-Jacobite hegemony of the political public sphere and the fixed binary of gender difference. Although Haywood's subsequent erasure from literary history is usually cast in moral terms, we should recognize that this narrative itself may be the product of a Whig ideology that was reluctant to accommodate a Jacobite politics of difference.

HAYWOOD'S RESPONSE TO COFFEE-HOUSE POLITICIANS

Although many twentieth-century scholars view Eliza Haywood as a hack writer of sexually scandalous domestic fiction, a few critics have recently come to recognize the political import of her novels.[9] As I have argued elsewhere, Haywood's strong political voice is particularly evident in the two periodicals that she penned during the mid 1740s — *The Female Spectator* (1744–46) and *The Parrot* (1746).[10] In the opening issue of *The Female Spectator*, a periodical that appeared in monthly issues between 1744 and 1746, Haywood adopts the narrative personae of a coterie of four women, alluding directly to the male "club" to which Addison and Steele refer in *The Spectator*, and thus positioning herself within the periodical literature that helped to define the Enlightenment public sphere. At the same time, the different domestic positions occupied by her coterie of narrators echo the organizational structure typical of eighteenth-century conduct books for women, in which different chapters prescribe behavior appropriate to the different roles of daughter, wife, and widow. Interestingly, Haywood ultimately reserves editorial decisions to her own controlling narrator whose position within the proper life scheme of women's life remains ambiguous.

As she begins her self-styled reflections on the world around her, Haywood flatteringly describes her first contributor, Mira, as "a Lady descended from a Family to which Wit seems hereditary, married to a Gentleman every way worthy of so excellent a Wife, and with whom she lives in so perfect a Harmony." Her next is "a Widow of Quality, who not having buried her Vivacity in the Tomb of her Lord, continues to make one in all the modish Diversions of the Times, so far . . . as she

finds them consistent with Innocence and Honour." The third, Eur-
phrosine, "is the Daughter of a wealthy Merchant, charming as an
Angel, but endued with so many Accomplishments, that to those who
know her truly, her Beauty is the least distinguished Part of her."[11] In
establishing these paragons of conduct-book virtue as her advisers and
consultants, Haywood clearly positions her work both within the norms
for polite female behavior and generally within the confines of the domestic sphere. By contrast, the character she sketches of her own narrator, who will serve as the "Mouth" or voice for the whole group, is that
of someone who has acquired wisdom through a previous life of folly:

> —My Life, for some Years, was a continued Round of what I then called
> Pleasure, and my whole Time engrossed by a Hurry of promiscuous Diver-
> sions. — — —But whatever Inconveniences such a manner of Conduct has
> brought upon myself, I have this Consolation, to think that the Public may
> reap some Benefit from it: —The Company I kept was not, indeed, always
> so well chosen as it ought to have been, for the sake of my own Interest or
> Reputation; but then it was general, and by Consequence furnished me, not
> only with the Knowledge of many Occurrences, which otherwise I had been
> ignorant of, but also enabled me, when the too great Vivacity of my Nature
> became temper'd with Reflection, to see into the secret Springs which gave
> rise to the Actions I had either heard, or been Witness of, —to judge of the
> various Passions of the human Mind, and distinguish those imperceptible
> Degrees by which they become Masters of the Heart, and attain the Domin-
> ion over Reason.[12]

Haywood suggests in this passage that the very ability to offer insights
that might benefit the general public can only stem from a wealth of
experience that exceeds the range of behavior allowed a respectable
woman.

The conflicting goals Haywood sets for her periodical further emphasize the inconsistency between proper feminine behavior and political
commentary. She claims that she will have access to an "eternal Fund
of Intelligence," by placing "Spies . . . not only in all the Places of Resort in and about this great Metropolis, but at *Bath, Tunbridge,* and the
Spaw." Moreover, she will find the "Means . . . to extend [her] Speculations even as far as *France, Rome, Germany,* and other foreign Parts."[13]
The type of behavior her associates are likely to spy out in a resort town
suggests that the content of periodical will be sexual intrigue, while her
promise to keep spies in foreign countries suggests that she is also concerned with political intrigue and the movement of suspect characters
abroad. However, as is typical of Haywood's work, the line between
sexual and political scandal is often difficult to draw.[14] Her desire to
enter the literary public sphere as "to be in some measure both useful

and entertaining to the Public," is clear, but she makes equally evident the difficulty of offering political advice through the polite code of feminine behavior.

Fully acknowledging the inconsistent and shifting focus of her periodical, the *Female Spectator* includes an ostensible reader's complaint that she has not fulfilled her stated purpose of publishing a periodical "fit for the polite Coffee-Houses or to satisfy Persons of an inquisitive Taste," but instead has penned "Lucubrations . . . [which are but] fit Presents for Country Parsons to make to their young Parishioners; — to be read in Boarding-Schools, and recommended as Maxims for the well regulating private Life."[15] This distinction between "private Life" and the world of "polite Coffee-Houses" reminds readers of the gendered split within the literary public sphere between those texts deemed to be properly political and those concerned merely with domestic concerns. Her ostensible correspondent, one Curioso Politico, who first addresses her as *"Vain Pretender to Things above thy Reach!,"*[16] insists on the connection between the Female Spectator's failure as a political correspondent and her inability to confine herself to matters within the domestic sphere: "Tho' I never had any very great Opinion of your Sex as Authors," he writes, "yet I thought, whenever you set up for such, you had Cunning enough to confine yourselves within your own Sphere."[17]

Haywood's response to this possibly fictive correspondent is twofold: on the one hand she claims that the domestic anecdotes she includes are at least as politically relevant as newspaper reports of facts and figures; she insists that real politics lies in not in the factual reports of "News Mongers" describing details "such as Armies marching, — Battles fought, — Towns destroyed, — Rivers cross'd, and the like," but in more subtle reflections on morality and private life. At the same time, she offers evidence that women do have important contributions to make to political debate by including in the next issue "A DIALOGUE between An *English* and a *Hanoverian* Lady." In this extended debate, two highly articulate and knowledgeable women politely disagree as to whether or not the current Hanoverian monarch gains more by ruling England than the English do by having him rule them. Each woman offers pertinent legal, economic, and cultural reasons to support her cause, confirming the introductory remarks of the ostensible witness to the debate, one A.B., a man whose educational status may be inferred by his very initials: "I must confess, my Reason yielded to them both by Turns: — I was convinced, confuted, and convinced again as often as either of them spoke."[18]

Through this dialogue, Haywood constructs a model for civilized public debate that contrasts sharply with the more vituperative pamphlet wars that marked, for example, the anti-Jacobite tracts from the same period.[19] In complimenting the "Moderation and Sweetness" used by the debating women, Haywood denigrates those "who cannot hear themselves contradicted without Virulence and bitter Speeches."[20] Casting the impertinent Curioso Politico as an irrational and impolitic conversationalist, Haywood challenges his distinction between female discourse and male coffee-house debate by suggesting that the former may be more rational than the latter. But then again, a closer look at the history of coffee houses indicates that their culture may have had more to do with reinforcing gender difference and partisan political differences than with genuinely enabling a rational exchange of ideas.

COFFEE, TEA, AND ANTI-JACOBITE DISCOURSE

As coffee houses currently hold a privileged place in twentieth-century mythology of the Enlightenment public sphere, it is perhaps easy to overlook the fact they reinforced a culture accustomed to exclusion by rank, class, and profession.[21] Thomas Macaulay notes the importance of coffee houses during a period before the advent of modern newspapers: "In such circumstances the coffee houses were the chief organs through which the public opinion of the metropolis vented itself."[22] However, Macaulay also contrasts their apparent policy of openness with their actual clannish nature: "Nobody was excluded from those places who laid down his penny at the bar. Yet every rank and profession, and every shade of religious and political opinion, had its own headquarters." Describing a likely response to someone entering a coffee-house near St. James Park, where the preference was for snuff rather than smoking tobacco, Macaulay writes: "If any clown, ignorant of the usages of the house, called for a pipe, the sneers of the whole assembly and the short answers of the waiters soon convinced him that he had better go somewhere else."[23]

Not only did coffee-house patrons segregate themselves by rank or profession; they also, by contrast with customs on the European continent, excluded women altogether. Although women occasionally owned such establishments and were frequently employed as servers, they were not permitted entry as customers. Nor did this exclusion pass without comment; as early as 1674 a pamphlet appeared entitled, "The Women's Petition against Coffee, representing to public consideration the grand inconveniences accruing to their sex from the excessive use of the drying and enfeebling Liquor." The pamphlet's general argument is that public establishments serving coffee were luring husbands away from the company of their wives and, more importantly, from fulfilling their duties in helping to propagate the nation. Coffee, the petitioners insist, made men "as unfruitful as the deserts where that unhappy berry is said to be bought."[24] From the very start, then, allusions to coffee houses within the discursive fields of the public sphere were as sexualized as the partisan political language that issued forth from them.

Recognized as a force in excluding women from the public sphere, coffee houses were also generally recognized as potential hotbeds of political opposition. One year after the "Women's Petition," Charles II issued "A Proclamation for the Suppression of Coffee Houses" based on the claim that "false, malitious and scandalous reports are devised and spread abroad to the Defamation of his Majestie's Government, and to the Disturbance of the Peace and quiet of the Realm."[25] This royal proclamation raised so much protest that two weeks later, and just two days before the date on which the coffee houses were to be closed, Charles proclaimed his "royal compassion" and offered a reprieve. The monarch's inability to suppress the coffee houses points out not only the forces of opposition building against the Stuart succession but also the value that a significant portion of concerned citizens placed on their ability to meet and exchange ideas. If it is true that coffee houses permitted the discussions that may have helped build support for James II's exclusion from the throne, it is also seems to be the case that during Cromwell's time, "the king himself owed . . . no small debt of gratitude in the matter of his own restoration."[26] By the middle of the eighteenth century, however, the crown's interest in coffee would be affected less by political partisanship than by economic interest—having lost control of the coffee trade to France, the East India Company persuaded the government to encourage tea drinking. By the end of the eighteenth century, tea effectively would surpass coffee as the caffeinated beverage of choice.

Interestingly, the role that coffee houses played in fomenting opposition in times of crisis may have been less a result of their potential to foster open debate than their ability to nurture partisan bias. Macaulay describes certain venues frequented by "fops," others by men "of polite letters," others by "Puritans" or by Dutch or Jewish merchants, others by those of "Popish" sympathies.[27] Viewed within this partisan framework, it makes perfect sense that members of one party would attempt to marginalize members of another by rhetorically feminizing them, thus excluding them altogether from both coffee-house debates and the political public sphere. For example, in his *The Jacobite's Journal* (1747), the staunch anti-Jacobite Henry Fielding insists that whereas among Jacobite women, "the very Scandal at their Tea-Tables is political," a woman's "Whig principles" may be detected by her very "Silence on that Head."[28] Fielding's association of Jacobite discourse with women's tea-tables should be understood as part of a broader attempt by Whigs and opposition Tories to marginalize Jacobites by associating them with Amazonian women, and concomitantly with impotent men; at the same time, he manages to question the "femininity" of any woman daring to discuss politics openly.

Until the heaviest of the excise taxes on tea was lifted in 1746 and until the East India Company finally helped sway the British in favor of tea as a national drink, tea was favored by women, sometimes in mixed company, at afternoon tea tables in their own houses, and at pleasure gardens such as Ranelagh and Vauxhall. [29] In her 1725 publication *The Tea Table*, Eliza Haywood describes the conversation of five exceptionally erudite men and women, offering their moral analyses of various recent literary productions. What is striking about Haywood's sketches is the need to wait for the fops, beaux, and vain of both sexes to stop talking before any rational exchange can take place. She observes, "We had just began to enter into a Conversation, which wou'd have been very Entertaining, when a Titled *Coxcomb* came into the Room, and with an Inundation of Impertinence put a Stop to every Current of good Sense."[30] By contrasting this coffee-house fop with the rational erudition of her tea-table hostess, Haywood reminds us what an earlier broadside about coffee made all too clear—that what passed for rational conversation inside the smoke-filled rooms was frequently little more than gossip:

> Here Men do talk of every Thing,
> 　With large and liberal Lungs,
> Like Women at a Gossiping,
> 　With double tyre of Tongues.[31]

Thus even though she also scolds empty-headed women into rational discourse,[32] Haywood nevertheless insists in *The Tea Table*, as she would do again so eloquently two decades later in *The Female Spectator*, that a model for polite debate should include rational conversation between the sexes.

However, despite Haywood's wish that political debate could include women's voices, coffee houses continued as male preserves, increasingly associated with the status-quo politics of Whigs and anti-Jacobite Tories while Jacobite sympathizers were discursively associated with treasonous, Amazonian tea tables.[33] This association of marginalized political positions with Amazonian women of course raises the question of how loyal Whig and Opposition women might show support for their cause. Fielding's suggestion that Whig Ladies' tea tables were distinguished by their silence about political affairs is consistent with Haywood's own awareness, demonstrated in her choice of narrative personae in *The Female Spectator*, that any woman daring to participate in public political debate risked being labeled disreputable. Consistent with this is the anonymous 1746 pamphlet "The *Highlanders Salivated*, or the LOYAL ASSOCIATION OF *M— —ll K— —g's* Midnight Club: with The serious Address of the Ladies of *Drury*, to the batter'd strolling Nymphs of their Community." The band of Whig prostitutes, gathered as "THE LOYAL ASSOCIATION, OF THE *Amazon Society* At MOLL KING'S *Coffee-House*," raises the question of what "*Woman* can do, against these *Highland Rebels*." Voicing their fear that Jacobites would confine them "in *Nunneries, Convents* and other *Popish* Prisons," these Whig "strolling Nymphs" eloquently insist on the "Right and Privilege of keeping open House and hospitably entertaining Strangers" and to "the free Use and natural Right we have over our own Persons." Presuming this to be a pro-Jacobite pamphlet which is maligning Whig women in the terms usually reserved for Jacobite women, we may see how images of Amazons were deployed by both sides of the political divide in such a way as to denigrate any woman who dared to voice strong political convictions.

Within this rubric, we see why Haywood cast the narrator of *The Female Spectator* as a respectable woman but one with a less than reputable past: her previous history explains her political insight; her current respectability allows her to converse with the rest of her proper coterie. However, Haywood also obviously realized the dangers in associating her narrator with the one group of women allowed to speak freely about politics: her views would be mocked and discounted because of the perceived looseness of her moral behavior—a fate that Haywood herself had already experienced through the vituperative pen of Alexander Pope.[34] Not surprisingly, writing the final issue of *The Female Spectator* in the spring of 1746, Haywood suggests that her coterie's next publication might represent male voices as well, by adding Mira's husband to her cast of contributors. However, as the violence toward captured Highlanders increased over the summer, Haywood seems to have changed her mind; rather than casting herself as representative of a mixed group of men and women, she instead casts herself in the voice of an androgynous green parrot, whose feelings of exclusion from the dominant voices of the public sphere are marked by his very alienation from the human race itself.

PARROTS AND OTHER VULNERABLE ORACLES

While the title page announces that *The Parrot* is written by the authors of *The Female Spectator*—that is, the coterie of four women—the narrator takes on the guise of a male inheritor of what would sound like an aristocratic lineage: "In the first Place, I am a *Parrot*;—my Father, Grandsire, great Grandsire, and so back for near six thousand Years, were all *Parrots*."[35] While this parrot insists on his right to join the masculine fraternity of voices that marked the coffee-house public sphere, he simultaneously insists on his difference, or his position as outsider, having been born in Java and having lived in many different households in a variety countries. At a certain point, the narrator even suggests that he is neither human nor parrot at all, but an inanimate (if vocal) oracle: "Mark me then, and suppose me not a meer *Parrot*, which without Distinction utters all he hears, and is the Eccho of every foolish Rumour, but a Thing,—a Thing to which I cannot give a Name, but I mean a Thing sent by the Gods, and by them inspired to utter only sacred Truths."[36]

The androgynous quality of this disembodied voice offers Haywood the perfect foil for expressing views critical of the dominant political establishment. Casting herself as the Java-born parrot, she frequently comments on qualities typical of the English character; she suggests, for example: "That Impetuosity which is so natural to you, would, in all Probability, hurry you to Extravagancies, not all together allowable in a *good* Cause but monstrous in a *bad* one." The parrot continues: "It is a true Characteristic of the People of *England*, that they are easily *led*, but impossible to be *drove* to any thing;—they *yield* on *soothing*, but are *obstinate* on *controul*:—How careful ought they to be, therefore, that they imbibe no Notions, which to persevere in, would be either shameful of prejudicial."[37] The peculiar critique of Englishness the parrot narrator offers throughout the nine issues of the periodical may be understood through Haywood's likely Jacobitism and thus her concern that the English are being carried to an impulsive extreme in punishing the defeated Highlanders.

The parrot reminds readers that it is not only women such as the authors of *The Female Spectator* who would have difficulty being taken seriously within the dominant discourses of political debate, but also those who are recognized by the Jacobite demarcation of the color green—a color that Paul Kléber Monod explains was associated "so strongly with the oak bough of support for the exiled Stuarts that in 1717 and 1718, people were arrested for wearing a sprig of green."[38] Haywood's parrot observes: "THE Colour I brought into the World with me, and shall never change, it seems, is an Exception against me;—some People will have it that a *Negro* might as well set up for a *Beauty*, as a *green Parrot* for a *good Speaker*."[39] Haywood further protests the anti-Jacobite sentiments that marked the period through her parrot's complaint: "POOR *Poll* is very melancholy,—all the Conversation

I have heard for I know not how long, has been wholly on Indict-
ments, — Trials, — Sentence of Death, and Executions: — Disagreeable
entertainment to a Bird of any Wit or Spirit."[40] The Parrot finally protests that it feels itself "alien . . . in the Kingdoms."[41] The reference to
the plural 'Kingdoms' rather than a singular United Kingdom further
suggests a Jacobite preference for stressing the separate identities of
the different British nations even as the parrot recognizes that the prejudice against him is nevertheless prevalent throughout most parts of the
Kingdom.

Haywood's complex narrative positioning as alienated green parrot
reminds her readers of the exclusionary tendencies exhibited by the
presumably rational debates of the dominant political discourse. In the
"Compendium of the Times" with which she ends each issue, Haywood
(in a narrative voice more her own than her parrot's) frequently adds
postscripts about the wives and fiancées of Jacobite leaders who died
of grief when watching their loved ones hang. Haywood also has her
parrot describe a scene in which Oram, her code name for the Duke of
Cumberland (known to Jacobite sympathizers as "the Butcher of Cul-
loden"), enters the lodgings of a well-known courtesan. Oram becomes
annoyed by buzzing flies who do not show him due respect; he then
ensnares them with a lump of sugar from the tea-table and proceeds to
pull off their limbs — a clear allusion to the recently announced English
policy of disarming the Jacobites, to which the Parrot refers in the preceding issue of the periodical.

As he describes Oram "pulling off the Legs of some, the Wings of
others, and the Heads of the largest," the watchful parrot cannot help
observing that "with this he seemed highly diverted, and laughed very
heartily to see the severed Limbs and mangled Carcasses lye spread
upon the Field of Action." The cautious parrot, afraid of Oram's obvious predilection for violence against those who might dare even speak
out against his policies, explains "for my Part, I said nothing all the
while, for fear of incurring a Displeasure, which might have been no
less fatal to me." Notably, however, both the flies who had shown Oram
such a "want of Respect" and the green parrot himself are saved from
the threat of further violence when "a Summons from the Lady called
him up Stairs."[42] Within her subtle critique of anti-Jacobite abuses of
power, Haywood repeatedly suggests that the voice of wisdom and restraint necessary to temper the excesses of government policies may lie
in the quite observations of green parrots and the diverting actions of
female courtesans. And yet, Haywood's Parrot, like her Female Spectator is ultimately rendered a silent observer, for fear of itself becoming
the object of political violence. Although Haywood's 1749 arrest for seditious libel (for her publication and sale of a pamphlet about the Pre-

tender) did not result in conviction,[43] it must have underscored the urgent need for her to construct a safe paradigm through which women (and other marginalized creatures) might voice their political views. Haywood's sudden interest at the very end of her career in writing conduct books that seem to reinforce the split between male and female spheres must be understood as part of her ironic recognition that the domestically oriented literary public sphere might be the only sphere in which women's and other excluded political voices could continue to be heard.

In the Voice of the "Perfect Wife"

Judged only by her conduct book *The Wife* (1755), Eliza Haywood might seem to approve the increasingly hegemonic Whig discourses of property rights and separate spheres. In this text, whose title page announces it to be penned by Mira (the respectable wife who supposedly helped author *The Female Spectator*), Haywood includes a predictable delineation of duties: woman is responsible for the domestic sphere; men are expected to have political opinions that women should not contradict in public. Further supporting the impression that the spheres are separate and that men and women inevitably confront each other through a rehearsing of the battle of the sexes, Haywood ends *The Wife* with the suggestion that her female readers who "think my admonitions too strongly enforced . . . will have their full revenge when they read the duties I have enjoined a husband,"[44] referring to the companion volume, *The Husband* (1756), whose publication she obviously anticipates.

However, what at first glance seems yet one more discursive thread in the construction of the separate spheres proves to contain within it a challenge to that same binary. While a standard truism of a separate spheres ideology is that the control of property should rest entirely with the husband,[45] Haywood modifies this cliché slightly by insisting on the importance of the wife staying informed about the husband's financial dealings: "a Wife being the sharer in the fortune of her husband, whether it prov'd good or bad, has an undoubted right to be made acquainted with the whole truth of his affairs."[46] Moreover, although Haywood expects the husband to share knowledge with his wife, she does not expect that the wife should necessarily return the favor. Rather, she insists that the husband respect the wife's autonomy over her dominion within the house. Haywood even borrows the Whig language of rights to insist on a wife's right to control her own sphere of influence: "Nor does she look upon all this as a delegated authority, but as a lawful right to which marriage has entitled her." Yet, what seems at first a proto-feminist appropriation of Whig principles is soon shown to be of a piece with Haywood's larger argument—that separate spheres are not natural or God-given, but are simply practical ways of preventing inevitable squabbling within a family. Haywood thus instructs husbands to understand that it is not because the wife's dominion over the household is in fact "lawful," but because she *perceives* it as naturally hers that the wife is "more tenacious of it than of any other privilege whatsoever: a husband therefore, who has any regard for the peace of his family, or living in amity with his wife, will never attempt to break in on so darling a point." [47]

Haywood's delineation of separate spheres as not absolute or fixed accords with her suggestion that women not contradict their husbands about political matters. She again grounds her argument in pragmatism rather than fixed or natural differences by suggesting "that a prudent wife will find it no hard matter to avoid entering into any dispute with her husband on the score of politics." Furthermore, although Haywood seems to conform to the generally held belief that "there are so few women qualified to talk on those affairs, that most of those who do, would find it much more to the reputation of their understanding to be silent," she nevertheless refuses to limit women to a separate sphere of political ignorance. Instead, she allows for the exceptional woman who has plenty to contribute to political debate, even as she cautions her against showing up her husband in public:

> But supposing her to be endued with an uncommon genius,—a penetrating and sound judgment,—well vers'd in history and political tracts,—able not only to talk about also to reason well on the occasion, and have infinitely the advantage over her husband, will the secret heart-burnings, discontent, and ill-humour, which, in all probability, these debates may create in him, be atoned for by the applause her capacity may receive from others? [48]

Rather than ordering an intelligent wife to agree with her husband in all things, Haywood ultimately allows for a woman's right to her own opinion, as long as she is not too vocal about it: "If a woman cannot bring herself to the same way of thinking as her husband, nor ought always to endeavour it, she has it nevertheless in her power to forbear thwarting his opinion." [49] Haywood's insistence on the practicality of women not contradicting their husbands positions her not as an advocate of women's natural inferiority but rather as an advocate of conflict avoidance techniques—a position that also suggests an astute political strategy.

Haywood concludes her section on political discourse with the empirical observation that "Women being excluded from all public offices and employments, the men are apt to look on any attempt made by that sex to intermeddle with affairs of state, as an encroachment on their prerogative." She offers grudging recognition of the separate spheres when she acknowledges, "I think it must be allow'd, that she who busies herself too much that way somewhat transgresses the bounds of her own sphere." Yet the cautionary "somewhat" marks Haywood's resistance to accept the limiting designations of spheres as commonly defined, and she quickly observes, allowing a loophole to the single, the widowed, or those women separated by legal means: "the unmarried, however, are at liberty to act as they please."[50]

Haywood also suggests through an amusing anecdote about a Williamite woman who unwittingly married a Jacobite man that the best way to avoid political conflict within the household is to be certain to marry someone of the same partisan bias. She describes the scene once husband and wife have realized their mistake:

> Each by turns endeavoured to bring the other over to their own party; but that being a thing impracticable, created such inward discontents and heart-broilings . . . that if they do not absolutely hate, they cannot be said to love;—a peevish thwarting of each other, even in matters of the utmost indifference to either, or a sullen silence, are the least proofs of their mutual ill-humour:—in fine, the whole tenor of their behaviour affords too much reason to believe, that since they are not able to agree in one point, they are determined never to do so in any other.[51]

Haywood's focus on the importance of not crossing party lines in marriage provides advice not only for household peace but for a different kind of political rapport than the model of England's prominence within Great Britain.

Even as she recounts the squabbles of the mismatched marriage, Haywood refers more openly than she usually does to her own political preferences. When recounting the argument provoked by the Jacobite husband when he sees his wife dressed in yellow to celebrate the Hanoverian accession, Haywood slyly remarks:

> I forbear to repeat the reply he made to these words; because it is more than barely possible that some one or other, in this scrutinizing age, might take it into his head to imagine that I was glad of an opportunity of venting my own sentiments through the mouth of a third person;—it will be sufficient to inform my readers, that one reflection drew on another, till the husband and the wife seem'd equally to have forgot all the regard due to decency and good manners.[52]

Given her attempts to demand a political voice within the periodical literature taken seriously by the coffee-house public sphere, it is perhaps ironic that Haywood should make her most direct allusion to her own probable Jacobite sympathies within the safe confines of a text ostensibly about domestic conduct. Yet, considering her own 1749 arrest for seditious libel, Haywood no doubt felt obliged to camouflage her political sentiments within a text whose very genre denied its political intent. And as a rational, well-informed writer unshackled by a husband with whom she might disagree, Haywood certainly fits into her own category of women entitled to voice their political views in public.[53] She also offers her opinion within the context of a general guide to "good manners"—good manners that might help prevent bloody, irrational vengeance imposed by one national group on another, good manners that could set a paradigm for a new type of mutually tolerant political union.

As Murray Pittock has argued, one important facet of Jacobite ideology was its resentment of the force that English culture was bringing to bear on the other nations of Great Britain after the Union of 1707. Scottish nationalists especially had hoped for the right to maintain their own national identity within a loose amalgam of nations rather than the unequal dominion that England imposed. Pittock describes the "limited common purpose" sought by those who envisioned a "Jacobite Britain of multiple kingdoms."[54] Within this framework, we may understand Haywood's advice to women about marrying within their own political party: they stand a better chance of maintaining their own separate identity by avoiding a union that inevitably limits their right to express their political sentiments, just as Scotland and Wales might better protect their own identities through a less lopsided kingdom of Great Britain. We may similarly appreciate Haywood's career-long critique of the exclusionary forces that dominated the coffee-house public sphere—a critique enabled by the continuous self-transformation of her own narrative persona. Against the increasing hegemony of an Anglican, Whig, male national political identity, Haywood continued to demand a feminized, tea-drinking politics of difference within an Enlightenment public sphere that truly lived up to its claims for open and rational debate.[55]

WHIG HEGEMONY AND THE POLITICS OF RECEPTION

Having made the case that Haywood operated from a "subversive" Jacobite position, coyly critiquing the political public sphere through even her most apparently apolitical domestic conduct books, we may well ask: so what? Why should it matter that Haywood consistently protested the Whig and male hegemony of the eighteenth-century political public sphere if history has cast her in the apolitical guise of a novelist who started her career writing in the "licentious . . . style of Mrs. Behn" but finished by writing novels "by no means devoid of merit"?[56] The Jacobite undercurrent of Haywood's domestic conduct books may seem as noble but futile as her apparently unnoticed refusal to sign her own testimony never to have written anything "in a political way" when being examined for seditious libel.[57] After all, the trajectory of Haywood's oeuvre seems to fit a narrative of inevitably separate gendered spheres and increasingly distinct literary and political spheres.

On the other hand, the teleological evolution of the separate spheres in Stone's account, like the apparent inevitability of the literary public sphere's gradual detachment from the political only contributes to the perception of these as "natural" divisions. Whereas Haywood may have been ultimately unsuccessful in either convincing her Jacobite "friends" to rally effectively for their cause or in revising the domestic household so that the "good manners" of political tolerance became the norm, there is nevertheless value in acknowledging her attempts. The pessimism that we may feel in observing her powerful political message become silenced by the hegemonic forces of the mid-eighteenth-century public sphere should be tempered by our awareness that her efforts could yet help convince us to recognize the contingency of divisions long assumed to be natural.

Notes

1. *The Family, Sex, and Marriage in England 1500–1800* (New York: Harper and Row, 1977), 359.

2. Research for this article was supported by a faculty research grant from Cleveland State University.

3. *Structural Transformation of the Public Sphere: An Inquiry into a Category of Bourgeois Society*, trans. Thomas Burger (1962; Cambridge: MIT University Press, 1989), 55–56.

4. Ibid.

5. See my "It's Not Easy Being Green: Gender and Friendship in Eliza Haywood's Political Periodicals," *Eighteenth-century Studies* 32:2 (1998–99), 199–214. Elizabeth Kubek's persuasive account (elsewhere in this collection) of Haywood's connections to Bolingbroke's circle during the mid 1730s is not necessarily inconsistent with Haywood's taking up the Jacobite cause again more directly during the 1740s, when the Young Pretender became a rallying figure for his father's long-disaffected supporters.

6. See Jill Campbell's *Natural Masques: Gender and Identity in Fielding's Plays and Novels* (Stanford, Calif.: Stanford University Press, 1995) for a discussion of the brutal misogyny of many anti-Jacobite tracts in the 1740s. While I agree with Campbell's point about misogyny during this period, I do not view this as a new or different trend from earlier anti-Jacobite discourse, which had since the first Exclusion Crisis aligned pro-Stuart forces with negative stereotypes of both Catholics and women. See, for example, Elkanah Settle's misogynist, anti-Catholic Restoration tragedy *The Female Prelate: Being The History of the Life and Death of Pope JOAN* (London, 1680).

7. *Inventing and Resisting Britain: Cultural Identities in Britain and Ireland, 1685–1789* (New York: St. Martin's Press, 1997), 86.

8. *Women's Worlds: Ideology, Femininity and the Woman's Magazine* (London: Macmillan Education, 1991), 56–58. Ros Ballaster, Margaret Beetham, Elizabeth Frazer, and Sandra Hebron are the joint authors of this text, although they indicate in the preface that Ros Ballaster is largely responsible for Chapter 2, "Eighteenth-century Women's Magazines," to which I am referring.

9. In elucidating amatory fiction's relationship to party politics, Ros Ballaster delineates the obvious satire of the South Sea Bubble in Haywood's *Memoirs of a Certain Island Adjacent to the Kingdom of Utopia* (1727) and Haywood's anti-Walpole stance in *The Adventures of Eovaai* (1736). See *Seductive Forms: Women's Amatory Fiction from 1684 to 1740* (Oxford: Clarendon Press, 1992), 153–58. However, aside from these two obvious allusions to party politics, Ballaster describes the bulk of Haywood's work as "part of a struggle for power and, more particularly, a gendered conflict over the interpretation of the woman's body as amatory sign" (174). Ballaster also ignores the political import that Haywood claims for *The Female Spectator*, which she describes as containing "no veiled references to the sexual and political misdemeanors of the rich and powerful" (*Women's Worlds*, 58). For all their focus on social history, Helen Coon ["Eliza Haywood and the Female Spectator," *Huntington Library Quarterly* 42:1 (winter 1978): 43–55] and Deborah Nestor ["Representing Domestic Difficulties: Eliza Haywood and the Critique of Bourgeois Ideology." *Prose Studies* 16:2 (August 1993): 1–26], overlook the specific political allusions in *The Female Spectator*. *The Parrot* as of yet has scarcely been analyzed by scholars. More recently, Catherine Ingrassia's observations in "Additional Information about Eliza Haywood's 1749 Arrest for Seditious Libel" establish the need for broader recognition of Haywood as "producer and distributor of surprisingly political texts in a heretofore unrecognized way." See *Notes and Queries* 242:2 (June 1997): 202–4, 202. Ingrassia's *Authorship, Commerce, and Gender in Early Eighteenth-Century England: A Culture of Paper Credit* (Cambridge: Cambridge University Press, 1998) further elaborates the way that Haywood negotiates the "fundamental generic instabilities that characterize this literary period—was fiction 'political'? was political writing 'fictional'?" (125).

10. See note 3, above.

11. *The Female Spectator* (London, 1744–46), 4 vols., 1: 6–7. Future references will be by volume and page number.

12. Ibid., 5–6.

13. Ibid., 6.

14. See Ingrassia's *Authorship, Commerce, and Gender* for more details about this overlap.

15. *The Female Spectator*, 2: 121.

16. Ibid., 117.

17. Ibid., 117–18.

18. Ibid., 123, 135, 133.

19. The biting satire of Fielding's *The Jacobite Journal* (London, 1746) is a model of politeness when compared with the more vicious attacks in such pamphlets as *The Highlanders Salivated* (London, 1746) or *The Female Rebels* (London, 1747).

20. *The Female Spectator*, 2: 158.

21. In his *Structural Transformation of the Public Sphere*, Jürgen Habermas emphasizes the importance of coffee houses as places where men of different ranks could freely exchange ideas (28–57).

22. Thomas Macualay, *The History of England From the Accession of James II* (New York: Harper and Brothers, 1856), 6 vols., 1: 276.

23. Ibid., 1: 277.

24. Quoted in William H. Ukers, *All About Coffee*, 2nd ed. (New York: The Tea & Coffee Trade Journal Company 1935), 66.

25. Quoted in ibid., 68.

26. Comments by William Coventry quoted in ibid., 68.

27. Macaulay, *History of England*, 1: 277–78.

28. *The Jacobite's Journal* (London 1747), in *The Jacobite's Journal and Related Writings*, ed. W. B. Coley (Oxford: Oxford University Press), 99.

29. Ukers, *All About Coffee*, 70–78.

30. Eliza Haywood, *The Tea Table* (London, 1725), 3.

31. "New from the Coffee House" (London, 1667), quoted in Ukers, *All About Coffee*, 65–66.

32. "Were every Woman . . . but half as zealous in correcting the little Vanities of her Acquaintance, they would be as preferable to Men in *Understanding*, as they are allowed to be in Beauty" (5).

33. Although Macaulay describes "Popish coffee houses" in the London of 1685, it is likely that these would have been scarcer, and certainly less open in their support of the Stuart monarchy after 1688.

34. Pope's now famous reference in *The Dunciad* to Haywood's "two babes of love" (II.ii.158) is sometimes assumed to be a purely biographical allusion but in fact is probably a reference to two of her novels that particularly offended him. And yet, Pope's slander, along with Haywood's representation of herself in *The Female Spectator*, colored two centuries of critical reception of Haywood's life and work. Ros Ballaster refreshingly corrects the critics who interpret Haywood literally when she describes to herself as having "run through as many Scenes of Vanity and Folly as the greatest Coquet of them all" (1: 2) by reminding us that "in the knowledge that during the 1720s Haywood produced a novel on average every three months, it is hard to imagine she had much time for the 'promiscuous diversions' to which she refers" (*Seductive Forms*, 159–60).

35. *The Parrot* (London, 1746), no. 2. The magazine is not paginated; references are to issue numbers.

36. Ibid., 1.

37. Ibid., 2.

38. *Jacobitism and the English People 1688–1788* (Cambridge: Cambridge University Press, 1989), 204.

39. *The Parrot*, no. 2.

40. Ibid., 4.

41. Ibid., 8.

42. Ibid., 2.

43. See Ingrassia's "Additional Information about Eliza Haywood's Arrest for Seditious Libel" and her *Authorship, Commerce, and Gender*, 116–27.

44. Eliza Haywood, *The Wife* (London, 1755), 280.

45. While Lawrence Stone suggests that women's financial position and autonomy improved during the eighteenth century as contractual settlements replaced common law property arrangements, Susan Staves has recently demonstrated that women's real economic situation did not improve with this new reliance on written contracts. See *Married Women's Separate Property in England 1660–1833* (Cambridge: Harvard University Press, 1990).

46. Haywood, *The Wife*, 21.

47. Ibid., 27–28.

48. Ibid., 19–20.

49. Ibid., 22.

50. Ibid., 20.

51. Ibid., 27–28.

52. Ibid., 27.

53. Although some biographers have identified her as the Eliza Fowler Haywood who eloped from Rev. Valentine Haywood, Haywood herself suggests that she was widowed.

54. Murray Pittock, *Inventing and Resisting Britain*, 58.

55. As tea gradually became preferred to coffee and men's private clubs gradually replaced the coffee house, Haywood probably still would have chosen the mixed gender conversations of tea-tables to the exclusionary culture epitomized by the men's clubs.

56. Anna Barbauld, "On the Origin and Progress of Novel-Writing," *The British Novelists* (London, 1810).

57. All the booksellers questioned by Lord Stanhope in hope of identifying Haywood as the author of her anonymous *Letter . . . to a Particular Friend* (1749), for which she was accused of seditious libel, sign their names to their testimonies. Haywood's maid, however, refused to "swear to her examination," as is noted by the examiner on the document in the spot where the signature should be. The omission of Haywood's own signature is not similarly noted by the examiner. See PRO SP36/111 f.204–14 and PRO/SP36/112 f.24.

"To the Women of Both Sexes": Christopher Smart, Mrs. Mary Midnight, and the Voice of the Dissident Woman Writer

Chris Mounsey

VERY LITTLE RESEARCH HAS BEEN UNDERTAKEN ON CHRISTOPHER Smart's "less serious" prose: that is to say his periodical journalism. Robert Mahony and Betty Rizzo's *Annotated Bibliography*[1] lists no academic papers on *The Student*, *The Midwife*, or the *Universal Visitor*.[2] To begin to redress the balance, the present paper will consider *The Midwife* (1750–53), Smart's most successful journal. The two major biographies of this century take little interest in it. Christopher Devlin spares six pages of his *Poor Kit Smart*[3] for extracts from *The Midwife*, but they are left without critical engagement since he claims the writing was: "Deliberately ephemeral juvenili[a]: [which] never once [showed] the keen bite of intellectual satire, never the thrill of creative fantasy that can play on different levels, no sign that the author was a poet."[4] Though the magazine involved three years work by his subject, Devlin dismisses it, since: "This is a life of Smart, not a monograph on eighteenth century journalism, so we now say goodbye to Mrs. Midnight—except so far as she indicates the events in Smart's life."[5]

The index of Arthur Sherbo's *Christopher Smart: A Scholar of the University* lists seven references to *The Midwife*. Of these, only one has anything substantial to say:

> None of . . . [Mrs. Mary Midnight's wit] . . . is acidulous; all is conceived and carried out in a spirit of good clean fun, with the author enjoying his own wit and humour as much as anybody else. . . . This even extends to "The Midwife's Politicks: Or, Gossip's Chronicle of the Affairs of Europe," a concluding part to each issue clearly modeled on the "Historical Register" or "Foreign Intelligence" of other periodicals.[6]

In this comment, we see Professor Sherbo attempting to play down his scholar's association with Grub Street hackdom, so he avoids any lengthy critical appreciation of the magazine itself. Only John Sitter and Deborah Ayer Sitter draw attention to the need for closer study of *The Midwife* and, in a short article, describe the final section — *The Midwife's Politicks* — as "a mixture of shrewd observation and ludicrous speculation."[7]

My own biography of Christopher Smart follows the Sitters' suggestion, but goes further, by placing the production of *The Midwife* as one of several possible reasons why Smart was kept for seven years in a lunatic asylum: because he was involved in the publication of political satire and the magazine for which he wrote was the vehicle for opposition political ideas during the extended ministry of Henry Pelham and his brother Thomas Pelham-Holles. I do not intend to rehearse the arguments of the biography at any great length in this essay. Rather, I will comment upon the particular twist Smart brought to his *Midwife* journalism: that he was a man writing as a woman.[8] By this means it will be argued that Smart avoided entering the political contest as a man battling with other men. He dressed his prose style in feminine stereotypes in the same way he dressed himself in female clothes when he brought *The Midwife* to the stage in *Mary Midnight's Oratory*. I will argue that he presented himself as female in order to evade censorship, and get away with a depth of political comment for which he would have been jailed had he been open about his sex or open in the content of his essays. Furthermore, I will argue that his cross-gendered approach was not arbitrary but chosen since it was a tactic readily recognizable to his readers. Thus the secondary purpose of this essay is to argue that Mrs. Mary Midnight's writing shares characteristics with the female political writers active throughout the eighteenth century whose work is discussed in other essays in this volume.

The technique the *Midwife* employed to disguise its political comment was to juxtapose two articles under female bylines, which, although innocuous (or jumbled) in their message when read singly, comment upon each other in a way that produced a clear political message. To add another level of complexity, Christopher Smart and other contributors also wrote as a cast of different women, each with an individual persona and background. The particular experience of one character would then be used as a witness to support the speculations of another. When referenced against the newspapers and magazines that reported carefully self-censored versions of the news, the *Midwife* may be decoded following these guidelines and read to give news and comment critical of the Pelhamite ministry and Hanoverian monarchy. In this way, a network of female gossips[9] passed on Tory High Anglican political messages in carefully crafted numbers of a magazine that was thought, until the Sitters' work, no more than a blind alley in Smart's poetic career.

The Midwife was successful from its first number, demonstrating the usual thirst for opposition political comment during a long stretch of government that was undistinguished in its strength and direction. However, taken in isolation it is difficult to understand why a magazine with so complex a method of transmitting information to the reading public could be successful. Decoding a single number requires a great deal of cross-referencing. Without a key, such as that printed simultaneously with Delarivière Manley's *The New Alatantis*, furthermore, without obvious signs that there even was a hidden message, one might expect that *The Midwife* would have taken several numbers to become comprehensible to its target audience as political satire.[10]

On the one hand, it could be argued that surface humor carried the early numbers until the hidden messages were understood. However, in the first number, readers had to make their way through five sober articles to page 27 (that is, over halfway through) before coming upon the first unequivocally funny item: *A Journey to Paris*, by W. Boobykin. Even then, the letter from the eponymous country bumpkin to his papa was copied from an earlier book of jokes, *The Agreeable Medley, Or, Universal Entertainer*.[11] On the other hand, it could be argued that it was common knowledge that *The Midwife* was copying its style from the *Student*, which was also edited by Christopher Smart, and on which he wrote as the "Female Student." However, no connection was made between the two journals until the Female Student claimed that she was Mrs. Mary Midnight on the 21 November 1750.[12] In the meantime two numbers of *The Midwife* had appeared,[13] the first of which was reprinted four times.[14] Furthermore, the content of the two magazines is quite different and the *Student* offers little or nothing in the way of political comment. It is therefore necessary to explain the popularity of the first number of *The Midwife* without recourse to the suggestion that it was funny. Nor can it be argued that it carried easily recognized political messages: such signs would have been picked up by scholars before now. However, since the magazine was popular from the outset it must have borne hints about its content that were easily ascertainable by the contemporary audience who demanded reprints.

In *Women's Worlds*[15] Ros Ballaster, Margaret Beetham, Elizabeth Frazer, and Sandra Hebron argue that in general, the women's magazine was one of the tools of patriarchy's construction of the feminine. A second element to their analysis is the argument that: "The magazine functions as surrogate 'family,' providing an intimate and private space for the discussion of issues to which even, or perhaps especially, a mother cannot be made privy." Together, the women's magazine read as ideological project and intimate space for female debate would have announced *The Midwife* to its first audience as being no threat to patriarchy: at least superficially. In the case of productions nearly contemporary to *The Midwife*, the fact that the *Female Tatler*'s Mrs. Phoebe Crackenthorpe claimed that her magazine presented news gathered from the "scandal office" that was her drawing room, loudly proclaimed that her women's journalism was no more than tattling. In the same vein, the title, *The Midwife*, made out that what followed would be gossip since the word "gossip" refers to a woman's female friends who are invited to be present at a birth.[16] Furthermore, the idea of using Mrs. Mary Midnight as a strong journalistic persona to edit each number of *The Midwife* was borrowed from the *Female Tatler* as well as Eliza Haywood's eponymous "Female Spectator."[17] Thus, Smart's magazine can be seen to have been carefully located in a preexisting tradition of female magazine writing, and one that on its surface did not lend itself to political comment, but consisted of gossip.

However, as Jan Gordon argues in *Gossip and Subversion*,[18] "Gossip, . . . must find a place for its representations within more socially respected narratives, and for that reason, incessantly competes for our attention with other commodities that similarly lack completion and cry out for 'finish' in arenas so resistant to closure." In describing gossip as the archetypal expression of the uncloseability of discourse, Gordon points to its power. That is, it does not try to present a so-called fact and point toward an idea or a thing in the world. Rather, it "depends for its efficacy upon the circulation and speculation . . . of that which cannot be verified." To refer the idea of the indeterminacy of gossip to women's magazines, we can see that the very triviality of their essays becomes the source of their interest to readers. By eschewing the adherence to facts, which characterized men's magazines such as the *Gentleman's Magazine*, several possible referents are brought into play. In turn, the readers' task becomes a game of deciding exactly who or what is under discussion. The tactic is particularly relevant to women's magazines of the Pelham era, since, as Gordon concludes: "In a domain of very weak father figures, gossip alone has the authority of a given, at times, almost an assumed universal. . . . This illusion of a common understanding, often enhanced by the passive voice, is part of a complicated process by which the subject of a given discourse is either temporarily denied or rendered anonymous." That is to say, the game of guessing who is the butt of satire issuing from the women's magazines is not difficult since the target is universally assumed to be the weak patriarchs—albeit not said openly. In the present context, we may add to this, that the women's magazine might be argued to provide the obvious locus for the dissemination of political dissent. Superficially it provided no threat to patriarchy, but was one of its tools of domination. The magazine would limit its discussion to the intimate details that women spoke of to each other when they were away from the company of men. However, by the nature of such "gossip"[19] to resist closure of meaning, it could be a source of easily deniable innuendo about the failings of the men in power.

And it is political dissent in the form of gossip that we find in *The Midwife*. The first item of the first number[20] is called *Come Dame, light up your Lanthorn, and let us prowl*. It begins:

> Now fie upon seeking honest Men in Knaves Skins. There's not a Street, Lane, or Alley, in all the City, but I have trod, and can hardly meet a Man, worthy of giving the Good-Morrow to. Why what Rascals are these? Have they banish'd honest Men out of Town quite? Alas, poor Virtue! What hast thou done to deserve this Contempt? Thy Company is out of Request; and thou hast walk'd so long alone, that thou art even, at last, walk'd away with thyself. There is no Goodness to be found, all is set upon Villany. Yonder walks Knavery, Bribery, Cruelty and Extortion, in the habit of substantial honest Citizens: Perhaps they are of the Common Council; put off your hat to 'em, Sirrah![21]

The piece is passionate, perhaps, but not humourous. Mahony and Rizzo argue the story is adapted from "Diogenes's lost Labour" a short article in the *British Magazine*, no. 1 (October 1746),[22] and the first sentence bears this out. There is a direct reversal since Diogenes took his lantern about by day to seek "Knaves" in "honest Men's skins," but Mrs. Mary Midnight's ploy is recognizable enough. However, if Mary Midnight was simply referencing the *British Magazine*, the piece would be little more than a contribution to a debased philosophical tradition that had become a well-known form of travel writing. As such we might find further references as early as Thomas Dekker's *Belman of London* (1608) and *Lanthorn and Candle-Light* (1608). These texts were aimed at tourists to London to inform them of the sort of hoaxes that might be played on them by the various tricksters and sharps at work on the streets of the metropolis. However, the first person Mrs. Midnight and the boy meet on their night's ramble is the Bell-Man himself:

> Who is this coming? Oh! 'tis the Watchman. . . . — These are the People that are employ'd to guard the City, to preserve the Peace, and to wage War with the Thieves and Robbers! What hast thou a Night, good Man, for thy Care? Ninepence I suppose, that is, let me see, a Penny an Hour for freezing, and if you don't appear in Time, the round O is fix'd on your Name I suppose, and your Money forfeit to the Common Council Men, is it not? And who

keeps Watch and Ward the Night you are so discharg'd, no body? No, we are all bad I find at the Bottom.[23]

Although remonstration about morals is typical of a Diogenes text, Mrs. Midnight is not warning wary visitors about card-sharpers after their holiday money, she indirectly addresses city council corruption in her sympathy for the poorly paid watchman. The political angle she introduces at such an early stage in the *Midwife* must have set bells ringing in the minds of her audience, which suggested that Mrs. Midnight in the role of Diogenes was commenting upon current political issues. The only two other texts with the name Diogenes in their titles published between 1700 and 1750 are both by Dennis de Coetlogon, the first entitled *Diogenes's Ramble* (1743)[24] and the second *Diogenes at Court* (1748).[25] *Diogenes's Ramble* is a cynical account of various European courts. De Coetlogon holds up his lantern to the kings and queens of Spain, Morocco, France, and others, and finds all to be corrupt. However, *Diogenes at Court* brings the same methodology to England and several of its articles hint at the project of the *Midwife*. One examines *"The Characters of* English *News-mongers,"* who are criticized as:

> Jugglers and Fortune-tellers; particularly dexterous in *legere-de-main*, and skilful in interpreting the Intentions of Princes and their own Dreams. For, whenever they please, they make numerous Armies appear where there is none, and none where there are very numerous ones: They represent Princes pacifick, when they have not the least inclination for a Peace; and warlike, when they have not the least Thought of taking the Fields; always dreaming of Victories and Conquests, always victorious over their Enemies in the Manner of the Knight of the Awful Figure.[26]

Those who followed the Diogenes reference to de Coetlogon would thereby be alerted to Mrs. Mary Midnight's new publication being a magazine that would try to avoid the government position forced upon other newspapers. At the same time, the reversals the *Midwife* made to the Diogenes texts also spoke loud and clear. Clothing the philosopher in women's weeds suggested that there was something hidden beneath the stories that followed. *The Midwife* would be much more equivocal in its approach to the people described than the de Coetlogon texts, since the substitution of Diogenes for Mary Midnight altered the directness of a stereotypical masculine attack into stereotypical feminine gossip. The fact that day was swapped for night as the time of the ramble further suggested that Mary Midnight was not trying to see behind the public faces of her subjects, but behind their private faces. In this way, readers were also informed that they must look behind what appeared to be gossip for the political message.

Also in the first article, Mrs. Midnight addresses women's problems such as pregnant servant girls sleeping in shop doorways, who were ruined by "the Sons, and 'Prentices of the honest Citizens . . . or . . . by some of the Righteous Lads of the *Temple* and Inns of Court." On one level Mrs. Midnight is heavily ironic:

> However that may be, it need not affect us Boy. Lay still my Heart: Women are not of the Human Species, so down with them. Boy if ever thou livest to be a Man, (as in all probability thou wilt, if the Halter don't catch thee soon) do thou, whenever any poor Creatures tumble down, kick them about, 'tis the way of the World Boy, and all must conform to Custom. In this Case you are to imitate the Dogs, who all take a Snap at the Cur, that is calling for Mercy.[27]

Such irony in the feminine voice concurs with the idea that this is feminist critique of the type described by Ros Ballaster in *Seductive Forms*.[28] However, the reversal of the sex of the expected writer of a Diogenes text destabilizes the feminist irony. We expect Diogenes to be absolutely truthful and direct. However, since Mrs. Midnight is Diogenes in disguise, it is hard to say for sure when she is being like Diogenes, and when she is being ironic and feminine. Mrs. Midnight heaps abuse on Monsieur *Flutter-and-Fly*, a courtier who spends a thousand a year to ensure a sinecure worth five hundred. Next she hints at the sexual secrets of a woman in a hooped dress: "Nay, Malapert, you need not be out with me, I methinks have seen as much Virtue without a great Hoop in my Time Madam."[29] Then other female philanderers are mocked: "I am sure many of my poor Mistresses have been forc'd to lay in without the help of their Husbands."[30] By this time, the article appears to be no more than stereotypical feminine gossip. Mrs. Midnight, the midwife/gossip, has a tale to tell of the illegitimate babies she has helped into the world. But at the same time she also speaks with the directness of a Diogenes text as actions of those observed are criticized since they are held up to the general gaze. Therefore, the sum total effect is unstable and undecideable.

As in all Diogenes texts, Mrs. Midnight and the boy end up at a good man's house: "But this House is the Politician's, blow out the Candle Sirrah, the Sight of an Honest Man may frighten you. Take care of your Teeth Varlet, and put your Hands in your Pockets. *Good night* Boy."[31] However, if the politician is so honest why should he frighten the boy, why must the candle be snuffed, and why does the boy have to look to his teeth and keep his hands in his pockets? In the context of the politician's presentation with corrupt council officials, honest citizens who treat their woman worse than dogs, Flutter-and-Fly, the lady with the hooped dress and the philanderers, the politician may appear honest. But it is not clear where the irony stops and direct criticism starts. Whereas in a Diogenes text, the honest person is always described carefully so readers may learn what it is to be good, the substitution of Mrs. Midnight for Diogenes and gossip for philosophical comment destabilizes any univocal reading.

Thus, *Come Dame, light up your Lanthorn, and let us prowl* presents a complex textual pattern that gives and takes away meanings without privileging a particular interpretation. The technique is typical of the *Midwife* as it had to hide its political message in references between articles. However, those who recognized the source of the symbolism from de Coetlogon would already be aware of the political stance Mrs. Midnight took — she was a High Tory Jacobite.

As Murray Pittock argues, Jacobites were still active in the 1750s.[32] Although severely bruised by the failures of their attempts to secure the Stuart succession, High Anglican Tories nevertheless held faith with the divine right of kings. Their demands became very specific, but were generally anti-Gallican, anti-Catholic, anti-Scottish, and anti-Hanoverian. Although a Frenchman, de Coetlogon's writing shows all these facets, and thus acts as a model for *The Midwife*.

Diogenes at Court is carefully located as anti-Gallican (since de Coetlogon had been banished from France),[33] anti-Catholic (since English Catholics were mere observers of ceremonies),[34] anti-Scottish (since the Scots had reneged on promises made to de Coetlogon)[35] and scathingly anti-Hanoverian:

> But you Hanoverians were the Cause of all these Troubles and Calamities; for it was to protect you against your Enemies, or extend your Frontiers, we have been Engaged in a War. — To protect us against our Enemies! we had none, we lived in Amity with all our Neighbours, who had not the least Thought of attacking us, neither had we any of attacking them. It is you who wanted a War; how often and how long have you asked for one against *France* and *Spain!* How much murmuring, writing, caballing to oblige the King to enter into a War against those two Nations! And now that you are sick of it, you would make us responsible for it.[36]

When the *Midwife* is decoded with reference to *Diogenes at Court* as its key, the juxtaposition of articles begins to show a complete picture, and its popularity may be explained: it was the voice of the political opposition to the Pelham administration (the Hanoverians who led the King astray). The second article of the *Midwife* takes up de Coetlogon's theme of the disasters caused by over-reaching Ministers. "AMBITION. *An* ALLEGORY" tells how Philemon leaves his rural cottage and his sacrifices to the Gods to follow his "Thirst of Riches." By avaricious dreams he transforms the rivulet in his peaceful country setting into a river, and the river into an ocean on which his tiny boat becomes a treasure ship. Disaster strikes: "The Sea grew enraged; its Billows swell'd; a horrible Tempest assail'd the Vessel on all Sides; a furious Wave cast is against a Rock, the Ship split, and the Sea swallow'd up the Riches it had contain'd."[37] The allegory is easy to interpret when juxtaposed with the Jacobite and Tory sentiments of the de Coetlogon model. The little-England and God-fearing Stuart court that is underpinned by the divine right of Kings, is destroyed by the false prayers of the Hanover obsessed Pelhams. The Hanoverian ship of state had become too ambitious, with its divided loyalty between the Electorship and the British throne. By engaging in European politics with countries who had hitherto been allies, Britain will surely come to ruin. The moral drawn from the allegory is clear: "Let us leave the Gods the Arbiters of our Lot; Man alas! Is more dear to them than he is to himself. Let Prudence regulate our Wishes: Otherwise we shall have Reason to fear that we shall become, like *Philemon*, the Victims of our Rashness."[38] However, the allegory by itself does not make a clear statement about the British Government. The *Come Dame* article suggested the text might have another meaning, but by itself it reads as an innocuous if moralistic tale. It is unlikely to have been: the *Midwife* was too popular to have sold so well on such generalities.

The perpetrator of the approaching catastrophe is named in the third story, which is disguised as the gossip between two old nurses about the frightful treatment of a poor family by an unscrupulous landlord. Presented as a letter *"To Mrs.* Midnight," Martha Johnson tells her friend the tale of the evil effects of the laws concerning debt. The husband is imprisoned, his wife goes mad as she is unable to pay off the debt, and the children are left to the care of the parish. The particular facts of the story may be decoded to reveal comments about Hanoverian foreign policy:

> 'Twas he, [John Williams] Mrs. *Midnight*, that kept the Shop on the Green: He was always a very honest Man, and every Body thought him in a good Way: however, since this War, he lost so much Money by bad Debts, that he was unable to pay his Creditors so soon as they expected. Sir *Thomas* (who you know is a Brute of a Man, if we dared say so) seized his Goods first for Rent; upon which one of his Creditors arrested and sent him to Jail.

The "War," the war of Austrian Succession, centered around a squabble between the various electors of the Holy Roman Emperor. As such it was of little interest to non-Catholics and less to Tories. The *Midwife* article therefore suggests that the Hanoverian Court was spending money on a war that was of no interest to the citizens of Britain, though it was bankrupting them. The Duke of Newcastle, Thomas Pelham-Holles (Sir Thomas of the story) is blamed for exacting repayment via taxation, of the National Debt that was caused by the need to pay Hanoverian troops. In fact, he became the object of much hatred among taxpayers for perpetuating the divisions between the French and Austrians, and keeping the war going as long as he could, to secure his personal power.[39]

Other magazines commented weakly on Pelham-Holles's outrageous behavior. The *Gentleman's Magazine* publicly criticized a paper published "under the direction of the Ministry" called *"Observations on the* NATIONAL DEBT *and* PUBLIC CREDIT," but their comments were barely comprehensible:

> A distinction should be made betwixt the necessities of the *State* and the necessities of the *Ministers of State* . . . let indiscreet, corrupt, and profuse ministers encrease the national debt ever so much by ill-advised expeditions on the continent, or by any other impolitic extravagances, they should have the more credit in proportion to the debts they bring on the publick.[40]

The *Midwife* had no such scruples. In later numbers it went on to lambaste the Pelhams for the ruinous taxation of British woollen manufactories and the consequent establishment of a rival Spanish trade which succeeded under the direction of British émigrés. But it could not make such comments overtly, its political message therefore remained couched in stereotypical female gossip. The story of the Williams family jumps between gossip and political comment: "As soon as poor *Mary* [Williams, wife of John] was dead, I took the youngest Child, and put it to *Hannah Underwood* to nurse, and I believe she'll take Care of it. I fancy you knew *Hannah*, Mrs. *Midnight*; she is the young Woman who lived with me when you used to be at Madam *Dormand's*." By so doing, *The Midwife* took the heat out of its political comment, while allowing itself to go further than other magazines in decrying the British Ministry: "Oh Sir *Thomas*! Sir *Thomas*! I have a thousand Things to tell you of that wicked Man; but I must defer it till another Time; for I am afraid I have tired you with this long Letter." *The Midwife* went on to tell "a thousand Things" of Pelham-Holles in a monthly criticism of the Pelhamite government. But all was given disguised as old women's gossip. Mrs. Midnight's comment about Martha Johnson's letter gives her fictitious correspondent verisimilitude to hide the political nature of the message: "I have inserted this Letter of Mrs. *Johnson's*, *verbatim*, without the least Alteration; Her Diction is the pure Language of Nature; and her Sentiments carry more Weight in her own Words, than they would do mangled by the most masterly Hand. The Contents are too true; for I personally knew the poor deceased Woman she speaks of."[41] The technique deflects interest onto the story of the death of Mary Williams and renders the article innocuous when read on its own.

The female voice dominates the next two articles. The first is a *Rambler* essay about the tribulations of a young girl who is abandoned by her widowed mother who is attempting to remarry and finds that a grown up daughter ages her. The second is a darker story about a young woman who is seduced and abandoned by a married man. In a paragraph that introduces the story, Mrs. Midnight suggests that:

> As we have many more Male than Female Writers, it is not to be wondered at, that the Vices and Foibles of the Women are most maliciously satyrized; it shall be my Province sometimes to give my Sex their Revenge by laying open the Villany of these our Masters, these Lords of the Creation. In their Transactions with each other they are obliged to keep up an Appearance of Probity, but in regard to us, every Stratagem, every Deceit is put in Practice to corrupt the Innocent, and to betray the Unwary. But why it should be a less Crime to deceive an inexperienced Girl, whose Age and Situation render it impossible she should know the World, than it would be to direct a blind Man to the brink of a Precipice, I am at a loss to imagine, yet Custom, that Tyrant Custom, has taught us this, and many more Absurdities.[42]

Thus, she introduces her politics as one that reverses the erotics of customary heterosexuality and offers an alternative form that might be styled female revenge. Such discourse has been described by Ballaster and others, but is made more complex here by the fact that Mrs. Mary Midnight was written by a man, or by several men. The device therefore must be to recall earlier feminist critiques and places *The Midwife* in that tradition. Two effects may thereby be exploited. The first is that *The Midwife* asks to be read in the same vein as the *Female Tatler* and *Female Spectator*, as a magazine by and for women (as its title suggests) and thus declares it is not political or dangerous. The second, as the essays in this volume by Ruth Herman on Delarivier Manley, and Rachel K. Carnell and Elizabeth Kubek on Eliza Haywood suggest, flags the fact that women's writing is political even as it is delivering feminist critique, and alerts readers to another method by which they may decode the text.

Why the technique should be used by a group of men may be explained by the fact that masculine opposition ends up in homoerotic contests (what Luce Irigaray calls the domain of homosexual rivalry)[43] and in the subjugation of the feminine. This, in turn, frees the female voice to pour forth criticism in a way that is not thought coherent enough by patriarchy to put up serious opposition. The men use feminine voices to say what they cannot say, uncensored, in masculine voices.

The importation of the cloddishly masculine voice of William Boobykin in the next article demonstrates what is possible for men to say: they must support their country and toe the government line. In terms of Mrs. Midnight's comment about male writers, we are presented with a satire of masculinity that is put to use to show readers how to tackle the rest of the articles. Boobykin has been sent on a shortened version of the Grand Tour, but after a week in Paris desires to return home so he can "live and do well," since "they are all *Papishes*, or *Roman Catholicks*, and I like them at no Price." However, "The whole City have their Eye upon me, especially the Ladies, who I am told are all in Love with me."[44] As all eyes, of both French men and French women, are upon him, his British Protestant heterosexual masculinity is glorified over French Catholic homosexual effeminacy. Its relevance in a collection of articles in subversive female voices is twofold. It both bluntly states an anti-Catholic line, and alerts readers—if they had not already noticed it—to the fact that they should look for the important messages in the articles written by the more subtle women writers.

If the message had not been received, the next article by Mrs. Mary Midnight, *On Poetry*, continued to debate the relative merits of men's and women's writing. She declared that "Every Man scribbles poetry as every Woman curls her locks," and that "The ridiculous Figure which some Ladies make in their Finery, may be seen every Day in the Mall, the Streets, and Gardens, and to illustrate the Comparison, I shall also let you see how ridiculously Men appear in their Poetic Apparel."[45] The extracts of poems which follow (three by men and one by a woman) are undistinguished, and Mary Midnight, as their critic, describes them in terms of cookery: "Here the Flowers of *Rhetorick*, and the Nutmeg and Sugar of *Poetry*, are finely intermix'd."[46] Her language is disarmingly simple, but by using culinary metaphors she once again explains one of the disguises of her messages: they may appear in an inappropriate discourse.

She finds the first two men's poetry problematic because the rules of grammar are not followed. One calls his mistress to kiss him "With her dark and rolling Eye." The second mixes the metaphor of a "Flood of Darkness" around his protagonist's head which is apparently so "permanent and thick" it precludes him hearing "the Cock's shrill Din when Morn appear'd." The third poet is so direct in his address to his subject matter "the Distemper among the Horned Cattle," that the intended pathos is lost in comedy.[47] The poem was purportedly written by a squire to be sung by a congregation in Yorkshire, and acts as a reminder of the patriarchal-political nature of writing. The parson, faced with a hymn that describes "how the Intrails look Of Cattle dead and gean" must "stand Neuter, however stupid and ridiculous it may appear to him; for it is as much as his *Benefice* is worth to contradict the 'Squire."[48] In this inappropriate discourse, Mrs. Mary Midnight explains why other newspapers do not speak out about the government's poor record in foreign policy: they will face the retribution of the ruling class.

As is usual in miscellaneous magazines, the critical article introduces a selection of poems and epigrams. The first shows what a woman poet can do at the age of fifteen, in Nelly Pentweazle's *A Ballad*. Her poem displays a felicitous use of rhyme and numbers, does not mix its metaphors, and follows the rules of grammar. It is also noted to have been "borrow'd" from the *Student*, which is "publish'd with the Approbation and Assistance of those famous Universities." This footnote has a dual purpose. First, it claims that Nelly's writing is approved of by learned scholars, whereas the poetry by men in the article was bad. Second, it distances the *Midwife* from the *Student* as the *Student* had recently been involved in a dispute with the *Magazine of Magazines* and the *Grand Magazine of Magazines* which had also been "borrowing" its "original pieces." By openly acknowledging the theft of the poem, the *Midwife* set itself up as a random selection of articles from previously published sources. Anyone who tried to claim it was a carefully directed piece of political satire could be met with the claim that if the juxtaposition of articles produced a political meaning, it could only be accidental.

Two further thefts, occasional prologues for simultaneous productions of *Romeo and Juliet*, at Drury Lane and Covent Garden, are followed by a third occasional prologue on the two occasional prologues, which points out that the theaters are probably in cahoots with each other over the productions of the same play. The theatergoing audience had to see both performances in order to discuss a single play. Mrs. Mary Midnight thought it a ploy to make money. She puts the words of the deception into the mouths of both Garrick and Barry:

> And let's like *Peachum*, and his Brother Lockit,
> Our own Affronts — with others Money, pocket.[49]

Then she bursts forth onto the stage of her prologue, declaring:

> While *Garrick* smart, and blustering Barry jar,
> Like rough and smooth, or Oil and Vinegar,
> I, like an hard-boil'd Egg come in between,
> And mix their Matters, as I intervene;
> I form (*for Rhyme's sake add, with* Just Intention)

Betwixt the fighting Fluids a Convention;
Which being thus conjoin'd, please ev'ry Palate,
And make a pretty Figure in a Sallad.[50]

The word, "Convention," highlighted by the note in parentheses, may mean an agreement between parties,[51] but also draws in other possibilities. Mrs. Midnight may be setting herself up as a judge,[52] or be calling a parliament without the summons of the Sovereign.[53] The more obvious semantic link between the theaters and politics, in the common uses of the word "house," is brought to prominence in the epigram that follows:

Well—what's to Night? Says angry *Ned*,
As up from Bed he rouses:
Romeo again!—and shakes his Head.
Ah! Pox on both your Houses.

The fact that both these pieces are on the facing page of *The Midwife's Politicks: Or, Gossip's Chronicle of the Affairs of Europe*, on which Mrs. Mary Midnight gives her views on the treaty negotiations with Spain, all but openly declares that her role as egg bringing about the mixing of the matters of oil and vinegar is not the culinary reference expected from a woman. Furthermore, in order to mix successfully, oil and vinegar must be combined with raw egg. By declaring herself "an hard-boil'd egg" she declares that she will keep the oil and vinegar in the two Houses of Parliament apart from one other and never in agreement.[54]

Mrs. Mary Midnight's reason for keeping the political parties at each other's throats was her antipathy to the European dimension of British Politics. She declared: "Our Disputes with Spain are yet unsettled, tho' we have been assured, over and over, that both Parties are willing to make some Concessions for the sake of Trade. The Spanish Ministers are so slow and formal in their Deliberations, that I am afraid that artful Old Woman, the Queen Dowager, contributes to blunt the Edge of Mr. Keen's Arguments."[55] In her statement, the parties are England and Spain, but in the *London Magazine* earlier that year, the same treaty negotiations are described in a way that suggests that only disputes between the Whigs and Tories (or Whigs and opposition Whigs) can stop it being ratified:

When it is thoroughly understood, that no nation except Great Britain can Trade to mutual advantage with Spain, it will readily be assented to, that only a schism in politicks can possibly break the natural connection between us, hinder permanent union, or impede our obtaining from the court at Madrid, a reasonable exclusive preference, in some particular branches of commerce, and security to our hearts content.[56]

The fact that the treaty with Spain amounted to British meddling in European affairs would have annoyed the Tory Jacobite, Mrs. Mary Midnight, and this would give her a reason why she wanted to keep the parties apart. However, her reference to the negotiations about trade give her a chance to explain why the process was so protracted. The same article in the *London Magazine* went on: "Woollen goods, cutlery-ware, tin, lead, alum, saffron, &c. are properly British commodities, . . . and [some mixture] of Spanish wool, in the finer woollen goods." Their comment apparently ignores recent events concerning the woollen trade in England, though more probably reflects the government position: the Spanish Treaty could bring nothing but improvement to the British wool trade. The *Gentleman's Magazine* was careful, but told a different story. Their *Monthly Chronologer* for July 1750 noted: "Wednesday 4 July: Richard Metcalf was brought to the King's bench court, and pleaded guilty to an information exhibited against him by Mr. Attorney General, for seducing four artificers of the woollen manufactory to go out of this kingdom to *Spain*: (See vol.XIX p.473) when he was remanded to prison, for three months, and fined 100£".[57] Their *Foreign Advices* column in the same number remarked upon the growth of the Spanish trade, and the effect it would have upon British exports: "SPAIN: The king has just granted some privileges and exemptions to the manufactories lately established in this kingdom, which improve daily, and we doubt not bringing them to such perfection as that we shall no longer need to import foreign merchandize—To the success of these new manufactories, we ascribe the *English* . . . The number of manufacturers from Lancashire and other parts of *England* is about 500."[58] The *London's* position is that the British Wool trade is strong enough to stand up for itself, and would benefit from importing Spanish goods. The *Gentleman's* position is that the British Trade is strong, but weakening due to a drain of talent to Spain, though the drain is being halted by intervention of the courts. The *Midwife's* position, though not stated directly, is that the Spanish are trying to keep the treaty negotiations going for so long that there will be no British wool trade left. The view makes paradoxical Mrs. Mary Midnight's attempt to keep the parties from coming to an agreement, but for the fact that she notes that it is the Queen dowager of Spain who is trying to keep negotiations from concluding since "her Influence is not yet lost, as some pretend, her youngest Son being to exchange his Cardinal's Hat for a Temporal Sovereignty." Mrs. Mary Midnight's position is not coherent and logical. If it were, it would be open to accusations of being unpatriotic. As in her midnight ramble, information is presented in a haphazard way that avoids a univocal reading. But this is not arbitrariness or poor writing:

the power of gossip is not to be logical and coherent, but to make suggestive statements.

Mrs. Mary Midnight is equally indirect and suggestive about her own country. She will say nothing about it, but indirectly tells a great deal.

> There are two Reasons why I do not chuse to insert any Thing here relating to the Policy on my own Country; One is, that I know nothing new which can be spoken of much to its Advantage; The other, that what may be said of a contrary Nature, our Enemies and Neighbours are ready enough to publish. I am a true Briton, and wou'd conceal the Nakedness I cannot prevent.[59]

Of course, disclosures about British Politics have already been made. But there was another aspect of British nakedness to which she was alluding. The *Historical Chronicle* of the *Gentleman's Magazine* for July 1750 noted: "July 30 A general muster was made on board all the guard ships at *Portsmouth*, Admiral *Hawke* being present when 40 men out of each ship were pricked down to be discharged, in order to reduce the ships to their lowest compelments [*sic*]; the surgeons, boatswains, carpenters, gunners, and masters mates also to be discharged."[60] The next month, they reported the Spanish reaction to the reduction in the British navy: "Saturday 29 The *Spaniards* have begun to erect forts at the bay of *Campeachy*, for preventing any foreign ships, of whatever nation from cutting wood, or carrying on any traffick with the inhabitants; they also fitted out a fleet of small ships of war, which have taken several *English* vessels in that bay."[61] As before, the *Gentleman's* refrains from comment. Likewise, *The Midwife* makes no direct comment but the innuendo is clear that the British government has let its citizens down in pursuit of European gains.

In terms of Jacobite discourse, Mrs. Midnight's magazine both concurs with and marks a shift away from the mid-century forms described by Murray Pittock. While Mary Midnight continued to emphasize the democratic and even republican bias that reflected Charles Edward Stuart's popularity with the lower orders, her magazine was far removed from the highbrow "lost lover" poems and the "unique iconographical place" that mingled classicism, romanticism with the "virtuous patriot."[62]

The shift probably took place because of the failure of the '45. Mary Midnight decries all the actions of men, and the sexually promiscuous Prince is never offered as the poignant king across the water. Instead, he has become the noticeably Welsh John Williams, who has been imprisoned for debt, while his wife, Britain, has gone mad. Furthermore, Stuart's kilted heterosexual masculinity has now become the transvestite Mrs. Mary Midnight, who made no secret of her transgression in her addresses "the women of both sexes." Thus, in one respect *The Midwife* appears to be a lampoon of Jacobitism—which it may well have been in the true sense of the term—while remaining fiercely anti-Hanoverian.

The ambiguous figure of Mrs. Mary Midnight at the centre of the project, around which the whirlwind of meanings blow, is central to our understanding of the text. Like Charles Edward Stuart, Mrs. Mary Midnight is a man in a frock. However, Mary Midnight erases the dignity of Charles III's highland costume while at the same time mimicking it. Thus she both mocks him and supports him: she mocks his Catholicism as effeminate (as William Boobykin had) while she supports his divine right to the kingdom. At the same time, her anti-Hanoverian newspaper is protected from government censorship by her obvious lampoon of the man in the frock, while her demand for a divinely ordained British masculine Protestant monarch to replace German George (who was also tinged with the effeminacy of Catholicism as he was too bothered with the election of the Holy Roman Emperor) rings through the maelstrom of possible readings. The *Midwife* is calculated ambiguity. It is created of the illogicality of stereotypical female gossip like pieces of a jigsaw cast on the ground for readers to pick up and put together to make a picture for themselves. The writers were protected from punishment for, as Swift had said, readers would never see their own faces in the glass of its general satire, but only their enemies. If on the other hand it had followed the logic of stereotypical masculine thought, it would have been both closed down by the government and less popular since it would have estranged part of its audience. *The Midwife* was all things to all people—men and women—and thus went into many editions.

NOTES

1. Robert Mahony and Betty Rizzo, *Christopher Smart: An Annotated Bibliography* (New York: Garland, 1984).

2. There are several papers concerning the attribution of articles written in *The Midwife* that make up a fascinating argument about the use of internal evidence for this purpose. However, none discusses the contemporary significance of the material. [Ibid., items 82, 90, 97, 98, 99, 100, 101, 108, 111, 113]

3. Christopher Devlin, *Poor Kit Smart* (London: Rupert Hart Davies, 1961).

4. Ibid., 54.

5. Ibid., 56.

6. Arthur Sherbo, *Christopher Smart: Scholar of the University,*(Lansing: University of Michigan Press, 1967), 71.

7. *British Literary Magazines: The Augustan Age and the Age of Johnson, 1698–1758*, ed. Alvin Sullivan (Westport, Conn.: 1983), 226. Item on *The Midwife* by Deborah Ayer Sitter and John Sitter.

8. In my biography, I argue that Smart's was one of several hands that wrote under the byline Mrs. Mary Midnight. Other writers were probably Bonnell Thornton and Richard Rolt. I use Smart here as a shorthand for the conglomerate of men calling themselves Mrs. Mary Midnight, and throughout the essay will refer to the writer of the *Midwife* articles as Mrs. Mary Midnight.

9. Although the word "gossip" originally referred to both sexes in its original derivation of "god-parent" it was applied "only to women" from as early as the sixteenth century (*OED* definitions 1 and 2a).

10. For example, the satirical magazine *Private Eye* uses the name "Brenda" to write scurrilous satires about Queen Elizabeth II. The first few times the name was used it must have been difficult to know to whom the magazine was referring.

11. *The Agreeable Medley, Or, Universal Entertainer* (Malton: Joshua Nickson, 1748), 122–26. This connection is noted by Mahony and Rizzo, *Christopher Smart*.

12. *Student* II, Calliope, 52: "I am now forc'd to employ my pen, as others do their needle,—to get bread. I have written several poems, novels, &c. and at present am engaged in composing sermons for a bookseller , which he designs to sell for the MS. Sermons of an eminent divine lately deceased, warranted originals. And to tell you a secret, I am that very same MIDWIFE, who publishes the *Old Woman's Magazine*, which makes so much noise in the world. To conclude,—I am a perfect *Swiss* in writing; if therefore you think fit to take me into your service, I am ready. And you may henceforward enrol me in your services under the name of / *The* FEMALE STUDENT."

13. *The Midwife*, I.i., 16 October 1750. *The Midwife*: I.ii, 21 November 1750.

14. *Daily Advertiser, General Advertiser*: 17 October 1750. "The whole Impression of the Midwife or the Old Woman's Magazine, was Sold off Yesterday in four Hours, but a new Edition will be published this morning at Ten o'Clock, from Presses having been employed all last Night for the Prologue."

Midwife, I, 2nd ed. 18 October 1750: "The report rais'd of this Magazine being not to be had, was scandalous without Foundation and propagated with a malicious Design. 'Tis true the first Impression was sold out off on Tuesday, in about four Hours, but then it was immediately put to some Presses and a second Edition was published the next Morning."

Daily Advertiser, General Advertiser: 20 October 1750: "Pray observe, The Fourth Edition of the Midwife, or Old Woman's Magazine, will be published this Day at Noon, Price 3 pence; to which is added, the celebrated Epilogue spoken by Mrs Clive, on the Two Occasional Prologues."

Mahony and Rizzo, *Christopher Smart*, note that pp. 47–48 were blank until the 4th. They also note a 9th 14th ed. dated 11th and 16th Januuarty 1751.

15. Ros Ballaster, Margaret Beetham, Elizabeth Frazer, and Sandra Hebron, *Women's Worlds: Ideology, Femininity and the Woman's Magazine* (Basingstoke: Macmillan, 1991).

16. J. A. Simpson and E. Weiner, ed., *The Oxford English Dictionary* (Oxford: Clarendon, 1989) 2nd ed. 20 vols., VI:700, definition 2b.

17. Ballaster, *Women's Worlds*, 43, 55 and 57.

18. Jan B. Gordon, *Gossip and Subversion in Nineteenth-Century British Fiction* (Basingstoke: Macmillan, 1996), 58–60.

19. It must be pointed out here that the use of the term "gossip" for the discourse of

women attending a birth was not used until 1811 (*OED*). However, it is not necessary for the following argument that the term itself be employed in the eighteenth century, and I use it here for convenience.

20. That is, after the Preface, which announces two other characters in which Smart wrote, Ebenezer Pentweazle and Fardinando Foot.

21. *Midwife*, I.i., 6.

22. Mahony and Rizzo, *Christopher Smart*, item 325.

23. *Midwife* I.i., p.6–7.

24. Dennis de Coetlogon, *Diogenes's Ramble* (London: T. Cooper, 1743).

25. Dennis de Coetlogon, *Diogenes at Court* (London: J. Jeffries, 1748).

26. Ibid., 47.

27. *Midwife*, I.i., 7

28. Ros Ballaster, *Seductive Forms: Women's Amatory Fiction 1684–1740* (Oxford: Clarendon Press, 1992).

29. *Midwife*, I.i., 8.

30. Ibid., 8.

31. Ibid., 8.

32. See Murray Pittock, *Poetry and Jacobite Politics* (Cambridge: Cambridge University Press, 1994).

33. de Coetlogon, *Diogenes at Court*, 31–37.

34. Ibid., 50–51

35. Ibid., 53–58

36. Ibid., 60–61.

37. *Midwife*, 12.

38. Ibid.

39. See Paul Langford, *A Polite and Commercial People* (Oxford: Oxford University Press, 1992), 219–20.

40. *Gentleman's Magazine*, XVIII (1748), 170–71.

41. *Midwife*, I.i., 15

42. Ibid., 22.

43. Luce Irigaray, *This Sex which is Not One* (Ithaca: Cornell University Press, 1985).

44. *Midwife*, I.i., 31.

45. Ibid., 33.

46. Ibid., 34.

47. The subject may sound outlandish, but had been the subject of many articles in the *Gentleman's Magazine* the previous year.

48. *Midwife*, I.i, 36.

49. Ibid., 39.

50. Ibid., p.40

51. *OED* III: 864 definition 7.

52. Ibid., definition 3a.

53. Ibid., definition 5. The parliament that had declared the throne abdicated by James II was a convention parliament.

54. There is possibly an anachronism in this reading, as the *OED* dates the word "mayonnaise" after 1754. However, the verse so clearly implies knowledge of the property of raw egg yolk to bind oil and vinegar, that the sauce appears to have been known by Mrs. Midnight—though it is not described by Hannah Glasse.

55. *Midwife*, I.i, 41.

56. *London Magazine*,XIX, (1750), 455.

57. GM XX (1750), 328.

58. Ibid., 334.
59. *Midwife*, I.i., 45.
60. *Gentleman's Magazine*, XX (1750), 376.
61. Ibid., 427.
62. Pittock, *Poetry and Jacobite Politics*, 79ff.

Contributors

CONRAD BRUNSTROM is Lecturer in English at National University of Ireland Maynooth. He has published on James Beattie and Thomas Sheridan the younger and is currently preparing a full-length study of William Cowper.

RACHEL K. CARNELL, Assistant Professor of English at Cleveland State University, has published articles in *Eighteenth-Century Studies, Eighteenth-Century Fiction, Studies in the Novel,* and *Nineteenth-Century Literature.* She is currently completing a book on the relationship between eighteenth-century political discourse and the rise of the novel.

RUTH HERMAN is currently finishing her doctoral thesis on Delarivier Manley's political writing at the Open University, having worked for many years in the field of public relations and journalism. She has been previously published on Manley. Other work includes such diverse topics as brewing and popular history. She is also currently working on a book about early eighteenth-century political writing.

THOMAS A. KING is Associate Professor of Restoration and eighteenth-century British literature, performance studies, and l/g/b/t studies at Brandeis University and author of *Queer Articulations: Enacting Masculinity and Difference in Early Modern England* (forthcoming, University of Wisconsin Press). His essays and reviews have appeared in *The Image of Manhood in Early Modern Literature: Viewing the Male, LGSN, Monstrous Dreams of Reason: Writing the Body, Self, and Other in the Enlightenment, The Politics and Poetics of Camp, Strategic Sex, TDR (The Drama Review), Theatre Insight: A Journal of Contemporary Performance Thought, Theatre Journal, and Theatre Studies.*

ELIZABETH KUBEK is currently an Assistant Professor of English Literature at Benedictine University. Her work on the literature and culture of the Restoration and the eighteenth century focuses on the intersection between the development of modern political identities and gender epistemologies. The essay in this collection is an excerpt from a longer project on women's participation in the emergence of a "progressive" political discourse.

CHRIS MOUNSEY, Senior Lecturer in English at King Alfred's, Winchester, has published papers on Christopher Smart, Oliver Goldsmith, and Thomas Sheridan the younger. A biography of Smart will also appear from Bucknell University Press. Chris Mounsey is currently working on a project on eighteenth-century newspapers. His next biography will be on Defoe.

DAVID MICHAEL ROBINSON teaches lesbian & gay studies and eighteenth-century literature in the English Department of the University of Arizona. He received his Ph.D. from the University of California, Berkeley, and an M.F.A. in modern dance from Tisch School of the Arts, NYU. He is working on a book about the representation of lesbians and gay men in seventeenth- and eighteenth-century Britain and France.

JULIE SHAFFER is Assistant Professor at University of Wisconsin Oshkosh. She publishes on Austen, Edgeworth, Burney, Robinson, and noncanonical late eighteenth- and early nineteenth-century British female novelists. Her most recent essays appear in *Criticism*, *Studies in the Novel*, and *Disciplining the Body*, ed. Deborah Wilson and Christine Laennec (1997). She is currently preparing an edition of Mary Robinson's *Walsingham* for publication, and is also completing a monograph on illegitimacy in women's novels. Shaffer is associate editor of Corvey Women Writers on the Web, an Electronic Guide to Literature, 1796–1834.

CAROLYN D. WILLIAMS is a lecturer in the English Department at the University of Reading. She has written *Pope, Homer and Manliness* (1993), as well as a large number of articles on early modern life, sexuality, and literature.

KARINA WILLIAMSON is Honorary Fellow of the Department of English at Edinburgh University, Supernumerary Fellow of St. Hilda's College, Oxford, and has also lectured at the universities of Uppsala and New Mexico. She is principal editor of *The Poetical Works of Christopher Smart* (awarded the 1997 Rose Mary Crashaw Prize), contributor to the *New Dictionary of National Biography*, and author of articles on subjects including Shakespeare, Herbert, Marvell, Smart, eighteenth-century women's poetry, and Carribean fiction.

Index